DOWN DOWN DEEPER AND DOWN

Ireland in the 70s and 80s

DOWN DOWN DEEPER AND DOWN

Ireland in the 70s and 80s

EAMONN SWEENEY ～

Gill & Macmillan

Gill & Macmillan Ltd
Hume Avenue, Park West, Dublin 12
with associated companies throughout the world
www.gillmacmillan.ie

© Eamonn Sweeney 2010
978 07171 4633 8

Index compiled by Helen Litton
Typography design by Make Communication
Print origination by TypeIT, Dublin
Printed by Scandbook, Sweden

This book is typeset in Minion 11.5pt on 13.5pt

The paper used in this book comes from the wood pulp
of managed forests. For every tree felled, at least one
tree is planted, thereby renewing natural resources.

A CIP catalogue record for this book is available from
the British Library.

5 4 3 2

For Emily, Lara and Isabel

CONTENTS

ACKNOWLEDGEMENTS

Thanks to Fergal Tobin and Gill & Macmillan for their faith in and support for the book. The generosity of John Waters was utterly invaluable. Vincent Browne, Brian Hanley, Liam Reilly and the comrades at Cedar Lounge Revolution (cedarlounge.wordpress.com) provided vital help at crucial stages.

Thanks also to Vinnie Browne of Charlie Byrne's bookshop in Galway, and Des Kenny of Kenny's Bookshop in Galway.

Ronnie Bellew, as ever, was an ideal supporter, sounding board, advisor and friend. Without the support of Aengus Fanning and John Greene of the *Sunday Independent*, I wouldn't have been in a position to write the book. I am deeply grateful for the working environment they've provided over the past few years.

Most of all, thanks to my family in Galway, France and Cork who provided ceaseless encouragement and showed exemplary patience in listening to me talk about political controversies from days gone by. Without you I'm nothing.

Chapter 1 ∾

| INTRODUCTION

In June 2008 on the RTE television programme 'Questions and Answers', the Minister for Defence, Willie O'Dea, was asked his opinion of comments made by the Minister for Justice, Dermot Ahern, during the 1993 Dáil debate on the legalisation of homosexuality.[1] The Fine Gael TD Brendan McGahon had described homosexuals as 'sad' and suffering from 'abnormality' and a 'persecution complex,' adding that 'the Lord provided us with sexual organs for a special purpose. Homosexuals are like left-hand drivers driving on the right-hand side of the road.' Ahern, then a backbench TD, replied, 'I do not often find myself in agreement with my constituency colleague Deputy McGahon, but on this occasion I am,' before attacking the eventually successful proposal for legalisation made by the Fianna Fáil Minister for Justice, Máire Geoghegan-Quinn.[2]

What, one member of the audience wondered, did O'Dea think of this, given that Ahern might be responsible for piloting through legislation giving civil partnership rights to gay couples? O'Dea pondered for a moment. 'Ah, sure, you know, we can't all answer for what we said. We all said queer things—er, strange things, fifteen years ago.' The studio audience greeted this with hilarity and O'Dea appeared deeply embarrassed, his quick correction notwithstanding. Yet the most interesting thing about the answer was not the minister's verbal slip but his assumption that the mere passage of time sufficed to empty Ahern's statement of all meaning.

Many people were surprised that Dermot Ahern, a senior minister not associated in the public mind with moral conservatism, had made such comments. Perhaps this is because the years from 1973 to 1994, which are the subject of this book and its successor volume, are sometimes treated like an impossibly distant era, one barely relevant to today's Ireland.

The neglect of the more recent past is strange, because those years were so turbulent, dramatic and unpredictable. 'May you live in interesting times' is supposedly an old Chinese curse. Implied is the notion that interesting times are unlikely to be the most comfortable to live through; and it's indisputable that the period 1973–94 was one attended by a sense of crisis. Yet those years also seem like an atypically eventful period in Irish life, coming as they did between the long era of stagnation that had followed independence and the era of political and social consensus during the economic boom that began in the second half of the nineties. It was a time when cherished notions about the republican tradition, the place of women in society, the power wielded by the Catholic Church, sexual morality and the viability of the state itself were challenged. There was an impression of things being up for grabs in a way they had not been previously.

Perhaps that's why, at a time of consensus, there was a reluctance to look closely at the seventies and eighties. From the vantage point of the Tiger years, the main actors in the dramas of those times seemed almost gauche, their lack of irony and ferocity of commitment somewhat embarrassing in a society where apathy had largely replaced anger. The huge PAYE marches, the clashes between liberal and conservative elements over abortion and divorce and the street battles between republicans and the forces of law and order in the vicinity of the British Embassy seemed to have no contemporary analogues.

When Brian Lenihan, Dermot Ahern's predecessor as Minister for Justice, was asked about the possibility of a referendum on gay marriage he dismissed it as inadvisable, because it would be 'divisive.'[3] It was a very 21st-century answer. The partisans in most of the controversies described in this book welcomed division and in many cases seem to have deliberately sought it out.

The boom years also created the idea that we had reached a kind of end of history, enabling all previous events to be read as in some way leading to the inevitable consummation of the Celtic Tiger era. On this reading, even the most venal political behaviour could be seen as contributing to the blessed state we enjoyed in the first decade of the new millennium. It had all worked out in the end, hadn't it?

Such a statement could still have been made when I began writing this book, but I write this introduction at a time when the seventies and eighties do not seem so distant after all. Unemployment has risen above 10 per cent for the first time in more than a decade, the public finances are in crisis, trade union leaders are once more addressing large crowds in the streets, and the controversial Government rescue of the Insurance Corporation of Ireland in 1985 has unmistakable parallels with the bail-out of Anglo Irish Bank now. Rumours of our eternal prosperity seem to have been premature.

I have quoted extensively from the books, magazines and newspapers of the time, because I was interested in seeing how the era looked to those living through it. I believe that using the words of those writing about the period contemporaneously helps to guard against the enormous condescension of posterity. As far as possible I have tried to keep my own opinions out of the text, although, like all other books, it is surely skewed by the author's particular biases and predilections.

Hindsight can be misleading. For example, the mood of despair that swept the country during the years 1984–9, as unemployment stayed above 15 per cent, reaching a record of 17 per cent in 1986, had to do not merely with the prevailing economic conditions but with the notion that things would continue in this vein for ever, given that the number of people on the dole had increased every year from 1980 to 1987.[4] In the eighties the future seemed as much a cause for despondency as the present.

This sense of doom suffuses the final chapter of Dermot Bolger's novel *The Journey Home* (1990), which perhaps captures the *zeitgeist* better than any other.[5] It is easy to dismiss as alarmist his nightmare vision of a depopulated rural Ireland functioning mainly as a theme park for tourists, but he was tapping into a profound sense of national decline, triggered not just by unemployment but by emigration, which reached a peak in 1989 when 70,600 people—2 per cent of the population—left the country.[6]

This was merely a continuation of the long-standing problems of the Irish economy. When Ireland joined the EEC it was the poorest country in the Community, with an income per capita 42 per cent below the average.[7] Matters had improved somewhat in the sixties, but even so only the British and Luxembourg economies had grown at a slower rate between 1963 and 1971.[8] In 1973 inflation reached double digits for the first time, and it would remain there for almost the entire following decade, exceeding 20 per cent in 1975 and 1981 as global difficulties were made worse by economic mismanagement.[9] An apparent recovery in 1977 and 1978 proved to be merely a brief period of calm before a particularly destructive and persistent storm. That the seventies seem slightly less gloomy than the eighties is mainly because we now know there was even worse to come.

Yet it would be misleading to regard the period as unremittingly bleak. Irish society in the seventies and eighties was not in the same stagnant condition it had been in during the economically depressed fifties. It was in many ways a very exciting time.

The great political cliché of the age was that young people were the country's greatest asset.[10] This may have been no more than a platitude, but the unprecedentedly youthful composition of the population—almost half of which was under the age of twenty-five at the start of the seventies, compared with about a third at the present time—undoubtedly contributed to a continuous questioning of old standards and assumptions. This manifested itself in the persistent challenges to the status quo on women's rights, family planning, gay rights and divorce and also in the arts.

In 1973 Irish literature seemed moribund, living off the accumulated capital of the past and subject to the 'common wisdom that the Irish imagination and conditions in Ireland made it easier to write stories than novels.'[11] Over the next couple of decades, however, John Banville, John McGahern, Colm Tóibín, Patrick McCabe, Jennifer Johnston, Dermot Healy, Roddy Doyle and Dermot Bolger restored the Irish novel to a cultural centrality it had not enjoyed since the heyday of Joyce.

The theatre was similarly resurgent. Those were the years of *The Gigli Concert, Dancing at Lughnasa, Observe the Sons of Ulster Marching to the Somme, Talbot's Box* and *The Great Hunger*, of the emergence of Sebastian Barry, of the Druid Theatre and Passion Machine. U2's ascension to the status of not just the world's best-known rock band but perhaps the most consistently interesting merely marked them out as *primus inter pares* in a remarkably inventive generation of musicians. Meanwhile Planxty, Horslips, the Bothy Band, Moving Hearts et al. were engaged in a reinvigoration and reinvention of a traditional music that went from strength to strength in the aftermath of the Ó Riada era and the ballad boom. Neil Jordan and Jim Sheridan gave the country a world presence in cinema for the first time, yet they were only the most successful products of a hugely energetic and innovative film culture.

This book tells the story of the Republic rather than of the island as a whole. This is firstly because the same period in Northern Ireland has already been covered by several excellent books, and secondly because the experience of life in the two areas was very different. The election of Margaret Thatcher had as little direct effect on voters in the South as that of Charlie Haughey and Garret FitzGerald had north of the border.

That is not to say that the Republic was not profoundly affected by what happened in the North, particularly when—as with the Dublin and Monaghan bombings, the killings of Lord Mountbatten and of a number of gardaí, the notorious kidnappings of the time and the election of H-block candidates to the Dáil in the 1981 election—the conflict spilled over its usual boundaries. Politics in the Republic would have been very different without the influence of the Troubles.

The more closely I looked at the events and personalities of the time the more they contradicted my preconceived notions about the period. That's what happens, in interesting times.

Chapter 2 ～

A BOOT UP THE TRANSOM

1973

On New Year's Day 1973 Seán Kennan, Ireland's Permanent Representative at the European Economic Community in Brussels, handed a letter assenting to the changes in the Treaty of Rome that brought the country into the Common Market to André Dubois, Director of Foreign Affairs at the EEC's Secretariat-General. 'The ceremony', it was revealed, 'will consist of the handing over of the letter and the drinking of a glass of champagne.'[1] Eleven years after its first application, Ireland had become a member of the world's largest trading bloc.

Formal negotiations had begun in June 1970, and a referendum on whether to join had been held in May 1972. The two main political parties and the farmers' and employers' organisations had campaigned for a Yes vote; the Labour Party urged a No vote, as did the Common Market Defence Campaign, two of whose founders, the academics Raymond Crotty and Anthony Coughlan, would go on to prove thorns in the Government's side during future referendums on European unity. The Defence Campaign boasted an eclectic range of supporters: its inaugural meeting in the Mansion House was addressed by the War of Independence hero Tom Barry, while its patrons included the poet Austin Clarke, the playwright John B. Keane, the anti-apartheid campaigner Kader Asmal, the singer Luke Kelly, the actor Siobhán McKenna, the comedian Niall Tóibín, the painter Harry Kernoff and the novelist and veteran republican activist Peadar O'Donnell.

These impressive connections notwithstanding, the campaign was fighting a lost battle. On polling day the electorate voted by a five-to-one margin to enter the EEC. The No vote of 16.9 per cent bore a marked resemblance to the 16.6 per cent garnered by the Labour Party in the previous general election. The foregone nature of the conclusion, however, did not preclude some heady rhetoric. The Labour Party TD Justin Keating declared that

> the origin of the EEC lies in Hitler's New Order. There is no difference in the basic outlook, the morality, the social system between the Germany of 1914, the Germany of 1939 and the EEC of 1972.[2]

It was a line of argument that would not have found favour with the *Irish Farmer's Journal*, which informed its readers that

> most of the voices on radio and television against entry, you'll notice, have Dublin accents. One thing, though, that stands out very strongly, one and all are devoted disciples of Karl Marx. Do you find anyone among them who earns his living the hard way? Instead you'll find ESB officials, Gardiner Street Sinn Féin, teachers in vocational schools, Kevin Street Sinn Féin, university lecturers, parlour pinks and, over all, a motley collection of £5,000 plus a year white collar Dublin trade union officials.[3]

The electorate's decision to resist the blandishments of Marxist teachers and people with Dublin accents rested largely on 'an anticipation of major financial transfers from Europe, especially for farmers.'[4] Ireland would be joining at a time when the economies of western Europe were enjoying a golden age, which had begun a few years after the end of the Second World War.[5] Few people could have expected that 1973 was the year in which this era of sustained growth and low unemployment would begin to be replaced by an era of economic crisis and uncertainty.

Despite the improvement of the Lemass years, the Ireland that joined the EEC was the poor relation of the nine. After the stagnation of the fifties the economy had grown throughout the sixties, but the average annual growth rate from 1963 to 1971 had been the lowest of the EEC member-states, with the exception of Britain and Luxembourg.[6] A comparison with Italy is instructive. In 1955 Ireland's gross national product per head had been £239, compared with £229 for Italy. In 1971 the figures were £709 for Ireland, £864 for Italy.[7] The average Irish income at the time was 58 per cent of the EEC average, while the inflation rate was the highest.[8]

Yet the overall picture was less bleak than it had been at almost any time since the foundation of the state. The 1971 census had seen the first rise in population since independence,[9] the total income from farming had risen by 37 per cent in 1972 alone,[10] and a mining boom led to Ireland becoming Europe's leading producer of copper, lead and zinc.[11] The average hourly industrial wage had doubled between 1966 and 1973, and the average weekly agricultural wage had done likewise since 1968.[12] Between 1969 and 1973 the number of cars had jumped from 315,000 to 477,000.[13]

There was also optimism arising from the fact of Ireland's having the youngest population in western Europe. Those youngsters were the best educated in Irish history, university admissions and secondary school attendance having more or less doubled between 1961 and 1971, largely because of the introduction of free post-primary education midway through that period.[14]

It was a changing country. The 1971 census showed urban outstripping rural population for the first time. (Agricultural employment fell by 154,000 between 1958 and 1974, while the number employed in industry and services increased by 133,000.)[15] The number of people with a television licence had quintupled in the decade following the opening of the national television channel on New Year's Eve, 1961.[16] And, while 90 per cent of the Catholic population attended Mass at least once a week, a figure unrivalled in Europe, 30 per cent of those between twenty-one and twenty-five didn't, and almost half of those in the 18–30 age group disagreed with the church's teaching that the use of 'artificial' contraception was morally wrong, a figure that was the harbinger of battles to be fought over the coming decades.[17]

Yet the political issue that overshadowed all else was the conflict taking place north of the border, which had escalated hugely the previous year, with 479 people, 250 of them civilians, losing their lives.[18] The Troubles had exposed serious divides in the two main political parties, both of whose leaders had almost been ousted as a result.

Fianna Fáil's victory in the 1969 general election had seemed to place Jack Lynch in an unassailable position. It was the party's fourth general election victory in a row, its ninth in the eleven elections since 1932, a period during which Fianna Fáil had been out of power for only six years. That 1969 election, however, had taken place against the backdrop of increased civil unrest in the North, the year having begun with the attack by loyalists on a small group of civil rights marchers near Derry, which had seriously exacerbated tensions between the communities. Within a month of Lynch's re-election as Taoiseach the first deaths of the conflict occurred when a Catholic pensioner, Samuel Ferguson, died after an altercation between civilians and the RUC in Dungiven, and another Catholic, Samuel Devenny, died of injuries inflicted by the police in Derry during disturbances in April.

On 12 August the 'Battle of the Bogside' began in Derry, and rioting spread to other towns. The following day Lynch, addressing the nation on television, declared: 'The present situation is the inevitable outcome of the policies pursued for decades by successive Stormont governments. It is also clear that the Irish Government can no longer stand by and see innocent people injured and perhaps worse.'[19] A day later the British army was deployed in Belfast to quell riots, which had resulted in another half a dozen deaths.

Lynch's television speech seemed to imply the possibility of direct intervention by the Irish Government to protect the Catholic population of the North, and at a Government meeting earlier that day Charles Haughey (Minister for Finance), Neil Blaney (Minister for Agriculture) and Kevin Boland (Minister for Social Welfare) had in fact urged that the Irish army be despatched over the border.[20] There was a clear divide between Lynch, who in August condemned the IRA and the use of physical force, and a section of the party that viewed his cautious approach as a betrayal of its traditional republican values. The contradictions finally became undeniable when Lynch sacked Blaney and Haughey from his Government in May 1970 for their alleged involvement in an attempt to import arms for the use of the IRA. Boland resigned in protest, as did a parliamentary secretary, Paudge Brennan. The Minister for Justice, Mícheál Ó Móráin, had earlier resigned on the putative grounds of ill health, though his departure was also connected with his failure to inform Lynch about the arms plot.[21]

Thus began a rocky spell for Fianna Fáil and its leader. When, in October, Haughey was acquitted by the Central Criminal Court of involvement in the arms conspiracy he declared that 'those who were responsible for this debacle have no alternative but to take the honourable course that is open to them.'[22] Yet Lynch's ministers rallied round him, and he survived. He survived too the raucous ard-fheis of 1971, which featured fist fights near the podium, derisive chants of 'Union Jack' directed towards the Taoiseach by some delegates and the spectacle of Boland storming the podium and challenging the party hierarchy, 'Come up and put me down.' Minister for External Affairs Patrick Hillery's famous response to chants supporting Boland, 'You can have Boland, but you can't have Fianna Fáil,' seemed to sum up the majority mood.[23]

By 1973 Boland had resigned his seat and, joined by another Fianna Fáil TD, Seán Sherwin, formed a new party, called Aontacht Éireann, which he hoped 'would bring republicanism back into constitutional politics.'[24] Blaney had been expelled from Fianna Fáil, as had Brennan. A Dublin County North TD, Des Foley, had resigned. Haughey, alone of the dissidents, stayed within Fianna Fáil and 'ate humble pie until it came out of his ears, said *"mea culpa"* and was rehabilitated.'[25] The infighting was over, and Lynch seemed to have carried his party with him.

Then, on 30 January 1972, came Bloody Sunday. The shooting dead of thirteen unarmed demonstrators at an anti-internment march in Derry seemed at first as though it might have a seismic effect on public opinion south of the border. When thirty thousand people marched through Dublin in protest on 2 February and the British Embassy in Merrion Square was burned down it seemed as though Lynch's attempts to calm emotions might have been for nought. 'It was', said his Minister for Justice, Desmond O'Malley, 'the moment of greatest potential danger.'[26]

The irony was that the burning of the embassy may in fact have strengthened Lynch's resolve to clamp down on the republican movement. He appeared to agree with one of his biographers in seeing the incident, and the sight of IRA members openly giving orders in the vicinity of the blaze, as the work of 'a fascist element liable to take over unless radical action was taken.'[27] O'Malley, and the Gardaí, stepped up the campaign against republicans, and in June the non-jury Special Criminal Court was set up to try those accused of subversive offences. The extent to which O'Malley discomfited the IRA can be seen from the fact that the organisation's Army Council discussed a proposal for his assassination. 'Some of those present were in favour of it.'[28]

O'Malley brought the Offences Against the State (Amendment) Bill before the Dáil in November 1972. Surprisingly, it was Fine Gael rather than Fianna Fáil that plunged itself into utter turmoil over the legislation, with the party leader, Liam Cosgrave, coming closer to losing his job than Lynch had at even the most fraught moments in the previous three years. Tom O'Higgins, one of the party's senior figures, remarked on

> the suspicion with which Garret FitzGerald, with whom Alexis Fitzgerald and Jim Dooge frequently sided, was regarded by Paddy Donegan and Richie Ryan. Donegan and Ryan seemed to believe that Garret was trying to move the party so much to the left that traditional values would be ignored.[29]

FitzGerald was regarded as the leader of the wing that hewed to the values of the social-democratic document *Towards a Just Society*, produced by Declan Costello, son of the party's previous Taoiseach, and adopted by the party before the 1965 general election.

In contrast, Cosgrave, a knight of the Grand Cross of Pius IX, whose father, W. T. Cosgrave, had served for ten years as head of the Irish Free State government, seemed to be the epitome of an older, more conservative Fine Gael. His allies, observed O'Higgins, believed that 'some form of a move was always being contemplated against Cosgrave's leadership.'[30] O'Malley's bill precipitated its greatest crisis.

The bill provided for the conviction of suspects solely on the testimony of a Garda superintendent that they were members of an illegal organisation. This was described as 'inherently objectionable' and 'repressive' by FitzGerald, while Paddy Cooney said that the 'likes of the bill can only be found on the statute book of South Africa,' adding that 'there is a limit to the measures a democracy is entitled to adopt in order to protect itself.'[31] At a meeting of the Fine Gael parliamentary party the vote was 38 to 8 in favour of opposing the bill. After the vote only two TDs continued to argue in favour of supporting the Government. One was Paddy Donegan, the other was the party leader, Liam Cosgrave.

As Friday 1 December dawned it looked as though the votes of Fine Gael, the Labour Party and the former Fianna Fáil TDs would be sufficient to defeat the bill. The inevitable result would be a general election and the departure of Liam Cosgrave as leader of Fine Gael. Just before eight o'clock that night, with the Dáil still debating the proposed legislation, two bombs went off in the centre of Dublin. The one outside the Liffey Bar in Eden Quay injured thirty people, the one in Sackville Place killed two CIE busmen, George Bradshaw and Thomas Duffy. The contention of Bernadette Devlin, then MP for Mid-Ulster, that the British had been responsible for the bombs reflected a widespread unease at their politically timely nature.[32]

Fine Gael withdrew its amendment and abstained when the bill was voted on, enabling the Government—and Liam Cosgrave—to enjoy a narrow escape. The Labour Party TD John O'Connell felt that,

> had Jack Lynch yielded to the temptation to call the election the night of the bombing, I firmly believe he would have won a massive majority as his television appearance that night reassuring a frightened public won him overwhelming support. I felt he missed a great opportunity.[33]

In fact, one commentator wrote, it had been

> the government's intention to dissolve and go to the country precisely on the Amendment to that Act and it was only when Fine Gael's opposition collapsed following the bombs [that] it was judged more prudent to delay, since only a genuine confrontation over a key issue could justify a December campaign leading to a poll just before Christmas Day.[34]

Fine Gael, most of whose supporters had decried the party's opposition to the bill, would, in Cosgrave's opinion, have faced 'electoral disaster' had they brought down the Government.[35]

The Labour Party stuck to its original intention and voted against the bill; but it also suffered from a certain amount of disunity. It had been the focus of much excitement before the 1969 election, campaigning on the slogan 'The seventies will be socialist' and predicting an electoral breakthrough. In the event it lost four seats, but the party's profile remained higher than ever before, largely because of the presence in its parliamentary ranks of the writer and academic Conor Cruise O'Brien, David Thornley, who had become a household name as the presenter of RTE's main political programme, 'Seven Days', and Justin Keating, RTE's former head of agricultural programming.

The politically peripatetic Noël Browne, now in his fourth party, who had said that the only countries truly approaching James Connolly's brand of socialism were Albania, China, Cuba, Hungary, Poland, the Soviet Union and Yugoslavia,[36] was a figurehead for the Labour left. The 1973 election leaflet in Dublin North-West, which called for the nationalisation of banks, mines, building societies and building land and 'for socialism and unity,' reflected the increased radicalism of that section of the party.[37]

In those circumstances the Wexford TD Brendan Corish seemed an odd choice as leader. He had once declared himself to be 'a Catholic first, an Irishman second and a socialist third.'[38] But the Labour Party was not all about media figures and Marxism. The party's TDs outside Dublin, such as Seán Treacy in Tipperary South, Dan Spring in North Kerry and the Limerick East TD Stephen Coughlan, who had once described Jews as 'bloodsuckers' and 'extortionists', were in the main deeply conservative.[39] Perhaps the emblematic figure of this group was Jimmy Tully, the Co. Meath veteran who at the party's 1970 congress had poured scorn on 'smart alecs, with the sweat dripping onto their schoolbooks, talking about the workers of this country.'[40] At the beginning of 1973 Corish, like Lynch and Cosgrave, led a party whose different factions coexisted uneasily.

If Lynch's policy was to ensure that the Northern conflict did not spill over into the South, the new year dawned with a couple of reminders that this would not always be possible. At 2 a.m. on New Year's Day gardaí investigating reports of shots and screams between Muff and Burnfoot, Co. Donegal, discovered the bodies of an engaged couple, Oliver Boyce, a carpenter from Clonmany, and Breege Porter, a shirt factory worker from Buncrana, who had been shot and stabbed by members of the UDA. On the previous night gardaí had arrested two men from Derry in a field near Ballybofey as they fled from a car that was discovered to contain five thousand rounds of ammunition and 250 pounds of gelignite. One of the men, 22-year-old Martin McGuinness, was described as 'leader of the

Provisional IRA in Derry during the period of the "no-go" areas.'[41] He was sentenced to six months in prison by the Special Criminal Court for IRA membership.

The battle between the Government and the Provisional IRA took another twist on 17 January when Seán Mac Stiofáin, the organisation's chief of staff, ended a 58-day hunger strike at the Curragh Military Hospital, where he had been moved on 27 November after a failed rescue attempt at the Mater Hospital in Dublin.

Seán Mac Stiofáin was the most unlikely of IRA leaders. Born John Stephenson in London in 1928, his closest Irish relative was a Belfast great-grandmother. Yet an obsession with Irish culture and history led to an involvement with the IRA, and in 1953 he was sentenced to eight years in prison after stealing a hundred guns from an officer training school in Essex. One of his companions on the raid was Cathal Goulding, who was chief of staff of the IRA when, at the end of 1969, republicans who disagreed with the political emphasis and left-wing direction of the movement split to form the Provisional Army Council. The leader of the Provisional IRA was Seán Mac Stiofáin, who had moved to Ireland on his release from prison. Those who stayed loyal to Goulding became known as the Official IRA, whose indefinite ceasefire in 1972 presaged the move to democratic politics and would lead to 'Official' Sinn Féin ultimately becoming the Workers' Party.

Mac Stiofáin was regarded as the principal strategist of the Provisionals at a time when their campaign was at its most ferocious. In 1972 a total of 105 British soldiers were killed, more than in the entire period between 1980 and 1988. Mac Stiofáin is credited with having personally developed the strategy of random car bombings, which paralysed towns throughout the North in the early seventies, to have 'mastered the art of propaganda techniques' and to have been responsible for the regular use of press conferences to get the message out.[42] Urging the IRA to 'escalate, escalate, escalate,' he 'became the personification in the British media of the entire Provisional "terror network" . . . portrayed as either a blood drenched madman or an evil genius.'[43] His jailing was therefore seen as hugely significant and provoked immediate repercussions. The RTE journalist Kevin O'Kelly, who had interviewed Mac Stiofáin on the day of his arrest, was himself sentenced to three months in jail for contempt of court after refusing to identify Mac Stiofáin as the interviewee, citing the venerable journalistic principle of the protection of sources. The entire RTE Authority was then sacked by the Minister for Posts and Telegraphs, Gerry Collins, for failing to enforce the directive issued the previous year under section 31 of the Broadcasting Authority Act (1960), prohibiting interviews that might promote the aims of organisations that used violence. Seven thousand protesters marched from the GPO to the Mater Hospital, where a rescue mission was undertaken by eight armed men. Three gardaí were held at gunpoint by men disguised as priests before Special Branch detectives arrived and foiled the attempt after a shoot-out in a hospital corridor, during which four people were slightly wounded.

At his trial Mac Stiofáin had told the judge:

> I'm going to die in six days. I have taken no liquids and no food since my arrest. I'll not take liquids or food. I'll see you in Hell before I submit. You had no evidence against me. I repeat, I will be dead in six days. Live with that.[44]

Ten days later he had taken water, and it was announced that he was also taking glucose. On the fifty-eighth day he was reportedly ordered by the IRA to end his strike, because 'no useful purpose would be served by him continuing his protest against his unjust imprisonment.'[45] It was the end for Mac Stiofáin as a senior IRA figure, because, 'although he maintained that he did so on the order of the Army Council, his decision to come off was met with some derision in republican circles.'[46]

By the time Mac Stiofáin was released, Séamus Twomey of Belfast had taken over as chief of staff, and the 'evil genius' faded into the wings, though in 1979 he did decline the offer of becoming chief of staff of the INLA. When he died, in 2001, the memory of his hunger strike was long blotted out by that of the more famous ones, which would produce the kind of martyr Seán Mac Stiofáin had not become.

The end of Mac Stiofáin's hunger strike had provided the Government with a morale boost; but three days later came another bombing in Dublin. A 25-year-old bus conductor, Thomas Douglas, had just left his bus when a car containing twenty pounds of explosives exploded and killed him. It had been placed in the same street, Sackville Place, where one of the December devices had gone off. The culprits, who had stolen the car in the loyalist Shankill Road in Belfast that morning, seemed to be demonstrating that they could carry out such acts with impunity.

Given the background, it was not surprising that when, on 5 February, Lynch called a general election to be held on the 28th, security was the main theme of the Fianna Fáil campaign. Fine Gael and the Labour Party banked on the electorate being more concerned with bread-and-butter issues when they produced a fourteen-point election programme. The manifesto promised strict price control, the removal of VAT on food, the halving of rates, the building of 25,000 new houses a year, the abolition of the means test, an increase in old-age pensions and worker representation on the boards of state companies.

As important as the programme itself was the fact that it had been issued jointly by Fine Gael and the Labour Party: this time the electorate were being presented with a clear choice of alternative Government. The parties were running as the 'National Coalition', presenting joint policies and, crucially, as it turned out, a transfer pact. Noël Browne dismissed the joint programme as 'representing the humane platitudes of public life everywhere' and refused to endorse it, and he was deselected in Dublin South-East.[47]

In 1969 Fianna Fáil had won 75 seats out of 144 to 50 for Fine Gael and 18 for the Labour Party, with Joseph Sheridan of Longford-Westmeath the solitary independent. Since then the parliamentary party had shed Blaney, Boland, Brennan and Foley, as well as Seán Sherwin, who had won a by-election in Dublin South-West, and had 69 seats at the dissolution of the Dáil. Boland and Sherwin would run for Aontacht Éireann, as would the Arms Trial defendant James Kelly in Cavan. 'We're there', said Boland, 'to oppose a policy which is common to three parties, a policy of collaboration with the British side in the war of independence.'[48] Asked if he thought he would regain the Dublin County South seat he'd resigned in 1970, he was characteristically blunt. 'I've no idea. I stand for the same principles as I stood for the last time. I don't see why I should lose support.'[49]

The Government party stressed the law and order issue. 'All subversives are hoping for a coalition victory,' warned George Colley. 'They are quiet now but they would push a coalition around.'[50] Lynch took up the theme. 'Fine Gael would depend for its support in the Dáil on those who only a few months ago were openly running with the subversive hares and the anarchist hounds.'[51] Fine Gael retaliated, with the Dublin Central candidate, Michael Keating, stating that 'George Colley had dragged the broken bodies of six hundred dead into the election. But for Fine Gael pressure, Blaney, Ó Móráin and Haughey would be on the same platform as George Colley. The sickened and cynical people must reject the gravediggers.'[52] The Fine Gael TD for Longford-Westmeath, Gerry L'Estrange, reckoned that

> the house that Jack built after the last election, the Fianna Fáil government, has crumbled to a shoddy ruin. Two of its pillars, Mr Boland and Mr Blaney, have been rejected as unsuitable timber. Mr Haughey, having been rejected, is once again being appraised for structural solidity. Sherwin, Foley and Brennan have been adjudged to contain dry rot which has undermined the structure.[53]

In Carrick-on-Shannon protesters against the jailing of the president of Provisional Sinn Féin, Ruairí Ó Brádaigh, shouted, 'Jack Lynch traitor,' and threw a couple of eggs at the Taoiseach.[54]

Invective notwithstanding, the coalition's programme had set the election agenda, and an opinion poll showed them on course for 76 seats with a 10 per cent swing against the Government. But this survey had been taken before Fianna Fáil changed tack and unfurled its own list of promises six days before the election, including increased social welfare payments and children's allowances, the abolition of rates on dwellings and the provision of a monthly pound of butter for eight pence to all families on social welfare. Brendan Corish described it as 'a panic measure . . . something that was unprecedented in the whole history of politics in Ireland . . . the last throw of a desperate gambler.'[55] 'This is not a bribe,' said Lynch, 'it is the answer to a challenge which was put to us.'[56]

The election was held only a few weeks before young people benefiting from the lowering of the voting age from 21 to 18 would have been able to vote. This drew a furious response from the president of the Union of Students in Ireland, Pat Rabbitte, who urged the electorate to bear in mind 'the hypocrisy of the Fianna Fáil government in preventing 140,000 young people voting.' He also lambasted Fianna Fáil for 'a campaign of arrogance, contempt, slander and vilification.'[57]

In Dublin County South, Mervyn Taylor for the Labour Party stressed the plight of 'the caravan people', young families unable to find housing who ended up in caravan parks where 'the tenants pay high ground rent to the landlord as well as repayments for their caravans and are at the mercy of the owner.' At one park beside a river the tenants were 'plagued with rats.'[58]

Polling day was uneventful, with the exception of incidents in Co. Louth, where army bomb disposal experts were called to Dunleer to deal with what turned out to be a biscuit tin filled with stones, and in Mayo East, where the Labour Party candidate Tom Dillon-Leetch called the Gardaí when he claimed to have found an eleven-year-old boy acting as polling clerk at Callow National School in Foxford and three members of Fianna Fáil in the polling booth. Voting at the school was briefly suspended, and Dillon-Leetch accused Fianna Fáil of having obtained a thousand illegal votes in the constituency.[59]

When the counting ended, the country had its first non-Fianna Fáil government in sixteen years. But it had been close. After all the trauma of the past four years and the embarrassing departures, Fianna Fáil increased its vote slightly, from 44.6 to 46.2 per cent; yet it obtained only sixty-nine seats, four less than the combined total of Fine Gael and the Labour Party. The coalition's transfer pact had enabled it to win an extra five seats, despite its combined vote dropping by 1.1 per cent. This was most evident in three constituencies where transfers of remarkable precision from Fine Gael to the Labour Party produced a narrow victory for candidates who would not otherwise have been elected. In Kildare, Joe Bermingham got 95.4 per cent of the Fine Gael transfers, John Ryan in Tipperary North got 94.6 per cent and Tom Kyne in Waterford got 94.3 per cent. The corresponding transfer rates in the previous election had been 14.3, 35 and 53.4 per cent, and it's clear that those transfers had made the difference between victory and defeat for the new Government. John Ryan, for example, got home by 143 votes from Michael Smith of Fianna Fáil, having received 768 transfers to Smith's 44 from Thomas Dunne of Fine Gael.[60]

The biggest shock of the election was the defeat of the Minister for Foreign Affairs, Brian Lenihan, in Roscommon-Leitrim. Lenihan had served as Minister for Justice, for Education and for Transport and Power, and his eclipse by Pat Joe Reynolds of Fine Gael was remarkable. Three former Fianna Fáil ministers also bit the dust: Michael Hilliard in Meath, Mícheál Ó Móráin in Mayo West and Kevin Boland, whose vote dropped by two-thirds, in Dublin County South.

There was similar humiliation for Seán Sherwin and James Kelly, who came bottom of the poll in Cavan. But Neil Blaney, running as Independent Fianna Fáil, topped the poll in Donegal North-East, while Haughey, the dissident who had remained within the party, polled a spectacular 12,901 in Dublin North-East, more than his party leader managed in Cork City North. Only Cosgrave, the incoming Taoiseach, did better, garnering 13,054 votes in Dún Laoghaire-Rathdown.

The Labour Party was not so fortunate in trying to hold on to Noël Browne's seat, with the newcomer Ruairí Quinn losing out by thirty-seven votes to Fergus O'Brien of Fine Gael. The Fine Gael newcomer Peter Sutherland got to the last count in Dublin North-West before losing to the Fianna Fáil veteran Dick Gogan, who believed the Northern Ireland situation 'would only be solved when Catholics and Protestants got together under the workers' flag.'[61] The new Fianna Fáil TD Ray Burke raised a few eyebrows by topping the poll with 10,652 votes in Dublin County North.

The big surprise in the new Government was that Garret FitzGerald did not become Minister for Finance. Instead this post went to Richie Ryan, with FitzGerald given Foreign Affairs. Corish was Tánaiste and Minister for Social Welfare, while the Labour Party also had control of

Industry and Commerce (Justin Keating), Posts and Telegraphs (Conor Cruise O'Brien), Labour (Michael O'Leary) and Local Government (Jimmy Tully). The Cosgrave loyalists Dick Burke and Mark Clinton were given Education and Agriculture, respectively, with Paddy Donegan in Defence. Declan Costello was a surprise choice as Attorney-General, while Paddy Cooney, as Minister for Justice, would have to operate the Offences Against the State Act that he had condemned with such passion. Peter Barry of Cork in Transport and Power, Tom Fitzpatrick of Cavan in Lands and Tom O'Donnell of Limerick as Minister for the Gaeltacht completed the line-up.

The most eye-catching junior appointment was that of John Bruton of Co. Meath, twenty-five years old and the son of the prominent National Farmers' Association activist Joe Bruton. The most surprising omission was that of David Thornley, who, it seemed, was paying the price for following the lead of Noël Browne in refusing to agree to the coalition agreement, before changing his mind a day later. Speculation that the Government might be bold and appoint Eileen Desmond of the Labour Party or Brigid Hogan O'Higgins of Fine Gael as the first woman minister since the foundation of the state proved to be off the mark.

The new Government was famously described by the *Irish Times* political correspondent, Michael McInerney, as 'the government of all the talents.'[62] There were minor reservations: the appointment of Costello as Attorney-General 'was a major disappointment because it deprived the country of the opportunity to witness one of the most innovative social reformers at work in a ministry like Health, Social Welfare, Labour or Education';[63] but in general the new Government was seen in a benign light. 'The change after sixteen years of Fianna Fáil was welcomed on all sides. Expectation was high; the talent available was widely recognised and extolled.'[64]

There was certainly an intellectual air about several of the new ministers. FitzGerald was a lecturer in political economy at UCD, had written economic journalism for a number of international publications and published a thoughtful and influential book, *Towards a New Ireland*. Keating had taken first place in every examination he sat in UCD before becoming the youngest veterinary surgeon to qualify in Ireland at the age of twenty-one.

But perhaps the most notable intellectual in the new Government was Conor Cruise O'Brien. A former Chancellor of the University of Ghana and professor of humanities at New York University who had written well-received books on Catholic novelists, Albert Camus and the Congo crisis, in which he had himself been embroiled as a UN diplomat, was always going to be something of an exotic flower in the world of Irish politics. But it was his crusade against what he saw as the self-deceptions and myths of Irish nationalism, most notably in his book *States of Ireland* (1972), that had made him one of the most polarising public figures in the country. His conclusion in that book—'I believe at this moment none of the main sections of the population of Ireland actually wants unity'—would have created a fuss at any time, but given the context of the strife in the North it was political dynamite.[65] The opportunities for controversy were increased by Cruise O'Brien's position as Labour Party spokesman on Northern Ireland. John Hume's comment, in his review of the book for the *Irish Times,* that *States of Ireland* was 'the best statement of the Ulster Unionist case ever written' was the kind of backhanded compliment unlikely to endear Cruise O'Brien to his political colleagues.[66] There was even a proposal to expel him from the Labour Party after he had disagreed with an SDLP suggestion that Britain and Ireland should exercise joint authority over Northern Ireland. Seamus Heaney praised Cruise O'Brien for

> creating some kind of clarity in Southerners' thinking about the Protestant community in the North. And it is not enough for people to simply say, 'ah they're all Irishmen' when some Northerners actually spit at the word Irishmen. There is in O'Brien a kind of obstinate insistence on facing up to this kind of reality which I think is his contribution.[67]

But John A. Murphy, who thought Cruise O'Brien's attacks on nationalist shibboleths performed 'a very great public service which will one day be appreciated as such,' still felt that 'he concentrates his attack on the excesses of nationalism and the ambivalences indubitably inherent in Irish nationalist attitudes but in so doing he indicts the whole nationalist population and especially anyone who articulates a unity aspiration.'[68] Before the end of 1973 Bobby Molloy would say of the new Government that 'the nearest thing they could get to Hitler's Dr Goebbels was Doctor Conor Cruise O'Brien.'[69] Few other politicians of the era excited the same kind of visceral response.

There were only four female TDs out of 144 in the new Dáil: Joan Burke and Brigid Hogan O'Higgins of Fine Gael, Celia Lynch of Fianna Fáil and Eileen Desmond of the Labour Party. In the circumstances it's arguable that an event that took place two days before their election was of greater long-term significance for Irish women.

The report of the Commission on the Status of Women, headed by the senior civil servant Thekla Beere, recommended an end to all forms of discrimination and to the civil service marriage bar. It also came out in favour of family planning information and advice being provided by the Department of Health, of nursery schools and creches being provided in each new housing estate and of the bar on women doing jury service being lifted.

The commission's recommendation of equal pay for women was prompted by some extraordinary statistics. In manufacturing industry, women, who made up a third of the work force, received 43 per cent less in hourly pay than men. Women teachers were paid 20 per cent less than married male teachers, though the same as single men. Female civil servants received 20 per cent less than both their married and single male colleagues.[70] The relative situation had actually disimproved for women, who were earning less compared with men in 1971 than they had done in 1938.[71]

The report's conclusions were 'accepted in principle' by the outgoing Government, though largely because of the requirements imposed by membership of the EEC. The Government undertook to remove the marriage bar, by which female civil servants were forced to resign their jobs on getting married, within two years. And in that year's budget the Minister for Finance, Richie Ryan, brought in the first unmarried mother's allowance. This change in policy was the result of campaigning by a single mothers' organisation, Cherish, and in particular by its founder, Maura O'Dea, one of a number of remarkable activists who put women's rights on the political agenda for the first time. A single mother herself, O'Dea had founded Cherish to put an end to the stigma of single parenthood at a time when there was 'always the terror of who might have the heart attack, or of the father who might die, or of the somebody who might die if this girl didn't disappear. They didn't tell their parents anyway. I remember the terror and how everything had to be hidden.'[72]

A significant document of the time was *Chains or Change*, produced in 1971 by the Irish Women's Liberation Movement, a group that included the journalists Mary Maher and Nell McCafferty of the *Irish Times* and Mary Kenny of the *Irish Press*, the Communist Party activist Máirín Johnston, the anti-war campaigner Dr Máire Woods and the general secretary of Official Sinn Féin, Máirín de Búrca. The pamphlet called for equal pay, equality before the law, access to contraception, and justice for deserted wives, unmarried mothers and widows.

On the fringe of the group was Mary Robinson, a young Trinity College senator who had been one of the guests when the IWLM received the ultimate media accolade of the time: an appearance on 'The Late Late Show', presented by Gay Byrne. The group made an even greater imprint on the public consciousness in May 1971 when members travelled to Belfast to buy contraceptives, demonstrating the anomaly by which contraceptives were illegal in the Republic but could be purchased in the North and brought home without interference from Customs officers. The arrival of the women in Connolly Station, their contraband cargo in hand, on the 'Condom Train,' to the cheers of their supporters and the puzzlement of the Customs officers, was a spectacle that could scarcely have been imagined in previous decades.

In the same year Robinson introduced a private member's bill in the Seanad to legalise the sale of contraceptives but found herself politically isolated and personally vilified, some imaginative souls sending her anonymous letters containing the severed fingers of gardening gloves. Despite Jack Lynch's immortal statement that he 'would not like to leave contraception on the long finger for too long,' the three main parties shied away from legislation.[73] In this they were undoubtedly influenced by the opposition of the Catholic Church, typified by the 1971 Lenten pastoral of Archbishop John Charles McQuaid, in which he declared: 'Contraception is evil; there cannot be, on the part of any person, a right to what is evil.'[74] It was the kind of pronouncement that a few short years earlier would have passed unchallenged. Instead, 'the following Sunday when the letter was being read in the churches, the Irish Women's Liberation Movement formed a forty foot chain across the entrance to the Archbishop's house in Drumcondra.'[75] Battle had been joined.

The Irish Women's Liberation Movement broke up shortly afterwards, but most of its principal members would be among the protagonists in the struggles for women's rights that would play such a central part in national life over the next couple of decades.

The battle would, however, take place without John Charles McQuaid. On Saturday 7 April 1973, shortly after 11:45 a.m., one of the most influential figures in Irish life since independence died at the age of seventy-seven. He had felt too ill to say Mass that morning and had been rushed to hospital by ambulance. Staff Nurse Margaret O'Dowd described how he had been given pain-killing injections but never complained.

The son of a doctor from Cootehill, Co. Cavan, McQuaid had been Archbishop of Dublin from 1940 to 1971 and had assisted Éamon de Valera in drawing up the 1937 Constitution. The *Irish Times* observed that, 'with Mr De Valera, perhaps more than the President, he shaped an epoch.'[76] Few people would have argued with that assessment; but whether such huge influence had been entirely positive was more debatable. 'Dr. McQuaid', wrote his adversary Noël Browne, 'ruled his archdiocese with an unbending conviction that his rigid, triumphalist, conservative approach to Catholicism was the only appropriate stance.'[77] He had been rigid in his insistence that Catholics could attend Trinity College only with permission from their diocesan authorities. He had campaigned against the decision of the National Athletic and Cycling Association in 1934 to allow women to compete at the same sports meetings as men, which he described as 'a social abuse outraging our rightful Irish tradition.'[78] Like most of McQuaid's opponents, the NACA had backed down. He was responsible for the sacking of the writer John McGahern from his teaching post after the publication of the novel *The Dark*; he had expressed opposition to the legalisation of tampons, in case they might provide sexual stimulation for women; and at the 1957 Dublin Theatre Festival he caused the withdrawal of plays by Samuel Beckett and Seán O'Casey, who vowed that he would 'never return to Ireland as long as the Arch Druid of Drumcondra is alive.'[79] Most significantly, he had been the central figure in the church's opposition to Browne's Mother and Child health scheme in 1951. 'McQuaid boasted that the bishops' condemnation of the Mother and Child Scheme, and the condemnation of it by the Inter-Party government led by Taoiseach John A. Costello was the most important event in Irish history since Daniel O'Connell had achieved Catholic Emancipation in 1829.'[80] He was also a fierce opponent of ecumenism and an anti-Semite, who in 1932 had preached that

> from the first persecutions till the present moment, you will find Jews engaged in practically every movement against Our Divine Lord and his Church . . . How many of you who saw *Ben Hur, The King of Kings* and *The Ten Commandments* realised that these films were based on this very desire to show Christ as only a great man and a member of the Jewish race? I hold here copies of the telegrams by which the powerful Masonic and Jewish group, the Benai Berith, compelled the Jewish film producers to alter the sacred history of the gospel.[81]

McQuaid's admirers pointed to his undoubted achievements, his setting up of the Catholic Social Service Conference, which had provided meals and clothes for the poor of Dublin, his encouragement of the provision of halting sites for Travellers, and the eighty new churches and 250 new national schools built during his time in charge of the diocese. But the frequent references to his love and care for the marginalised sat strangely with his wondering aloud to Browne at the time of the Mother and Child Scheme 'why it was necessary to go to so much trouble and expense simply to provide a free health service for the 10 per cent necessitous poor.'[82] This came at a time when 'infant mortality in the lower income groups was 133 per 1,000 compared with 29 per 1,000 in higher income groups.'[83]

McQuaid had seemed notably undisturbed by the Second Vatican Council, telling his parishioners on his return home that 'no change will worry the tranquillity of your Christian lives' and preventing two well-known liberal theologians from speaking in the diocese.[84] Yet the reforming current in the church was to sweep him away. McQuaid had been shocked when, on 27 December 1971, the resignation he had submitted to Pope Paul VI as a matter of form, because he had turned seventy-five, was accepted. Worse was to follow when he was succeeded not by his preferred choice, Joseph Carroll, but by Dermot Ryan, the 47-year-old professor of eastern languages at UCD and one of McQuaid's greatest critics.

His final years were a change from the halcyon days of 1961, when the streets of Dublin had been decorated to celebrate the supposed 1,500th anniversary of the death of St Patrick, for which McQuaid had celebrated Mass in Croke Park for ninety thousand people. The broadcaster Father Joseph Dunn saw that McQuaid had 'moved quite suddenly from a position of great power and activity to one where he was powerless, unemployed and semi ostracised. Rightly or wrongly some seemed to suggest that to call at Killiney, where John Charles lived, might be taken as a symbol of opposition to the new regime.'[85] On the Sunday before he died the *Sunday Press* published a report on the chaotic diocesan financial position inherited by Archbishop Ryan. McQuaid felt the report was 'putting my whole period in office in question.'[86]

The day after his death Noël Browne observed that while the archbishop 'adversely influenced the pattern of life adopted by our political leaders, this may have been a fault in them, rather than in Dr McQuaid.'[87]

The question of whether bishops were wrong to throw their weight around in political matters or whether politicians were wrong to let them do so would not disappear with the death of the man who more than anyone else had embodied the immense power of the Catholic Church in twentieth-century Ireland.

A significant victory seemed to have been gained by the state in its battle against the IRA when, on 28 March 1973, the *Claudia,* a 298-ton motor vessel containing 250 rifles, 248 revolvers, 7,600 rounds of ammunition, 100 Russian-made anti-personnel mines, 600 pounds of gelignite, 300 hand grenades and a quantity of Cortex fuse wire was apprehended half a mile east of Helvick Head by ships of the Naval Service. The boat had been tracked by the armed fishery protection vessel *Deirdre* and two other naval ships, *Gráinne* and *Fóla.* Among the six men arrested on the *Claudia* and a thirty-foot angling launch that had gone to meet it were Joe Cahill, who had become IRA chief of staff after the arrest of Seán Mac Stiofáin, and Donal Whelan, the headmaster of Kilmacthomas Vocational School. Cahill had been sentenced to death in 1942 for his involvement in the killing of an RUC policeman in Belfast, but the sentence had been commuted to life imprisonment, and he was released in 1949.

A jubilant Minister for Defence, Patrick Donegan, memorably informed the press that the *Claudia* would 'get a boot up the transom' and be sent out of Irish waters.[88] On 22 May the Special Criminal Court found Cahill guilty of conspiracy to import arms and ammunition. He told Mr Justice Thomas Finlay:

> If I am guilty of any crime it is that I did not succeed in getting the contents into the hands of the freedom fighters of this country. And I believe that national treachery was committed off Helvick Head when the Free State forces conspired with our British enemies to deprive our freedom fighters of the weapons of war.[89]

His fellow-defendants, Seán Garvey and Denis McInerney, were equally defiant, McInerney telling the judge to 'earn your thirty pieces of silver' and Garvey urging him, 'Do your damnedest.'[90] Mr Justice Finlay's damnedest turned out to be three years in jail for Cahill and two apiece for Garvey and McInerney. Whelan received a two-year suspended sentence and was suspended from his job for seven years.

The arms had come from Tripoli, where they had been loaded by Libyan soldiers on the orders of Muammar al-Gaddafi. It was believed that American intelligence sources had learnt about the shipment and passed the information to British intelligence, which then notified the Irish authorities.

———

When Éamon de Valera stepped down as President of Ireland in 1973 at the age of ninety, after fourteen years as President, Erskine Childers was nominated by Fianna Fáil. He began the campaign as underdog against Tom O'Higgins of Fine Gael, who in 1966 had come within 10,700 votes of defeating de Valera.

Fianna Fáil adopted a strategy of arguing that the election had nothing to do with party politics and appealing for votes for Childers personally. 'He was packed into a bus and began to tour the country,' wrote Brian Lenihan, Childers' campaign manager. 'A wag christened the bus "Wanderly Wagon" after a popular children's television programme of the time . . . Erskine made short inspirational speeches, all on the same themes of community, leadership, practical patriotism and an open Áras. It was great stuff.'[91] The strategy proved to be a winning one, and Childers won by 48,096 votes, coming out on top in 27 of the 42 constituencies and becoming the state's second Protestant president. Educated in England, at the age of sixteen he had suffered the loss of his father, who was executed without trial by the Free State government during the Civil War. The older Erskine made his son promise to seek out the men who had signed the death warrant and shake their hands in a spirit of reconciliation. The new President had become an Irish citizen only in 1938, the year in which he also became a TD for Cavan. A Lynch loyalist, he had held several ministries and been Tánaiste from 1969 to 1973. He said that he believed 95 per cent of his votes had been personal rather than party-political ones.

'I still feel a little bewildered at the great honour bestowed on me by the Irish people,' he said. 'I feel like a humble clerk in an office who has suddenly had a magic wand waved over him and finds himself occupying a palace.'[92] Asked about his plans for the future, the defeated O'Higgins said: 'I notice the grass in my garden is rather long and I intend to cut the grass.'[93]

If the presidential victory had given Fianna Fáil a boost, the party was soon back in turmoil, with Jack Lynch arguably going closer to political oblivion than he had even at the time of the Arms Trial. It was a complicated saga, including, among other things, hot pants, Joe Bugner and various shady machinations that seemed to be plucked from the pages of a John Le Carré novel.

On 12 October 1972 the biggest robbery in the country's history took place in Dublin at the Grafton Street branch of Allied Irish Bank. Three armed men kidnapped the wife, sister-in-law and two children of the manager and forced him to help them, and another three armed men, rob the premises. Staff members were locked in the strongroom by the gang, who proceeded to fill bags and trunks with banknotes. The thieves asked the porter to make tea for the staff and talked to them about the European heavyweight boxing championship fight won by Bugner and the poor quality of Ireland's telephone service. They remained in the bank for more than two hours, addressing each other by military ranks.[94]

On 21 December 1972 two English brothers, Kenneth and Keith Littlejohn, were arrested in London. They were extradited to Ireland, where on 3 August 1973 they were sentenced to twenty and fifteen years' imprisonment, respectively, for the Grafton Street robbery after a trial at the Special Criminal Court during which Kenneth claimed that the brothers had been working for the British Ministry of Defence. One of their contacts had been John Wyman, an agent of the Secret Intelligence Service (popularly called MI6), who the previous year had been discovered receiving secret information on the IRA from Detective-Sergeant Patrick Crinnion of C3, the Garda security and intelligence section. Wyman was sent back to England; Crinnion, released from custody,

> was driven to Dublin Airport by his solicitor, together with Wyman. En route, the disgraced garda asked the solicitor to stop his car in the Dublin suburb of Whitehall. He got out, and disappeared.[95]

Kenneth Littlejohn had arrived in Ireland with a prison term for robbery and a dishonourable discharge from the British army already under his belt. His first port of call was Co. Kerry, where he claimed to be a businessman who was keen to manufacture hot pants under the company name of Whizz Kids (Ireland) Ltd. The hot pants never materialised, but Littlejohn had more luck when he sought to set up a meeting in London with the Under-Secretary for Defence, Geoffrey Johnson-Smith. At this meeting, which the British confirmed had taken place, Littlejohn offered his services as an informant on IRA activities. Moving to Clogherhead, Co. Louth, Littlejohn met former members of the Official IRA who had been expelled for involvement in 'unofficial' bank robberies, notably Brian Mathers from Newry, who was later given ten years' imprisonment for his part in the Grafton Street robbery, the Court of Criminal Appeal doubling his original sentence. He also claimed to have carried out bank raids and other robberies on the instructions of his intelligence handlers.

> The objective, according to Mr Littlejohn, was to stir trouble in border areas and to the South so that the Dublin government would be forced to take action against the IRA. If that were so, the plan succeeded. After these incidents, and a riot in Dundalk which republicans disclaimed, [the] Minister for Justice Mr O'Malley began to draft his amendment to the Offences against the State Act.[96]

The Littlejohn story was an embarrassment for the Irish and British Governments, while the SDLP worried that the affair might give the IRA a propaganda triumph. But it was Jack Lynch who suffered the greatest embarrassment of all. He said that during his time in Government the only contact he had with the British concerning the Littlejohns was when their extradition was being sought. But he had in fact been told about the activities of the Littlejohns. On 3 January he had received a report from the Irish Ambassador in London, Dónal O'Sullivan, that the British Government had accepted the offer of information on the IRA from the brothers but had not sanctioned any illegal actions. Two days later, at a meeting in Dublin, the Attorney-General, Colm Condon, and the Minister for Justice, Desmond O'Malley, had asked the British Director of Public Prosecutions, Sir Norman Shelhorn, if there was any connection between Wyman and the Littlejohns.

Garret FitzGerald instructed the Secretary of the Department of Foreign Affairs, Hugh McCann, to contact Lynch and remind him that he had known the Littlejohns were in touch with the British authorities since January. Caught out in what could have been construed as a lie, a shaken Lynch gave a press conference at which he revealed that he was considering resigning as leader of Fianna Fáil. His colleagues rallied round. Brian Lenihan described Lynch as suffering from 'a lapse of recollection which did not warrant any action (such as resignation) within Fianna Fáil.'[97] O'Malley said the mistake was his fault, as he had been on holiday when Lynch denied knowing about the Littlejohns and so had been unable to remind Lynch about the meeting of 3 January.[98] But what probably saved Lynch was the fact that the opposition didn't seem interested in taking the matter much further. Lynch's biographer feels that this showed 'a fundamentally decent side to Irish politics.'[99] Yet the whole saga raised questions about the extent to which the British intelligence services had manipulated the political situation within the Republic, questions that have never been conclusively answered.

In May 1974 the Littlejohn brothers scaled the walls of Mountjoy Prison, and, while Keith was recaptured almost immediately, Kenneth eluded the authorities for the next twenty months, during which time he gave interviews describing his work for the Secret Intelligence Service. In 1981 the brothers were released, on condition that they leave Ireland, thus ending an association with this country that had almost ended the career of one of the most popular politicians in its history.

The coalition's unwillingness to damage Anglo-Irish relations was a result of the growing hopes of a political breakthrough in Northern Ireland. On 20 March the Conservative government, headed by Ted Heath, had produced a white paper, *Northern Ireland: Constitutional Proposals*, which proposed the setting up of a 78-member power-sharing Executive as well as a Council of Ireland, a 32-county body whose powers were as yet undefined. The white paper had the support of the Ulster Unionist Party, the SDLP, the Alliance Party and the Irish Government. It was opposed by Ian Paisley's Democratic Unionist Party as well as a new unionist party, Ulster Vanguard, led by William Craig, which had links with the UDA. Sinn Féin and the IRA also declared their opposition.

The elections for the new assembly on 28 June gave the Official Unionists 24 seats, the SDLP 19 and the non-aligned Unionists, DUP and the Alliance Party eight each, with Vanguard winning seven. On 17 September, Heath became the first British prime minister to visit the Republic on official business since independence. After a nine-hour meeting, Cosgrave and Heath agreed to hold a conference of the two governments and the Northern political parties to decide the structure and form of the Council of Ireland. Cosgrave wanted to assure unionists that the council was 'no trick to win a United Ireland.'[100] Jack Lynch, who met Heath for two hours, said that 'a lasting peaceful solution can only be found in the context of a United Ireland.'[101] Official Sinn Féin burned an effigy of Heath outside the GPO, where thirty people were arrested after an attempt to take over the RTE studios, then housed in the building.

On 28 October the Standing Committee of the Ulster Unionist Party voted to take part in the Executive, the margin of 132 to 105 showing the dissent that its leader, Brian Faulkner, faced within his own party, quite apart from the implacable opposition of the other strands of unionism. On 22 November the Executive was formed, with Faulkner as Chief Executive and the SDLP leader Gerry Fitt as deputy. In the Dáil, Cosgrave described this as 'momentous', Lynch as 'historic.'[102] And on 6 December the participants in the tripartite talks began their four-day conference at Sunningdale in Berkshire.

The Taoiseach led a team of thirty ministers and officials to the talks, which were given a somewhat ominous cast by the fact that members of the Ulster Unionist delegation bore the bruises inflicted the previous day at the Assembly by representatives of Paisley and Craig's parties, 'beating and kicking them and attempting to propel them bodily through the doors.'[103] A Canadian-born academic and member of Ulster Vanguard, Prof. Kennedy Lindsay, had laid out both Peter McLachlan and Lloyd Hall-

Thompson during the attack, which the perpetrators said had been caused by their not receiving proper invitations to the Sunningdale conference.[104]

The problem for the negotiators was that

> they all wanted different things. The British wanted the Republic to co-operate in security and agree to mutual extradition, and most of all they wanted a broadly based coalition to outface terror and extremism in Northern Ireland. The Unionists wanted the Republic to recognise the legitimacy of their state, and the British to let them continue governing it with minority representatives who, in this new climate, would give up their tiresome insistence on Irish unity. The Republic wanted a Council of Ireland which would count, and be consulted. So did the SDLP, who saw this as their guarantee, portrayed as the first stage in all-Ireland institutions, when they went back into their communities to face out the gunmen . . . Two different accounts had to come out of Sunningdale. The Unionists had to say that the Council of Ireland had scuppered Irish unity, the SDLP that it advanced it.[105]

Nevertheless, after four days of talks it was agreed that there would be a Council of Ireland, consisting of seven ministers each from the Dáil and the Northern Executive, a secretariat and a consultative assembly of thirty members each from the Dáil and the Executive. Policing, both North and South, would come under the umbrella of the Council, which would also deal with the development of natural resources, electricity generation, tourism, transport, health, agriculture and fisheries. The Irish Government 'fully accepted and solemnly declared that there could be no change in the status of Northern Ireland until a majority of the people of Northern Ireland desired a change in that status.'[106]

All sides seemed optimistic. Faulkner, Fitt and the Alliance Party leader, Oliver Napier, declared themselves satisfied with the outcome. The *Irish Independent* published a five-column photograph of Faulkner clasping the hand of Fitt on one side and of Cosgrave on the other.

Opposition to the agreement was not confined to pugilistically inclined Unionists. The IRA vowed to wreck the Executive, while at a function to mark his twenty-fifth year as a member of the Dáil, Neil Blaney was scathing.

> I am disgusted, sick and tired of the antics of the SDLP. I am ashamed of them now as I have never been ashamed of Irish representatives before . . . The SDLP have sold the heritage and the traditional aspirations of the Six and Twenty-Six counties . . . We are worse now than ever before, and the struggle will have to go on.[107]

Sunningdale was seen as a political success for the coalition Government, as something that, as Desmond O'Malley later remarked, 'would have worked, it would have lasted, it would have changed the whole sorry story of the North had it not been for a change of government.'[108] But three separate problems that arose late in the year would between them derail the Government's economic policy, damage its reputation for competence in security matters and eventually lay bare the division between liberals and conservatives within the coalition.

The oil crisis that would herald the end of the golden era of European capitalism seemed to come out of the blue. Even the invasion of Israel by Egypt and Syria on 6 October did not ring many economic alarm bells. Yet when, on 15 October, the petroleum-producers' organisation OPEC imposed an embargo on crude-oil supplies to the United States and the Netherlands to penalise those countries for supporting the eventually victorious Israelis, a general price increase of 17 per cent and an export cut of 5 per cent, the effect on Western economies was profound. By 1974 the price of oil on the international market had quadrupled; and one of the first casualties was the huge economic optimism that had attended Ireland's entry into the EEC.

The immediate effect was an increase in the price of petrol, electricity, central heating and public transport. In December the Minister for Finance, Richie Ryan, told the Seanad, 'our entire future is threatened by a combination of the oil crisis, inflation and soaring interest rates.'[109] In the same month the country's motorists were asked to apply immediately for petrol ration books, which would be issued to everyone by the new year in case rationing became necessary.[110]

ESB workers had done their bit for energy conservation with two industrial disputes at the beginning of November, first a work to rule by shift workers at power stations and then a strike by members of the Amalgamated Union of Engineering Workers. The resulting power cuts seemed to make Galway Chamber of Commerce blow a fuse as it appealed to the public to boycott those involved in the engineers' strike. 'We suggest that the majority of people suffering show their feelings by ostracising those concerned from the community; shops should refuse to serve them, neighbours to talk to them, milkmen call on them.'[111] The strike ended shortly afterwards, though this probably had to do with the ICTU's threat to suspend the union for breaking the terms of the National Wage Agreement rather than a fear of locally imposed starvation.

It was a militant time. The Association of Combined Residents' Associations greeted an increase in mortgage interest rates by building societies from 10 to 11½ per cent by threatening a mortgage strike, whereby members would withhold their mortgage payments and instead pay them into bank or post office accounts.[112] They demanded a return to the old rate, the merging of all the building societies into one and the publication of payments to the societies' directors. Anti-apartheid protesters demonstrated at the World Ploughing Championships in Wellingtonbridge, Co. Wexford, against the presence of teams from Rhodesia (Zimbabwe) under the Smith regime, whose participation led to the withdrawal of the Kenyan and Czechoslovak teams.[113] And at the Labour Party conference in Galway, Noël Browne pleaded with delegates to support the nationalisation of mining companies, closing with the words of James Connolly, 'We only want the Earth.'[114] The conference agreed with nationalisation as a long-term aim. The delegates were divided on whether 95 per cent nationalisation should be made a condition of the Labour Party continuing in government, and the motion was referred back to the Executive.

Petrol crisis notwithstanding, enough fuel was available on 31 October for Irish Helicopters Ltd at Dublin Airport to facilitate the request of a Mr Leonard who wanted to be flown to Stradbally, Co. Laois, to photograph an ancient monument. But when the pilot landed in a field at Stradbally at 2:30 p.m. two armed men emerged from the trees. 'Mr Leonard' and one of the armed men left the scene, but the other armed man instructed the pilot to fly the helicopter to Mountjoy Prison.

At 3:31 p.m. the helicopter landed in the yard of Mountjoy, where the political prisoners were exercising, watched by about half a dozen prison officers. The prisoners surrounded the helicopter and prevented the prison officers from approaching it, while three prisoners—Séamus Twomey, Kevin Mallon and J. B. O'Hagan—clambered aboard. The thirty-odd prison officers who ran from the main block into the yard were unable to prevent the escape. Within ten minutes the helicopter was landing at Baldoyle Racecourse, where a car was waiting.

Twomey, who had been sentenced to three years' imprisonment in October for possessing money taken in an armed robbery in Co. Kerry, was believed to have been chief of staff of the IRA at the time of his arrest and O'Hagan to have been its quartermaster-general. The escape of three such senior figures proved gravely embarrassing for the Government, with Fianna Fáil criticising its 'incompetence' and questioning whether the Ministers for Justice and Defence should resign.[115] The Minister for Foreign Affairs, Garret FitzGerald, was subjected to a belligerent inquisition by viewers of a BBC Northern Ireland television phone-in programme and suggested that the prison officers should have been armed.[116] Neil Blaney, meanwhile, claimed that most members of the Dáil were delighted that the men had escaped.[117] Whether this was true or not, the feat certainly elicited enough admiration to propel a quickly recorded ballad by the Wolfe Tones, 'Up and Away', more popularly known as 'The Helicopter Song', to the top of the Irish charts for four weeks.[118] It was not, however, heard on the radio, as the song was banned by RTE, which meant that 'for weeks Larry Gogan's top three climaxed prematurely with the number two hit in the land.'[119]

It remained to be seen whether the success of 'The Helicopter Song' and the anti-internment ballad 'The Men Behind the Wire' by Barleycorn, which had spent five weeks at number 1 the previous year, confirmed Blaney's theory of widespread republican sentiment, or whether Kevin Boland had it right with his suggestion, after a final humiliation in the 1976 Dublin South-West by-election, that republicanism for people south of the border merely meant being able to 'salve their consciences by singing rebel songs in the pub at night.'[120] Maybe the truth was somewhere between these poles, as suggested by a survey of attitudes in 1973 which showed that 35.3 per cent of people in the greater Dublin area agreed that 'violence, though regrettable, has been necessary for the achievement of non-unionist rights in Northern Ireland.'[121]

———

The final shock of the year for the coalition Government came on 19 December when the Supreme Court ruled that the ban on the importing of contraceptives was unconstitutional. The case had been taken by Mary McGee, a 29-year-old fisherman's wife from Skerries, Co. Dublin, after Customs officers had seized contraceptive jelly sent to her through the post from England. The court heard that Mrs McGee, the mother of four children, during each pregnancy suffered from toxaemia, during her second pregnancy developed a serious cerebral thrombosis from which she nearly died and which left her temporarily paralysed on one side, and during her last pregnancy suffered from toxaemia complicated by hypertension. She had been advised by her doctor that if she became pregnant again there would be a serious risk that she would again suffer a cerebral thrombosis. Because of this the doctor advised against an oral contraceptive and instead recommended an intra-uterine device, to be used with a contraceptive jelly.[122]

A majority of the court—Justices Brian Walsh, Frederick Budd, Séamus Henchy and Frank Griffin—ruled in favour of Mrs McGee; the Chief Justice, Mr Justice William Fitzgerald, dissented, describing the risks to her health as 'natural hazards which must be faced by married couples with such fortitude as they can summon to their assistance.'[123]

Strictly speaking, Mrs McGee's victory did not change a great deal. The sale of contraceptives within Ireland remained illegal. (There was also the anomalous position that by 1973, 38,000 Irish women were taking the contraceptive pill, which was being prescribed as a cycle regulator.)[124] But it did produce pressure on the Government to finally legislate in favour of permitting some form of contraception. This was something that would prove problematic for a Government made up of two parties in which the liberal and conservative wings were deeply divided, though the ludicrous way in which this division would eventually manifest itself was not foreseen.

The Supreme Court judgement was yet another obstacle for the coalition to surmount; yet all the problems might be forgotten should the Government play a part in bringing peace to the North.

Sunningdale was the one bright spot on the horizon.

Chapter 3 ∾

┃ WALK ON HOT COALS

1974

In the early hours of Saturday 12 January 1974 several days of bad weather culminated in the worst storm to hit the east coast in seventy-one years. The wind gusted to hurricane force, up to 112 miles per hour, and in Finglas, Dublin, a woman died when her car was swept off the road and into a lamp-post. In Ballymun a night watchman died of a heart attack in his storm-damaged shelter.[1] 150,000 houses lost electricity supply and 30,000 of those, mainly in Cos. Cork, Limerick and Tipperary, would remain without power for days.

These were not inappropriate auguries for a year that would be characterised by destruction and chaos and the struggle to contain forces that seemed too powerful for the authorities to master. It was a year in which the conflict in the North spilled over the border to an unprecedented degree. It was a year of roadblocks and checkpoints, one when the coalition Government sometimes seemed convinced that the very survival of the state was at stake.

Two particular periods seemed to encapsulate the spirit of the year: the month of June, which saw the death and funeral of Michael Gaughan, the kidnapping of Lord and Lady Donoughmore and the trials of Rose Dugdale and the killers of Senator Billy Fox; and the ninety seconds on 17 May during which three car bombs exploded in Dublin.

At half past five on that Friday afternoon 24-year-old John O'Brien, his wife, Anna, and their two baby daughters, Jacqueline (17 months) and Ann Marie (5 months), were in Parnell Street when 150 pounds of explosive packed into the boot of a car exploded near them. The whole family was killed instantly, as were six other people. Less than a minute later 100 pounds of explosives in a car went off outside O'Neill's shoe shop in Talbot Street, killing twelve people: two more would die later. A third car bomb, in South Leinster Street, exploded last and killed two people.[2]

In Talbot Street, Dr John Cooper, a Belfast anaesthetist who was in Dublin to attend a conference, saw 'a woman decapitated and another with a piece of car engine embedded in her back. He also saw a man dying with an iron bar through his abdomen.'[3] At the same site someone saw 'a gutter literally running with human blood. A few feet away was a human leg and next to it a head.'[4] There were 'bodies covered by newspapers from a newsboy's stand at the corner of Gardiner Street . . . two bodies in Guiney's window so badly mutilated they were fused together.'[5] The body of one of the O'Brien babies was discovered in the cellar of a pub near where the blast had happened.

The dance hall of Moran's Hotel in Talbot Street 'was turned into an emergency centre where scores of injured men, women and children, many with limbs missing and covered with blood, were brought from the street by hotel staff and members of the public. Two Indian student doctors staying in the hotel were summoned from their rooms to the basement to render what medical aid they could.'[6]

Eighty-eight minutes after the Dublin blasts a car bomb containing 'a number of items of farm machinery, including heavy gauge aluminium and brass cog wheels, designed to inflict maximum death and injury,'[7] went off outside Greacen's Bar in Church Square, Monaghan, killing six people instantly. A seventh died later. In all, thirty-three people perished in the bombings of 17 May.

In Dublin that night more than two hundred people came to the City Morgue to see if their friends or relations had been caught in the blast. The response to the appeal for blood donations was so great that Pelican House turned several hundred people away.[8] Among the victims were an Italian man whose brother owned a fish-and-chip shop in Parnell Street and a French woman studying in Dublin.[9]

Jack Lynch's response was to state that every organisation involved in bombing over the previous four years 'has the blood of those innocent victims on their hands.'[10] This sentiment was echoed by the Attorney-General, Declan Costello, who said that 'a very heavy burden of responsibility' lay on the Provisional IRA.[11] In a telegram to the Foreign Office three days after the bombings the British ambassador, Sir Arthur Galsworthy, observed that, though the general assumption was that loyalists were responsible, there was no 'anti-Northern Protestant reaction. Perhaps surprisingly it was the Provisionals themselves who were attracting most of the opprobrium on account of their own long standing association with violence.' He described this belief as 'helpful' and 'healthy' for the British Government.[12]

North of the border the Official Unionist MP John Laird gloated that 'the people who are suffering are people who have quietly condoned a terrorist campaign against the people of this country and sought to gain political ends through violence and indeed have succeeded in making political gains through violence.'[13] Sammy Smith, a member of the Ulster Workers' Council and press officer of the UDA, was more succinct. 'I am very happy about the bombings in Dublin. There is a war with the Free State and now we are laughing at them.'[14]

Within three months the Garda investigation was being scaled down. No-one has ever stood trial for the bombings, although it is generally accepted that they were carried out by the Mid-Ulster UVF.[15] The men identified in 1993 by Yorkshire Television as the chief planners of the Dublin operation—Billy Hanna, Harris Boyle, Robert McConnell and Robin Jackson, all former members of the British army's Ulster Defence Regiment—are all dead, despatched by their own comrades, their own bomb, the IRA and cancer, respectively.[16]

The great unanswered question is to what extent, if any, British forces were involved. Among the observations that contributed to public unease were those by the former head of British army bomb disposal, Lieutenant-Colonel George Styles, that in 1974 the loyalists were not 'at a level that would equate to the sort of techniques that were used here in Dublin' and by the former Garda Commissioner Éamonn Doherty, who led the investigation at the time, that he 'didn't think at the time and I don't think now that any loyalist group could have done this on their own in 1974. I believe that if they did participate in this operation they must have been helped.'[17]

Campaigning by a tenacious group set up by those who had lost family members, Justice for the Forgotten, eventually led to two official inquiries, which resulted in the Barron Report of 2004 and the MacEntee Report of 2007. Suggestions of collusion between British intelligence and the bombers were not found to be proved, but, in the words of the MacEntee Report, the inquiry was 'limited in the scope of its investigations by not having access to original security and intelligence documents in the possession of the British government.'[18] The full story, it seems, may never be told.

The Fianna Fáil TD Vivion de Valera (a son of the former Taoiseach) accused the Government of being almost exclusively focused on the threat posed by republican violence, even though 'it was not the IRA who bombed Dublin.'[19] Certainly the rhetoric employed by senior coalition figures was far more stringent than anything that had issued from the

Lynch Government. Liam Cosgrave said that the Northern Troubles were 'killing here the desire for unity which has been part of our heritage . . . Unity or close association with a people so deeply imbued with violence and its effects is not what they want.'[20] Séamus Mallon, chairperson of the SDLP group in the Northern Ireland Assembly, thought it was unfair to describe Northerners in general as being imbued with violence when only a small minority were involved.[21] The SDLP let it be known that it thought silence from Cosgrave would have been more valuable than the comments he had made.[22]

The Minister for Justice, Paddy Cooney, was even more forthright in describing republicans as being, literally, insane. 'The mentality of the IRA is mindless and savage. It is so irrational that it prohibits us from understanding the mentality of the person who can support or be a member of the IRA.'[23] Vivion de Valera protested in the same Dáil debate:

> Violence in the North did not start with the IRA. The IRA are the symptom and the product of an unnatural situation in the North, a very unnatural state of affairs, the B Specials, the later extremist elements up there and the persecution of the Catholic and Nationalist minority up there. That was not the IRA. I do not like saying this because I have no brief for the IRA.

This met with a response from the Parliamentary Secretary to the Minister for Foreign Affairs, John Kelly: 'I am sick hearing people say that they have no brief for the IRA, *but*.'[24]

When Neil Blaney asked if the Government had made any representations to the British in connection with the Price sisters from Belfast, then on hunger strike, the Minister for Foreign Affairs, Garret FitzGerald, answered: 'I am not concerned with his selective sympathy. In fact it turns my stomach,' to which Blaney replied by calling the minister 'a whited sepulchre' and 'a gutty'.[25]

It may well be that the ferocity of Government rhetoric was connected with the events of the night of 11 March, when a Fine Gael senator, Billy Fox, became the first member of the Oireachtas to be murdered since Deputy Pat Reynolds of the same party had been shot in Sligo-Leitrim during the 1932 election campaign. Fox was visiting the farmhouse of his girl-friend's father, Richard Coulson, at Tircooney, three miles from Clones and a mile and a half from the border, when a group of armed and masked men burst into the house and said they were looking for arms. They held the family prisoner, then burned the house and also a caravan in which Coulson's son lived with his wife and two young children. At ten the next morning Fox's body was discovered hidden behind a hedge two miles from Clones. He had been shot.[26]

There was some initial confusion about the identity of the culprits. The Provisional IRA denied involvement and extended 'the sympathy of the republican movement' to Fox's family, while a phone call to RTE claimed responsibility on behalf of the Ulster Freedom Fighters, a loyalist paramilitary group.[27] The IRA turned out to be responsible all the same, the irony being that Fox, a Protestant, was one of the most republican members of the Fine Gael parliamentary party. He had criticised the British army's cratering of border roads and had produced a rubber bullet in the Dáil to publicise their use in the North.[28]

On 7 June in the Special Criminal Court three men from Clones—Seán McGettigan, George McDermott and James McPhillips—and two from nearby Legnakelly—Seán and Michael Kinsella—were sentenced to life imprisonment for the murder of Senator Fox. Seán Kinsella said he had recruited the other local men on the request of IRA men from the North, who claimed that George Coulson was a UVF quartermaster.

> The North men seemed to have gone berserk, and with the shooting and the burning I decided to pull the Clones men out immediately. We all profoundly regret the death of Senator Fox. There was a clear understanding that under no circumstance were any shots to be fired.

The words of Michael Kinsella, as reported by his brother, 'For fuck's sake don't burn the house. There's no sense in that,' seemed to capture the disastrous flavour of the night.[29]

The following day the body of Michael Gaughan arrived in Dublin and began its remarkable journey to Co. Mayo. Gaughan, a 24-year-old from Ballina, had died in the hospital wing of Parkhurst Prison in the Isle of Wight after developing pneumonia while on hunger strike. A member of a family that had moved to Manchester six years earlier, he had been jailed for seven years in December 1971 for his part in a bank robbery in London. The medical verdict was that Gaughan had died of pneumonia, though republicans claimed he died of 'complications from force feeding; the tube deposited liquid in his lungs, not his stomach.'[30]

The previous December Gaughan's fellow-Mayoman Frank Stagg had arrived at Albany Prison, also in the Isle of Wight, to serve a ten-year sentence for IRA activities. When Stagg refused to do prison work and demanded treatment as a political prisoner, Gaughan joined him in protest. They were then kept in the eight-foot-square cells of the punishment block, which Stagg claimed were not 'slopped out' regularly and had rats coming through the windows. On 31 March, having been transferred to Parkhurst, they went on hunger strike to demand, among other things, transfer to a prison in Ireland, and on 10 April they were moved to the prison hospital.[31]

By the time Gaughan's body reached Dublin on Saturday it had already caused a furore. On the Friday night the coffin had rested in the Sacred Heart Church, Kilburn, London, and on Saturday morning a parade took place along the Kilburn High Road, an area of London associated with the Irish community, the coffin followed by men in the standard IRA funeral garb of dark glasses and black berets, young women in green Cumann na mBan uniforms and several thousand mourners.[32] Questions were asked in the House of Commons by irate Tory MPs about the spectacle, while an Irish priest based in Wolverhampton, Father Michael Connolly, was stripped of his duties for telling the mourners that the parade was 'a fitting tribute to a great man.'[33]

Thousands of people lined the route from Dublin to Ballina, and 'tricolours and black flags flew from houses.'[34] In Mullingar the town band preceded a colour party through the town, and in Longford a guard of honour led by the president of Provisional Sinn Féin, Ruairí Ó Brádaigh, walked alongside the coffin.[35] In Charlestown, where the cortege crossed into Co. Mayo, it was led by local men who had been interned for IRA membership during the forties.[36]

At the requiem mass in St Muiredach's Cathedral, Father Michael Keane made a call for conciliation. 'England is always seen as our enemy. But we may think how good a country it has been to us in the past by giving us work, opportunity and money. It is a pleasant land, and it is a sad thing to see the fighting going on and on. Can we not sit down and talk?' At this point one of the congregation stood up and shouted, 'This is not the sermon to offer a true Irish soldier. It is an offence and insult. You should try living in the North and see what it's like there. You wouldn't like that.' The man then led a walk-out from the cathedral.[37] Among those who walked out was Dáithí Ó Conaill of Provisional Sinn Féin, who gave the graveside oration to ten thousand mourners, inveighing against 'the British opportunists, the well-heeled politicians in the South, the hired scribes and the venal churchmen,' and saying that Gaughan's death 'had given purpose to the struggles of all people throughout the world.'[38]

The outpouring of emotion at the Gaughan funeral was a propaganda triumph for the republican movement. It had also been an embarrassment for the Government, and Fianna Fáil sought to embarrass it even further when David Andrews was 'instructed to raise a question in the Dáil about the lack of action by the authorities in relation to the Gaughan funeral on

Sunday last where subversives had blatantly paraded and fired volleys.'[39] The Government would react very differently on the occasion of the next big republican funeral.

In the early hours of the Sunday morning following the Gaughan funeral a member of the Ard-Chomhairle of Sinn Féin, Phil Flynn, who was also assistant general secretary of the Local Government and Public Services Union, drove a couple of passengers to Dublin.[40] He dropped them off in the Phoenix Park at 3 a.m., and they made their way to the gate lodge at the Parkgate Street entrance and asked that the Gardaí be contacted. They gave their names as Lord and Lady Donoughmore. A kidnapping saga that had gripped the country's attention for several days was over.

On the previous Tuesday night a group of armed kidnappers had arrived at Knocklofty House, near Clonmel, where they beat up the chauffeur and his wife in an effort to make them divulge the whereabouts of guns and money before waiting for the Donoughmores to return home. When they did, as Lord Donoughmore explained after his release, 'one put a gun to my ear, and I struggled. I was hit on the head five times with a revolver. I think they call it pistol-whipping in the Wild West.' Lord Donoughmore, Conservative MP for Portsmouth from 1943 to 1945 and Grand Master of the Freemasons' Grand Lodge of Ireland, had lived at Knocklofty since 1947.

The kidnapping was an attempt to secure the repatriation of Dolours and Marion Price, two student teachers from Belfast who had been arrested in connection with IRA car bombs that had killed one person in London in March the previous year. That week the Prices had been more than two hundred days on hunger strike and were being forcibly fed.

Emotions were running high. Gardaí escorted vans delivering the *Kerryman* in Tralee after an anonymous phone call warned that 'serious action' would be taken against the paper's editor, Séamus McConville, if he published an editorial critical of the Prices.[41] The editorial was published, and the Irish Council of the NUJ condemned the attempt at intimidation, as it did an article in *An Phoblacht* signed by 'Cormac Mac Airt' that described the broadcaster Liam Nolan as an 'enemy agent' and 'a good employee of the British propaganda machine.'[42] Conor Cruise O'Brien 'blew his top' when the 'Seven Days' programme showed parts of an independently made film, *Behind the Wire,* containing interviews with some Northern Catholics who had been subjected to sensory deprivation by the British army in 1971. He summoned the Director-General to his office, and the producer of 'Seven Days', Eoghan Harris, was moved from current affairs to the agricultural department.[43]

At eleven o'clock on the Friday night after the Donoughmores had been kidnapped the Price Sisters ended their hunger strike, after 205 days, when the Home Secretary, Roy Jenkins, agreed that they would be transferred to an Irish prison within the year.[44] Phil Flynn had made contact with one of the kidnappers, and on Sunday morning he turned up at their hideout and subsequently drove the couple to the Phoenix Park.

The kidnapper whom Flynn had contacted was Eddie Gallagher, a farmer's son from Ballybofey who in April had been involved in the most spectacular robbery of the entire Troubles. One of his accomplices was Rose Dugdale, later his wife, one of the most exotic recruits ever to the cause of Irish republicanism.

Rose Dugdale was the daughter of a millionaire underwriter at Lloyd's of London who owned a 600-acre estate in Devon. As a debutante in 1958 she had been presented to Queen Elizabeth.[45] She had graduated from Oxford University before earning a master's degree in philosophy from Mount Holyoke College, Massachusetts, and a PhD in economics from the University of London.[46] She became disenchanted with her privileged background, giving away money she had inherited to the poor and becoming involved in left-wing causes, including the civil rights movement in Northern Ireland. 'For years my family has been taking money from the poor,' she said. 'I'm just trying to restore the balance.'[47]

In October 1973 Dugdale was found guilty of stealing hundreds of thousands of pounds' worth of paintings and silverware from the country house of her parents. Her then partner, Walter Heaton, a radical shop steward, received a six-year prison sentence, but the judge suspended Dugdale's two-year sentence on the grounds that the likelihood of her committing further crime was 'remote'.[48] By January the following year Dugdale and Gallagher were involved in an unsuccessful attempt to bomb Strabane RUC station with explosives contained in milk churns dropped from a helicopter that had been hijacked in Co. Donegal.[49]

On 27 April 1974 a woman knocked on the door of Russborough House, an eighteenth-century Palladian mansion near Blessington, Co. Wicklow. Four armed men rushed in and bound the owner, 71-year-old Sir Alfred Beit, his wife and his staff before removing nineteen paintings from their frames with screwdrivers.[50]

Beit, a member of a wealthy South African diamond mining family and a former Tory MP, had bought Russborough in 1952 and possessed one of the finest private art collections in the world. The stolen paintings included a Vermeer, *Lady Writing a Letter with Her Maid,* valued at £1½ million, and Goya's *Woman in a Mantilla,* considered one of the master's finest paintings, as well as works by Hals, Velázquez and Murillo. The total was valued at £8 million, making it the biggest art robbery in history.[51] A letter sent to the director of the National Gallery, Dr James White, said that five paintings would be returned when the Price sisters, as well as Hugh Feeney and Gerard Kelly, also convicted for the London car bombings, were transferred to the North. The other fourteen would be returned on payment of a ransom of £500,000. Unless those conditions were met by 14 May the pictures would be destroyed.

On 4 May gardaí called at a cottage near Glandore, Co. Cork, as part of a nationwide check of rented accommodation. In the cottage was a woman who gave her name as Mrs Merrimee, with an address in London. Ten minutes after the gardaí left, the woman arrived at the farmhouse of Connie Hayes, from whom she and a male companion had rented the house two days previously, and asked him if she could borrow his car. The gardaí returned and informed Hayes that they suspected his tenants of having something to do with the Russborough robbery. At six o'clock the woman drove to the cottage at high speed, only to find three Garda cars waiting. Three of the stolen paintings were in the house; the remaining sixteen were in the boot of the car she had borrowed from Hayes. Rose Dugdale, wearing an auburn wig, was arrested, but Eddie Gallagher did not return to the cottage.[52]

Rose Dugdale was sentenced to nine years' imprisonment. She told the court: 'I hold that the whole people of Ireland have and are solely entitled to the wealth of this land, which they laboured to produce. The wealth of this land may not be appropriated from them.'[53] The RTE News duty editor, Rory O'Connor, ordered that further statements by Dugdale—'We have a right to take up arms in reclaiming the wealth of Ireland to her own,' and 'Where was the right of the court to deprive them of their freedom to fight for Ireland? The Republic owed its existence to the fact that others had fought and died for this principle'—were not to be broadcast, whereupon the National Union of Journalists directed its members not to report any more court cases for RTE.[54]

In Limerick Prison on 12 December, Dugdale gave birth to a son, whose father, Eddie Gallagher, she married on 24 January 1978, also in Limerick Prison, which made them the first serving prisoners in the history of the state to get married.[55] On leaving prison in 1980, Dugdale, unlike many of the radicals of the time, did not return to the milieu from which she had come. She became a Sinn Féin activist and in 2007 could be found supporting the Shell to Sea campaign and, at the Sinn Féin ard-fheis, speaking in favour of the leadership's decision to recognise the PSNI.

Eddie Gallagher found himself in Port Laoise Prison in August 1974 awaiting trial on charges of possessing firearms. As it turned out, he would serve only a single day in prison before he played his part in the most embarrassing security lapse yet for the coalition Government, the escape of nineteen IRA prisoners, including the recently recaptured Kevin Mallon, and Michael and Seán Kinsella, who were serving life sentences for the murder of Senator Billy Fox.

The escape began at 12:25 p.m. on 18 August when a group of prison officers were overpowered and their keys taken. The prisoners put on the uniforms and retrieved explosives they had hidden nearby. They used the keys to reach an adjoining flat roof and ran a short distance to the wall surrounding the governor's house, where they used gelignite to blast through a gate; a second charge blew open a gate in the perimeter wall. The escapers piled into three cars that they hijacked on the Borris road.[56]

There were suggestions of a security situation spiralling out of control. The biggest armed robbery in the country's history took place in Tralee on 27 September when two armed men robbed a Post Office van of £74,000 destined for the Bank of Ireland in the town.[57]

What made the Gaughan funeral, the Port Laoise escape and the various exploits connected with Eddie Gallagher all the more galling for the Government was that they came in the absence of political progress to end the conflict in the North. Before the year had even reached the half-way point the Sunningdale Agreement, signed with such high hopes the previous December, and the power-sharing Executive that issued from it lay in ruins.

They had arguably been doomed as early as 3 January, when the Ulster Unionist Council voted to repudiate the agreement, signed less than a month before by their party leader. Faulkner was replaced by Harry West, and on 23 January the Official, Democratic and Vanguard Unionist parties withdrew from the Assembly. Faulkner's position was made even worse when, on 7 February, Edward Heath called a general election, which his Conservative government would lose. The results were disastrous for the Executive, with eleven of Northern Ireland's twelve parliamentary seats going to the Unionist parties opposed to the power-sharing Executive, the odd man out being Gerry Fitt of the SDLP, who held his seat in West Belfast.

The *coup de grâce* arrived in May when the Ulster Workers' Council, an umbrella body of unionist organisations in which the paramilitary Ulster Defence Association played a central role by supplying the kind of intimidation that proved crucial, called a general strike against the agreement. After two weeks of civil and industrial chaos Faulkner and the other Unionist members of the Executive resigned when they were refused permission to negotiate with the strikers. 'It was apparent', said Faulkner, 'from the extent of support for the strike that the degree of consent needed to sustain the executive did not at present exist.'[58] The power-sharing experiment came to an end. It would not be repeated for more than two decades.

Various culprits were blamed for the failure of the Executive. In the Dáil, Liam Cosgrave fumed, 'As we warned it would, the campaign of the IRA has provoked a massive sectarian backlash. This has undermined the only solution that can bring peace to Northern Ireland and security to the minority in the area.'[59] It has also been argued that 'fear of the Republic moved the strikers far more than fear of republicanism. The deference that the British and moderate Unionists had shown towards Catholic aspirations and which had led to power-sharing was largely conditioned by the climate of violence created by the IRA. In the drama itself the IRA played only a small part, providing the noises off.'[60]

Jack Lynch held 'loyalist intimidation' responsible.[61] Seán Donlon of the Department of Foreign Affairs, the Government's main link with the Catholic community in the North, found the SDLP 'traumatised by what they considered to be a British failure to face down an anti-democratic strike whose goal was to undo what had been solemnly agreed at Sunningdale by the British and Irish governments.'[62] Desmond O'Malley later concurred in blaming the British Government: 'Wilson did not seem to have the bottle to stand up to the loyalist workers in the way I think a Conservative government would have.'[63]

Brian Faulkner, who reckoned that the agreement had initially commanded the support of 60 per cent of Northern Protestants, claimed that this had been eroded by the Irish Government's defence of a case brought by Kevin Boland, which claimed that the agreement's acceptance of the right of the North to remain part of the United Kingdom until a majority decided otherwise was unconstitutional, and by a botched swoop on sixteen IRA suspects, all but one of whom had to be released within two days because of insufficient evidence.[64] The Boland case was lost in both the High Court and the Supreme Court, but the Government's defence, that its statement at Sunningdale was not a binding agreement but a matter of policy, 'totally destroyed the value of the declaration, undermining Faulkner's already shaky position and leaving a legacy of distrust.'[65]

Harold Wilson, who had replaced Heath as Prime Minister after the general election and may not have been convinced that complete co-operation would be forthcoming from the RUC or the British army, made a famously counter-productive speech during which he railed against 'people who spend their lives sponging on Westminster and British democracy and then systematically assault democratic methods. Who do these people think they are?'[66]

The leader of the Alliance Party, Oliver Napier, thought the people of the Republic were to blame, and told them so in an open letter.

> You do not want a United Ireland now or in the immediately foreseeable future. Stop claiming that you own Northern Ireland and stop pretending that you want a United Ireland tomorrow. What has your attitude to Northern Ireland achieved in 54 years. It wrecked a Council of Ireland in 1921 and 1974. It helped to wreck the first attempt at partnership government in the North. It helped to maintain bitterness and tension within Northern Ireland. It sowed the seeds for the propagandists of the Provisional IRA and sent young boys and girls to be killed for a mythology, not a cause.[67]

Garret FitzGerald felt that BBC Northern Ireland had much to answer for.

> The BBC was very much in support of the strike, so much so that Conor Cruise O'Brien finally rang the BBC in London to ask what the hell was happening ... They were running basically a rebel radio station.[68]

Cruise O'Brien, on the other hand, blamed FitzGerald.

> I think he was too much under the influence of John Hume ... he made a hash of Sunningdale. The problem was that, supported by some of his colleagues, he built up the Council of Ireland element of Sunningdale on quite unrealistic lines. It had three tiers, executive powers and God knows what else. He put on so much Council of Ireland sail that he capsized the power-sharing boat.[69]

This and similar statements, however, raise more questions than they answer. As the historian Joseph Lee has pointed out,

> the proposed Council of Ireland had a somewhat elaborate structure but it was unlikely to wield any real power for the foreseeable future ... more than half of the popular unionist vote in June supported parties opposed to the power-sharing principle. Once the Council of Ireland vanished from the agenda after 1974, Unionist opinion remained resolutely opposed to the principle of power-sharing.[70]

A speech given that August in Dungarvan by the Rev. Martin Smyth, Imperial Grand Master of the Orange Order, gave an audience in the

Republic a rare opportunity to hear the voice of mainstream unionism at first hand.

> Many of us Ulster Protestants regard the Irish Republic as a very sick country. We do not think that just because people drink too much. We see it as a place from which too many people emerge with an anti-social Mafia type attitude.

The Republic, he went on, was

> the place of origin of many extremists, people unable to settle down to any form of stable, public-spirited and responsible living. In the South of Ireland, however, there is one factor lacking which in Ulster evokes acute conflict. There is not in the Republic a large number of non-Roman Catholics whose performance Roman Catholics have to measure themselves against.
>
> The troubles in Northern Ireland have arisen from the fact that the Roman Catholic part of the community has imposed upon itself many of the same social and psychological handicaps that have also been imposed in the Republic: a bad, sectarian education system, lack of acceptable qualifications for the better types of employment, unplanned families leading to the seeking of dead-end jobs by early school-leavers. Their Protestant neighbours ... tend to achieve more and are marginally more successful in certain directions. Unwilling to attribute some of their disadvantages to their own way of life, the Roman Catholics attribute all failures of achievement to discrimination against them.[71]

It seems unlikely that people holding such a view of a neighbouring community would feel it incumbent upon them to grant civil rights, let alone a share in power, to that community.

Under these circumstances, it was perhaps unfortunate that less than a month before the Smyth speech the debate on the Government's Family Planning Bill—a response to the previous year's judgement in the McGee case—did not show the Dáil at its best. It featured memorable contributions from the Fianna Fáil spokesperson on Justice, Desmond O'Malley ('Our duty as a legislature is, so far as we can within the Constitution, as interpreted by the Supreme Court, to deter fornication and promiscuity, to promote public morality'[72]), the Fianna Fáil backbenchers Michael Kitt ('As soon as we have contraception in, there will be abortion, divorce, euthanasia, all the other evils of venereal disease ... Contraception and all that comes in its wake is not going to have our people living the life that God desires that man should live'[73]) and Hugh Gibbons ('There is an old phrase which says that a taste of the grass makes a rogue of the cow, and with sex experience, being such as it is, having been experienced once, the tendency is to wish to experience more of it, particularly where there is no fear involved'[74]) and Oliver Flanagan for Fine Gael ('There are many of us who believe still that which was taught two thousand years ago is still right . . . What will happen in the case of a dealer who becomes a sex speculator as a result of this section of the bill? We have already heard of the amount of money coming here to keep sex propaganda alive and before the public mind today'[75]).

The bill itself—the Control of Importation, Sale and Manufacture of Contraceptives Bill—provided for the supply of contraceptives to married people only; there had even been a suggestion, from the Attorney-General, Declan Costello, that there be a provision to allow a garda to ask people suspected of carrying contraceptives if they were married. Among letters the Taoiseach received from opponents of the bill one from Dr Patrick Cassin of the Central Mental Hospital warned that 'the present transition of our people is toward a humanist society with the consequent loss of their faith. As such they would be no different from English people.'[76]

On 16 July the Taoiseach and the Minister for Education, Richard Burke, 'amazed even their closest colleagues' by voting against their own Government's bill.[77] With them went the Fine Gael backbenchers Oliver Flanagan, Des Governey, Martin Finn, Joe McLoughlin and Tom Enright (who had been lined up with the Yes voters before he saw his party colleagues taking advantage of the fact that, unlike Fianna Fáil, Fine Gael had permitted a free vote).[78] The bill fell by 75 votes to 61.

———

The political failure to deal with family planning was thrown into sharp relief by the strides made the same year in connection with another once-taboo issue by one of the leading women's rights campaigners of the time. Nuala Fennell, a Dublin journalist, had been involved in the Irish Women's Liberation Movement before bidding farewell to it in a sulphurous open letter that lambasted it as

> an elitist and intolerant group who are using women's liberation as a pseudo-respectable front for their own various political ends . . . if you are not anti-American, anti-clergy, anti-government, anti-ICA, anti-police, anti-man, then sisters there is no place for you either . . .

women's lib has not only lost her virginity, but turned into a particularly nasty harlot.[79]

Fennell founded her own group—Action, Information, Motivation (AIM)—which

> has come to be recognised as one of the most effective women's pressure groups ever to come out of the women's liberation movement. The group was highly influential in securing some of the most important legislation for improving the condition of women's lives and expanding their rights throughout the seventies. The Social Welfare Act of 1974, which transferred the legal right to the Children's Allowance from only the father to either parent or guardian, and the Family Home Protection Act of 1976, which prevented one spouse from disposing of the family home without the consent of the other, are among the most important laws that AIM's lobbying was instrumental in getting passed.[80]

The catalyst for Fennell's next project was a documentary produced by Harlech Television, 'Scream Quietly or the Neighbours Will Hear,' about the Chiswick Women's Aid Centre in London, which offered a refuge for battered wives and their children. On 29 April the Irish Women's Aid Society was set up, with Fennell as chairperson. A business acquaintance leased her a derelict city-centre house that in its first month of existence provided shelter for 40 women and 135 children, 40 per cent of the latter being classed as emotionally disturbed. A visiting journalist heard the women tell,

> with great calm and dignity, how they had been held over the stove and burned, kicked around the floor while pregnant, dragged out of hospital while still ill and beaten again as soon as they got home, given black eyes and had their children battered, all by their husbands.[81]

Even her erstwhile sparring partners in the IWLM paid tribute to Fennell's achievement, Nell McCafferty commenting that

> it was Nuala Fennell who rolled back the stone on domestic violence against women . . . I watched her scrub out the shit encrusted toilets before the first women and children arrived seeking refuge. I knew, of course, that it would not work—that Nuala would not last the pace. I was, of course, wrong . . . Women's Aid refuges, with state funding, are now established throughout the country.[82]

The wider implications of domestic abuse did not escape Fennell. In a speech to the Galway branch of Care, the campaign for the care of deprived children, she lamented that 'with our national self-righteousness we imagined that any kind of divorce in our culture was more unacceptable than the glorified misery of our broken homes.' Many of the women her organisation dealt with, she said, were in their early twenties yet they could never remarry and hope for a better life. Irishwomen had nothing to thank this government, or any Irish government for, while they continued to prevaricate and vacillate on urgent changes. In a topsy-turvy way we find public compassion and involvement operating for the drug addicts, the ex-criminal, the homeless, to which causes the clergy, academics and top people will lend their names, but the root cause of most of these social problems, the broken or unhappy home, goes untreated because the same people are unsure of the implications of involvement in this pseudo sacred area.[83]

AIM also organised a campaign for family law reform, which included representatives of Adapt (the association for deserted wives), the Free Legal Advice Centres, the Society of St Vincent de Paul, the Council for the Status of Women, Cherish (a support group for single parents), the Women's Political Association, the Samaritans and Care. The campaign called for the District Court to be given the power to impose non-molestation orders and to make husbands pay maintenance, for family cases to be heard in private, and for legislation to protect a wife's right to live in the matrimonial home and to prevent its sale against her wishes—all of which subsequently came to pass. The campaign noted that between January and October 1974 there had been 148 matrimonial assault cases in the Dublin metropolitan area and 250 maintenance cases. Three thousand wives were receiving deserted wives' allowance, while there were believed to be another six to eight thousand deserted wives in the city.[84]

———

The morale of the Irish women's movement might well have been boosted by the idea of having a woman President of Ireland. Rita Childers briefly seemed a likely successor to her husband, who died of a heart attack while addressing a dinner of the Royal College of Psychiatrists in Dublin.

Erskine Childers had not enjoyed a particularly brilliant ministerial career. One commentator regarded him as 'tardy, incompetent, vacillating and pedantic, and held in contempt by several of his colleagues, notably Haughey.'[85] Yet the same writer observed that Childers had been 'an exceedingly energetic and popular but unhappy president. When he died suddenly the mourning was general and genuine and his state funeral in Dublin a fine piece of theatre.'[86] By contrast with de Valera, who had taken up Presidential office at the age of seventy-seven and left it only when he had turned ninety, Childers had been a very visible and accessible head of state. He was also popular because of the Panglossian optimism that led him to declare that Ireland was 'the happiest place in the world to live in for almost all the people here.'[87]

On 21 November 'Cosgrave suggested to Lynch that Rita Childers should be named as President by agreement . . . Lynch agreed to sound out Fianna Fáil.'[88] Unfortunately a Fine Gael member of Skibbereen Urban District Council, who had no idea of Cosgrave's proposal, also suggested Rita Childers as a candidate. The *Cork Examiner* published the story, and as a result Noel Smith of the *Irish Independent* rang the Minister for the Gaeltacht, Tom O'Donnell, for a comment.

> O'Donnell mistakenly thought the word of the government decision was already out so he explained to Smith that the government was prepared to back her. The following day the *Sunday Independent* carried the story under the headline: Mrs Childers for President. Smith quoted a government source as saying that Mrs Childers could have the nomination if she wished. Lynch was furious. He considered this a breach of confidentiality as it looked like the coalition was using her candidacy to upstage Fianna Fáil. That killed the possibility of having her as an agreed candidate as far as Fianna Fáil was concerned.[89]

Lynch despatched David Andrews and Michael O'Kennedy to meet Mrs Childers. She was not at home, but they met her son, who

> made it absolutely clear to O'Kennedy and Andrews that both Rita and he were negotiating with the government to ensure that a smooth transfer to Rita would take place to the satisfaction of everybody, many of whom did not want another election. O'Kennedy and Andrews were offended by the tenor of the meeting . . . Lynch set about letting Liam Cosgrave know that under no circumstances whatsoever would Rita Childers be acceptable as an 'agreed' candidate.[90]

Both T. K. Whitaker, the former Secretary of the Department of Finance who had been behind the First Programme for Economic Expansion of the Lemass years, and Dónal Keenan, president of the GAA, were mentioned as possible agreed candidates before the parties eventually settled on Cearbhall Ó Dálaigh, the former Chief Justice and President of the Supreme Court, then serving as Ireland's representative at the European Court of Justice in Luxembourg.[91] The choice would prove to be a fateful one.

If 1974 was a fraught year for the Government on the security front, it was scarcely less troublesome from an industrial relations point of view. The nine-week Dublin bus strike was the most notable of the numerous strikes. It had begun on 5 May, when Dublin's busmen were due to begin working a five-day week for the first time. Members of the National Busmen's Union, which had gone on strike in 1965 for the five-day week and been defeated after a lock-out, were in favour of the new schedules, but members of three other unions—the ITGWU, Workers' Union of Ireland and National Association of Transport Employees—were not, because they had not been balloted on them. This inter-union disagreement complicated the dispute. When the Labour Court recommended on 12 May that a ballot be held on the new schedules, this was accepted by the three other unions but rejected by the NBU. A compromise was eventually reached on 8 July when it was agreed that union members would be allowed to work either a five or a six-day week.

The same year saw the first strike in 215 years at the Guinness brewery in Dublin, which began in May and lasted for three weeks as 1,700 general workers pursued a claim for an extra £2.25 a week. By 11 June apocalypse loomed, as 'most public houses in Dublin have now run out of Guinness draught stout and although bottled Guinness is now available, the pint bottle of Guinness is also becoming scarce.'[92] Three days later the dispute was settled. On the same day conciliation talks were going on to avert a strike by nine hundred workers at Dublin, Shannon and Cork Airports. Members of the AUEW employed by the Institute for Industrial Research and Standards stopped work at UCG and in the water pollution monitoring centre at Shannon Industrial Estate, and the night staff of St Andrew Street telephone exchange in Dublin threatened to strike 'in protest against oppressive conditions . . . Permission from the Night Telephone Supervisor had to be received, according to the Post Office Officials' Association, even for visits to the toilet.'[93]

The *Limerick Weekly Echo and Shannon News* advanced a time-honoured explanation for this rise in industrial unrest. 'The ICTU has moved from the right wing position it held under [the] Limerick man Maurice Cosgrave to the extreme left under Andrew Barr, Chairman of the Communist Party of Ireland.'[94] The *Munster Express* blamed union officials, who it described as 'a few tough and not too educated bargainers.'[95] However, the rash of pay disputes may have been connected less with Red subversion than with the huge price increases engendered by rapidly increasing inflation, which from an already high figure of 11.4 per cent in 1973 had soared to 17 per cent in 1974.[96] There was also the assertion that the ITGWU 'had lost all confidence in the coalition and is no longer all that pleased to support the Labour rump of it.'[97] The union's general secretary, Michael Mullen, a former Labour Party TD, complained that 'the whole concept of public ownership had been played down and they were left with not a socialist vision of the future but milk and water liberalism.'[98] Trade unionists claimed angrily that 'Labour had sold out the working class to implement Fine Gael policies.'[99]

Militancy was not confined to the shop floor. In Cork a rent strike that had been going on for four years reached crisis point, with strikers being jailed, the city council chamber being invaded by protesters and a sympathetic strike briefly closing down the city's docks. The tenants' continued action was sparked by the fact that four hundred new council houses built by Sisk Construction Systems in the Glen and Mayfield had immediately developed 'dampness and black mould or fungus growing on the walls.'[100] An inspection carried out by the British Standards Institution on behalf of the Department of Local Government upheld the complaints.[101]

When the City Manager, Patrick Clayton, urged a council meeting on 25 March to have the tenants who refused to pay rent committed to prison, the motion was carried by 25 votes to 2, only Councillor Gerry Carroll (Aontacht Éireann) and the former Lord Mayor Thomas Leahy (Labour Party) voting against.[102] A fortnight later three of the strikers, Thomas O'Sullivan and John Smyth of Togher and Thomas Lynch of Ballyphehane, began two-week sentences in Limerick Prison. The following night a council meeting was broken up by fifty striking tenants, who filled the public gallery and sang 'We shall overcome' and 'We're on the road to freedom,' until the councillors and officials walked out of the chamber. Two women began a hunger strike on the steps of City Hall, which continued in 24-hour shifts until 12 April.[103]

Next day the city's five hundred dockers called a one-day strike and marched on City Hall with the rent strikers, council lorry-drivers and bin-lifters refused to work and thirty building workers from a city site also joined the picket.[104]

The confrontation continued until 1976, when the city council began to evict striking tenants. It finally ended in October, with the council owed £415,000 in unpaid rent, which it was agreed would be repaid over time. An extraordinary dispute, during which the tenants felt they had opposed 'civil disobedience' to 'institutional violence,' was over.[105]

———

Not far from the housing estates of the Glen and Mayfield is Mac Curtain Street, the home of a young man, born in Co. Donegal, who is the subject of the most compelling visual document of Ireland in 1974 and perhaps one of the finest cinematic records of the country in the entire decade. There remains something infinitely beguiling about *Rory Gallagher: Irish Tour, 1974*, a film during which 'young girls with lank hair reach out their arms to the stage, someone in a suit roves among the young men, motioning them to sit down and a backdrop of waves crashing onto the rugged coast bleeds into "Walk on Hot Coals" a crescendo of live noise and the face of an ecstatic 25 year old with sharp sidies and a wrecked guitar.'[106]

Gallagher, filmed in Belfast, Cork and Dublin during his January tour, was perhaps then at the height of his popularity. He had turned down invitations to join Deep Purple and the Rolling Stones, and the judgement of Jan Akkerman of the Dutch band Focus that Gallagher was 'the king of the white blues players,' would have found wide agreement, not least among the two million people who bought the live album of that Irish tour.[107] He was fortunate to be filmed by one of the great documentary-makers, the Englishman Tony Palmer. The result is a film that gives both a sense of the excitement generated by Gallagher on stage and a sense of place and time as the singer walks around the streets of Cork, signing a jacket for a fan, trying out new instruments in a local music shop and playing at an after-hours party.[108]

It would be easy to regard Rory Gallagher, 'the first Irish rock star', as the antithesis of the showbands that had dominated the entertainment scene in the previous decade.[109] Yet he had begun his musical career in 1964 with one such outfit, taking to the road with the Fontana Showband, later the Impact, as a sixteen-year-old guitarist. At the apogee of the showband era, in the mid-sixties, the Royal and Miami Showbands were drawing crowds of three and four thousand to the big ballrooms. In Cork twenty buses lined up on Grand Parade to take dancers to the Majorca in Crosshaven.[110] But by the mid-seventies the day of the Majorca and of the string of venues operated by an enterprising promoter, a former CIE clerk named Albert Reynolds, which included the Jetland in Limerick, the Dreamland in Athy and the Fairyland in Roscommon, was over, their audience having been lured away to pubs and hotels offering cabaret and the chance to get a drink, which had never been possible in the alcohol-free ballrooms.[111]

The showbands were replaced by rock groups such as Rory Gallagher's and Phil Lynott's Thin Lizzy, by the bands that emerged from the sixties folk boom, the best and most successful of which, Planxty, broke up in 1974, and by the bands playing a specifically Irish, critically derided but immensely popular version of country and western music, the likes of Big Tom and the Mainliners, Philomena Begley and Country Flavour, Ray Lynam and the Hillbillies, and Larry Cunningham and the Mighty Avons.

The urban entertainment phenomenon of the year was not, however, a band at all but one of the most successful shows ever to hit the Dublin stage, Andrew Lloyd Webber's *Joseph and His Amazing Technicolor Dreamcoat*, produced by the impresario Noel Pearson. With Tony Kenny as Joseph, Fran Dempsey as Potiphar and a promising comedian named Brendan Grace as narrator, it opened at the Olympia, did a brief spell in Cork Opera House and celebrated its 250th performance at the Gaiety in October. The producer struck gold again with *Jacques Brel Is Alive and Well and Living in Paris,* starring John Kavanagh, which opened at the Eblana Theatre during the Dublin Theatre Festival to critical acclaim before embarking on a lengthy run of its own.

Yet even the extraordinary Pearson didn't provide the city with its most spectacular show of the year. The impresario behind that was Kevin Heffernan, who had taken on the apparently thankless task of managing the county's football team. Heffernan had been perhaps the outstanding figure on the charismatic Dublin team that had won the all-Ireland championship in 1958. However, the memories of those glory days were now a thing of the past. Dublin had not won an all-Ireland title since 1963 and in 1973 had been ignominiously relegated to the second division of the National League. In the battle for the affections of city youngsters Gaelic football seemed to have conclusively lost out to soccer, then enjoying a golden age, thanks to such television programmes as 'Match of the Day' and 'The Big Match'. In much of the city the GAA was seen almost as an alien organisation, to the extent that on the great Dublin team of 1977 only the corner-forward Bobby Doyle had two Dublin parents.[112] Heffernan would be the driving force behind a sporting miracle and a cultural upheaval.

Dublin's form early in 1974 had been predictably unimpressive. After an undistinguished win over Wexford in their first-round Leinster championship Heffernan pulled a master-stroke by cajoling out of retirement Jimmy Keaveney, an overweight veteran full-forward, who despite his unathletic appearance would end the year as the team's top scorer. Dublin chugged on past Louth, Offaly and Kildare before beating Meath to land their first provincial title in nine years. This, it was almost universally agreed, was as far as the team would go, because the semi-final pitted them against the reigning all-Ireland champions, Cork.

Instead the Dubs swept Cork aside by 2-11 to 1-8 in front of forty-two thousand fans, a respectable number of supporters but an unimaginably low one for an all-Ireland semi-final featuring Dublin in the contemporary, post-Heffernan era. The stage was set for an all-Ireland final against Galway, who had lost two of the previous three deciders.

The audience at Croke Park included Charles Haughey, 'almost totally obscured in a blue and white rosette of gigantic proportions,' and the Soviet and American ambassadors, who 'seemed to be conversing in a most animated fashion about the merits of Galway and Dublin footballers,' as well as the youthful army of Dublin supporters who made up the majority of the attendance of seventy-two thousand.[113] So unusual was it to see such a huge crowd from the city at a match that

> the fear of trouble on the terraces of Hill 16 clouded the great occasion in a restive, unreal atmosphere . . . the atmosphere was unreal because the dangers were minimal. They were exaggerated, for example, by the huge phalanx of Gardaí which faced Hill 16 from the Railway goal-line, causing reaction among a small section of the crowd who threw cans and other missiles, possibly more in protest at their view of that end of the field being obstructed than in any mood of rowdyism.[114]

On the field Dublin won by 0-14 to 1-6, the recalled Keaveney contributing eight points of the total. It was perhaps one of the most unexpected championship victories of all time. Jack Lynch's post-match comment that there was 'too much whistle' probably didn't cut much ice with his rosette-wearing party colleague.[115]

When the team paraded the Sam Maguire Cup from the Mansion House to the GPO on 23 November a planned reception by the Lord Mayor, James O'Keefe, and the Artane Boys' Band had to be cancelled as Dublin fans swarmed all over the route, chanting 'Heffo for Pope' and 'We're at the GPO, let's have a rising!' There was one ominous moment on a joyous night as gardaí tried to move fans away from a car with a Northern registration parked in Sackville Place. The panic was stilled by the arrival of the owner of the car, who drove it away.[116] It was a minor incident but one that indicated the extent to which the Northern conflict continued to overshadow life in the Republic.

———

With the collapse of the Sunningdale Agreement the Government had adopted an 'underlying law and order approach which became a dominant factor of the National Coalition and a form of substitute policy for Northern Ireland initiatives.'[117] Disheartened SDLP members told Seán Donlon that the downfall of the Executive had resulted in 'a massive swing away from support of their party to support of both wings of the IRA.'[118] Paddy Devlin and Austin Currie told Donlon there could be no settlement without the involvement of the IRA.[119] Yet it appeared that the Government, 'set in rigid law and order mode, regarded talking to the Provisionals as something akin to deliberately spreading a life threatening infection.'[120] Garret FitzGerald would later complain that 'the British were a long time learning the lesson that you do not talk to a terrorist organisation as long as they are continuing terrorism.'[121]

When contact was made with the IRA it was by a group of Protestant clergymen, who met the IRA and Sinn Féin leadership in Smyth's Village Hotel, Feakle, Co. Clare, on 10 December. The group included Dr Arthur Butler, Church of Ireland Bishop of Connor, Rev. Jack Weir, clerk of the General Assembly of the Presbyterian Church, Rev. Eric Gallagher, former president of the Methodist Church in Ireland, Rev. Ralph Baxter, secretary of the Irish Council of Churches, and his assistant, Rev. William Arlow, who had been instrumental in setting up the meeting.

The clergymen met Ruairí Ó Brádaigh, Máire Drumm, Séamus Loughran, Billy McKee, Dáithí Ó Conaill, J. B. O'Hagan, Séamus Twomey and Kevin Mallon.[122] Arlow was surprised by the attitude of the republicans.

> Twomey said he went back to the area where he lived and was astonished to discover what was happening. Young people had been running wild, creating a nuisance, especially for old people at night. They were caught up in drink, caught up in drugs and he suddenly thought to himself 'why don't the police do something about this' and then he remembered that he had been one of those who had helped to drag the police out of the area and he said 'well now, is this the kind of new Ireland I'm fighting for' and the answer was 'it isn't' ... and when they started to talk in these terms, men concerned with their children and men concerned with their church, then I began to see that these men were not the monsters I thought them to be.[123]

At four o'clock the republicans got word that gardaí were on their way to raid the meeting. They passed this on to the clergymen and told them that Ó Conaill, Mallon, Twomey and O'Hagan, who were on the run, were leaving. The clergymen returned to their caucus while Ó Brádaigh, McKee, Drumm and Loughran sat by the fire and chatted. At about 4:30 a large force of gardaí, armed with submachine guns, arrived. Seeing Ó Brádaigh

and company, they asked where the others were. McKee replied, 'Upstairs.'
Assuming they had captured the entire leadership of the republican
movement, the gardaí raced up the stairs, lined the clergymen up against
the wall, and then learnt their identities. Ó Brádaigh, McKee, Drumm and
Loughran were highly amused.[124]

The upshot of the Feakle meeting was that Arlow met the British
Secretary of State for Northern Ireland, Merlyn Rees, and presented a list
of demands from the IRA, who wanted a declaration from the British that
they had no strategic interest in the North and that their prime concern
was peace, guarantees that the British army would be removed from
policing duties and eventually withdrawn in the event of a ceasefire, and
that a united Ireland would be recognised as a legitimate political
aspiration.[125] The British Government responded, and there was a further
response from the Provisionals, who then declared an eleven-day ceasefire
on 22 December. A second year in a row would end with the hope that the
Northern conflict might soon draw to a close.

Chapter 4 ~

| INFLATION ONCE AGAIN

1975

Perhaps fittingly, the papally decorated Liam Cosgrave is the only Taoiseach to have been present at the canonisation of an Irish saint. On 12 October in St Peter's Square in Rome, Cosgrave, 'dressed in an evening suit and wearing a blue and red striped sash as a Knight of the Grand Cross of Pius IX came forward to the lectern near the high altar to read a lesson in Irish' at the Mass to mark the canonisation of the former Archbishop of Armagh, Oliver Plunkett, who had been hanged, drawn and quartered in London in 1681.[1]

Twelve thousand pilgrims had travelled from Ireland. President Cearbhall Ó Dálaigh was not present, the civil service having advised that 'the presence of both the Taoiseach and the President at the canonisation ceremonies would create too elaborate and top heavy a delegation.'[2]

The occasion would undoubtedly have been a personal highlight for the deeply religious Cosgrave at any time, but it must have come as an added relief after a year of almost unremitting bad news on the economic front. Ireland's 17 per cent inflation in 1974 had been the second-highest in Europe; but 1975 was the year it reached a record annual rate of 21 per cent, still unsurpassed.[3] But that figure tells only part of the story, as in May inflation was running as high as 24½ per cent.[4] Even the farmers, who had been expected to be the main beneficiaries of EEC membership, had cause to complain. Farm incomes had declined by 24 per cent in the previous year, largely because of falling prices for small cattle and the rising cost of fertiliser. The president of the Irish Creamery Milk Suppliers' Association, James O'Keeffe, reckoned that small farmers had been disproportionately affected, their income dropping by as much as 60 per cent.[5] Matters were made worse by a dispute between the Irish Veterinary Union and the Department of Agriculture, which resulted in brucellosis and TB testing being suspended for the year.

Yet the strange thing was that by-election results suggested that the Government was actually increasing in popularity. This may have had something to do with a run of good fortune on the security front, with the prison escape that didn't happen, the train that wasn't derailed, the kidnappers who didn't get away and the hunger-strikers who didn't die. The coalition also benefited from the weakening of Jack Lynch's position as leader of Fianna Fáil.

The worsening economic climate was a worldwide phenomenon. The United States was suffering its worst unemployment rate since 1941 and West Germany its worst since 1959.[6] Yet Ireland was particularly badly affected, its rate of 8 per cent in January the second-highest in Europe— though there would come a time when Governments would look back with envy at the days of single-figure unemployment.[7] In February unemployment passed the 100,000 barrier, reaching 101,734.[8]

Anti-EEC campaigners were quick to say I told you so, Michael Mullen commenting:

> 'Markets in Europe, jobs at home.' You remember the Government's forecasts of huge job increases as a result of the Common Market? Where are they? Our textile industry and other industries have been hit by a flood of dumped imported products, let in without control under EEC regulations. Employment has been savagely hit in these and in other industries, just as we foretold and warned the people against.

Perhaps the most telling statistics given at the public meeting organised by the Irish Sovereignty Movement in the Mansion House and addressed by Mullen were that since Ireland joined the EEC the price of milk had increased by 60 per cent and that of butter by 70 per cent, with the price of meat almost doubling.[9]

The Government came under severe criticism for its failure to control inflation, the most serious being that implied by T. K. Whitaker's announcement on 15 October that he would relinquish his position as governor of the Central Bank after only one term. Whitaker—who a year earlier had been considered as a candidate to succeed President Childers— was typically diplomatic.

> As governor, and on behalf of the Central Bank, I have, of course, offered advice and criticism and have expressed the bank's concern about inflationary trends and developments, especially in relation to money incomes and the public finances. These criticisms have been conveyed to successive ministers . . . the discharge of this duty has had no adverse effect on personal relations.[10]

But economic experts saw his departure as arising from the fact that the bank's, and Dr Whitaker's, major recommendations on economic policy have fallen on governmental deaf ears over the past two years. During that period the bank has consistently emphasised that much of our inflation is created by ourselves and that the very high rate of price increase is not simply due to external events such as rising oil and commodity prices.[11]

The beleaguered Minister for Finance, Richie Ryan, was forced to bring in a second budget as early as June, when he brought down the consumer price index by 4 per cent through subsidising the price of bread, flour, butter, milk and gas, taking VAT off electricity, clothes and footwear and reducing bus and train fares by 25 per cent. Budget number 2 met with an initially sceptical reaction, but Garret FitzGerald felt that Ryan did work the oracle in reducing inflation.

Ryan's first budget had been notable mainly for increases of 21–23 per cent in social welfare payments, to keep them in line with inflation, and the imposition of a 3p rise in the price of a pint of Guinness, which would now cost the Dublin drinker 26p in the bar and 28p in the lounge. Cigarettes also went up, ranging from 30p for twenty Gold Bond to 40p for twenty Players.[12]

The Government's economic policy was criticised not only by the guardians of financial orthodoxy in the Central Bank but also by sections of the Labour Party, whose Administrative Council 'called twice for a change in the direction of government economic policy.'[13] Yet the party played a central part in the renegotiation of the National Pay Agreement in July, when the ICTU accepted an embargo on special claims by the public sector. The renegotiation meant that the average pay rise of 29.4 per cent under the 1974 agreement fell to 16.6 per cent in 1975.[14]

Whatever about his economic nous, Ryan did show tremendous political will in piloting through the country's first wealth tax, something that Fianna Fáil might have thought would go the way of the family planning legislation when the pressure came on. The measure, which proposed a levy of 1 per cent on married people earning more than £100,000 per annum and single people earning more than £70,000, was fiercely opposed by Fianna Fáil, which adopted the venerable policy of brandishing the S word in the Dáil. 'This vicious tax is typical of what you would expect from a Socialist government,' said the Meath TD Brendan Crinion, who predicted that the tax would 'force farmers to sell their land not to individual landlords but to multinational organisations such as insurance companies.' Vivion de Valera detected in the bill 'doctrinaire socialism', which was 'diabolically dangerous' and driven by a 'perverted form of jealousy.'[15] The former Minister for Labour Joseph Brennan was apocalyptic in tone, predicting that the Government was

on the brink of meeting the wishes of those who would like to move over to complete state ownership. The small number who were seeking to create a revolution in addition to the many on the periphery of that school of thought would find it easy to take over.[16]

But no-one attacked the bill with more gusto than Charles Haughey, who described it as 'a socialistic juggernaut' that was 'squeezing the rich to pay for the poor' and criticised the Government for 'trying to create some sort of super welfare state.'[17] The wealth tax was seen as a measure driven by the Labour members of the coalition, and the party's attitude was perhaps best captured by the statement of the Kildare deputy Joe Bermingham that 'the minister had been very lenient in the whole matter. The very rich should contribute to the relief of the needy. This Wealth Tax should be higher than 1% and the minister had been very generous with the thresholds.'[18] There was

a most unscrupulous campaign by some among the wealthy people affected by it. The campaign had been designed to arouse irrational fear amongst people of quite modest means who were in no danger of ever being found liable to pay wealth tax.[19]

Fine Gael maintained its discipline to get the bill passed, with one abstention, that of Cosgrave's constituency colleague Maurice Dockrell, who had also spoken against it in the Dáil.[20] Even though it subsequently proved to have 'generated more controversy than income,' being 'so riddled with loopholes, successfully engineered by powerful interest groups that in practice it was hardly worth the exercise,' its successful passage was a morale boost for the Government, an important gesture towards some form of tax equity and a personal triumph for Ryan.[21] Justin Keating recalled:

It was hard to convince Richie initially on the need for a Wealth Tax, but once he was convinced, he fought for it bravely. Without Richie's commitment, it could not have happened. Once he made up his mind on the issue, he was like a lion.[22]

Ryan's reward was to be dubbed 'Red Richie' by the satirists.[23]

The Government would also bring in a capital gains tax and a capital acquisitions tax, and it is generally accepted that 'it was in the areas of social welfare and taxation that the coalition could register some modest achievements.'[24]

Improvements in social welfare were something of a personal triumph for Frank Cluskey, Labour Party TD for Dublin South-Central. Though officially only Parliamentary Secretary to the Minister for Social Welfare, he found himself functioning as a 'de facto minister',[25] and his party leader, Brendan Corish, whose portfolio encompassed both health and social welfare, broke with precedent by bringing him into Government meetings to argue his case.[26]

Another area in which the coalition achieved its aims was that of housing. The Government announced its intention of building twenty-five thousand houses a year, and this target was exceeded in 1974 and 1975.[27] Most were built by the private sector, but the total of 8,794 local authority houses built in 1975 has not been surpassed.[28] The person responsible as Minister for Local Government was Jimmy Tully, who his fellow-Labour TD John O'Connell described as having 'surprised everybody by being one of our most active ministers, pushing through a housing programme the likes of which we had not seen in years.'[29] Tully was also the object of one of the most inept attempts at a smear in Irish political history and one that backfired completely.

Bobby Molloy, who had previously shadowed Tully from the Fianna Fáil front bench before becoming spokesperson on Posts and Telegraphs, accused Tully of having rezoned land in Cos. Dublin, Waterford and Galway for the benefit of a Kells builder, Robert Farrelly, with whom he had a business relationship to the extent of paying cheques of £600 and £700 into Farrelly's account from an account in a bank in Drogheda and paying the wages of Farrelly's workers. Tully, said Molloy, had given Farrelly 'permission to build on land which the county council had zoned as agricultural land at Rockfield Road, Kells.' He also alleged that the minister 'had an involvement with the builder which was in conflict with his office, and he asked the minister to agree to a police investigation of his accounts to clear up the matter.'[30]

Tully replied that he would be 'only too glad to have an investigation into my bank accounts immediately . . . There is absolutely no truth whatsoever in the statement.' However, Molloy received the support of his party colleague and Meath TD, Brendan Crinion, who chipped in, 'It was well known in Kells that the cheques had arrived.'[31]

The following day it was announced that the Government had set up a judicial tribunal to examine the allegations. But the plot thinned somewhat when both Molloy and Crinion told the Dáil they had got it wrong. Molloy said that since the announcement of a judicial tribunal he had been in touch with three people. Two of them refused to have their names disclosed or to give evidence; 'the third person has satisfied me that the allegations made by the other two, upon whose information I primarily relied, were not correct.' In the circumstances, he would be withdrawing the allegations.[32] Crinion also joined in the climb-down. Molloy resigned from the Fianna Fáil front bench on 7 July, to be replaced by Tom Fitzpatrick. 'It was authoritatively understood that if Mr Molloy had not voluntarily offered his resignation, it was the party leader's intention to dismiss his front bench.'[33]

It was a stunning reverse for Molloy. The judicial inquiry reported on 1 August that there was no truth in the allegations, and on 4 December the Dáil Committee on Procedure and Privileges found that Molloy and Crinion 'had committed a grave breach of privilege.'[34]

But other examples from 1975 may help explain why Tully has been described as 'the worst Minister for Local Government in the history of the state' and one whose time in office 'marked the very nadir of planning in Ireland.'[35] In May

> he granted retrospective planning permission for a half-finished bungalow at a well-known beauty spot near Glencullen, in the Dublin Mountains, despite the fact that the owner had built it without the County Council's permission, had been fined in court for breaking the law and had then defied an order to demolish it. Conservationists were appalled, accusing the minister of making a mockery of the Planning Act.[36]

Tully defended his decision on the grounds that

> it was an opportunity for someone who had never owned a house to own their own house . . . I am following policies in relation to planning control which command the support and approval of the general public.[37]

The Glencullen case followed hot on the heels of an earlier decision that seemed to encapsulate everything that was wrong with Tully's attitude towards planning. This time the beneficiary was not an individual citizen but a state-sponsored body, and the affair would create huge controversy. In March 1975 he granted full planning permission to Bord na Móna for the demolition of five early nineteenth-century houses at 28–32 Upper Pembroke Street, on the edge of Fitzwilliam Square. The scheme had been turned down by Dublin City Council, but the fact that Bord na Móna wanted a modern office block for its head office instead of the Georgian houses seemed to trump all other considerations. 'Despite overwhelming evidence from no less than five architects and eight structural engineers that the Bord na Móna houses were sound enough to last for another century, Tully continued to insist that they were "entirely unsuitable for repair of any kind".'[38]

The objectors included An Taisce, the Dublin Civic Group, the Living City Group and the Arts Council. But it was the action of seventy architecture students from UCD and Bolton Street College of Technology that proved crucial. They occupied the building, and began repairing damage already done by the builders. In the fourteenth week of the occupation Bord na Móna announced that it was selling the property to Allied Irish Investment Bank for £250,000. The purchasers promised that they would not demolish the building and instead restored it before letting it to a law firm.[39] Direct action had triumphed.

Such was Tully's contempt for planning regulations that one of his advisers would write:

> You would be standing in front of his desk arguing that such and such an appeal should be rejected out of hand on all sorts of planning grounds, but he would just sit there smiling malevolently at you while he signed an order granting permission. Almost every appeal that came from Meath was granted, especially for bungalows in the countryside, because he apparently saw this as part of a service for his constituents.[40]

——

It was in Tully's Co. Meath bailiwick that a huge mineral find had been made that seemed to give the lie to the old schoolbook cliché about Ireland being a country poor in natural resources. But the discovery in 1970 of one of the largest lead and zinc deposits in the world at Nevinstown, near Navan, was only the beginning of a heady few years. In 1974 it was confirmed that the gas field found thirty miles off the Old Head of Kinsale was commercially viable, and by 1975 there seemed to be a serious possibility that a significant oil find would be made in Irish waters.

Yet from the start these discoveries were plagued with complications. The Nevinstown find was made by Tara Exploration and Development, a Canadian company formed by expatriate Irishmen involved in the mining industry. The most prominent of these was Pat Hughes, whose companies in 1961 discovered the Tynagh mineral body in Co. Galway, which became the largest lead, zinc and silver mine in western Europe after it opened in 1965, and a major copper and silver mine at Gortdrum, Co. Tipperary.[41] The only problem regarding the Navan find was that a sixth of the ore lay under the 120-acre farm of Patrick Wright. While the price was being argued over, Michael Wymes, the solicitor who was advising the farmer, bought the land himself for £800,000 and set up a company named Bula Mines, whose investors included his father-in-law, Tom Roche, head of Cement Roadstone Holdings.[42]

In the Dáil the Bula people were accused of being 'claim-jumpers.'[43] The state tried to acquire the land by compulsory purchase order, but Bula won a case in the Supreme Court that allowed it to retain the property, which left the unsatisfactory situation whereby 'the orebody would be worked by separate companies, between which there was much antagonism, whereas joint working would be more logical, technically, economically and environmentally.'[44]

On 14 February 1975 the Minister for Industry and Commerce, Justin Keating, announced that he had agreed the terms of the state mining lease to Tara Mines, which up to that had been engaged in a legal action against the Government. Tara would hand over a 25 per cent share in the company and give the state a flat 4½ per cent royalty on profits as well as the normal 50 per cent company tax.[45] But it was the deal with Bula the same year, when the Government paid £9½ million for 24 per cent of the company to add to the 25 per cent it had been given free, that would come back over the following couple of years not only to haunt Keating but to overshadow what had been one of the most promising careers in Irish politics.[46]

The previous year Keating had abolished the tax exemptions for the mining industry brought in by the inter-party Government in 1956 and renewed by Fianna Fáil in 1967, but he was still heavily criticised by those who felt that the state was not getting sufficient return from the various mineral finds. The case for nationalisation was strongly put by the Resources Protection Campaign and adopted as policy by the Irish Congress of Trade Unions and the Labour Party.[47]

The discovery of the Kinsale gas field in 1971 by Marathon Petroleum Ireland, a subsidiary of Marathon Oil of Ohio, was relatively straightforward compared with the shenanigans at Nevinstown, but there was still disagreement about the Government's proposed use for the gas.

> It had been decided by the government that of the projected annual output . . . over 40% would be allocated to the state fertiliser company Nítrigin Éireann for the production of ammonia in a new factory at Marino Point in Cork Harbour and the remainder to electricity generation. It was argued, by the Dublin gas company and others, that a more efficient and economical use would be in town gas supply.[48]

Yet the pleas of the town gas companies for the immediate construction of a national pipeline were largely ignored by the Minister for Transport and Power, Peter Barry, whose only concession was to agree to supply Kinsale gas to 37,000 homes in his native city of Cork.[49]

A possible Irish version of Britain's North Sea oil strike was the most tantalising prospect of all. Hopes centred on the area off the coast of Co. Cork where the gas had been discovered. By 1975 the oil giant Esso had begun operating in the area, and Shell, Chevron, BP and Texaco would join it the following year. The sense of anticipation about the Seven Heads area, twenty miles south-west of the Kinsale gas field, was palpable.[50]

———

For all the problems faced by the coalition, there was still a feeling abroad that Fianna Fáil had not particularly troubled the Government in its first couple of years. 'Complaints flowed into headquarters about the alleged inactivity of our new front bench, of our failure to get publicity, and of our propensity for letting the government away with everything,' admitted one front-bench spokesperson.[51] Fianna Fáil's dynamic young press secretary, Frank Dunlop, saw the party, coping with a spell in opposition after sixteen unbroken years in government, as

> totally lost. At sea. Rudderless . . . Senior members of the party had become so used to having everything done for them—in some instances even their thinking—and it was cataclysmic for them not only to lose office and to have to organize themselves on their own initiative, but also to have to begin to think about how they should react to the policies of the new government.[52]

It was this perceived weakness that prompted Lynch to carry out the reshuffle in January that confirmed the rehabilitation of Charles Haughey, less than five years after the Arms Crisis had appeared to sound his political death knell. The eating of humble pie, derided by his old ally Kevin Boland, had paid off.

The recall of Haughey did not, however, lead to a burying of the hatchet. 'Haughey was excluded from the party's inner councils which were dominated by George Colley, now Finance spokesman, Martin O'Donoghue, economic adviser to Lynch and Desmond O'Malley.'[53] Colley had been opposed to Haughey's promotion, and there would have been others who agreed with the view that

> it was the biggest political mistake Lynch ever made. What is baffling is that he did not really need to do it. There was certainly pressure from the grass roots for Haughey's return but nobody in

the parliamentary party would have dared to challenge Lynch if he had stood his ground and refused. Instead, he handed Haughey the platform from which he would be able to build himself into a leadership contender again.[54]

The most pointed comment on Haughey's return came from Rita Childers, who in February refused to attend a commemorative Mass for her husband, for Sinéad de Valera, who had died on 7 January, and for five Fianna Fáil TDS and senators who had died since the dissolution of the previous Dáil.

> The late President would not benefit from the prayers of such a party. Happily for him, he is closer to God and will be able to ask his intercession that his much loved country will never again be governed by these people.[55]

Erskine Childers had been the most outspoken critic of Haughey during the Arms Crisis, and 'when Mr Haughey was elected joint Honorary Secretary of the party at the Ard Fheis of 1973, Mr Childers was the one member of the top echelon who did not congratulate him and shake hands with him when he took his place on the platform.'[56]

Haughey himself did not seem to be in a humour to forgive and forget.

> A clash of views between Jack Lynch and Charlie Haughey resulted in Haughey leaving the room. I met him later in the corridor and, as I was returning to the meeting room, I suggested that he should return with me. On the way back we called in at another meeting where Haughey launched into a vitriolic attack on Jack Lynch. This embarrassed many of those present, including myself. The bad feeling on Haughey's part was suspected, but the verbal attack was so unexpected that nobody commented.[57]

The chief immediate interest in Haughey's return was the extent to which he might challenge Lynch's policy on the North, something Lynch anticipated on the day of the reshuffle, stressing that Haughey had given him a personal undertaking that he fully supported and was committed to the party's policy 'as enunciated by me as party leader and endorsed at successive Ard Fheiseanna.'[58] Haughey pledged his support, adding that he was 'basically a pacifist, opposed to violence in any shape or form.'[59]

This contention might have been challenged by Noel O'Loughlin of Raheny, Dublin, who told Dublin District Court that on 25 October he had been standing in Molesworth Street talking to a friend in a double-parked car when a navy-coloured car pulled in behind and sounded the horn. When his friend drove away, the navy car accelerated towards him.

> I was quite shocked. I froze. The car came towards me a second time and I jumped out of the way. As the car moved off, I struck at the

windscreen and hit my knuckles off the car. I reported the incident immediately to the Gardaí.

Charles Haughey was fined £100 for dangerous driving and £2 for assault.[60]

The radical change in Fianna Fáil's Northern policy later in the year has been described as 'a vital ingredient in Haughey's strategy to succeed Lynch,' and the party was criticised for ending the bipartisan approach that had operated since the beginning of the Troubles.[61] Yet this ignores the fact that 1975 also saw a change in Government policy that may well have influenced Fianna Fáil's move to a harder line.

After the collapse of Sunningdale the coalition seemed to become possessed by an *idée fixe* that British withdrawal was a real possibility. From being prime movers in the previous initiative in the North, the Government seemed to adopt the attitude that, as stated in one Department of Foreign Affairs memo, 'the more we participate, the more we facilitate the British in any plans they may be developing for shuffling off the Northern coil.'[62] In the words of one historian, 'Above all they were wary of giving the British an excuse to make a precipitate, self-interested withdrawal.'[63] This meant that 'far from conducting a "Brits Out" campaign it was secretly wedded to a policy of Brits In . . . this was an incredibly weak negotiating position for an Irish government to proceed from.'[64]

The Government seemed obsessed with the idea that Harold Wilson and his Labour Party government were ready to cut and run, a notion probably exacerbated by Wilson's reputation as a slippery operator. On 23 August, Garret FitzGerald attended a dinner party given by the Home Secretary, James Callaghan, at the house of his son-in-law Peter Jay (later British Ambassador to the United States) in Glandore, Co. Cork. Jack Lynch was there too; but it was FitzGerald who sought to impress on Callaghan the appalling consequences of a British withdrawal, telling him that it could eventually 'threaten democratic government in the Republic . . . a situation in which extra-European powers such as the Soviet Union, China or Libya could meddle.'[65]

Far-fetched as these ideas now seem, they reflected real fears within the coalition at the time. But the consequent 'easy does it' attitude to the North had a notably demoralising effect on the SDLP, which depended on the backing of the Government in the Republic for much of its credibility.[66] It was therefore a singularly inappropriate time for Conor Cruise O'Brien to tell an RTE interviewer who asked him about the possibility of power-sharing, 'I think it's not on. In fact I think there isn't going to be a power-sharing Executive.'[67] The SDLP's response was furious, with Séamus Mallon stating:

> Dr. O'Brien's definition of attitudes has given a blank cheque to the UUUC [United Ulster Unionist Council] and the British government to disregard the rights and aspirations of the minority community in the North. By the timing and contents of his statement he has clearly demonstrated that some members of the Irish government have not the will to honour their responsibility towards the North. Over the past two years he has consistently contributed to the demoralisation of the minority community and his latest statement puts the seal on a remarkable catalogue of political perfidy.[68]

John Hume pointed out that it was 'unacceptable that a spokesman for the Dublin government should without consultation with them have announced, on the heels of the election results, that the policies to which that government and the SDLP were committed were unattainable.'

The crisis brought into focus Cruise O'Brien's anomalous position within the Government.[69] Despite his new portfolio as Minister for Posts and Telegraphs, he retained his position as Labour Party spokesperson on Northern Ireland, something that made him the party's only official spokesperson on anything and resulted in him speaking more often on Northern policy than either Cosgrave or FitzGerald, whose responsibility it was within the Government. The problem was that 'even those who agreed with almost everything he said felt that what had once been a courageous challenging of sterile orthodoxy had now become an obsession.'[70]

The effect of Cruise O'Brien's rhetoric on many members of the Northern Catholic community is encapsulated in the reaction of a 24-year-old academic from Belfast, Mary Leneghan, who had arrived in Dublin to become the youngest Reid Professor of Law at Trinity College (succeeding Senator Mary Robinson, who had held the same distinction at the age of twenty-five).

> When I first arrived in Dublin, Conor Cruise O'Brien was at the height of his political power and influence. I found it difficult to believe I was listening to an Irish government minister when everything he said about the North and about the nationalist people had the ring of unionism about it. His arrogance, as he blatantly rewrote Irish history, was almost frightening. He created and nourished an attitude to Northern nationalism which some people in the Republic are still trying to grow out of.[71]

Prof. Leneghan would become Mary McAleese after her marriage the following year.

What made life even more difficult to bear for the SDLP was that, after the thwarted promise of the power-sharing Executive, the party had been rendered more or less politically impotent in its successor, the Constitutional Convention, 'which had no legislative function, only a mandate to produce within six months an agreed constitution for the North.' The British Government undertook to accept any constitution it drew up if it could be shown to have 'widespread support within both communities.'[72] Elections to the Convention were held on 1 May. Of 78 seats, 46 went to anti-power-sharing Unionists, 17 to the SDLP and only 5 to Faulkner's Unionist Party of Northern Ireland. Despite this,

> mindless optimism persisted in some quarters, a number of respected British commentators making the curious argument that because the Loyalists had an overall majority and could feel secure, they might now agree to make concessions. This left out of consideration the relevant fact that the Loyalists had won their overall majority on a platform of making no concessions whatever.[73]

What happened next was predictable.

> The UUUC drew up a report which was essentially a Unionist wish-list, seeking a return to majority rule and ruling out any new Council of Ireland. The report wanted a new Stormont with even greater powers, a doubling of Northern Ireland seats at Westminster, and the introduction of an oath of allegiance to the Queen for all major appointments.[74]

With Government policy comprehensively stalled, it was perhaps not all that surprising that Fianna Fáil executed a change of tack, revealed on 14 October by its foreign affairs spokesperson, Michael O'Kennedy, when he 'spoke in favour of a declaration by Britain of its intention to withdraw from Northern Ireland: such a declaration he described as an essential element in any package designed to solve the problems of the North.'[75] This was an implicit rebuke of Lynch's Northern policy, and there were suggestions that should O'Kennedy's line be adopted by the parliamentary party it would leave Lynch and the Fianna Fáil spokesperson on the North, Ruairí Brugha, virtually isolated, and 'Mr Lynch's resignation would be inevitable.'[76] Yet when, on 29 October, the party issued a statement calling on the British Government

> to encourage the unity of Ireland by agreement, in independence and in a harmonious relationship between the two islands, and to

this end to declare Britain's commitment to implement an ordered withdrawal from her involvement in the six counties of Northern Ireland,

Lynch did not resign but instead chose to describe the change in direction as 'an evolution.' His critics within Fianna Fáil, however, 'greeted the outcome of the party's deliberations on the North as a considerable weakening of his position and an encouragement to his more nationalistic opponents.'[77]

That the old bipartisan days were dead and gone was graphically illustrated when in November and December the Dáil debated the Criminal Law (Jurisdiction) Bill, which provided, among other things, for the trial in the Republic of certain alleged offences committed in Northern Ireland. The legislation had been agreed as part of the Sunningdale Agreement, and Lynch wondered why the bill was being proceeded with when the Unionists had rejected power-sharing, describing it as 'an uncontrollable, unworkable and divisive piece of legislation.' Law and order, he said, 'does not constitute a Northern policy. Relying on it solely means either total abandonment of any concern for the Northern minority or else abject surrender to undemocratic elements.'[78]

Paddy Cooney insisted that 'those who criticise the bill and condemn it run a serious risk of placing themselves on the side of the terrorists,' while Conor Cruise O'Brien was similarly uncompromising, saying that Lynch's speech had

> a touch of blackmail and collusion with violence in it. If it was looked at from the Northern side, Mr Lynch seemed to be saying that unless the government in the South got what they wanted they could not proceed against the fugitives.[79]

By the time the bill was passed it was clear that the IRA ceasefire was as good as dead. The original ceasefire, declared in the aftermath of the Feakle talks, had lasted from 22 December to 16 January. A new ceasefire began on 10 February and officially ran until 23 January 1976, though it had effectually ended several months before that. It had got off to a promising start. 'Only a few violations were reported by either side during its initial phase. Just one British soldier was killed during the first six months of 1975.'[80] But there was a catch.

> Unnerved by the IRA's contacts with the British, Loyalist paramilitary groups began murdering Catholics in often gruesome fashion and in a way that challenged the Provisionals' claim to be the defenders of their community. The Loyalist logic was terrifyingly simple: the more Catholics they killed and the more

horrible the manner of their deaths the stronger the pressure would be on the IRA to stop its activities.[81]

The awful irony was that, rather than leading to a decrease in violence, the IRA truce ushered in

> the darkest period of the troubles, nearly two years of slaughter in which the Loyalists and the IRA vied with each other in an often indiscriminate sectarian killing game ... By the end of 1976 Loyalists had killed nearly 250 people, most of them innocent Catholics, while 150 protestants similarly unconnected to those who were directing the murder campaign had also met violent deaths, a majority of them at the hands of the IRA.[82]

In the same way that the truce saw civilians take the place of combatants as the most common casualties, it also effected a geographical shift. Rural areas, most notoriously the 'Triangle of Death', which Fathers Denis Faul and Raymond Murray described as being bounded by Portadown, Moy and Dungannon in Cos. Armagh and Tyrone, began to rival Belfast as a murder site.[83] Three notorious incidents near the border, all involving people travelling to or from the Republic, seemed to sum up the new nature of the conflict. That the people murdered were coming from such innocent events as a dog show, a pop concert and a football match added to the feeling that the conflict had begun to plumb new depths.

On 3 June a golden Labrador belonging to an electrician from Portadown, David Thompson, won two first prizes at a dog show in Cork, while his friend John Presha from Hillsborough won 'best of breed' with his Labrador. The two men, who had been travelling to dog shows in the Republic for a number of years, set off for home accompanied by Alfred Doyle, a butcher from Portadown who was also a member of the UDR.

At 12:30 a.m. the car containing the three men's bodies was discovered on the side of the road, 150 yards on the Northern side of the border, by another group who had attended the Cork dog show. Sixty spent shells were found on the road and forty-seven bullet holes in the car. The deaths were claimed by the 'People's Liberation Army', a hitherto unknown republican group, which claimed that the dead men had been members of the Protestant Action Force.

On 31 July the Miami Showband played at a dance in the Castle Ballroom, Banbridge, Co. Down. The original Miami, with its singer Dickie Rock, had been one of the most successful showbands of all;[84] it had broken up in 1967, but a new Miami had emerged. The members of the band were travelling home on the main Belfast–Dublin road when they were stopped at what appeared to be a British army roadblock five miles from Newry. The five men in the van—Fran O'Toole, Brian McCoy, Tony Geraghty, Steven Travers and Desmond McAlea—were asked to step out onto the road while the vehicle was searched, unaware that the soldiers were actually UVF members in disguise.[85] As two of the UVF men, Harris Boyle and Wesley Somerville, attempted to plant a bomb in the back of the van it went off, killing them instantly. Their accomplices then opened fire on the band, killing O'Toole, McCoy and Geraghty and seriously wounding Travers in the chest and abdomen. McAlea made a run for it in the dark and somehow managed to escape.[86] The following day the scene was one of carnage.

> Bits of bodies—including an arm with the tattoo mark UVF—were strewn with the wreckage of the van over the roadway and the adjoining field . . . Around the wreckage were strewn many of the personal belongings of the musicians—photographs, playing cards, a pair of high heeled brown boots, a torn map, a gramophone record and a book 'The Who' by Garry Hermann. The flyleaf of the book was marked . . . where the group members had been keeping the score of a card game.[87]

It appears that the UVF plan was

> to stop the minibus at the roadblock and, while the musicians had their backs to the vehicle, for Boyle and Somerville to plant a bomb under the driver's seat . . . The device would be set to explode after the vehicle crossed the border . . . Not only would the band members be killed but they would be judged to have been transporting explosives . . . The suggestion that a band was 'carrying' the explosives would have led unionists to feel justified in arguing that all Nationalists were potential terrorists.[88]

The Miami Showband massacre came as a profound shock to public opinion, not least because showbands from the Republic had crossed the border to play to Northern audiences without any problems.

> Many other incidents in the twenty five years of the Troubles which followed would be said to show that things could not really get much worse, that innocence could be no more deeply sullied. But the Miami was the first. After that it seemed that no-one was considered untouchable and nothing was considered unthinkable.[89]

The killings raised worrying questions about the Ulster Defence Regiment, at the time the largest infantry regiment in the British army. Both Harris Boyle—one of the men who had planned the Dublin bombing—and Wesley Somerville had been members, as had James

McDowell, Thomas Crozier and John Somerville, the men eventually convicted of the murders.

There was also the question of possible British army involvement. In 1987 Ken Livingstone 'caused an outcry in the British House of Commons during his maiden speech when he claimed that Robert Nairac was quite likely to have been one of the names behind the Miami Showband massacre.'[90] Nairac was a captain in the SAS who would later be killed by the IRA. Steven Travers, who recovered and played an emotional comeback gig at the Seapoint Leisure Centre, Galway, in November, has continued to maintain that the man leading the patrol had an English accent.[91]

A ghoulish postscript is that the day after the killing Lillian Presha, whose husband was one of the men killed on their way home from the Cork dog show, was approached in Hillsborough and told that the Miami had been killed in revenge for her husband's death.

> She was very distressed that her husband's name should have been linked with the showband killings. Like everyone else, she abhorred the killings. Her husband had not been associated with politics or paramilitary organisations and she did not want her name associated with revenge.[92]

Seán Farmer and Colm McCartney were also returning from a day out in the Republic. The two workmates had attended the Dublin v. Derry all-Ireland football semi-final on 24 August and were stopped at a bogus UDR checkpoint near Newtownhamilton in south Armagh, where they were shot dead. An RUC constable who happened across the checkpoint earlier in the night suspected it not to be genuine, but when he informed his local station about this no action was taken,[93] and the fake roadblock 'remained in place on the main Newtownhamilton–Castleblayney road outside Armagh for over an hour.'[94] Colm McCartney's second cousin, Seamus Heaney, wrote about the death in his poem 'The Strand at Lough Beg'. Its description of the moment when the two men encountered their killers could stand as an epitaph for all the people fatally waylaid on country roads in those terrible years.

> Leaving the white glow of filling stations
> And a few lonely streetlamps among new fields
> You climbed the hill towards Newtownhamilton.
> The red lamp swung, the sudden brakes and stalling
> Engine, voices, heads hooded and the cold-nosed gun.[95]

There seems little doubt that the IRA felt that the truce might eventually lead to a British withdrawal. But as time went on, 'the refusal of the British to put flesh on the bones of the secret offer to talk about "structures of disengagement" from the North,' as Ruairí Ó Brádaigh had been promised by the intermediary, led to an increasing disenchantment.[96] The leadership seemed to be tactically outmanoeuvred by the British authorities, whose plan

> was to link the release of detainees to the level of IRA violence. If they behaved, the flow was brisk. If they did not, it slowed to a trickle or stopped. The leadership of the IRA seemed to be mesmerised by this process.[97]

In the middle of June the Secretary of State for Northern Ireland, Merlyn Rees, told the House of Commons that the truce was at breaking point. In the first week of July

> the IRA held an operational meeting in South Armagh. All the active service units were represented. The participants were told that the truce was as good as over, that it appeared to be leading nowhere, and that preparations should be made to pass gradually into a resumption of the campaign. On September 20th Rees publicly denied that there was or ever had been a bilateral truce. Two days later the truce was over. The Provisionals set off 18 bombs in Northern Ireland. Another bomb went off at the Portman Hotel in London.[98]

The repercussions within the republican movement were so severe that 'to a large extent the history of republicanism in the subsequent years is the history of the consequences of the ceasefire.'[99] The end of the ceasefire was also the beginning of the process whereby the IRA leadership would be transferred from a generation of older figures, mainly from the Republic and with their roots in the 1956–62 border campaign, to a younger generation from the North. The men who would eventually take over would be scathing about the consequences of the ceasefire.

> To Danny Morrison, who was then a volunteer in Belfast, it was a 'disaster.' According to Martin McGuinness, it was the most critical stage . . . and if changes had not taken place in the short time then the IRA would have been disbanded.[100]

The coalition Government enjoyed a better year on the security front than in 1974, though 1975 almost began with the creation of a new republican martyr. Eight IRA prisoners had embarked on a hunger strike in Port Laoise Prison on 3 January in pursuit of special status, and by the middle of February the condition of Patrick Ward, a 27-year-old from Burtonport, Co. Donegal, and former commanding officer of the Fermanagh IRA, who was on his third hunger strike, was giving cause for grave concern. Ward had previously had a lung removed and suffered from pleurisy and pneumonia. He was brought to the Intensive Care Unit in Jervis Street Hospital, Dublin. Tension was added by an IRA threat to shoot two Government ministers if any of the hunger-strikers died.[101] The actor Siobhán McKenna, recently nominated to the Council of State by President Ó Dálaigh, embarrassed the Government by joining with Séamus Sorahan SC and Senator Michael Mullen in calling for an inquiry into conditions at Port Laoise, saying, 'We are always talking about the bad conditions at Long Kesh but we should put our own house in order.'[102]

On 16 February, Joe Cahill met the hunger-strikers, who were divided between Jervis Street, the Curragh Military Hospital and Port Laoise Prison, a second group of six having begun a hunger strike on 13 January. It was announced later that day that 'a satisfactory settlement' had been reached between the Government and the prisoners. Sinn Féin claimed that the prisoners' demand for segregation from other inmates had been granted, though Garret FitzGerald argued that

> it was policy to separate prisoners who didn't get on with each other. Because of problems of space there had been no possibility of segregation before but after releases last week it had become possible. There was no question of political status being given to the republican prisoners.[103]

The result was that the prisoners ended their strike, six of them— Patrick Ward, Joseph Buckley, Colm Daltún and Nicky Kehoe from Dublin and Gearóid Mac Carthaigh and Dónal McCarthy from Cork—having spent forty-five days without food; and the Government was spared the prospect of another republican funeral.

There were fatal consequences, however, when the IRA staged its latest escape attempt at Port Laoise on St Patrick's Day. Its secret weapon was a four-wheel-drive sand and gravel dumper stolen in Blessington, which had been subjected to an elaborate engineering and welding operation.

> It was fitted out all over with half-inch thick steel plates, which even protected the wheels. Huge girders formed a battering ram on the front of the vehicle which had also been roofed with steel to make a virtually impregnable tank-like compartment. This awesome machine thundered down the Dublin Road towards the prison some time shortly after 8.30pm on Monday night.[104]

Among the would-be escapers was the future Sinn Féin TD for Kerry North, Martin Ferris, who remembered later that he had

> crouched with seventeen others, while two of our comrades placed explosives as we tried to blow the gate. Brian Keenan was shot in the

head and leg; the charge went off and the gates burst open. We dashed outside the door and took cover against the pumphouse wall. Other prisoners dashed down the exercise yard. The place was alive with bullets. I saw Jap Murphy being wounded badly in the leg. He stumbled and stumbled badly, and two of our comrades got up and dragged him to cover. We heard outside the wall the truck, armour-plated, in the distance, but the sound of the lorry was dying; then there was no sound. Something had gone wrong. All they had to do was hit the gates and we were out. I know now what went wrong. The engine overheated and she ceased, only twenty feet from the wall, only twenty feet from the big double doors that she had just to touch and we were out.[105]

Seemingly convinced that they were under attack, soldiers on duty at the prison had fired a total of fifty-eight rounds, one of which killed 27-year-old Thomas Smith from Harold's Cross, Dublin, who was serving a life sentence for murdering a security man during a payroll robbery in 1973.[106]

It is noteworthy how much of an all-Ireland organisation the Provisionals were in the mid-seventies. Not only Thomas Smith but the six hunger-strikers and the two men captured fleeing from the juggernaut—Gerard Quinn and Éamonn O'Sullivan, both from Dublin—were all from the Republic.[107] The latter two were sentenced to four years' imprisonment for the attempt.

Smith's funeral was a fraught affair. On the Friday about a thousand gardaí prevented it from travelling through the city centre from a funeral home in Thomas Street to St Joseph's Church, Berkeley Road. On the Saturday morning,

> as the coffin was being taken into the cemetery what appeared to be a starting pistol was fired into the air. Gardaí shouted at each other to get the man who had fired it . . . at the same time plain clothes detectives struck a number of people with their batons. One man was hit on the back of the head and knocked to the ground. Another emerged from the melee with blood streaming down his face from a cut on his forehead. An *Irish Press* photographer, Mr Dick Rowley, was hit on the back of the head and then on the forehead by a baton wielded by a Special Branch officer.[108]

The NUJ chapel at the *Irish Press*, three of whose photographers had been batoned, sought an inquiry into the policing of the funeral, but the Government was bullish about both Smith's shooting and the aftermath. Paddy Cooney told the Fine Gael ard-fheis that those who had organised the escape attempt were responsible for the prisoner's death, while Richie Ryan compared republicans to the Ku Klux Klan and the Mafia, described them as 'protection racketeers' and declared that 'the lowest depths of indecency were reached last week when the dead body of the misfortunate victim of the criminal attack on Portlaoise prison was hawked through the country draped in the tricolour.'[109]

However, it was the UVF that continued to pose the biggest threat to civilian life in the Republic. On Sunday 22 June six of its members, including Harris Boyle and Wesley Somerville, who later came to grief in the back of the Miami Showband's van, attempted to carry out another 'spectacular' by planting a five-pound bomb on the Dublin–Cork railway line near Sallins, Co. Kildare, to derail a train carrying three hundred members of Official Sinn Féin to the annual Wolfe Tone commemoration at Bodenstown.[110] The bomb exploded eight minutes after the train had passed, and the only casualty was a local man, Christopher Phelan, who happened on the saboteurs and was then stabbed to death. At first it was suggested that responsibility lay with the Irish Republican Socialist Party—a new organisation that had split from Official Sinn Féin and had been engaged in a bloody feud with it, which included the attempted murder of the Official IRA adjutant-general, Seán Garland—before the Gardaí discovered that it was the UVF.[111]

The UVF would kill another person in a bombing at Dublin Airport on 29 November and yet another with a bomb left outside a pub in Dundalk on 19 December; but there would be nothing to match the Dublin and Monaghan bombings.

It was Eddie Gallagher who would give the Government its biggest security triumph, confirming his knack for the spectacular operation by following Strabane, the Donoughmore kidnapping and the Beit robbery with a final kidnapping that would focus the attention of the world on a small town in Co. Kildare.

The kidnapping had its roots in Gallagher's desire to secure the release of Rose Dugdale. To this end he had teamed up with Marian Coyle, a 21-year-old IRA member from Derry. On 3 October, with two Offaly men, Brian McGowan and Vincent Walsh, they waited near the house of Dr Tiede Herrema in the Limerick suburb of Monaleen. Herrema was the managing director of Ferenka, a plant that manufactured steel cord for tyres and was the city's biggest employer. Gallagher, wearing a postman's uniform with badges sewn onto it to pass himself off as a garda, flagged down Herrema's car as he set off for work. He stopped and wound down the window. Gallagher asked him his name; 'Dr Herrema,' he replied.

Gallagher drew a revolver, pointed it at his head and ordered him out of the car.[112]

On 11 October it was decided to move Herrema to a cottage in Kildangan, Co. Kildare, but Coyle was apparently unhappy with this, because the house had no bathroom.[113] They moved instead to 1410 St Evin's Park, Monasterevin.

On 4 October six thousand Limerick workers had marched through the city with placards reading *Release our boss, Jobs not violence* and *Dr Herrema is a co-worker*. Meanwhile there was controversy as Phil Flynn, the trade union official and Sinn Féin member who had secured the release of the Donoughmores, became involved as a negotiator. Harold O'Sullivan, general secretary of the Local Government and Public Services Union and Flynn's immediate superior, recalled that 'Flynn was highly thought of within Fianna Fáil but the government parties regarded him as a pariah.'[114]

On 13 October a tape from the kidnappers, dropped into a priest's house in Monkstown, Co. Dublin, contained a warning from Herrema: 'If you ask for proof that I am alive again, they threaten to cut off my foot and send it to you.'[115] The following day Flynn accused the Government of putting a man's life at risk by refusing to talk. Later that day he eluded members of the Special Detective Unit who were following him and met Gallagher at a house near the Heath in Co. Laois. Gallagher, convinced that the IRA was after him (he was now operating independently of the republican movement, and the kidnap had been denounced by Ruairí Ó Brádaigh at the Sinn Féin ard-fheis), decided on a change of plan for himself and Coyle. 'Ferenka would hand over £2.5 m sterling to them . . . A pilot, whom Flynn knew, would land a light aircraft on Kilbeggan racecourse in County Westmeath and fly to a small airstrip in France. From there, another transport would take them and the money to their eventual destination . . . Tanzania.'[116]

Astoundingly, on the 16th the Gardaí searched the house in St Evin's Park but managed to miss Gallagher, Coyle and Herrema, who were hidden in the attic. Two days later one of the gang, Brian McGowan, was arrested. He was released on the 20th and began to hitch-hike from Port Laoise to Tullamore. Detective-Inspectors John Courtney and Myles Hawkshaw picked him up on the road, and 'McGowan, according to evidence offered later in court, had a change of heart during the journey and decided to confess everything.'[117]

At 6:50 the next morning four plain-clothes detectives kicked down the door of 1410 St Evin's Park.

Gallagher, with a gun in each hand, started shooting indiscriminately. He fired off six shots, hitting doors, walls and window frames upstairs and screamed, 'fuck off, you cowardly, dirty cunts. Come up and get me. If you come up the stairs I'll blow your fucking heads off. I'll blow the head off this fucking Dutchman.[118]

The gardaí withdrew, and the siege began. It would last seventeen days, conditions in the house deteriorating to the extent that Coyle, Gallagher and Herrema, restricted to an upstairs bedroom, tried drinking their urine, because of a lack of water, while Gallagher became convinced he was suffering from meningitis.[119] At 9:05 p.m. on Wednesday 6 November, Coyle and Gallagher emerged from the house and surrendered.

The plan was to bring Herrema to the Curragh Military Hospital, but he told his Garda driver that he wished to go straight to Dublin to meet his wife, the result being that, while the Minister for Justice, the spokesperson of the Government Information Bureau and the Dutch ambassador set out for the Curragh, he passed them on his way to Dublin. His car arrived at the ambassador's house only to find it empty. The only person there was the Minister for Foreign Affairs, Garret FitzGerald, who had by chance gone to the house to express his congratulations. 'The people in a neighbouring house very kindly took us in,' he reported, 'and Dr Herrema had coffee and biscuits.'[120]

That the siege had ended without bloodshed was seen as a triumph for the Government, and there was international praise of the way the kidnap had been handled.[121]

The Taoiseach told a meeting in Belcarra, Co. Mayo, where he was campaigning in the Mayo West by-election, that 'this episode blackened the name of Ireland, but because of the national will it has now been removed from the reputation of the country.'[122] Five days after the surrender of Gallagher and Coyle, Fine Gael won a decisive victory in the by-election, with 24-year-old Enda Kenny retaining the seat formerly held by his late father, Henry, and increasing the party's vote by 3 per cent, despite the unemployment and inflation figures. The successful conclusion to the kidnap saga was cited among the main reasons.[123]

The only blot on the landscape was the suggestion that, despite all the rhetoric about not negotiating with terrorists, a deal concerning their sentences had in fact been made with the kidnappers to get them to surrender. This suggestion came from a pretty impeccable source, Dr Herrema himself, who made it in a radio interview with Gay Byrne.

The Department of Justice followed this sensational disclosure up by making it clear that any guarantee made during the Herrema kidnapping on the length of sentence Eddie Gallagher would serve, were null and void because Gallagher broke the conditions, most important its confidentiality.[124]

Yet Dr Herrema would regret that the agreement had not been honoured. He believed that Gallagher had been promised a light sentence, 'it may have been four years,' instead of the twenty years imposed upon him and the fifteen-year term given to Coyle, and that this had been ratified by the Government. Before Gallagher left the house he handed a copy of the agreement to Herrema and asked him to keep it safe. But as Herrema was enjoying coffee and biscuits with Garret FitzGerald, Chief Superintendent Larry Wren, the main negotiator with the kidnappers, came to the door and asked Herrema if he could have the vital piece of paper.

> I gave it him and I regret very much that I did that now. Because the next thing I heard about the agreement was when Wren was on the news the next day denying that it ever existed. That made me very angry because I trusted him. He let me down . . . I couldn't keep my word and that is something I have regretted for thirty years.[125]

———

A married couple living in Raheny, Dublin, would become the closest thing Ireland had to Germany's Baader-Meinhof movement or America's Weathermen, making the jump from political activism to armed violence, with tragic consequences.

Marie Murray would have seemed an unlikely candidate to end up being sentenced to death for the murder of a garda. From Castlepollard, Co. Westmeath, she achieved straight honours in her Leaving Cert and became a civil servant in the Department of the Gaeltacht. She left on the eve of her marriage in 1973 to Noel Murray, a metal fabricator from Celbridge. They had met as members of Official Sinn Féin but 'were not republicans in the traditional sense. Anarchists would be a more accurate description.'[126] By 1974 Noel was on the run to avoid charges of robbery and possessing explosives and firearms. In July that year Marie received a two-year suspended sentence for receiving the proceeds of a payroll robbery in Dublin.[127]

On 11 September 1975 the Murrays were part of a four-person armed gang that stole £7,059 from the Bank of Ireland branch in Killester. As they made their escape by car they were pursued by Garda Michael Reynolds, who was off duty and had been bringing his wife and two-year-old daughter to the shops. When the robbers abandoned their car and ran into

St Anne's Park, Raheny, he pursued them on foot. He dived on one of the men, and the two fell struggling to the ground. One of the other raiders fired a revolver at Reynolds's head. A witness heard the shout 'Let go of my fellow!' before the shot was fired. Reynolds died that evening in Jervis Street Hospital.[128]

When gardaí raided the Murrays' house on 8 October they found guns, pipe bombs, sticks of gelignite and bags containing thousands of pounds, which Noel Murray claimed was 'from collections made for the anarchist movement Black Cross.'[129]

The couple were found guilty of capital murder in June 1976. So disruptive were they during the trial that they were removed from the court and 'listened to the proceedings through specially installed speakers in the holding cell underneath the dock.'[130] They became the first people to be sentenced to death in Ireland since the abolition of the death sentence for ordinary murder in 1964; but the conviction for capital murder was quashed by the Supreme Court in December, on the grounds that, as Michael Reynolds was not in uniform, the Murrays could not have known he was a garda.

———

The sense that Ireland was entering a new era, in which many of the old certitudes would be questioned, was given symbolic weight when the man who had to a large extent both created and embodied the ethos of the state died. On 7 January, Sinéad de Valera, Éamon de Valera's wife, had died on the day before their sixty-fifth wedding anniversary. 'As he sat in his Rolls Royce behind the hearse bearing a simple light oak coffin, he appeared a lonely figure and furtively wiped a tear from his eye with a gloved hand.'[131]

Less than eight months later, on 29 August, the former Taoiseach and President died, at the age of ninety-two. Tens of thousands of people filed past the coffin in St Patrick's Hall, Dublin Castle, where the man who had been Taoiseach or its equivalent for twenty-one years and President for fourteen lay, dressed in the habit of the Carmelite Order. Among the mourners was Liam Kavanagh, who had been in Boland's Mills with Commandant de Valera in 1916 and estimated that there were now 27 of the 170-man garrison still alive.[132]

The state funeral was a slightly less dignified occasion.

Chaotic scenes were caused by a group of Fianna Fáil politicians who broke ranks in the funeral cortege . . . these reached a climax when the graveside area in Glasnevin Cemetery was 'invaded' by Fianna Fáil deputies, closely followed by party supporters and members of the public, thus leaving little space for the then Taoiseach Liam Cosgrave and other state dignitaries.

Reporters sent to Bruree, Co. Limerick, where de Valera had attended national school, heard that his 'opponents still blame him for the Fianna Fáil government's refusal in 1953 to build a chocolate crumb factory in Bruree.'[133] The *Irish Times* wrote:

> In one respect, there will be no disagreement about Éamon de Valera: he was a great man. Great in controversy, it is true, but great also in his love for Ireland, in his vision, his tenacity, his independence of mind, his feeling for the people and his generosity. In a large measure his monument is the Republic of Ireland of today, with its weaknesses, its imperfections, its ends tied off; but also its national pride, its stability and its old divisions largely eradicated.[134]

Yet it is also difficult to ignore the element of truth in other judgements. Declan Kiberd: 'A man who had once fought for a poets' republic but who, in more recent times, had come to regard poets with almost as much distrust as he displayed towards women.'[135] Noël Browne: 'Far from being the high minded statesman which he was believed to be, under pressure [he] showed himself to be a commonplace politician intent on retaining cabinet office in the Republic.'[136]

It says a great deal about the changes the world had endured during the century when de Valera came of age that anyone looking for the house in which he was born, 61 East 41st Street, New York, where his mother worked as a maidservant, would find that it had disappeared, swallowed up by the construction of the 77-floor Chrysler Building. And it said something about the way the world continued to change that on the day of de Valera's death the Chrysler Building was taken over by an insurance firm, because its owners had defaulted on their payments as a result of the world recession that had proved such a torment for his latest successors in government.[137]

Chapter 5 ~

| THE WAR ON TERROR

1976

1976 was the year of the hijacked hunger-striker, the murdered ambassador and the insulted president; of the great train robbery and the Heavy Gang; of banned parades, censored television and a file on suspect letters to the newspapers. Even at the time it was regarded as 'a bad year for Irish politics, maybe the worst in decades.'[1]

Above all it was the year in which the Government declared its very own War on Terror. Whether or not the measures taken by the coalition were justified was a subject of much debate; but it is hard to disagree with the argument advanced by Desmond O'Malley during the Dáil debate on the Emergency Powers Bill that the threat to the state had been much greater when he, as Minister for Justice, had brought in the Offences Against the State Act (1972), previously considered to be the last word in draconian legislation.

> Referring to the differences between the period of November 28 and 29 1972 and September 1st and 2nd 1976 he said that there were at that time in 1972 6,000 people howling to burn the house [Dáil Éireann] and everyone in it down; there were 1,100 unarmed Gardaí at the front and back gates of the house and 100 armed troops were ready to be called in if the Gardaí had to give way . . . If one went down Molesworth Street today, there were three Gardaí, who were not even needed.[2]

Nevertheless, the Government insisted on the correctness of its stance and, as with the subsequent 'War on Terror', was not slow to suggest that those troubled by the legislation were soft on, or even supportive of, the terrorists. In the end there was indeed a constitutional crisis; but it was caused not by subversives but by a Government minister.

The year's watershed is usually held to be the assassination on 21 July of the new British ambassador, Christopher Ewart-Biggs, by a landmine placed outside his official residence in Sandyford, Co. Dublin. Liam Cosgrave specifically mentioned this killing, along with an attempted escape by five prisoners from the Special Criminal Court six days earlier, as motivating his Government to declare a state of emergency.[3] Yet there had been signs before then of a hardening in Government policy. This was perhaps most graphically demonstrated by the different attitudes adopted towards the funeral of Michael Gaughan in 1974 and that of his fellow-Mayoman Frank Stagg in 1976.

Stagg was thirty-five years old when he died just after 6 a.m. on 12 February, after sixty-one days on hunger strike, in Wakefield Prison, Yorkshire. He had been seeking a transfer to a prison in Northern Ireland, which had been turned down by the Home Secretary, Roy Jenkins, on the grounds that Stagg had no connection with the North. It was his fourth hunger strike in less than two years. He had been sentenced to ten years' imprisonment in November 1973 for his involvement in the activities of an IRA unit in Coventry, which also included Father Patrick Fell, a priest born in England, who was sentenced to twelve years.

A week later, Stagg's family waited in Dublin Airport for the arrival of the coffin from London, accompanied by Stagg's brother George. As the plane landed, George Stagg realised that he was not at Dublin Airport. Two members of the Special Detective Unit who had been on the plane but had not previously revealed their identity told him that the flight had been diverted to Shannon, and that they were arresting him under the Offences Against the State Act.[4]

When the family were informed of the diversion they travelled to Shannon, where they found that the coffin had been locked inside the airport mortuary, surrounded by approximately sixty gardaí, supported by a contingent of armed soldiers spread throughout the surrounding area.[5]

There had been some dissension in the family about the funeral arrangements, with Stagg's wife, Bridie, and his brother Emmet (a Labour Party member who would himself later be a member of a coalition Government) apparently disagreeing with the idea of a republican funeral. It was this that Garret FitzGerald would later use to explain the Government's decision to take control of the funeral.

> The IRA wanted to repeat the propaganda exercise of the Gaughan funeral despite the fact that Frank Stagg's widow, who lived in England, desired a private funeral . . . We were told that the authorities in Britain had refused to accord her a police guard on her home and had entered into a deal under which it was agreed to

ignore her right to her husband's remains and to hand them over to the IRA ... His widow approached me on the matter. I was appalled by the British actions.[6]

Yet the suggestion that the massive security operation was prompted solely by concern that the wishes of the widow be honoured seems somewhat disingenuous. At the time, the Government justified the decision differently, a spokesman explaining that

fears for the security of the city had influenced the government's decision which followed advice by senior Garda officers who had studied the possibility of a funeral through Dublin provoking action that would endanger the lives and property of citizens. Shannon would be secure, viewed by loyalists as the place where the government asserted its will to downface the Provisionals. The whole picture will be one of hostility to the Provos.[7]

Indeed this notion of a Government with eyes firmly fixed on potential loyalist reaction is borne out by FitzGerald's reply when he was asked why Government policy had changed since the Gaughan funeral.

A lot of people have died in Dublin since as a result of bombs and we have to make our decision based on what information we have and our assessment of the situation. And our assessment was that to allow this funeral to take place in Dublin would have created a danger.[8]

Perhaps, from a practical point of view, the Government's decision could be construed as being the right one. Yet this does not explain why the family had to be left waiting at Dublin Airport for a coffin that did not turn up, or indeed why Stagg's mother and brothers were not allowed into the mortuary to sit with the coffin. George Stagg recalled:

We spent the whole night there in parked cars outside the door of the morgue. We pleaded for his mother and one member of the family to be let in to spend the night with the coffin in the old West of Ireland way. But no, no, no, no, under no circumstances. They were vicious about it.[9]

There seemed to be a certain gratuitously punitive element in the behaviour of the authorities, something that would surface again during the year and give 1976 its peculiarly unlovable flavour.

While Bridie and Emmet Stagg supported the Government, the dead man's mother and ten of his twelve siblings issued a statement declaring that they would not attend the funeral, and that 'we do not expect any of our friends or relations in Hollymount or elsewhere to attend.'[10] Meanwhile the body was taken from Shannon by Air Corps helicopter to the parish church in Robeen, near Hollymount, where a local priest, Father Louis Berry, 'recited some prayers before the audience of Special Branch men and a small group of uniformed Gardaí.'[11] A detachment of soldiers surrounded the church, backed by two armoured cars.

On the Sunday 'the funeral procession was led by armoured cars and van loads of Gardaí.'[12] Meanwhile 'five thousand sympathisers marched from St Muredach's Cathedral through the town centre to the cemetery' in an alternative to the state-organised funeral. More than a thousand gardaí and soldiers in riot gear patrolled the streets of Ballina, where all shops, pubs and hotels had been advised to close. 'There were scuffles in the cemetery and soldiers later fired rubber bullets to disperse a group of youths who were stoning them. Eleven people were taken to hospital with minor injuries, involving seven Gardaí.'[13] Members of the Special Detective Unit dug the grave, as the local gravediggers refused.[14] Whether all this constituted a propaganda defeat for the republican movement is perhaps questionable.

The authorities placed a concrete slab two feet thick over the grave to prevent the body being removed; but the following year a group of republicans dug underneath the concrete and reburied the body in a nearby plot.[15]

Though by today's standards the Government's actions may seem extraordinary, it is worth pointing out that no criticism was heard from Fianna Fáil. In fact at the party's ard-fheis the previous weekend Jack Lynch declared that Stagg's life

> could have been saved by a word from his putative leaders. These men are only too willing to sacrifice the lives of their young subordinates just as they order the indiscriminate taking of many innocent lives in the pursuit of an objective which, by their evil deeds, they desecrate. They disgrace the name of Ireland.[16]

Evidence that the old-time republicanism was on the wane within the party came when the ard-fheis

> rejected the suggestion that Mr Neil Blaney TD should be invited to rejoin the party ... Mr Lynch put Mr Blaney's refusal to subscribe to the party's policy on the North third of his three reasons for rejecting the motion. The first was Mr Blaney's spurning of the party line in a crucial Dáil division; the second was his disloyalty, and loyalty was an essential qualification for membership of Fianna Fáil.[17]

Charles Murray from the Donegal Comhairle Dáilcheantair said that Blaney 'as an individual has done more harm to Fianna Fáil than Cosgrave and his Blueshirts or even the Cruiser [Conor Cruise O'Brien] and his fascist friends.'[18] Blaney was not to enjoy the same rehabilitation as Charles Haughey, who told the ard-fheis that

> there is no leadership crisis in Fianna Fáil. We are not casting around for a leader. We have a leader democratically chosen and as such commanding the support and allegiance of the party.[19]

Lynch nodded at Haughey's oratory, though there were those who wondered 'was it in agreement or in perplexity?'[20]

Ten years after the huge celebrations for the fiftieth anniversary of the 1916 Rising there was no attempt by the mainstream political parties to mark the sixtieth anniversary. A commemorative parade from St Stephen's Green to the GPO was organised by Sinn Féin for 25 April, but it was banned by the Gardaí. Despite this, ten thousand people turned up, among them David Thornley, who appeared on the platform. Three days later he was expelled from the Parliamentary Labour Party. His intention had been

> to sustain the principle of the right to dissent in the public space ... Even though he disagreed with the political aims and tactics of Provisional Sinn Féin he felt that they should be allowed a place in the public space, and in public discourse, to air their views.[21]

His stand for civil liberties impressed republicans no more than it had his party colleagues.

> Some of the organisers were against his appearance on the platform and all, it would appear, were agreed that he should not be allowed to speak ... Newspaper reports contained accounts of booing from the audience at Dr Thornley's presence.[22]

There was a time when such a parade would not have been banned, but there was now a sense of a progressive strengthening of state security. Yet it was the Ewart-Biggs killing, and the fleeting escape of five prisoners from the Special Criminal Court in Green Street, Dublin, six days previously, that prompted the Government to declare a state of emergency.

The Green Street escape was another one of those semi-farcical incidents that suggested that the state was better at guarding dead IRA men than living ones. On 16 July 'a young man, carrying a green haversack, posed as a tourist to pass through the tight security cordon' that surrounded the court.

> According to Gardaí the man said that he wished to see the outside of the courthouse because of its historical connections. He unslung the haversack from his shoulder, leant it on the wall and ran off

seconds before the explosion.[23]

At the same time two other bombs went off inside the cells where Michael O'Rourke, Jim Monaghan, Joe Reilly, Dónal Murphy and John Hagan were being held. Monaghan and Reilly were on trial in connection with the discovery of a bomb factory in Donabate, Dublin, and had asked for the other three men to be brought from Port Laoise Prison to give evidence in their defence.[24] After a chase through the streets four of the men were soon recaptured, but O'Rourke got away, fleeing eventually to the United States, from where he was deported as an illegal alien in 1984. Monaghan would later find fame as a member of the 'Colombia Three', arrested by the Colombian government in 2001 while returning from a visit to the guerrilla organisation FARC, while Reilly would become a Sinn Féin councillor and finish fourth in the three-seat Meath West constituency in the 2007 general election.

The escape seemed to give credence to the British Foreign Office opinion that Ireland's internal security was 'moderate to poor' by British standards.[25] Britain's new ambassador, Christopher Ewart-Biggs, apparently shared this feeling. On 12 July he met officers of the Gardaí to discuss his personal security. He wrote in his journal:

> They are not very reassuring. They do not seem to have given much thought to the scenario of attack. They thought for some reason that an attack on the car was unlikely. ('It hasn't happened yet.') It seems to be the department of fingers crossed.[26]

Nine days later he was dead.

At 9:40 a.m. on 21 July a convoy of four cars left the ambassador's official residence, 'Glencairn', in Sandyford to drive to the new British Embassy in Ballsbridge.

> It rounded a left hand bend, went down a hill and, at the bottom, the explosives were detonated in a drain crossing under the road . . . The size of the bomb was clearly evident from its effects. It demolished the road, leaving a crater thirty eight feet long across the road, thirty feet wide and nine feet deep . . . The bombers apparently set off the charge from a vantage point on a hill overlooking the hollow in the road. From behind a thick hedge there they would have had a clear view of the gates of Glencairn and of the convoy approaching the drain. A long length of flex led from the drain, along the road wall, up by a ditch and through a gap, where it continued along on the other side of the hill to their vantage points.[27]

The explosion killed Ewart-Biggs and Judith Cook, the secretary of

Brian Cubbon, Permanent Under-Secretary at the Northern Ireland office, who was also in the car. Cubbon and the ambassador's driver, Brian O'Driscoll, were seriously injured but survived. The IRA's motive for the attack was apparently that they believed Ewart-Biggs

> to be a British spymaster, an important link in the sophisticated intelligence network the British had now built up on both sides of the border: he was believed to have been attached to Century House, an anonymous office block on the south bank of the Thames that houses Britain's Special Intelligence Services [Secret Intelligence Service].[28]
>
> This first assassination of a serving foreign diplomat in Ireland provoked a great deal of public outrage. Perhaps the most powerful indicator of how attitudes in the Republic had changed came when twenty women representing residents from Leopardstown handed in wreaths at the British Embassy . . . Most of the women in the group had taken part in a protest march to Glencairn following the Derry Bloody Sunday shootings in January 1972.[29]

The fact that the pendulum of public opinion had swung in such a fashion, that the 'Peace People' had attracted twenty thousand people to a march in Dublin and that 1976 was the year the IRA set up a separate Northern Command, on the grounds that 'the IRA's principal business was to fight a war against British forces in Ireland,' would suggest that the idea that the institutions of the Republic might be toppled by the IRA no longer held much water.[30] Grisly as the killing of the ambassador was, it did not appear to have the state-threatening resonances of the burning of the British Embassy in 1972 or of the Dublin bombings two years later.

The Government, however, decided that drastic action was called for, and on 1 September a state of national emergency was declared. (Though confusingly it turned out that the state of emergency that had been declared on 2 September 1939 had never been brought to an end by the Dáil.) Liam Cosgrave told the Dáil that

> the legal measures would cause the government to derogate from the Convention on Human Rights but this it was allowed to do, 'in time of public emergency threatening the life of the nation' . . . If people obey the law they need not fear the effect of these measures.[31]

The measures included giving the Gardaí the power to detain people for seven days without charge.

The Government was bullish about the new measures, which passed in the Dáil by 70 votes to 65. Senator Michael O'Higgins, the leader of the Seanad, asked rhetorically were they going to pussy-foot with violence for the sake of ensuring that they did not stand on the toes of those who were concerned with civil rights and so that they would not be criticised?[32]

John Kelly described the objections of the Irish Commission for Justice and Peace as 'pathetic' and accused the Irish Council for Civil Liberties of putting them up to it, something that led David Thornley to describe him as 'a fascist hyena.'[33] Patrick Cooney hit a similar note when he stated that

the Gardaí were dealing with sophisticated modern ruthless gangsters and one must realise that it was impossible to fight these people 'with one arm tied behind one's back.' There had been a recent barrage of allegations and accusations against the Gardaí and he wished to say that the allegations had originated with terrorists or from their organisations.[34]

The language is strikingly similar to that of a more recent War on Terror.

Yet the opposition were unconvinced. Jack Lynch feared that

in a state of emergency the rights of the individual were suspended and the door was opened to a police state . . . He did not believe that the threat to the nation was so serious as to warrant the suspension of constitutional safeguards . . . He honestly thought that this reason was primarily a propaganda exercise on behalf of the coalition government.[35]

Brian Lenihan, Fianna Fáil's leader in the Seanad, felt that it was 'the kind of ham-fisted reaction of dictators in South American governments.'[36]

Mary Robinson, the Trinity College senator who had just joined the Labour Party and was a member of the Executive of the recently formed Irish Council for Civil Liberties, felt that

we have not got a deep concern about civil liberties . . . We have no value on democratic structures and therefore we had cheapened the values in this regard. We stood accused of cheapening the values of our democratic state by allowing an unreal state of emergency to remain for reasons of political convenience.[37]

She was not the only Labour Party representative to express unease. The expelled duo of David Thornley and Senator Michael Mullen joined her in voting against the Emergency Powers Bill, while John O'Connell and Senators Michael D. Higgins and John Horgan abstained. Although Conor Cruise O'Brien was the only Labour TD to speak in favour of the measures, the great majority of Labour Party members stood by their senior coalition partner. Justin Keating, then Minister for Industry and Commerce, would later state that we responded, I am afraid, by becoming more authoritarian. This was a grave mistake. It is in difficult times that the test of liberal conscience really comes.[38]

Claud Cockburn, the famous English journalist, then living in Co. Waterford, mocked the emergency as being 'rather of the kind experienced by inmates of clinics for those suffering from persecution mania or similar delusions.'[39] But perhaps the most devastating summation came from another Englishman, Bruce Arnold, then parliamentary correspondent of the *Irish Independent* and someone who could scarcely have been regarded as a republican fellow-traveller.

> It was a largely cosmetic response to a single shocking act of terrorism which had not fundamentally changed the level or degree of security threat in the country. Politically, it represented an opportunity to wrong-foot the opposition. A law and order election would then be on the cards with the real emergency, the economic one, left on the sidelines.[40]

If this was indeed Cosgrave's reasoning, it was not without political astuteness, because the Government's hard-line stance did not seem to be an electorally unpopular one. In an opinion poll taken in December, 49 per cent of voters felt that the coalition was doing well on security matters, with only 16 per cent feeling they were doing badly and a mere 7 per cent thinking Fianna Fáil would do better. This is in contrast to the disastrous figures for the coalition on economic matters, where only 8 per cent thought they were doing well on prices, as opposed to 75 per cent who thought they were doing badly. On unemployment the outlook was not much better: 14 per cent to 68 per cent.[41] The majority of the electorate seem to have been untroubled by the emergency legislation, something acknowledged in Mary Robinson's comment at a meeting in Trinity College on 5 September that 'it did not take much courage to denounce the IRA in the Ireland of September 1976.'[42] It was at the same meeting that Liam de Paor, a lecturer in history in UCD, made the obvious but largely ignored point that 'the murder of the British Ambassador represented a failure on the part of the security forces and, rather than sack the security forces, the Government was now giving them extra power.'[43]

One reason for the opposition of civil liberties campaigners to the Gardaí being given extra powers was that there was growing unease about the manner in which the force was employing the powers it already possessed. When Rev. Terence McCaughey, vice-chairperson of the Irish Council for Civil Liberties, said that 'the Government would have to explain what it was that the Gardaí could do better in seven days that they could not do in two,' there would have been knowing smiles in certain quarters.[44]

Despite Cooney's suggestion that accusations of ill-treatment 'emanated from the subversive side and their fellow-travellers . . . the whole tradition of the Guards showed that they did not abuse people who came into their custody,'[45] there is no doubt that in the mid-seventies there was

> an impromptu 'heavy gang' within the Gardaí that specialised in interrogations . . . The 'gang' had a floating membership around a nucleus of detectives attached to the Garda Technical Bureau's Special Investigation Unit. As well as beatings they used crude psychological measures similar to highly publicised techniques that had been used in Northern Ireland in the early 1970s. They had been formally described by the European Commission of Human Rights as torture after Ireland initiated a case against the United Kingdom. The techniques included apparently simple devices like depriving people of sleep and food and disorientating them through the use of hoods over their heads and high-pitched 'white noise.' Suspects were also forced to stand spread-eagled against walls for long periods.[46]

The existence of the Heavy Gang became public knowledge when, in late 1976,

> two Gardaí separately approached the News Features Editor [of the *Irish Times*] Conor Brady and told him that suspects were being mistreated in custody to secure incriminating statements, which in turn were used to secure convictions. A team of reporters was assigned to dig deeper. On 14 February 1977 under the headline, 'Gardaí using North-style brutality in interrogation techniques,' the paper began a week long series of articles by Don Buckley, Renagh Holohan and Joe Joyce that outlined the activities of a 'heavy gang' of interrogators within the Garda Síochána.[47]

Forty members of the Irish Republican Socialist Party had been questioned following the robbery of £130,000 in used banknotes and £20,000 worth of postal orders from the Cork–Dublin mail train at 3 a.m. on 31 March 1976.

> The train was stopped near Hazelhatch, County Kildare by one of the 12 strong gang, standing on the line waving a red light. The gang then came up alongside the train, some covering the driver and crew and others jumping into the mail van. They threw down registered mail bags to more members of the gang who loaded them into a van.[48]

Four IRSP members—Osgur Breatnach, Nicky Kelly, Brian McNally and John Fitzpatrick—were eventually charged with the robbery at the Special Criminal Court on 17 December. The subsequent trials, appeals and releases would lead to their case being seen as the emblematic one of the Heavy Gang era. After being interrogated in the Bridewell Garda Station on 6 August, Kelly told doctors that he had been punched, had his ears slapped, had his hair pulled and had been spreadeagled against a wall and knocked from behind. Injuries found by Dr Seán Ó Cléirigh were consistent, in his opinion, with Kelly's claim that he was beaten while in custody.[49] Kelly would later claim that he received between thirty and forty blows from a blackjack during questioning.[50] In all, 'within a few days of their arrest fifteen of the IRSP men reported being beaten and nine of them alleged grievous assault.'[51]

The saga of the Sallins mail-train robbery would drag out longest of all for Nicky Kelly, subsequently a Labour Party councillor in Co. Wicklow who failed to be elected to the Dáil in 2002 by a mere four votes.

The extent of the Government's knowledge of the Heavy Gang's activities remains a mystery. We do know, however, that one minister was aware, and approved, of them. In his autobiography, Conor Cruise O'Brien recounts how, during the search for Tiede Herrema in 1975,

> one of the gang had been arrested and we felt sure he knew where Herrema was. So this man was transferred under [Special] Branch escort from a prison in the country to a prison in Dublin, and on the way the car stopped. Then the escort started asking him questions and when at first he refused to answer, they beat the shit out of him. Then he told them where Herrema was. I refrained from telling this story to Garret or Justin because I thought it would worry them. It didn't worry me.[52]

It has been pointed out that Cruise O'Brien's admission is something of a smoking gun. Gene Kerrigan and Pat Brennan wrote that, in October 1975,

> sixteen months before the Irish Times made public the Heavy Gang allegations at least one Government member believed that the beating of suspects was acceptable. The culture of violence appears to have been so acceptable in certain quarters that detectives had no qualms about casually telling a Government minister about a specific beating. The detectives must have felt confident that O'Brien would not report that conversation or make an official complaint. It must also have been comforting to the detectives who discussed this with O'Brien that a Government minister saw

nothing wrong with beating up a prisoner. This approval can only have encouraged those within the force who engaged in such violence.[53]

There is no reason to doubt Cruise O'Brien's assertion that Garret FitzGerald and Justin Keating would not have received such a confidence with the same equanimity as himself. FitzGerald tells us that when the *Irish Times* series came out he was

> distressed by these reports which appeared to me to warrant investigation. Several of my colleagues shared my anxiety. Having reflected on the matter during our holiday in France in August, I decided to raise it in government and, if necessary, to force the issue to a conclusion by threatening resignation. In the event I was deflected from my purpose by a consensus in the government that we would be sending very conflicting signals to public opinion if at the same time as enacting legislation that, among other things, extended to seven days the maximum period for which suspects could be held under the Offences against the State (Amendment) Act, we instituted an inquiry into the interrogation of suspects being held by the Gardaí.[54]

The explanation seems profoundly illogical, as presumably the best time to examine the behaviour of gardaí towards suspects would be when enacting legislation that puts suspects in the custody of the force for an extra five days without a charge having to be preferred. FitzGerald concludes that

> I allowed myself to be persuaded to leave this sensitive issue over for several months, and my recollection is that I raised it again in November and/or January to no effect.[55]

The Heavy Gang's activities would not be investigated, checked or questioned by the coalition. Perhaps the most telling statistic about the period is that

> between 1970 and 1974 two people died in the Republic's prisons or in Garda custody. Between 1975 and 1979 that figure rose to 20. All were described as suicides.[56]

Patrick Cooney's response to suggestions that prisoners should be given immediate access to medical attention and legal representation was the facetious suggestion that if that were the case 'they would also require access to hairdressers, dentists and opticians.'[57]

There are some other odd incidents from 1976 that epitomise the tenor of the times. In June the Gardaí's own newspaper, the *Garda Review*, carried an editorial critical both of the government and of the Garda Commissioner Edmund Garvey. Garvey had the editorial referred to the Director of Public Prosecutions in an unsuccessful attempt to have the editorial board charged with subversion and incitement to violence.[58]

Subversives, it seemed, were everywhere. They were to be found, for example, in the letters pages of national newspapers, as Conor Cruise O'Brien explained to a journalist from the *Washington Post*, Bernard Nossiter, who visited Dublin to write about the newly declared emergency. A clause in the Criminal Law Act recently passed by the Dáil declared that

any person who recruits another person for an unlawful organisation or who incites or invites another person (or other persons generally) to join an unlawful organisation or to take part in, support or assist its activities shall be guilty of an offence and shall be liable on conviction on indictment to imprisonment for a term not exceeding 10 years.[59]

Tim Pat Coogan, editor of the *Irish Press*, had told Nossiter that 'this clause could bar him from sending a reporter to interview anybody in the IRA or its fronts and might even stop him from publishing charges of brutality levelled against British soldiers in Ulster.'[60] Hoping to explain to the American visitor about the legislation, Cruise O'Brien

pulls from his files letters to Coogan's *Irish Press* that denounce contributions to a memorial fund for the murdered Ambassador as an insult to the patriots who died for Irish freedom. 'With this kind of language,' O'Brien says grimly, 'you induce young people to join the IRA, putting youths at the disposal of men who may order them to kill and maim.' Would he use the law to jail the letter writers? No, but he hints that he might use it against the paper that gave them space. O'Brien acknowledges that the measure could punish music teachers who lead classes in IRA ballads or even history teachers who glorify the Irish revolution heroes.[61]

In the Dáil, John Kelly dismissed Fianna Fáil's right to comment on the implications of such censorship on the grounds that in 1922 republicans had damaged the printing press of the *Freeman's Journal*.[62]

Cruise O'Brien, once the courageous challenger of nationalist shibboleths, had metamorphosed into someone who believed that 'anyone who favoured a United Ireland, or who maintained that such an outcome to the national problem was a valid political position, was a Provo supporter if not the Real McCoy.'[63] On 18 October he made his most lasting contribution as a minister when he used section 31 of the

Broadcasting Authority Act (1960) to ban from radio and television 'any matter which is an interview, or report of an interview, with a spokesman or with spokesmen' for the Provisional or Official IRA, any organisations classified as unlawful in the North, and Provisional Sinn Féin. The decision followed an interview on RTE Radio with the PRO of Provisional Sinn Féin, Seán Ó Brádaigh, at the party's ard-fheis, during which he was asked to comment on an incident in Co. Laois in which the Provisional IRA had attacked the Republic's forces of law and order in a previously unprecedented manner.

The Provisional IRA was responsible for the deaths of six members of the Garda Síochána during the period 1970–94.[64] Four killings occurred when gardaí tried to capture IRA men who had just carried out robberies, one when they sought to recover a kidnap victim. Only once was there clearly a premeditated plot to murder a member of the force.

Just before midnight on Friday 15 October an anonymous phone call was made by a woman to Port Laoise Garda Station, claiming that men were acting suspiciously at a disused house in Garryhinch, near Mountmellick. At 12:50 a.m. five gardaí—Sergeant Jim Cannon, Garda Michael Clerkin, Garda Gerry Bohan, Detective-Garda Ben Thornton and Detective-Garda Thomas Peters—arrived at the house.

> The five Gardaí checked the outside of the house as best they could, using high powered torches. They saw nothing suspicious and then moved in to check the interior of the house. Cannon, Clerkin, Bohan and Thornton went to the back of the house, while Peters remained at the front. Thornton then went to the back of the house, while Peters remained at the front. Thornton went around to the front again. Cannon and Bohan were still at the back of the house, at the gable end, when Thornton and Peters went in through the front door. Seconds later, Clerkin got in through a ground-floor window at the back. The young Garda turned slightly to his left and stepped onto a flagstone when, suddenly, there was an enormous explosion. Clerkin had stepped directly onto a bomb that had been planted underneath a flagstone slightly to the left of the rear door.[65]

The blast, which was heard six miles away, reduced the house to rubble. Garda Bohan sought help at the house of a farmer, Billy Moore, who lived 250 yards from the blast site. With two of his brothers he went to the scene and joined in removing the debris. Bohan was able to find the spot where Thornton was buried, and the group were able to dig him out.[66] He survived but Clerkin's body had to be identified by reference to his signet ring. Peters was left blind and almost deaf for life.

Though Seán Ó Brádaigh denied republican involvement, there is no doubt that IRA members were responsible. 'There are some suggestions that Mountmellick was a "solo run" although others reject this and say the bombing had to have been sanctioned.'[67] The IRA had not carried out such an attack on the Gardaí before: the organisation's standing orders expressly barred them. 'Clerkin's killing did not go down well within certain sections of the IRA and those responsible for the outrage were subsequently isolated.'[68]

One writer believes that 'this flagrant breach of Standing Order Number Eight was an expression not merely of IRA anger at the situation in Portlaoise jail, but at the activities of what became known as the "heavy gang".'[69] It has also been suggested that

> the Mountmellick blast occurred against a backdrop of heightened tension between republicans and the Gardaí in Portlaoise. There had been several incidents involving Provos and the Special Branch in the town . . . culminating in the arrest of three IRA men in the area shortly beforehand. Neither Michael Clerkin nor any of the other Gardaí who responded to the call were the intended targets of the bomb. It was meant for another plain clothes officer in Portlaoise against whom certain Provos had a grudge. The Provos who planted it had expected that this detective would respond to the phone warning and be lured to his death.[70]

Garda Clerkin, in fact, had been unhappy with having to work at Port Laoise Prison and had applied for a transfer, which tragically came through a week after his death.[71] The prison had been the site of a struggle of wills all year between the authorities and the prisoners, who had made frequent allegations of mistreatment and poor conditions. The device that killed Christopher Ewart-Biggs and Judith Cook was believed to have been made at the same place as the bomb which killed Garda Clerkin, a house between Tullamore and Clara.[72]

Thousands of people attended Garda Clerkin's funeral in Monaghan; yet his death was quickly overshadowed by an event that, once it had happened, seemed like the consummation the coalition had been heading towards all year. This also took place in the midlands, and the repercussions proved to be politically seismic.

———

Patrick Donegan, the Minister for Defence, had been in Columb Barracks in Mullingar on 18 October to open a new army cookhouse. He did not, however, stick to his script.

On 24 September President Ó Dálaigh had referred the Emergency Powers Bill to the Supreme Court, because he wanted to be sure it was not repugnant to the Constitution. Having received confirmation that it was not, he signed the bill into law shortly after midnight on Saturday 16 October. It had not been a particularly controversial move by Ó Dálaigh, but Donegan decided it was worth a diatribe. He told the assembled soldiers:

> It was amazing when the President sent the Emergency Powers Bill to the Supreme Court ... In my opinion he is a thundering disgrace. The fact is that the army must stand behind the state. The army stands behind the state but too often was put behind it as a minor force.[73]

By stressing the necessity of the army 'standing behind the state' Donegan was implying that in this case the President had not. By that evening the Fianna Fáil defence spokesperson, Joe Dowling, was calling for the minister to be sacked.

> I consider today's remarks of the Minister for Defence to be a flagrant breach of both the spirit and letter of the constitution, compounded by the fact that they were delivered publicly before members of the Irish Army of whom the President is Commander in Chief. The remarks Mister Donegan made are totally unworthy of a member of the government.[74]

It seemed that Donegan had signed his own political death warrant. Though he quickly issued a public apology, Ó Dálaigh implicitly rejected this by refusing to meet the minister.

Donegan, Fine Gael TD for Louth, had a previous record in the realm of unfortunate behaviour. 'In 1969 when he was Fine Gael's spokesman on Industry and Commerce, he was fined £20 at Drogheda District Court after he admitted trying to run some traveller families out of Monasterboice by firing his shotgun outside their caravans.'[75] He had suggested that the unemployed should be conscripted into the army.[76] The previous year he stated that 'in the months ahead I will have to ask the army to perform things which they will not like but because of their tremendous loyalty the army will go ahead and perform them.'[77] The alcoholism for which he would subsequently be hospitalised was common knowledge in political circles, and 'the assumption of many people was that the Minister had too much to drink.'[78]

Yet Liam Cosgrave not only refused to dismiss the errant minister but refused to accept his offer of resignation, managing to turn a minor political drama into a constitutional crisis. On 20 October, Fianna Fáil moved a Dáil motion calling for Donegan's dismissal.

> There was a cold, cutting edge to Jack Lynch's voice in the Dáil as he demanded Mr Donegan's head for 'the gross insult offered to the President and the grave reflection on his integrity, capacity and constitutional status as head of state.'[79]

Fianna Fáil was further infuriated by the contrast with events the previous year, when Lynch would have sacked Bobby Molloy from the front bench for making false allegations against Jimmy Tully had Molloy not resigned.

The Government won the vote by 63 to 58, with John Kelly, in his now-familiar role of defender of the indefensible, declaring that Donegan's speech 'was the product of a hot and generous temper, in contradistinction to the whey-faced, cold-nosed Puritanism of the opposition and outside commentators.'[80]

Ó Dálaigh wrote a letter to Donegan, criticising

> the insinuation that the President does not stand behind the state ... Have you any conception of your responsibilities as a Minister of State and, in particular, as Minister for Defence? If the office of President, as I conceive it to be, is to have any usefulness a President would be failing in his duty 'to maintain the Constitution of Ireland and uphold its laws' if he were not vigilant in his scrutiny of legislative proposals.

On 22 October he resigned.[81] His wife, Máirín, said: 'I feel he really had no choice but to resign. Nobody could hold any respect for him or his office if he stayed.'[82] What Claud Cockburn termed 'the coup d'état of the yahoos' was complete.[83]

Desmond O'Malley observed that

> the real culprit in this matter is not Mister Donegan but the Taoiseach. He deliberately stood over a serious denigration of the highest office of this state. He must now carry full blame for today's event.[84]

There is little disagreement that the affair was a disaster for the Government.

> The Donegan affair marked a low point in the term of the national coalition. The government of all the talents had begun with so much hope and optimism. It was a ragged and dispirited group by the time Ó Dálaigh resigned.[85]

And the damage was lasting.

> The 'thundering disgrace' remark, with the constitutional crisis which followed, clung like some malodorous marsh gas to the remaining days of coalition rule.[86]

Given that the mess was made infinitely worse by Cosgrave's failure to cut Donegan loose, the question remains why the Taoiseach acted in the way he did. Charles Haughey asserted that 'what the minister said reflected accurately the views of the government and that the Minister, in his usual outspoken way was doing no more than echoing what his cabinet colleagues were saying.'[87] On this reading, the Mullingar speech was less an extempore performance from a political wild man than a deliberate shot across the bows of the President, with Donegan employed as a kind of stalking donkey, 'to inform the President, at one remove, that he was not performing his tasks in a helpful way.'[88] Credence is lent to this notion by the admission of the Labour Party's chief whip, Barry Desmond, that

> there was a growing suspicion towards Cearbhall O'Dalaigh. I was shocked that Cosgrave did not accept Paddy Donegan's offer of resignation from the government for his insult to the President. When I raised the issue at a Parliamentary Labour Party meeting I was greeted with a show of great hostility from all Labour ministers towards O'Dalaigh.[89]

After the President resigned, Desmond revealed,

> he told me that Liam Cosgrave as Taoiseach had only called on him on four occasions during his two years in the Áras to brief him on affairs of the state. He regarded this level of briefing as insulting. I agreed with him. Liam Cosgrave could not overcome his deep distrust of him.[90]

It may be that Paddy Donegan was a present-day equivalent of the knights who, hearing King Henry II wondering out loud 'Who will rid me of this turbulent priest?' headed to Canterbury to put Thomas Becket to the sword. Given the Government's increasing tendency to treat any dissent as a declaration of enmity, the President could be seen as a victim of collateral damage in the coalition's War on Terror.

Cosgrave's offer to replace Ó Dálaigh with a successor of Jack Lynch's choosing may indicate some belated contrition, not least because Ó Dálaigh's successor turned out to be Patrick Hillery, the outgoing Irish member of the European Commission, who earlier in the year had gravely embarrassed the Government in another controversy that the coalition had approached in its trademark scorched-earth fashion.

———

On joining the EEC, Ireland had agreed to implement equal-pay legislation by the start of 1976. But as the day drew closer there was a concerted campaign against implementation, led by the Federated Union of Employers, which claimed that equal pay for women would lead to an increase in unemployment, then at 10½ per cent. This argument was taken up by the Government, which announced its intention to postpone equal pay. 'The enforcement of equal pay now,' said Richie Ryan, the Minister for Finance, 'could cause unemployment in the private sector and cost £12 million in the public sector, money which could be used to create jobs for those already out of work.'[91] For the private sector the Government adopted the policy proposed by Michael O'Leary, the Minister for Labour, who sought to allow firms to defer equal pay for two years wherever 'the viability of companies or the maintenance of employment would be put at risk.'[92]

There was a problem. 'If the government with its Minister for Labour, Mr O'Leary, had deliberately planned how to give the women's movement a whole new impetus at the end of International Women's Year they couldn't have done it any better.'[93] Such disparate organisations as Irishwomen United, the Irish Widows' Association, the Council for the Status of Women, the Irish Housewives' Association, the Labour Women's National Council, the Irish Countrywomen's Association and the Sinn Féin National Women's Committee banded together to oppose the Government.[94] It was pointed out that 'the gap between [the] basic wages of men and women workers in manufacturing industry is on average about 30% and the difference between average earnings about 50%.'[95] Irishwomen United occupied the head office of the Federated Union of Employers in Fitzwilliam Place in protest.

The Government's big idea for the public sector was to announce

> that it proposes to abolish sex discrimination but not discrimination between married and unmarried workers in the public service, and to establish mechanisms by which unions and managements might arrange exemptions from equal pay in the private sector. The proposal for the public service would reduce the cost of implementation from £12 million to £2 million and a change from equal pay to the abolition of sex discrimination would reduce the number of workers affected from 35,000 to 9,000.[96]

The move was described as a 'confidence trick' by Dan Murphy, secretary of the Public Services Committee of the ICTU.[97] Máirín de Búrca, general secretary of Official Sinn Féin, noted that

> the vast majority of women teachers in both the public and private sectors were single women while the majority of men were married. The government's claim that its compromise abolished

discrimination against women was patently untrue.[98]

The man charged with assessing the merits of Ireland's claim for exemption was the EEC Commissioner for Social Affairs, who happened to be Dr Patrick Hillery, appointed to the post by the previous Government. Hillery had been partly responsible for the equal pay legislation.

> He pointed out that the entire argument for postponing equal pay rested on an assumption that some industries could survive only by maintaining lower wages for the female section of their workforce; trade unions rejected the general argument that raising wages would lead to [the] collapse of industries and he saw no reason why it should be any different for female workers. Moreover, while the economic conditions were far from favourable for any new initiative on pay, there was no ideal time to introduce pay increases and indeed there was no guarantee that conditions would be any better in two years.[99]

Such arguments might have been expected to strike a chord with Labour ministers, but Michael O'Leary defended the Government's decision throughout,

> pointing out that the major problem within the community at present was lack of jobs and this the EEC had simply failed to solve ... It was quite obvious, he said that while there was a right to work and a right to equal pay for work of equal value, the Commission's interpretation suggested the superiority of the right to equal pay.[100]

The Government's feeling that Hillery should have privileged its needs over that of the country's women was expressed with most rancour by Richie Ryan, who thundered that

> Ireland's name on the international stage has been damaged by the irresponsible antics of the Fianna Fáil appointed Commissioner to the European Communities and the Fianna Fáil members of the European Parliament who have abused their position in Europe to damage Ireland's reputation.[101]

So eager was Ryan to get this point across that he claimed, in the script supplied to the newspapers, to have made it at a meeting of the Executive of Rathmines West Branch of Fine Gael in Terenure. In fact the meeting had never taken place, which left the minister open to a certain amount of ridicule.[102] What is striking is the resemblance of this attack to that of Paddy Donegan on President Ó Dálaigh. Seven months before the Mullingar speech, a man who was only doing his job had been attacked by a minister for political reasons.

With the trade unions, the EEC Commission and the women's

organisations against it, the Government might perhaps have been cheered by the support of the Irish Family League, which congratulated it

> on the abandonment of equal pay for women which is contrary to Catholic teaching . . . [It] could lead to the EEC being used to promulgate directives imposing contraception, divorce and abortion, says the league. It also criticises the ending of the marriage differential in public servants' pay which, it says, is a breach of the constitution as it would force wives to go back to work.[103]

Such support was not enough, and

> the demands for a partial exemption from equal pay or full reimbursement of the economic cost of the directive were quietly dropped . . . The dispute over equal pay resulted in a considerable victory for Hillery and an embarrassing capitulation for the Irish government.[104]

It was also a considerable victory for the women's movement, whose campaign had been hugely effective.

In 1976 another broad campaign began with the founding of the Contraceptive Action Programme, which

> synthesised a coalition of various women's groups, the Labour Women's National Council and family planning organisations. The structure of the campaign and repertoire of strategies broadened in scope from 1976 and received support from different constituencies—trade unions, students' unions, community and tenants' organisations, the Council for the Status of Women, Bray Women's Group, Limerick Women's Action Group, Young Socialists of the Labour Party and the Women's Group of the Socialist Labour Party and individual activists.[105]

Its aims included the legalisation of contraception, the provision of contraceptive advice and the introduction of sex education in schools.[106]

There were further gains in the field of women's rights. The Juries Act (1927), which effectually excluded women from jury service, was found to be unconstitutional by the Supreme Court following a case taken by Mary Anderson and Máirín de Búrca. The Family Home Protection Act (1976) prevented the family home being sold by one spouse without the knowledge of the other.[107] And there was a further erosion of the old conservative hegemony when RTE broadcast an interview that 'was not simply the first time that homosexuality had been discussed on national television; it was also the first time that an interview with an openly gay man had been shown.'[108] The producers had offered the interviewee anonymity by filming him facing away from the camera. He declined the offer. 'If I'm there saying I'm a perfectly normal, ordinary person, I have to be seen, so people will realise I don't have horns,' said David Norris, a 32-year-old lecturer in Trinity College.[109]

That this programme drew 'a ruling from the RTE Complaints Advisory Committee that the programme broke their broadcasting code as it did not represent social mores' was one indicator of the struggle faced by Irish homosexuals for tolerance—let alone acceptance.[110] So was the fact that 'even the owner of Bartley Dunne's, the most famous and oldest gay bar in Dublin, was not prepared to admit to an RTE crew that his was a gay pub,' and that the English magazine *Gay News* was banned by the Censorship of Publications Board in April the same year.[111] Homosexuality was illegal, and

> during 1973 and 1974 alone forty three men were sentenced in the District Court for acts of gross indecency under the Labouchere Amendment to the Criminal Law Amendment Act 1885. Gross indecency remained undefined and could be interpreted broadly as any intimate contact between men . . . Between 1962 and 1972 there were 455 convictions under the legislation, undermining the view that the legislation was largely dormant in this period.[112]

It was to challenge this state of affairs that in December 1976 David Norris, Edmund Lynch, Brian Murray and Bernard Keogh set up the Campaign for Homosexual Law Reform.[113] 'There was a tiny number of people involved,' Norris would recall,

> and our facilities were half a filing cabinet in my office in Trinity and some headed note paper and I got some distinguished people, like the Dean of St Patrick's Victor Griffin, Hugh Leonard, Victor Bewley, these sorts of people, Noël Browne, to act as patrons. Well, that was a wonderful coup because the newspapers took us seriously. They gave us wonderful credibility and there was only four of us and a couple of pages of headed paper! And we were still seen as an international conspiracy which was going to corrupt the Western world.[114]

Among those who may have been inclined to view it in that way were the members of the Society to Outlaw Pornography, set up in October by Niall Darragh, a prominent member of the Knights of Columbanus, an all-male secret Catholic organisation.

> Between November 1976 (one month after the founding of Darragh's STOP organisation) and March 1977, no fewer than 117 books and three periodicals were banned. There is little doubt that the direct influence of [the] Knight of Columbanus, Darragh, was a

major factor in the heightened activity of the board.[115]

It was a year in which the foundations of a backlash began to be laid, as 'three significant speaking tours took place all around Ireland, all instigated by the Knights of Columbanus.'[116] The speakers were all of a fundamentalist Catholic hue, the most famous being Father Paul Marx, professor of sociology at St John's University, Minnesota.

> Father Marx had paid a brief but infamous visit to Ireland in 1971, gaining notoriety by displaying a preserved foetus in a bottle to schoolchildren. Now he and the foetus were back.[117]

In December

> an anonymous member of the public complained about the Irish Family Planning Association pamphlet, *Family Planning*. The Censorship Board moved with alacrity to ban it on the grounds of indecency and obscenity.[118]

Yet the move backfired when a High Court appeal by the IFPA was upheld and a subsequent appeal to the Supreme Court by the Censorship Board failed. The IFPA's appeal had been 'the first such challenge brought under this legislation for fifty years,' and its victory seemed like a milestone.[119]

Yet the backlash was not confined to shadowy organisations like the Knights. Amid rising unemployment figures,

> the objections to jobs for married women had reached a veritable crescendo at the end of the year. Civil servants, religious brothers, local councillors, VEC members, farmers, all leapt with incredible agility onto the bandwagon. There were times when you would think that every job in the country was being held down by a married mother of nine while thousands of starving unemployed male school leavers roamed the countryside destitute.[120]

Even Government ministers got in on the act. 'Dr. Garret FitzGerald annoyed the Council for the Status of Women when he stated recently that gentle persuasion should be used to discourage married women from working while high unemployment continued.'[121] In reality only 14 per cent of married women were working in 1975, and by 1979 the figure would only be 15 per cent.[122] Factors other than a flooding of the labour market by erstwhile housewives were obviously contributing to the unease felt by the male establishment. The women's movement marched on regardless, and 1977 would see more important landmarks. The contrast between political venality and incompetence on the one hand and the energy and radicalism of those seeking social change on the other is one of the defining features of the period. And so is the contrast between economic

stagnation and cultural vitality, epitomised in 1976 by the Irish Writers'
Co-Operative, whose founders would publish both accomplished and
influential first books by the end of the year.

Provoked by a local literary world so moribund that 'in a traditionally
literary country only one novel, Peadar O'Donnell's new one, has been
published in three years,' Desmond Hogan and Neil Jordan and the
brothers Jim and Peter Sheridan set up their own publishing co-op.[123]
They were joined by Ronan Sheehan, Lucile Redmond, Fred Johnson and
John Feeney.

> All of them were also writing and realised that the thing that was
> hampering the publication of fiction above all was the economic
> situation. This could only be defeated by getting involved in the
> production themselves.[124]

They decided that the co-op's first publication would be Hogan's debut
novel, *The Ikon Maker*. The venture appeared quixotic, as 'it seemed
unlikely that an outfit run primarily by voluntary effort could manage to
bring out a book at all, let alone sell it and get reasonably good reviews.'[125]
Yet in June the paperback best-seller charts showed *The Ikon Maker* in
second place, and it would stay in the top six for a month until its print
run of 1,500 was sold out.[126]

It was a remarkable achievement; but then *The Ikon Maker* was a
remarkable book. Elizabeth Bowen had spotted Hogan's promise when
giving him the first Hennessy Literary Award in 1971 and noting the
'unique quality' of his work.[127] There was something unique about
Hogan's blend of lush imagery, impressionistic narrative and locally
specific description of his native west of Ireland. The stereotypical Irish
first novel would have been a *bildungsroman* narrated in the first person
by a young man; *The Ikon Maker* was instead told from the viewpoint of a
middle-aged woman. It immediately indicated the birth of a distinctive
new voice. In the seventies and eighties, during which Hogan produced
three further novels and four critically lauded collections of short stories,
his work 'dominated discussions about the future of Irish writing.'[128] A
generation of readers would have agreed with the *Cork Examiner* reviewer
who said that 'like no other writer just now, Hogan sets down what it feels
like to be a disturbed child of what seems like a Godforsaken country in
these troubled times.'[129] An obvious influence on writers such as Colm
Tóibín and Colum McCann, Hogan would become one of the most
important Irish artists in these years. Yet today his former editor at Faber
and Faber, Robert McCrum, can write that Desmond Hogan 'is a name
that means almost nothing now.'[130] Two decades of a nomadic and isolated

existence meant that Hogan may be best known now as a kind of J. D. Salinger figure in Irish literature, as famous for the books that were never written as for the ones that were.

The author of the other book published by the Irish Writers' Co-Op in 1976, Neil Jordan, would become, as a film director, as ubiquitous a figure in Irish life as Hogan is an elusive one. *Night in Tunisia*, the collection of short stories that appeared in December, is every bit as extraordinary a debut as *The Ikon Maker*, a book that 'changed the face of Irish fiction . . . being cinematic, half American in its rhythms and full of post 1960s angst . . . [It] offered a beginning which had an impact on many young writers.'[131] Jordan himself spoke of how he had needed to find a new mode of expression for a new type of Irish experience.

> How was I to write about the experience I knew, as someone born in Sligo and growing up in the suburban streets of the sixties? The great books of Anglo-Irish literature had very little to do with this; they had no real resonance at this level . . . The only identity at a cultural level that I could forge was one that came from the worlds of television, popular music and cinema which I was experiencing daily.[132]

Jordan's and Hogan's second books would be published by English publishers, and the Irish Writers' Co-Operative would not publish anything else that made the same impact as *The Ikon Maker* and *Night in Tunisia*. It did, however, publish *Macker's Garden*, the first novel by a young writer named Sebastian Barry, and promising books by Ronan Sheehan and Adrian Kenny. Its real significance, however, may have been the sense of possibility it gave to young writers and the impetus it gave to the creation of a new literary scene in the same year in which the definitive account of an old one, Anthony Cronin's magnificent *Dead as Doornails*, with its warts-and-all portraits of Brendan Behan, Flann O'Brien and Patrick Kavanagh, was published.

The book of the year, however, was *The Book of Invasions: A Celtic Symphony*, the acknowledged magnum opus of Horslips, the rock band whose impact on Irish life may well have been larger than that of any other. U2 and Thin Lizzy may have enjoyed greater international status, but it is questionable whether even their influence equalled that of Horslips.

> They put Irish tunes to a rock beat and wrote songs based on the folk tales of Irish mythology . . . Refusing the diktats of both trad purists and rock snobs, they sang rock songs in Irish and folk songs in English. . . . This was not merely a rocked up version of a

traditional tune but a reinvention of the medium for a different version of history.[133]

Between 1972 and 1980 they played a staggering two thousand gigs and somehow found the time to release a dozen albums as well.[134]

It was part of the group's appeal that it was a team with each member an integral cog in the machine. Barry Devlin was the band's front man on stage and most frequent lead singer; Jim Lockhart provided the traditional chops with his expertise on uilleann pipes, flute and tin whistle; Johnny Fean was a guitar hero in the Rory Gallagher mould; Charles O'Connor was an expert multi-instrumentalist; and, while Eamonn Carr stayed behind the drums, his flamboyant personality and extravagant wardrobe meant that to this day he is the first member of Horslips to come to mind for many people.

By the time they came to record *The Book of Invasions* it seemed as though Horslips had run dry artistically, perhaps exhausted by their brutal touring schedule. Instead they produced an album that is 'widely regarded as the band's crowning achievement.'[135] Yet when Fean sang

Trouble, trouble, I try to chase trouble but it chases me,
Trouble, trouble, trouble with a capital T,[136]

he might have been providing the Government, if not the country, with the perfect theme tune.

——

Trouble was not confined to the struggle against the IRA or to women and the EEC. There was trouble on the trade union front as the Government failed to agree a national wage agreement with the ICTU. It was the third-worst year for strikes since the beginning of the previous national emergency, with 777,000 working days lost.[137] A national bank strike ran from June to September, while a dispute involving thirty carpenters and painters at RTE was supported by all 1,800 employees at the station, resulting in a two-week blackout of television and radio, with the exception of Raidió na Gaeltachta and local radio in Cork and the Liberties of Dublin.[138] Given the single-channel nature of much of the country, this returned it to a pre-electronic media age, which must have pleased the puritanical Laois-Offaly TD Oliver Flanagan (elevated to the post of Minister for Defence in a reshuffle in December that saw Patrick Donegan become Minister for Lands), who had once complained that there 'had been no sex in Ireland before RTE.'[139]

One good-news story was that the anticipated new prosperity for farmers in the wake of EEC membership had come to pass. Average farm incomes had grown by 34 per cent in 1975, and increases of 20 per cent in 1976 and up to 30 per cent in 1977 were predicted.[140] Yet even this bonanza was not greeted with universal joy. The increase in farm prices at the end of the year was predicted to 'add about 9 per cent to the cost of food, raising the prices of butter and beef by 4p or 5p a pound,' at a time when inflation was already high.[141] And news of the farmers' good fortune led to calls for them to be taxed, amid revelations that 'in the 1974 budget only 5% of the total number of farmers were brought into the tax net.'[142] The National Income Tax Reform Organisation pointed out that 'the farmer pays an annual £8 income tax, [while] the industrial worker pays £300 income tax.'[143] The Economic and Social Research Institute suggested that

> the whole community should receive at least some benefit from agriculture's gain and . . . this redistribution should be effected through taxation . . . Ability to pay income tax should remain the sole criterion for inclusion or otherwise. On an equity basis it is unfair to the rest of the community to exclude a group or groups from the taxation system simply because of their profession.[144]

The president of the Irish Creamery Milk Suppliers' Association, James O'Keeffe, responded: 'Certain elements in the country are always looking to grab more from the farmer.'[145]

An awful year for the Government ended with one final, galling disaster. On 12 November came the news that an independent arbitration board, the London Institute of Arbitrators, valued the Bula Mines deposit at Nevinstown at £39.75 million.

> As a result, the state which had been granted a 25% stake free of charge, will pay out £9,785,000 for a further 24% equity stake in Bula, bringing the total state holding to 49% . . . Both parties to the arbitration proceedings agreed in advance to accept the Institute's valuation as binding. It appears that the state is paying slightly over the odds for the 24% stake which is purchasing from Bula.[146]

This turned out to be something of an understatement. On 18 December it emerged that the minister had threatened to use the Official Secrets Act to prevent the *Irish Times* publishing documents relating to the valuation.[147] The paper refrained from publishing the documents but revealed why the minister might have been unhappy about it.

> The government will shortly start paying the best part of £10 million for an investment which it had valued at not much more than £3.1 million . . . Moreover the £9.7 million which the government has to

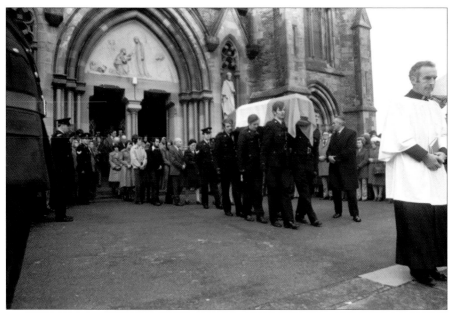

The coffin of Garda Michael Clerkin is borne from St Macartan's Cathedral, Monaghan, on 19 October 1976. Garda Clerkin had been killed by an IRA bomb at Garryhinch, Co. Laois, three days earlier. (*Irish Times*)

A scene from 'The Spike', the RTE drama series that was axed in 1978 after public protests about a nude scene involving the actor Madeleine Erskine that caused the founder of the League of Decency, J.B. Murray, to suffer a heart attack. (*RTE Stills Library*)

Bob Geldof proving that the first item on the agenda of any Irish rock band is the splits. The Boomtown Rats hit number one in England with 'Rat Trap' in 1978 and 'I Don't Like Mondays' in 1979. (*Ian Dickson/Rex Features*)

The largest march in the history of the country. Up to 400,000 people marched through Dublin on 22 January 1980 to demand reform of the tax system, which they felt placed an unfair burden on PAYE workers. Another 300,000 took part in thirty-six other marches that took place in every county. (*Irish Times*)

Anti-abortion campaigners march through Dublin in 1981, the year that both Fianna Fáil and Fine Gael agreed to hold the constitutional referendum demanded by the Pro-Life Amendment Campaign. (*Irish Times*)

The gutted interior of the Stardust nightclub in Artane, Dublin, where forty-eight young people died in a fire on 14 February 1981. An inquiry chaired by Mr Justice Ronan Keane found that there had been 'reckless disregard for the safety of the people in the premises.' The Director of Public Prosecutions, Éamonn Barnes, decided against prosecuting the owners of the club. (*Press Association Images*)

Members of the National H-Block Armagh Committee on a protest march during the 1981 H-block hunger strikes, which cost the lives of ten republican prisoners. In 1977, fourteen republican inmates of Port Laoise prison spent forty-eight days on hunger strike before abandoning their fast in disputed circumstances. 'The vast, emotive political funerals of republican hunger strikers, which eventually brought Sinn Féin to power in the North, could easily have occurred in the South also,' wrote Tim Pat Coogan, whose *On the Blanket* is the definitive account of the H-block struggle. (*Crispin Rodwell Photography*)

From the 1981 election campaign, a graphic illustration of the way the personality of Charles Haughey would overshadow everything else about Fianna Fáil during the eighties. This was the last election of the era when Haughey's leadership would be seen as an asset rather than a hindrance to his party. (*Irish Times*)

The aftermath of the explosion in Talbot Street, Dublin, that killed fourteen people on 17 May 1974. Ten people were killed by a bomb in Parnell Street and two by a bomb in South Leinster Street. Later that day another car bomb killed seven people in Monaghan. The bombing is believed to have been carried out by the Mid-Ulster UVF. Nobody stood trial, and allegations of British collusion have yet to be proved. (*Peter Winterbach/Press Association Images*)

The coffin of the IRA hunger-striker Michael Gaughan is paraded along the Kilburn High Road in London on 8 June 1974. Gaughan, from Ballina, Co. Mayo, died in Parkhust Prison after sixty-four days on hunger strike. The show of public support at his funeral prompted attempts by the coalition Government to deny the republican movement such propaganda triumphs in the future. (*Frank Barratt/Keystone/Getty Images*)

An apposite comment on the great taboo subject of the era, police brutality. From the Heavy Gang activities of the mid-seventies and the death of Peter Matthews in Shercock to the Kerry Babies case, allegations of questionable behaviour by the Garda Síochána would recur again and again. (*Irish Times*)

Joanne Hayes and her family outside Tralee Courthouse during the Kerry Babies Tribunal of 1985. What began as an inquiry to see why perfectly innocent people would confess to a crime they had not committed ended up as an inquisition into the character of Joanne Hayes. She nevertheless emerged as a heroic figure in the eyes of many people. (RTE *Stills Library*)

The strike by eleven workers at the Henry Street, Dublin, branch of Dunne's Stores who refused to handle South African goods lasted two years and nine months before the Government banned the import of South African goods. The trade union official Brendan Archbold described it as 'probably the finest example of trade union solidarity ever.' (*Irish Times*)

pay will not go towards the development of the mine but straight into the hands of the present Bula shareholders who, it seems, have completely outmanoeuvred the Department . . . Is it not prudent to reserve the right not to take up the investment if the final valuation is wildly out of line with what the government thinks it is worth? . . . It seems equally prudent to ensure at least that the person who is going to spend the money i.e. the state, is told the basis on which the consideration was calculated. Under the contract, it seems, no such details will be divulged.[148]

The former head of farming programmes at RTE had, it seemed, bought a pig in a poke. His opposite number, Desmond O'Malley, remarked: 'It was incredible that any minister would pay more for 24% of something than his own professional advisers think 100% of it is worth.'[149] His relish at the prospect of pursuing the matter further was obvious.

The hapless Keating had perhaps only one defence: 1976, he could have told O'Malley, was just one of those years.

Chapter 6 ～

| LET'S MAKE IT YOUR KIND OF COUNTRY

1977

One of the most fascinating books to deal with 1970s Ireland is a 634-page tome published by the College of Industrial Relations in 1977. The author of *Prejudice and Tolerance in Ireland* was Mícheál Mac Gréil, a Jesuit who lectured in sociology at St Patrick's College, Maynooth. His ground-breaking survey was meant to cover the entire country, but the security situation in 1972 and 73, when the research was carried out, ruled out work in the North, while a 'failure to attract sufficient financial support' made a representative sample of the Republic also prohibitive.[1] Mac Gréil and his researchers were left with a sample of three thousand people in the greater Dublin area.

What they found was 'a relatively high and severe degree of racial prejudice among a large proportion of the respondents' and 'a considerable degree of general intolerance and authoritarianism.'[2] The figures do not make for pleasant reading, not least because the confinement of the sample to the Dublin area may, if anything, have skewed them in the direction of tolerance, as Mac Gréil found that prejudice tended to be highest among people brought up outside the city.[3]

One of the questions involved subjects' willingness to admit members of various minority groups to their family. Only 22 per cent would have welcomed Africans. The figure was 26 per cent for Asians, dropping to 24 per cent for Pakistanis and 21 per cent for the general category of 'blacks.' Only 29 per cent would have admitted itinerants (Travellers) to their family.[4]

The results were not much better for political or religious dissenters. Communists would be a welcome addition to only 23 per cent of families (placing them well behind criminals, on 29 per cent), while only 38 per cent would welcome atheists. Perhaps the most encouraging figure was that for unmarried mothers, whose 79 per cent appeared to show that their status as social pariahs was becoming a thing of the past.[5]

In relation to general social attitudes, 58 per cent of those questioned thought that marriage between whites and blacks, even if there were no cultural or religious differences, was a bad idea. 44 per cent believed that men whose doctrines were 'false' should not be allowed to preach, 54 per cent believed that advocating communism should be outlawed, 39 per cent that skinheads should be locked up. 40 per cent believed that homosexual behaviour between consenting adults should be a crime (which was in fact the legal position at the time), and 58 per cent believed that premarital sex was always wrong.[6]

The practical consequences of prejudice and general intolerance became obvious in 1977 during two highly publicised incidents in which members of the settled community tried, by any means necessary, to deny housing to members of the Traveller community. That the incidents took place in Galway was perhaps no surprise, though there were also attacks on and intimidation of Travellers in Clondalkin, Carrickmacross and Wicklow the same year.[7] The City of the Tribes had been the scene of the most infamous manifestation of anti-Traveller bigotry, in 1968, when an encampment was violently attacked in Rahoon, and the issue of the housing of Travellers was a regular source of political tension.

In February, Bishop Éamonn Casey had proposed a plan 'to house a small number of itinerant families, say three or four, housed in each parish in Galway City.'[8] The response was not encouraging.

> When Reverend John O'Connor, the Parish Priest of Renmore, the city's biggest suburb which mixes working class and middle class homes, put out feelers to find out how his parishioners would like itinerants moving among them, he got an unsettling answer. He was plagued by anonymous phone calls threatening to burn down his house.[9]

That the mores of Rahoon and Renmore were shared elsewhere in the city became obvious when in July the news broke that

> a 24 hour picket is being maintained at the entrance to Galway Corporation's newest housing estate by the members of the Bohermore Tenants Association because of a Corporation decision to allocate three of the new houses to itinerant families ... They will keep up this action until they are given assurances that no itinerant families will be allocated houses in the new estate.[10]

The protesters gained the support of the Mayor of Galway, Sheila Jordan, who turned up at their barricade, accompanied by three other councillors, and said, 'I will back you 100 per cent . . . If I am branded anti-itinerant, okay, then I brand those who force them on the people anti-settled community.'[11] There was also political support from Máire Geoghegan-Quinn, recently appointed Parliamentary Secretary to the Minister for Industry and Commerce, who 'fully supported the stand of the Bohermore Residents and Tenants Association in their refusal to house three itinerant families in the Bohermore estate.'[12] She said that

> she believed the matter had been blown out of proportion by the press. The Chairman of the Residents Association Mr Billy Matthews had been pictured as someone unreasonable and prejudiced whereas he was, she said, 'a very reasonable individual.'[13]

After a month 'a settlement was made possible by the generous gesture of the mother of one of the itinerant families involved, Mrs Theresa Mongan, in volunteering to accept alternative accommodation in another part of Galway.'[14] The two other Traveller families moved in, as did forty other families who had been kept out of their homes by the protest.

Worse was to follow when Mrs Mongan, her husband and their children tried to move into the house allocated to them in the Ballybane area on 28 October. When they arrived

> they had to push their way through a crowd of protesting residents to get in. They were forced to lock the windows and doors and were left without furniture after residents refused to let anything through.[15]

On the 31st

> two friends of the beleaguered itinerant family . . . were badly beaten up by local residents when they tried to visit the family. Mr Paul Donovan, one of the most prominent workers for itinerant settlement in Galway, and Mr James Raftery, a lecturer in the Regional Technical College, were attacked by the pickets outside the house and efforts were made to overturn their motorcar.[16]

The threat of a High Court injunction by Donovan secured the lifting of the siege, though not before the protesters had refused even to allow food into the house.[17]

A similar wish to impose a majority view on those considered undesirable was evident during the saga of the Project Arts Centre's funding from Dublin City Council. The Project had staged 172 arts events during 1976 that attracted forty thousand people.[18] Yet the performance of two plays by the London theatre group Gay Sweatshop drew the wrath of city councillors when a deputation from the centre, headed by the chairperson, Jim Sheridan, attended a meeting of the council's Cultural

Committee 'to press for a grant for £6,000 for the improvement of the centre and to answer allegations that they were putting on "obscene" plays at the centre.'[19] Councillor Patrick Cummins (Fianna Fáil) warned that

the whole fabric of our society was being threatened by works of this type . . . There should be greater concentration on good plays and good music. They would bring in the crowds and then they would not need to come to the Corporation looking for a grant.

His party colleague Gerard Brady complained that

the deputation had made no apology for the plays. They should be taken down a peg or two. No theatre had the right to put on such plays. They had put the Council into an awkward situation and had forced them to moralise.[20]

Councillor Frank Sherwin (independent) was worried that

if they glamorised such things as homosexuality it would make people interested and they might even want to experiment. Sex up to a point was all right; if it wasn't none of them would be here. It was just like if you had too much drink you became an alcoholic. There was such a thing as toeing the line. There were people who could stomach that sort of thing but others could not stand it.[21]

The committee duly turned down the application, claiming that they had taken this step because the Project had not got a long-term lease for their premises. This seemed a slightly less convincing explanation after Councillor Kevin Byrne (independent) pointed out that the Olympia Theatre, which operated on a similar lease and from the same landlord, had received £200,000 from the city council.[22] Two small right-wing organisations, the Irish League of Decency and Parent Concern, were mentioned as having influenced the decision.[23]

With the centre's future in danger, Gay Sweatshop returned to stage repeat performances of the two offending plays, *Mister X* and *Any Woman Can*, at the Eblana Theatre, playing to full houses, the £700 raised going towards the Project.[24]

With the chairperson of the Arts Council, Colm Ó Briain, describing the city council's decision as 'the worst thing that had happened in the Irish art world in the last twenty years,' and the Labour Party group on the council decrying 'the spurious arguments put forward about the lease and the tenure of the Project,' the council seemed to get cold feet about its role as a moral watchdog.[25] In October the Project received a grant of £4,000. Councillor Jim Mitchell (Fine Gael) said that 'the Council was not a censorship board and if anybody was offended they could go to the Department of Justice.'[26]

The Mac Gréil survey also gauged attitudes towards republicans, which revealed that they too had become something of a pariah group. Only 31 per cent of respondents declared themselves willing to admit a member of the Provisional IRA to their family, which meant that militant republicans rated 2 per cent higher than Travellers and criminals, trailing atheists and heavy drinkers.[27]

Perhaps it was such attitudes that emboldened the coalition Government to take an increasingly hard line with republicans. 1977, however, was the year in which the stories about the Heavy Gang moved from the realm of rumour to that of public record.

The first embarrassment for the forces of law and order came when Thomas Connors, a member of Provisional Sinn Féin from Co. Tipperary, apparently attempted to commit suicide by jumping from a third-floor window in Cahir Garda Station on 26 January while being questioned by gardaí from Dublin. Connors and the three men who were arrested along with him

> said that they were punched, kicked and pulled by the hair. They were deprived of sleep and lost track of time by being kept in rooms with the blinds drawn and the electric lights on day and night. One said that the Gardaí had told him, 'we'll break you mentally and physically on the seventh hour of the seventh day—that's when they all break.'[28]

One of Connors' companions, Dónal Wills, was admitted to hospital on being released from custody, while Connors, who suffered a cracked pelvis after his twenty-foot fall, spent three days in intensive care.[29] On 15 February, Timothy Henchy from Cashel, who alleged that he had been severely beaten after being arrested under the Emergency Powers Act, 'collapsed in the courtroom and was taken to hospital by ambulance' after charges against him were dismissed in the Special Criminal Court.[30]

This was the background against which the *Irish Times* series revealing the existence of the Heavy Gang appeared. One of the outstanding journalistic achievements of the era, it met with blanket denials from the Government and somewhat bizarre suggestions from Fine Gael backbenchers. They claimed that the *Irish Times* was part of a conspiracy to distract attention from the case being taken by the Government at the European Court of Human Rights against the British Government over the torture of prisoners in the North during the early seventies. The Kerry North TD Gerry Lynch suggested that

> it is no coincidence that these charges get prominence in a section of the press that has been traditionally hostile to Irish institutions

and who never cease to attack the moral and political standards by which Irish people live. Neither is it a coincidence that such charges are levelled with increasing ferocity at the very time when the nation from which such organs would have us take our standards is on trial before the world for activities that more properly belong to Cromwellian days or the era of the pitch cap for the mere Irish.[31]

Why members of the Provisional IRA and Sinn Féin would have colluded in this dastardly British plot was not explained. Yet it is indicative of the unwillingness of Fianna Fáil to be portrayed as soft on subversion that the response of their spokesperson on justice, Gerry Collins, was that

in allegations such as this one must be extremely careful, otherwise one could be used and used wrongly in an effort to possibly help those who would try to make propaganda against the government of the day and more especially against the Garda Síochána . . . I have nothing but the utmost confidence in our Garda police force . . . It could be a deliberate propaganda effort by subversives to try and embarrass the Garda force.[32]

There were not many votes in civil liberties.

One big battle remained for the coalition to fight, and it took place at Port Laoise Prison, where 'the confrontational policy of the government created a situation parallel to that which at the same time was building up North of the border in the H-Blocks.'[33] More incidents of strip-searching, solitary confinement and restrictions placed on visits led to increased tensions between prison officers and prisoners.[34] The new hard-line approach advocated by the Department of Justice was not universally welcomed, even by prison officers, one of whom explained:

You must have a live and let live approach between prison officers and prisoners . . . That's why so many of our people are now resigning or getting into trouble with the people at the top. We are being asked to do things which make that kind of co-existence impossible and which a civil prison service cannot and shouldn't be expected to do.[35]

The outcome was a hunger strike involving twenty IRA prisoners, which began on 6 March, the main demand of the strikers being a public inquiry into conditions in the prison. Those on strike included that ubiquitous figure in IRA dramas of the time, Kevin Mallon, the vice-president of Sinn Féin, Dáithí Ó Conaill, the future Sinn Féin TD Martin Ferris, and one of the men convicted for the murder of Senator Billy Fox, Seán McGettigan.

Prisoners from all over the country refused food, and perhaps this wide geographical spread accounted for the large number of appeals made to the Government to settle the strike.[36] Members of the Society of African Missions at Maynooth, thirty Co. Meath farmers who had been imprisoned a decade previously during a National Farmers' Association campaign, workers at Tara Mines, 120 building workers in Clondalkin, Conradh na Gaeilge, fifty-five members of the staff and Governing Body of University College, Galway, workers at the Fiat assembly works in Ballyfermot, Navan Trades Council, forty-one ESB workers at Ardnacrusha Power Station, forty-two residents of the Bayside area of Sutton, Co. Dublin, and the Cork County GAA Board were among those who called for a public inquiry.[37]

Tensions inside the prison spilled outside on a couple of notable occasions. On 3 April a demonstration by a thousand supporters outside the prison ended in a riot as

> stones were thrown at the Gardaí who then made a dash towards the crowd who were near the Hospital entrance. This was the start of a running battle as the Gardaí with riot shields and using their batons ran along the road pursuing the stone throwers. Many people in their way got rough treatment.[38]

When one member of Provisional Sinn Féin, speaking from a loudspeaker van, said, 'We didn't come here for a confrontation: we came here to hold a peaceful protest in Port Laoise' and urged the rioters to stop their stone-throwing and return to the meeting,

> one young Garda went to the back of the van and started trying to rip the wires from the loudspeaker. He took out a man, Mr Michael Hegarty from Clare, who was in the van, and as they exchanged words the Garda then hit Mr Hegarty with his baton. He staggered to the roadside and collapsed with blood coming from a wound above his right eye.[39]

When the fracas ended, forty-eight people had to be treated in hospital for injuries: eight gardaí and forty demonstrators.[40]

Another incident came after two Dublin footballers peacefully helped gardaí remove demonstrators from the pitch at Croke Park before the National Football League final against Kerry on 17 April. The chairperson of the North American GAA Board, Tom O'Donoghue, said that

> Irish Americans in general and the GAA within the jurisdiction of the North American Board in particular were shocked and outraged . . . Photographs showed two members of the Dublin team, David Hickey and John McCarthy, violently attacking persons pleading for mercy for the hunger strikers at Croke Park . . . These two players disgraced the uniform of the Dublin team and the spirit of the GAA

by using Croke Park to violently express their political hostility to the hunger strikers.[41]

By 6 April all twenty hunger-strikers, now thirty-two days without food, had been moved to the Curragh Military Hospital. Fourteen of them remained on the strike when on 22 April

all the men agreed to accept medical care and nourishment after direct intervention with them by the Auxiliary Bishop of Dublin, the Most Rev. Dr James Kavanagh. The fast was thus terminated apparently without any concessions by the government to the prisoners' basic demands concerning conditions in Portlaoise prison. Several of the hunger strikers were said to be in a critical condition.[42]

Senator Michael Mullen acted as an intermediary between the bishop and the hunger-strikers, who would later claim that

the communication between Michael Mullen and Bishop Kavanagh was misinterpreted or misunderstood. When the prisoners ended their fast, they did so in the belief that core issues which led to the hunger strike would be addressed.[43]

Whatever the truth of this,

the ending of the hunger strike without tragedy appeared to add up to significant victory for the government strategy. However, over the weeks, the affair has led to the spotlighting of the prisoners' demands and allegations concerning prison conditions and to the building up of considerable pressure from many quarters for an impartial inquiry into these conditions.[44]

The Government's strategy had been a high-risk one, as

the vast, emotive political funerals of Northern republican hunger strikers, which eventually brought Sinn Féin to power in the North, could easily have occurred in the South also.[45]

Yet this sense of a Government victory may well have informed the speech by Liam Cosgrave at the Fine Gael ard-fheis a month later. Along with Patrick Hillery's 'You can have Boland but you can't have Fianna Fáil' comment in 1971, Cosgrave's speech is probably the most famous of all ard-fheis moments. It was one of those that went down a bomb with people in the hall while doing untold damage to the party with the general public. Cosgrave's speech was regarded as being 'well to the right of anything any party leader had attempted since the nineteen thirties.'[46] All his resentment about the criticism the Government had endured burst forth, and 'the crowd that filled the Mansion House loved it. They stomped and roared approval.'[47] Cosgrave attacked a malicious campaign of vilification . . . that was conducted in one newspaper against the Garda and against the prison service. That wasn't the only paper. There are journals in this country with articles in them week in week out, vilifying the Garda and the army and vilifying the prison staff . . . The great thing in vogue with some of these commentators and writers is civil rights. What civil rights did Guard Fallon or Guard Reynolds get? . . . Not for the first time has this party stood between the people of this country and anarchy, and remember, those people who comment so freely and write so freely, some of them aren't even Irish. No doubt many of you are familiar with an expression in some parts of the country where an outsider is described as a 'blow-in.' Some of these are blow-ins. Now as far as we're concerned they can blow up or blow out.[48]

At times Cosgrave's anger rendered the speech barely coherent.

Did the two thousand people killed in Northern Ireland get civil rights? Did they get legal, medical or spiritual advice? The easiest thing for some of these commentators or do-gooders, I don't mind do-gooders operating so long as they don't do any harm, and I should have mentioned, did Billy Fox get civil rights?[49]

He had little respect for demonstrators, because 'any thick can carry a placard.'[50]

It was a remarkable performance, one that perhaps added to the impression that Cosgrave 'seemed to take deliberate pleasure in repression for its own sake rather than treating it, like Lynch, as a disagreeable necessity.'[51]

The speech took on a greater political relevance less than a week later, on 25 May, when Cosgrave asked President Hillery to dissolve the Dáil and announced that a general election would be held on 16 June.

Fine Gael knew from the start that the Government faced an uphill battle. A private opinion poll commissioned by the party's election committee showed that an incredible 59 per cent of the electorate intended to vote for Fianna Fáil.[52] And the party was forced further on the back foot when the opposition produced an election manifesto on the first day of the campaign that promised

to abolish rates on private dwellings and road tax on cars up to 16 horse power. There were to be increases in personal tax allowances and a reduction in the social welfare stamp for low-wage earners.[53]

The notion that the manifesto won the election for Fianna Fáil has become part of the conventional wisdom concerning Irish politics, with voters berated for accepting 'a massive give-away which would have been deemed totally imprudent and unpatriotic by a previous generation.'[54] But that is to oversimplify somewhat. It has been pointed out, after all, that 'Fianna Fáil's proposal to abolish rates on domestic dwellings was matched by a broadly similar National Coalition proposal.'[55] As for the first-time buyer's grant, 'a week after the publication of the manifesto only 11% of the respondents could spontaneously identify the proposal and this figure rose to a mere 16% in what was presumably the target group, the age group eighteen to thirty-four.'[56] The fact is that 'largesse may have played some small part but was certainly not a major factor.'[57]

The Government's problem was that the areas in which it was perceived to be least competent were those the electorate found most important. An opinion poll published in the *Irish Times* on 2 June found that the issues rated most important were prices and inflation (by 76 per cent of respondents), unemployment (76 per cent) and tax (54 per cent). Security and Northern Ireland (both 20 per cent) were in joint sixth place, behind social services and housing. Fianna Fáil was judged to be better able to tackle unemployment by 50 per cent of respondents, with the coalition only earning 21 per cent. On prices and inflation Fianna Fáil led by 48 per cent to 22 per cent.[58] For the second election in a row a Government that wanted to fight an election on its security record would find that economic issues mattered far more to the voters. Garret FitzGerald put it most succinctly: 'This explosion of promises was politically superfluous: Fianna Fáil would have won the election if they had promised nothing, for the people were tired of us.'[59]

Fianna Fáil was able to capitalise on this public mood to the full, because its organisation had been completely overhauled after the 1973 defeat. Playing a significant role in this reorganisation were three extremely capable young men: the head of the party's new policy support unit, Esmond Smyth, the press secretary, Frank Dunlop, and, by far the most important, the general secretary, Séamus Brennan, who had been charged with revitalising the party by Lynch when he had been appointed in 1973. Brennan had implemented

> a careful if unostentatious plan of reorganisation . . . The party HQ was updated and a new communications system installed. A review was made of the party's financial structure, new methods of fund raising were examined and implemented and the £100 a plate dinners of the palmy days of the nineteen sixties were firmly quashed.[60]

Come election time, Brennan drew on the lessons he had learnt when he visited America the previous year to observe Jimmy Carter's successful presidential election campaign at close quarters. Brennan explained afterwards:

> It was an incredible exercise in professionalism, scheduling, publicity, press relations, stage management, the lot. I came back and said to myself, 'if it'll work out there, why won't it work here?'

Despite a certain amount of resistance, he managed to persuade the party to have a campaign record, T-shirts printed with the slogan *Bring back Jack* and car stickers that read *Put Jack back.*

> There were also baseball or jockey caps with 'Get Ahead with Fianna Fáil' written on them. These were distributed at Lynch's rallies around the country to maximise the photo opportunities. The campaign record was played to give a degree of American-style razzmatazz to the campaign rallies that Lynch held in each of the constituencies.[61]

The campaign record was a ditty by Des O'Meara and Partners, music by Tommy Ellis, and sung by Colm Wilkinson. Its chorus ran:

> So let's make it your kind of country
> Get out there and show them that you're free
> Show them that you care a damn and that you'll win somehow
> Help us to make it your country now.[62]

No-one was going to mistake it for 'The Times They Are a-Changin'', and it's doubtful whether it contributed much to the swing towards Fianna Fáil; but it did illustrate a couple of significant features of the 1977 election. One was that unemployment was an issue in a way it had not been in previous campaigns. At 8 per cent when the coalition took office, it was at 12½ per cent when they went to the country.[63] The other was that first-time voters seemed particularly disillusioned with the Government. An opinion poll in April had revealed that only 7 per cent of voters thought the coalition was doing well on the provision of jobs for school-leavers, with 71 per cent thinking it was doing badly.[64] And a survey of voting intentions drawn from the combined opinion polls of May and June showed that only 32 per cent of 18 to 24-year-olds intended to vote for the coalition parties, compared with 44 per cent of those over sixty-five. Fianna Fáil's 17 per cent lead in this category was its largest among any age group.[65] With almost 20 per cent of the electorate due to vote for the first time, this was ominous news for the coalition and reflected the fact that 'Fianna Fáil was seen as the only major party which made any serious effort to attract the support and votes for the young.'[66]

The continued rise in unemployment was blamed on

> the combined forces of oil prices, high inflation, balance of

payments deficit, increasing capital investment and significant alterations in demographic and labour force numbers. The latter was due to the twin factors of increased immigration and a population explosion.[67]

The coalition could not be held responsible for all these factors; but the week before the election *Business and Finance* described the Government's economic performance as deplorable.

Unemployment is a festering sore, and despite the announcement of new industrial projects with heightening enthusiasm ... the race to provide the jobless and school-leavers with employment while maintaining existing jobs is not being won. Inflation is still too high. So are borrowings.[68]

Yet, unemployment aside, there had been something of an economic recovery. Richie Ryan's budget in 1977 was notably less harsh than those of the previous two years. And the 14 per cent inflation rate of the second quarter of the year, when the election was called, was the lowest since the beginning of 1974.[69] Later that year Jack Lynch would observe that

our growth rate, at five per cent, had been 'near the top of the league internationally,' investment has been dynamic; exports had risen at three times the average rate for industrialised countries; and there had been an average rise of 7,000 in manufacturing employment during the year. The volume of agricultural output was up nine per cent.[70]

The only problem for the coalition was that when Lynch delivered this implicit tribute to their handling of the economy he did so as Taoiseach.

Fine Gael was damaged during its campaign by an amateurishness that contrasted starkly with the display of the Fianna Fáil organisation streamlined by Séamus Brennan.

The party headquarters continued to be housed in an inadequate and ramshackle building in Hume Street which had extremely poor communications facilities for a national party. The headquarters remained understaffed especially in such areas as public research and press relations.[71]

The lack of professionalism was epitomised by the fact that

the party had no press officer to oversee the vital business of relations with the media. Cosgrave rang up Moore McDowell, a young UCD economist, and asked him to do the job for the campaign. McDowell's foremost political qualification was that he was a grandson of the 1916 Volunteers leader Eoin MacNeill. Liaising with the Leinster House press corps was a total novelty for him.[72]

The Labour Party's preferred method of shooting itself in the foot was internecine warfare. In the Cabra constituency in Dublin 'eight members took a High Court action contesting the legality of the selection conference . . . The party was not so much split as in splinters.'[73] In Artane, Noël Browne

> was nominated for this constituency as a Labour candidate by the local constituency executive. However, the Administrative Council of the party refused to endorse him and he stood as an Independent. He was expelled from the party.[74]

In Limerick East, supporters of the sitting TD, Stephen Coughlan,

> vetoed the nomination of a second Labour candidate. It was widely believed that they were trying to block Alderman Mick Lipper, a locomotive engine driver and Mayor of Limerick 1973–74 . . . so that Coughlan could eventually be succeeded by his son Thady . . . Lipper stood as Independent Labour.[75]

And in Rathmines West,

> in an atmosphere of some confusion and not a little recrimination, Mary Robinson was added to the list by the administrative council. David Neligan promptly withdrew his nomination in protest and vanished across the Liffey to help Noel Browne's campaign in Artane.[76]

All the while, the Fianna Fáil campaign gathered momentum, with its leader proving yet again to be the consummate campaigner. To make things worse for Fine Gael, its leader developed laryngitis early in the campaign and for a few days had to stand idly by while his son, Liam Cosgrave Junior, read out the speeches.[77]

It may have indicated a certain desperation on the part of the Government that the old 'soft on subversives' weapon was brought into play. Conor Cruise O'Brien told the *Times* of London that if Haughey were to become a minister again

> there would be a feeling that certainly existed in 1969–70, among members of the Gardaí that if you saw 'the boys' preparing for some exercise in Northern Ireland you really did not see them.[78]

Fianna Fáil's Northern policy opened up 'a vista of potential violence,' said Garret FitzGerald.[79] 'Do the people of Ireland really want Mister Haughey in the next cabinet?' wondered Tom Fitzpatrick, Minister for Transport and Power.[80] Some of them obviously did, as an *Irish Times* opinion poll showed him coming top as the preferred leader of Fianna Fáil should Lynch resign, with 34 per cent, as opposed to 26 per cent for George Colley and 18 per cent for Desmond O'Malley. The problem was that

Haughey also came top as the *least* preferred choice, with 25 per cent to Brian Lenihan's 19 per cent, something that graphically demonstrated the polarising effect he had on Irish politics.[81]

Yet despite the economic woes of the coalition's time in power, the greater public appeal of Lynch and the professionalism of the Fianna Fáil campaign, most people still expected the coalition to retain power. This had something to do with 'the results of the seven by-elections held during the lifetime of the last Dáil, in all but two of which Fianna Fáil dropped its share of first preference votes.'[82]

But the main reason why anything other than a Government victory seemed unthinkable was the redrawing of constituency boundaries by the Minister for Local Government, Jimmy Tully. The 'Tullymander' was designed to maximise the number of seats gained by the coalition in relation to share of the vote. It was 'a naked response to the previous Fianna Fáil revision before the 1969 general election which had been denounced as, 'Boland's gerrymander.'[83] For example,

> in the Greater Dublin area—where Fianna Fáil, with 40% of the votes, could hope to get 50% of the seats in the existing four seat constituencies—thirteen three seat constituencies were created; in these, the coalition, with slightly more than half the votes, hoped to gain two-thirds of the seats.[84]

As the coalition had won 55 per cent of votes in Dublin in the previous election, 'Fianna Fáil seemed likely to win only about fourteen of the forty-three seats up for grabs throughout Dublin,' something that would make it impossible for it to win a majority.[85] On the eve of the election, the pundits had little doubt about the result. For the *Irish Times*,

> according to our reporters, who have visited all 42 constituencies . . . Fianna Fáil is likely to win a minimum of 63 seats and a maximum of 71 seats. Fine Gael will win a minimum of 53 and a maximum of 60. They think Labour will have 21 to 24 seats and that two independent candidates will be elected.[86]

The general expectation was summed up by the political correspondent of the *Irish Press*, Michael Mills, who concluded that it was 'highly probable' that the result would be determined 'not by manifestoes or credibility, but by the redrawing of constituencies.'[87] Lynch's prediction that Fianna Fáil would win seventy-seven seats and an absolute majority was judged to be wildly optimistic. 'If his forecast were to prove correct . . . Fianna Fáil would have succeeded in overcoming a division of constituencies generally judged to be the most efficient in the history of the state.'[88]

Yet overcome it they did, to the extent that the 1977 general election can be regarded as a watershed. The rout of Fine Gael led to the resignation of Liam Cosgrave and the arrival as leader of Garret FitzGerald, who would reinvent the party in a social-democratic form that would bring it to its greatest popularity. The removal from the Dáil in one fell swoop of Conor Cruise O'Brien, David Thornley and Justin Keating, the trio of intellectuals elected with such fanfare in 1969, marked a kind of end to optimism in the Labour Party that led to a gradual and debilitating loss of electoral support over the next decade.

Things would never be the same again for Fianna Fáil either. In the hour of Jack Lynch's greatest victory were sown the seeds of his downfall. On the night of the election Charles Haughey met Geraldine Kennedy, the young *Irish Times* political journalist (now its editor), with whom his fate would later become intertwined to ultimately fatal political effect. Kennedy

> was perplexed by the attitude of Haughey who was 'absolutely thrilled.' She thought that his chances of ever becoming leader were well and truly buried by the Lynch landslide. 'What are you so pleased about?' she asked. 'Sure this is the biggest election victory ever.' 'Yes,' Haughey replied, 'but they're all my people. Now I know I'll be leader.'[89]

When Haughey defeated George Colley in the 1979 leadership election he had the support of seventeen of the twenty-eight TDs elected for the first time in 1977. Two of them, Albert Reynolds and Mark Killilea, would be members of the 'Gang of Five' that masterminded his campaign for the leadership.[90] On the day the twenty-first Dáil convened, on 5 July, Jack Lynch got to see the face of Fianna Fáil changing before his very eyes. As Frank Dunlop described it:

> There was a particular hullabaloo as a man in a white suit and polka-dot shirt was shouldered to the front door. 'Who in the name of God is that?' asked an incredulous Lynch. 'That,' I said, 'is the one and only Pádraig Flynn from Mayo' ... Though he would never have believed it that day, Jack was looking at one of those who would soon change the profile, and in some instances, the nature of Fianna Fáil for ever.[91]

Fianna Fáil's 51 per cent of the vote was its second-highest share, exceeded only by the 52 per cent obtained in 1938. Fine Gael's 31 per cent was its worst since 1957, the Labour Party's 12 per cent its worst since 1961. Fianna Fáil gained 15 seats to make a total of 84, Fine Gael lost 11 to achieve a total of 43 and the Labour Party dropped from 19 to 17. Four independents were elected.[92]

What was most striking was the status of some of the coalition casualties. Among those who lost their seats were three ministers: Conor Cruise O'Brien, Justin Keating and Patrick Cooney. In several constituencies Fine Gael's performance was spectacularly poor. In Carlow-Kilkenny it won only one seat out of five for the first time since 1933, while in Galway East, Galway West and Louth, Fianna Fáil took three seats out of four. In the three-seat constituencies of Dublin Artane, Kerry North, Kildare and Tipperary North, Fine Gael took no seat at all.

David Thornley lost his deposit, the first Labour Party TD to do so since 1923. Justin Keating blamed his own defeat on the fact that 'the work of his department had taken him out of the country, travelling the world seeking foreign investment for this country and in pursuit of new and expanded markets for Irish goods.'[93] But it may have owed just as much to events earlier in the year, when 'he was devastated in the Dáil by a searing enquiry into the entire background of the [Bula] deal by Desmond O'Malley.'[94] The ungrateful voters' rejection of Conor Cruise O'Brien earned them a rap on the knuckles from the *Observer* of London.

> Individual ministers, most notably Conor Cruise O'Brien, have lost their seats because they were outspoken and honest in facing the Irish people in ambiguities in Irish attitudes. Hypocrisy, it seems, is the best policy. Ireland has wounded herself by losing Dr O'Brien from the Dáil.[95]

Ireland's loss would be the *Observer's* gain, as the former minister would become the paper's editor-in-chief the following year.

Noël Browne scored an unexpected victory in Artane, while Mick Lipper (Independent Labour) ousted Stephen Coughlan in Limerick East. Lipper would later be welcomed back into the party; Browne would not.

The great irony of the election was that the Tullymander had completely backfired. T. Ryle Dwyer has pointed out:

> Had the old four seat constituencies been used the coalition would probably have got two seats in each as the Fianna Fáil vote was well short of that needed to secure three of the four seats. The coalition members had outsmarted themselves.[96]

Tully himself suffered the indignity of having to wait till the last count in the Meath constituency before he was elected, transfers from his party colleague Frank McLoughlin pushing him past Michael Lynch of Fianna Fáil.

Lynch's Government was largely along expected lines, with George Colley in Finance, Des O'Malley in Industry, Commerce and Energy,

Charles Haughey in Health and Social Welfare, Michael O'Kennedy in Foreign Affairs, John Wilson in Education and Jim Gibbons in Agriculture. The one intriguing appointment was that of Martin O'Donoghue to the new post of Minister for Economic Planning and Development, something that made him the third TD to be appointed a minister on his first day in the Dáil (the others being Noël Browne in 1948 and Kevin Boland in 1957). O'Donoghue had left school at fourteen and worked as a waiter before joining the clerical staff of the Dunlop Tyre Company in Dublin. He attended evening classes at Trinity College and obtained a degree in economics, in 1962 he became a lecturer and by the time of the 1977 election he was dean of the Faculty of Economics and Social Science. In 1970 he had become Lynch's economics adviser, but he returned to Trinity despite being asked to stay on in the Department of the Taoiseach by Liam Cosgrave.

O'Donoghue was regarded as 'a key figure in the planning of the 1977 general election campaign and manifesto. Indeed the entire economic strategy of that manifesto was his.'[97] As Minister for Economic Planning and Development

> the responsibilities he was then given were more far reaching, at least in theory, than those accorded an individual minister, other than Taoiseach. Apart from the responsibility for planning, he was given authority over negotiations with international agencies on economic issues and, most critically, planning units were to be set up in each department, each to be responsible to his Department.[98]

On O'Donoghue's strategy would rest the responsibility of leading the country back to economic health. As laid out in the white paper *National Development, 1977–1980*, published at the end of the year, this strategy

> offered to the 'social partners', the employers and trade unions, economic recovery and social advance in exchange for moderation in wage demands. And such moderation, spelt out in the post-election period, meant an annual wage round target of less than five per cent . . . Moderation of wage demands was critical to Lynch's administration . . . The 1977 agreement, negotiated under the national coalition, was ratified in February, and covered 14 months, three months of which was a wages freeze. But the increases for the 11 months was 9.4%, which presented a somewhat threatening background against which the new Fianna Fáil government was required, by its overall economic package, to impose wages restraint.[99]

Early signs were encouraging; yet there were warnings of possible problems. Critics argued that

> the emphasis on increased public expenditure, financed by foreign
> borrowing, would result in the creation of jobs abroad, not at home
> (this being because of the 'high propensity to import' characteristic
> of a small open economy).[100]

The course embarked on by Fianna Fáil was regarded as

> a brave strategy but a risky one. It gambled on continued growth in
> the rest of the world; and it gambled on Irish workers being willing
> to accept lower wage increases than our competitor countries, so
> that we could increase our share of growing world trade.[101]

———

An immediate result of the change of Government was the lessening of
tension in Port Laoise Prison,

> Once in power Fianna Fáil moved discreetly to defuse the situation.
> The Department of Justice adopted a more flexible attitude towards
> the prisoners, and the situation was gradually eased to a point
> where, although a judicial inquiry was refused, the national
> newspaper editors were invited to visit the jail in November 1977. By
> then the prisoners were back doing handicrafts, had their own areas
> within the prison, were wearing their own clothes, and the custom
> of strip searching was a thing of the past . . . The prisoners were
> being held, not humiliated.[102]

Yet style was one thing, substance another. The new Government

> set up a three man committee chaired by a judge, Barra Ó Briain, to
> recommend safeguards for people in custody and to safeguard the
> Gardaí from untrue allegations. The committee was excluded by its
> terms of reference from looking into the allegations of ill-treatment.
> Practically all of the recommendations, published a year later, were
> rejected by the government.[103]

The new Minister for Justice, Gerry Collins, even promoted many of
the gardaí whose names had been linked to the allegations.[104]

Meanwhile a demoralised Fine Gael set out on the long road to
recovery. Cosgrave's resignation was followed by the unanimous election
of Garret FitzGerald as party leader. He appointed Peter Prendergast, a
marketing consultant and unsuccessful election candidate, as general
secretary, with a brief to carry out a Brennan-style reorganisation.[105] He
also set about dispelling the harsh image the party had acquired during its

time in office. In a television interview on the evening of his election

> he issued an open invitation to people to join Fine Gael and to write
> to him personally if they did not know whom to contact locally. It
> was a vintage FitzGerald gesture, signalling and symbolising an
> open approach; getting people involved, making them feel welcome.
> Equally important, the new leader was making excellent use of
> television.[106]

The Labour Party also had a new leader after Brendan Corish's
resignation. The contest between Frank Cluskey and Michael O'Leary was
a draw (Seán Treacy not being allowed to vote, as he remained Ceann
Comhairle until the Dáil reconvened). The suggestion by the new TD
Ruairí Quinn that everyone vote again resulted in a 9-7 victory for
Cluskey, with Liam Kavanagh believed to be the deputy who changed his
vote.[107] The voters 'split partly on union lines . . . Cluskey belonged to the
Workers' Union of Ireland, all three members of which supported him,
while six of the eight ITGWU members supported O'Leary, a long-time
member of the union.'[108]

———

A union split of a far more serious nature would be a decisive factor in one
of the most controversial labour disputes in the country's history, which
began when a production worker at the Ferenka plant in Limerick refused
to clear a blocked toilet on a day when cleaning workers were not available.
A fortnight later

> a number of plant operators walked out and picketed the factory
> following some suspensions. The Chairman of the Shop Stewards'
> Committee, Mr Philip Byrnes, who led an unofficial strike two
> weeks ago following an incident about who should clean the toilets
> was among those suspended. Five other shop stewards were also
> suspended. Some of the shop stewards who were suspended by the
> company had decided by a large majority to join the Marine Port
> and General Workers' Union, but it is understood that Ferenka will
> only deal with unions who have an agreement already signed with
> the company.[109]

Less than two months later Ferenka would be closed for good, the 1,400
jobs thus lost making this the biggest factory closure in Irish labour
history. The rivalry between the ITGWU and MPGWU would be portrayed
as a major factor in the dispute; but the seeds of trouble had been sown by
working conditions within the plant.

Ferenka's work regime was notoriously authoritarian . . . Many commentators who ascribed industrial conflict to the 'cultural unpreparedness' of a rural workforce did not pause to reflect on the kind of education system required to persuade workers to adjust themselves placidly to conditions inflicted on migrant labour on the continent.[110]

The four-cycle shift pattern meant that workers got their two days off per week consecutively only ten times a year.[111] Among the things commonplace in most factories forbidden by Ferenka's management were 'running raffles, selling lottery tickets, advertising football matches and the like on the company boards, lending money to another worker, distributing any political or religious literature.'[112] Workers could be dismissed or suspended for smoking in prohibited places or for taking photographs of the plant.[113]

Byrnes claimed that the ITGWU 'was aiding the company in keeping the men on low wages and in bad conditions.'[114] The result was that,

> dissatisfied with the ITGWU's apparent passivity, two-thirds of Ferenka's workers opted for the Marine Port and General Workers' Union whereupon the ITGWU threatened a strike if the company recognised the 'interloper'.[115]

On 13 October 'only a few members of the ITGWU attended a meeting of the workers called for the Savoy Theatre. In the afternoon, however, hundreds of Ferenka workers attended a meeting called by the MPGWU.'[116] At that meeting Séamus Redmond, general secretary of the MPGWU, declared that the unofficial strike would be made official.

By November it was being suggested that 'the key to the decision at the plant is the securing of a workable relationship between the two unions.'[117] And on 20 November the strikers turned down a proposal for returning to work by a huge margin when they heard that it involved returning to the ITGWU.[118]

Three days later ENKA, the factory's Dutch parent company, warned the Minister for Industry, Commerce and Energy, Desmond O'Malley, that the closure of the plant (which was in his constituency) might be imminent.[119] On 27 November the MPGWU members voted to return to work after the intervention of the acting president of the ICTU, Harold O'Sullivan. Séamus Redmond 'hoped that peace and good will would obtain once the workers were back.'[120]

The following day ENKA announced that Ferenka was to close. Desmond O'Malley was not inclined to join in the union-bashing, observing that it is surprising and most disappointing that this decision should be announced when the workers had agreed to return. Labour relations was a two way exercise and he did not think it would be fair to say the workforce were the only people at fault.[121]

There was suspicion that the closure may not have been so much because of inter-union conflict but more

because the emergence, and near victory of the MPGWU heralded immediate demands for higher pay and less onerous factory regulations. MPGWU shop stewards planned to ask for an increase sufficient at least to bring Ferenka up to the national average unskilled industrial wage.[122]

A strike with a somewhat more cheerful denouement was the result of a situation where, in the words of one worker,

to get to the toilet I have to pull up a trap in the floor, climb down a steep ladder which has no hand-rail and make my way past rubbish in the basement. The walls of the toilet are green with rot. On wet days I bring an umbrella, because rain drips down through the broken glass set into the pavement above.

It was remarked that this woman, employed in Kilmartin's betting shop in Trinity Street, Dublin,

is luckier than many of her colleagues who work in betting premises in poor districts. To get to the outside toilet in Kilmartins in Sheriff Street, another woman has to climb through a window to reach the yard. There is no back door. She again is luckier than her colleagues in fourteen other Kilmartins shops where there are no toilets at all.[123]

On 11 March, 220 clerks picketed the seventy-two Dublin offices that made Kilmartin's the largest bookmaking business in the country. The strike was the result of a process that, since the clerks joined the ITGWU in 1973, had seen starting pay rise from £7.50 to £21.80 a week and annual holidays from two to three weeks. Kilmartin's responded by closing down and selling their offices and leasing them out piecemeal. Most of the strikers took redundancy money, but a hard core of twenty-eight held out for eight months before claiming victory when they were given a guarantee of employment in the former Kilmartin's offices.

———

Another woman defying the status quo was Josie Airey, who in July took a case against the Government to the European Commission of Human Rights, charging it

> with violation of the article in the Convention guaranteeing citizens' rights to access to civil and criminal courts and also with failing to protect her family right against her husband in a broken marriage and for discriminating against her rights on the basis of property.[124]

A judicial separation was available only through the High Court and cost several thousand pounds. Airey and her barrister, Mary Robinson, contended that

> the absence of a civil legal aid system in Ireland effectively denied her, as a person of limited means, access to the courts to achieve a judicial separation from her husband. Mrs Airey could not find a solicitor or a counsel to take her case in 1972 because she lacked the necessary money.[125]

In September the Commission found in favour of Mrs Airey, but in November the Government decided that a free civil legal aid system would be too expensive, something that prompted the Commission to refer the case to the European Court of Human Rights. She would fight on.

The women's movement also saw the opening in Dublin of the country's first Rape Crisis Centre; and the election of six women to the Dáil, though it may seem pitiable by today's standards, was in fact the highest number yet recorded. In contrast to Cosgrave, who had not included a single woman among his eleven appointees to the Seanad in 1973, Lynch included three: the founder of the Central Remedial Clinic, Lady Valerie Goulding, the Kildare Fianna Fáil activist Eileen Cassidy and 24-year-old Mary Harney, who had been an unsuccessful candidate in Dublin South-East and who became the youngest member ever of the Seanad.[126]

Before the election the Women's Political Association had circulated a questionnaire to deputies from the main parties. Among those who failed to reply were Liam Cosgrave, Charles Haughey, Brendan Corish, George Colley, Frank Cluskey and Tim O'Connor (Fianna Fáil, Kerry South), who remarked that

> in my own county the women are doing a great job of work in keeping their homes going and bringing up families. This I think is what Almighty God intended them to do. After all, they are by and large the commanding officers in the home and long may they retain this role.[127]

Yet more than half the deputies did reply, and their replies were graded.

Among the top scorers were John Ryan (Labour Party), with 29 out of a possible 30, Bobby Molloy (Fianna Fáil), with 28¾, and John O'Connell (Labour Party), with 28. Bringing up the rear were Paddy Harte (Fine Gael), with 7¾, and the Government ministers Richie Ryan, Oliver Flanagan and Tom O'Donnell, all with 10½.[128] 100 per cent of Labour Party TDs supported the introduction of a comprehensive family-planning service, with the figure dropping to 31 per cent for Fine Gael and 12 per cent for Fianna Fáil.[129]

A magazine opinion poll indicated 64 per cent support for the legalisation of contraception, though 43 per cent believed this should apply to married people only. In the same survey 65 per cent were in favour of the availability of divorce.[130] The magazine was *Magill*, whose first issue appeared in October 1977, one of an influential quartet of publications that came into being at this time, something that indicated significant intellectual, cultural and social ferment. In the words of John Waters, who would later edit two of the magazines, *In Dublin* and *Magill*, and contribute some of the best interviews to a third, *Hot Press*,

> the connection between *Hot Press*, *In Dublin* and the current affairs magazine *Magill* was less to do with content or objectives than with attitude and style. But together they amounted to an Irish counterculture. This was the first time there had been general interest feature magazines in Ireland, in which you could write about anything, from wrestling to politics to country and western music, all in the same way. *Magill* was concerned with the government, with electoral politics, while *In Dublin* looked to what was going on outside of that—women's issues, the inner city, media and general culture issues, while *Hot Press*, in the early days at least, concentrated on rock 'n roll and other forms of contemporary music culture.[131]

The circulation of the *Crane Bag*, founded by Richard Kearney, 'an energetic young philosopher at UCD and his former teacher Mark Patrick Hederman, a Benedictine Monk, with the support of Seamus Heaney and Seamus Deane,' was smaller still.[132] But that would not have worried the editors, who declared in their first issue that it is, 'if anything, an anti-journal. Its purpose is to alienate the reading idler.'[133] The *Crane Bag* was to publish some of the most intellectually distinguished and stimulating writing on Irish culture produced over the next decade before it folded in 1984.[134] The first issue included an interview by Deane with Heaney and one by Kearney with Herbert Marcuse and articles on art and politics from Francis Stuart and Peter Sheridan.

Yet even the most successful of these publications only reached a minority audience. They could not hope to fire the public imagination—or indignation—in the way that two of the best plays by two of the finest Irish playwrights did when televised on RTE in 1977.

King of the Castle by Eugene McCabe, who was born in Glasgow and reared in Co. Monaghan, had first been performed at the Gaiety Theatre as part of the Dublin Theatre Festival in 1964. Louis Lentin, who would direct it for RTE, called it 'the best Irish play for a quarter of a century.' It is 'an uncompromising, honest and devastatingly unflattering picture of Irish society. In this production RTE also pushed to the limits of what it would dare in its raw and explicit exposure of the darker side of human sexuality and all the predatory and vicious emotions surrounding it.'[135] Its characters have a genuine tragic grandeur and vitality and truth about them, and the production stands as one of RTE's greatest achievements.[136] Yet what made the headlines was the outraged response of local politicians, such as Joe Mooney of Leitrim County Council, who called the play 'a slander on the people of Leitrim . . . He asked why McCabe hadn't the guts to locate this filth in his own county,' while Richard Morrin of Castlebar Urban District Council claimed that 'the majority of people working in RTE were depraved minds, dropouts from society and winos.'[137]

The White House by Tom Murphy, first performed at the Abbey Theatre in 1972, created a similar furore. In Cashel 'a notice criticising the moral standards of RTE was read out at all Catholic masses at St John the Baptist Chapel,' while the play drew motions of condemnation from local authorities in Cos. Mayo, Cork and Tipperary.[138] The irony is that Murphy's lacerating tale of small-town disillusionment and compromise as the optimistic dreams of the sixties are revealed to be largely meaningless set out to attack the very attitude that revealed itself in these attacks. One character's mockery of 'this eejit, this bollocks, with his auctioneering and travel-agenting and property dealing and general greedy unprincipled poncing and Sunday night dancing—Mr successful-swinging-Ireland-in-the-Seventies,' perfectly described a species represented above all by the kind of local politicians who attacked the play.[139]

It is a long time since RTE produced drama of this quality, and it is arguable that even today it would shy away from anything as close to the bone. Yet 1977 was something of an *annus mirabilis* for RTE. The political satire 'Hall's Pictorial Weekly', with the comic genius of Eamonn Morrissey and Frank Kelly to the fore, was never as sharp as it was in the dying days of the coalition.

So sharp and constant was its satirical send-up of the government ministers of the time, that it was generally accepted that the programme played an important part in bringing the coalition into disrepute and perhaps even contributed to bringing it down.[140]

Then there was 'Time Now, Mr T.', a highly praised sketch show featuring Niall Tóibín. He believed there was 'a huge amount of self-righteousness in the country that needed to be pulled up by laughing at it.' In doing so he encountered 'criticism such as he had never faced in his career. He was beset with accusations of trying to pervert, corrupt and deprave the entire Irish nation.'[141]

The year was something of a false dawn for RTE, whose adventurous spirit was soon replaced by institutional timidity. There would be no second series of 'Time Now, Mr T.', and 'Hall's Pictorial Weekly' too would be gone by the end of the decade.

For the moment, though, signs of cultural change were everywhere. On Sunday 21 August, Dalymount Park staged Dublin's first major outdoor rock concert. Topping the bill were Thin Lizzy. The authorities adopted a *laissez-faire* attitude: 'there were no police on duty inside the ground, so the young people happily enjoyed their little wrong-doings such as the odd marijuana joint and open cuddle and kiss in the shady corners of the pitch.'[142] Among the supporting acts were the Boomtown Rats, who 'displayed a total lack of inhibition coupled with forthright aggression.'[143] By the end of the year they had scored two top twenty hits, 'Looking After Number One' being followed into the charts by 'Mary of the Fourth Form', and the lead singer, Bob Geldof, had earned a reputation for being as supremely confident in interviews as he was on stage.

After the Boomtown Rats, the Radiators from Space were the best known of the bands on an Irish scene inspired by the English punk rock movement, though neither band liked to describe themselves as punk. Fronted by Philip Chevron, the band had begun the year with a gig at the Asgard House in Howth at which the entire audience walked out, but by April they were playing to two thousand people at the Stardust Club in Cork.[144] Their album *TV Tube Heart* was acclaimed by perhaps the most influential of all punk critics, Mark Perry, in *Zig-Zag*, as 'the best new-wave album next to "The Clash"', while the single 'Television Screen' was single of the week in *Sounds*.[145]

Yet the band came close to splitting up after an eighteen-year-old from Cabra, Patrick Coultry, was stabbed to death at the UCD punk festival in June, which also featured the Undertones, Revolver, the Gamblers and the Vipers.[146] This isolated incident gave punk a popular reputation for violence that would later dog the Boomtown Rats as they tried to play the same kind of triumphal homecoming concert as Thin Lizzy had at Dalymount Park.

That Dalymount gig featured the odd spectacle of the crowd chanting 'Dublin, Dublin.' The uninitiated would have been appraised of the reason for this when 'an extra 2,000 people came after the match in Croke Park.'[147] The wise two thousand were attending one of the great Irish rock occasions immediately after a Dublin v. Kerry all-Ireland football semi-final of such excellence that

> as the crowd left the stadium groups of people, friends and strangers, stopped and talked in a hundred places—and the uppermost topic of conversation was almost universal: who could remember a greater semi-final, a greater game at any stage of the championship.[148]

Kevin Heffernan had departed as manager after Dublin won the 1976 all-Ireland final, their second victory in three years; but the hold his team had on the popular imagination was evident from the crowd of fifty-five thousand at the semi-final, the biggest at that stage of the competition since 1962.[149] Dublin, now managed by the centre-half-forward Tony Hanahoe, trailed by 1-6 to 0-6 at half time and were still 1-13 to 1-11 down with six minutes to go. That was when David Hickey, the subject of so much abuse earlier in the year after the Port Laoise protesters incident, scored a great goal to turn the game. Pat O'Neill, Anton O'Toole, Brian Mullins and Hickey were *primus inter pares* for Dublin, but it had been an extraordinary game, a kind of apotheosis for both that particular team and for Gaelic football itself. Even now few people would challenge the contention of the Dublin corner-back Gay O'Driscoll that it was 'the greatest game of football ever played.'[150] Dublin went on to win the all-Ireland final against Armagh, but that game has something of the quality of a footnote. That there were thousands of GAA fans whose world view could also include the Boomtown Rats and Thin Lizzy was another indicator of changing times.

——

One man who would not be there to see those times change was Séamus Costello, leader of the IRSP. Two years previously he had taken part in a forum on Northern Ireland at the University of Massachusetts. Noël Browne, not normally a fan of republicanism, described him as giving a scintillating display of good humour, history, politics and hard facts ... They will have to shoot him or jail him or get out of his way but they certainly won't stop him ... I've never heard his brand of republicanism before ... Is it not a triumph of our radio, television and newspapers, and of the venomous Dublin political denigration machine that none of us has ever read, heard or seen this man's remarkable dialectical skill and political ability?[151]

Yet 'by the summer of 1977 Costello was at the lowest political ebb he had ever reached.'[152] The IRSP, launched with such high hopes in 1974, was severely weakened as a political force, having lost Bernadette McAliskey, *née* Devlin, in its first year following a dispute over the party's direction. Costello's vote in Co. Wicklow had dropped from 6½ per cent in 1973 to 3 per cent in that summer's general election, which devastated him.

Costello's potential as a political leader was, however, forever compromised by the fact that he was engaged in an underground conspiratorial organisation that robbed banks, supermarkets and trains and that bombed and shot people. That is, he was a very Irish phenomenon: nowhere else, at least in Western Europe, would one find a man of his obvious political abilities driving the getaway vehicle after robbing a post office van.[153]

On 5 October he was sitting in his car at the corner of Northbrook Avenue, off the North Circular Road. An Official IRA man from Belfast, Jim Flynn, walked up to the car and shot Costello three times. Costello 'had been under sentence of death by the Official IRA Army Council since 1975.'[154] He was the first leader of an Irish political party to be assassinated. Flynn himself would be shot by the INLA close to the same spot in 1982.

The irony of Costello's murder by an Official IRA gunman was that this was the year in which that organisation's political wing, Official Sinn Féin, had renamed itself Sinn Féin the Workers' Party following the publication of *The Irish Industrial Revolution*, a document that 'represented a forceful repudiation of the canon of Irish nationalist history.'[155] Over the next decade SFWP, later the Workers' Party and later again Democratic Left, would become a serious rival to the Labour Party on the Irish left, leave its republican past far behind and condemn the use of physical force for political ends. Costello's IRSP, however, would fade into political insignificance, while its military wing, the Irish National Liberation Army, grew in importance during the next few years. Whether this would have happened had Costello lived is an intriguing if ultimately unanswerable question.

Chapter 7 ∽

｜ BOOM BOOM BOOM BOOM

1978

We'd never had it so good.

Near the end of 1978 the assistant editor of the *Irish Times,* James Downey, one of the most respected journalists of his generation, surveyed the lie of the land. He noted the existence of

> a general mood of self-confidence which had little to do with what government was in power, or what specific policies it pursued. For all the nagging of the unresolved issue of the North, the shadow of Britain over Ireland had grown markedly less, with the decline in Britain and the new European orientation, the increase in travel and the future opportunities for the young. Co-education was flourishing. The fight for equality for women was slowly, with many setbacks and much humbug, but nonetheless certainly, being won . . . We were making money; some people, most obviously large farmers were making enormous amounts of money. After being poor for too long, we were getting rich quickly—perhaps too quickly.[1]

Optimism seemed universal. Who could argue with the figures?

> Not since 1967–1968 did the economy expand at such a fast rate as it has done over the past 12 months . . . total non-agricultural employment grew by about 17,000 which, while less than the government's White Paper target, was way above average annual job creation levels in the past. The Live Register [unemployment] figures steadily came down during the year . . . the year was another good one for the farmers whose incomes went up by 20% . . . investors by the end of the year found themselves earning a better real rate of return on their deposits than at virtually any time during the post-war period.[2]

There was even 'an unprecedented boom in house prices which, by mid-year, had risen by more than 30% over a year earlier.'[3] There was 'a real increase in the range of 10 to 12%' in output for the building industry, an increase in youth employment of 6,400, 1,400 more than the Government target, and a rise in manufacturing output of almost 10 per cent.[4] Tourism receipts were up 20 per cent in real terms, and consumer spending rose by 9 per cent.[5]

'We are well on the way to the attainment of the government's economic targets for 1979 and towards the attainment of full employment by 1983,' declared Martin O'Donoghue.[6] His utopian expectations were echoed by the Taoiseach, Jack Lynch, who predicted that soon 'employment could grow so that no-one was ever without work in his own country of his own volition.'[7] The previous year's manifesto commitments meant that, 'with the generous tax cuts, such as the abolition of domestic rates and car tax, the average worker earned 16% more in 1978 than in 1977, which translated to an increase of 8% in real earnings.'[8] At 7.6 per cent the inflation rate, that bugbear of the national coalition, was the lowest it had been since 1969.[9]

O'Donoghue and Lynch appeared to have wrought something of an economic miracle, and their mood of confidence quickly spread to the public.

> 1978 was a bonanza year. In the year to mid-August 1978, personal borrowings from the banks increased by an extra 45%. It was the year of the big spenders. In addition to the injection of purchasing power through the budget deficit, farmers revelled in the largesse of the CAP [common agricultural policy] . . . land prices leaped to unprecedented heights. The banks were only too happy to accommodate the demands of a clientele who could offer land as a security on the expectation of permanently rising prices. Many an improbable hacienda in rural Ireland dates from the year of the big spenders.[10]

Economic optimism was matched by social and cultural optimism. It was the year of the first Lisdoonvarna Festival and similar get-togethers, of the Boomtown Rats, of a trio of films that suggested the emergence of a significant Irish cinema movement and of the pirate radio boom. An opinion poll showed that 58 per cent of people between 18 and 24 and 56 per cent of those between 25 and 34 believed that sex outside marriage was not wrong.[11] In any other country these figures might have been taken as indicating conservatism; in a country where family planning, even for married people, had still not been legislated for, they revealed a telling deviation from officially sanctioned standards of sexual morality.

The Government both contributed to and benefited from the general air of possibility. An opinion poll in July indicated that Fianna Fáil's popularity had risen since the landslide victory in the previous year's general election, from 51 to 56 per cent.[12] 65 per cent of those surveyed thought the Government was doing a good job and 86 per cent believed Jack Lynch was doing well as Taoiseach—a figure that appeared to place him in an unassailable position for the remainder of his time in politics.[13] It is possible that no Taoiseach has been loved to the same extent as Lynch was in the year before his resignation.

There is something poignant about encountering the hopes of that halcyon year. They are akin to the predictions of men bound for the Western Front in 1914, that the war would be over by Christmas. The Ireland of 1978 looked forward to a future that would not transpire for another couple of decades. By 1983, the year for which Martin O'Donoghue predicted full employment, there would be 180,000 people without work, a total exceeded in every year but one of the following ten.[14] And eleven years after Lynch's prediction of a time when 'no-one was ever without work in his own country of his own volition' more than seventy thousand people—approximately 2 per cent of the population—would emigrate, the highest figure of the century.[15] 1978 was the last great year of national optimism, before the economy began to go rapidly and comprehensively downhill. Using it as a vantage point, we find ourselves looking at the road not taken. Almost twenty years would elapse before the economy once more gave grounds for hope.

A striking feature of the year was the number of battles between two differing concepts of Ireland. The authoritarian model, which held that the opinions of those in command trumped those of any number of dissenters and that the objections of the latter need not even be taken into consideration, found itself up against a variety of organisations and individuals reluctant to accept the diktat of the powers that be. Very different issues were at stake in the arguments concerning Wood Quay, Carnsore Point, Loughan House and pirate radio, but what united the various controversies was a conflict between the political establishment on one side and those who believed that there was a democratic deficit at the heart of the decisions taken on the other.

After all the political upheaval of the coalition years it seems incredible that the largest demonstration of the year, on 23 September, described by Denis Larkin (son of Jim) as 'the biggest march in Dublin since the workers came out in the great strike of 1913,' was about archaeology and heritage.[16] Between 17,500 and 20,000 people took part, led by the ITGWU Band.[17]

The cause was that of the city's heritage; but perhaps, aside from its own importance as a historic site, the site at Wood Quay was also 'the most potent symbol of the corporation's determination to have its way with the city, regardless of the costs and consequences.'[18] The year had already been marked by 'the destruction of two of the city's earliest and most distinguished Victorian buildings, St Anne's School and Molesworth Hall … Molesworth Hall was the forerunner of the Abbey [Theatre] and it was here under the guidance of Yeats and Lady Gregory that the first performance of Synge's *Riders to the Sea* was staged.'[19] The developer, Patrick Gallagher, was allowed to pull down both buildings and replace them with a complex of four office blocks designed by Desmond FitzGerald (brother of Garret).

Though there had been mounting concern about planning policies, Wood Quay was undeniably a special case. The site had been earmarked for new city council offices since the fifties, and planning permission had been granted in 1970. The city council had begun to clear the site of older buildings and had then invited the National Museum to carry out archaeological excavations until construction work began.[20] It was the archaeologists' findings that set the controversy in motion.

> When the extent, variety and significance of the archaeological material on the site became clear—and when the amount of time needed for adequate excavation began to be calculated—the four office buildings began to look ominous. The conflict was simple: down in the ground lay the original Viking town, the adequate excavation of which would take—there seemed to be a concerted effort to avoid using the word—years.[21]

The work at the site between 1974 and 1976 by a team headed by a young archaeologist from Co. Limerick, Pat Wallace—who later became director of the National Museum—turned up, among other things, 'padlocks, keys, scales, lamps, knives, bowls, hammers, axes, drill bits, fishhooks, horseshoes, spurs, grindstones, dice, game pieces, coins, pilgrims' flasks and what seemed to be part of religious reliquaries.'[22] 'What you have here,' said Wallace, 'is a total town—streets, houses, the layout, the original townscape, town planning. That's what's important.'[23]

The most spectacular find was 'a wooden structure paralleling the river. It was recognized as a seawall or quay built at the limit of one of the advances of the river. Its elaborateness and engineering struck the archaeologists at once.'[24]

Yet in September 1977 it became clear that building would soon begin on a part of the site 'where almost no excavation had taken place. The richest and most historically important part of the site, the main Viking area, was to be trucked out without archaeological investigation.'[25]

F. X. Martin, an Augustinian friar and head of the Department of Mediaeval History in UCD, would emerge as the figurehead of the Wood Quay campaign. It was he who brought the legal case that resulted in the Wood Quay site being declared a national monument by Mr Justice Liam Hamilton in the High Court on 30 June 1978.

At first glance this seemed a huge victory for the defenders of the site; but 'the fact was that national monuments could be destroyed. All that was required was the joint consent of the local authority, in this case the Dublin Corporation, and the Commissioners of Public Works.'[26] Martin and his supporters took solace in the fact that this had never happened. 'So there was a kind of moral injunction, it was bravely argued, against destroying this one.'[27] Yet, unknown to the protesters, this joint consent was in fact agreed, on 29 August. By the time of the huge march through Dublin, the fate of Wood Quay was already sealed.

Its fate was sealed despite Martin's protestation that the site could be used to re-create the old heart of Dublin, including a Viking museum, a gallery surrounding a portion of the earthen and stone walls, and a fine vista down from Christ Church. Two-storey red-brick houses, like those newly built in the Coombe, could be built on the perimeter. The Irish Hoteliers' Association estimated that such a project could earn £3 million a year in tourism income.[28] And it was sealed although the 'Save Wood Quay' forces 'grew fast and attracted a more varied membership than anyone would have expected; they were imaginative and original, they were relentless.'[29] Above all, its fate was sealed because

> the bureaucrats wanted new civic offices and they were prepared to stop at nothing to achieve their objective. It didn't matter to them that the office blocks were to be built on the most important Viking site ever unearthed in Ireland containing, as it did, the very story of Dublin's birth and early development . . . they spurned appeals to cease and desist from over eighty social and cultural organisations . . . and contemptuously cast aside a petition signed by more than 200,000 people. They shut their eyes to mass meetings in the Mansion House and protest meetings throughout the city. And when the High Court declared the site to be a National Monument they conspired with the Commissioners of Public Works to sabotage this judgement by drawing up an order for the monument's destruction.[30]

The authorities were similarly unimpressed by opposition to the proposed building of the country's first nuclear power station at Carnsore Point, Co. Wexford. The Minister for Industry, Commerce and Energy, Desmond O'Malley, warned that 'if there was widespread opposition to the Carnsore Project by the people of Wexford, there were other sites available.' The ESB had favoured Carnsore only slightly over sites in Cos. Mayo, Sligo and Clare, 'and the people of those areas would be very pleased to get the four to five hundred construction jobs involved in the building of such a plant.'[31]

Refusing to countenance a public inquiry, O'Malley poured scorn on opponents of the project.

> In environmental terms nuclear power was the cleanest and most scientific of all . . . Some hospitals in the country were using radio-active equipment which presented a greater danger than a conventional nuclear power station. If those opposed to the building of a nuclear power station here were consistent they would also want to close down St Luke's Hospital in Dublin because a great deal of equipment containing radioactive substances were used there every day on many patients. But no-one had ever suggested that the hospital was a source of danger to either residents of the locality or the patients.[32]

Nevertheless, a significant movement opposed to the station sprang up. In comparison with the Wood Quay movement, which featured prominent academics and politicians among its supporters, the anti-nuclear campaign was

> spontaneous and unstructured . . . composed largely, but by no means exclusively of young people . . . It was the first issue to stir the notoriously apathetic youth of the country—at least South of the border—since the student 'revolts' of the sixties.[33]

Co. Wexford members of the Irish Farmers' Association passed a motion against the building of the station, and the Irish Writers' Co-Op published *Nuclear Ireland*, a book by Matthew Hussey, a lecturer in physics at Kevin Street College of Technology, who said that the Government was 'preparing to take a chance on nothing less than the physical survival of the Irish people and our society.'[34] David Nolan, chairperson of the Nuclear Safety Association, predicted that 'in a few years time solar energy and wave power, which were now at an advanced experimental stage would produce all the energy required.'[35]

On an August weekend near Carnsore Point, in the words of one of the participants, Christy Moore,

> ten thousand people turned up and the weekend was a glorious

success. The best of Irish music performed at this free gathering, there was poetry, theatre, dance, performance artistes and more and more music. Everyone got fed and no-one was hurt . . . By the time the festival was over we had thousands of recruits into the anti-nuclear movement and had set in place 22 groups around the 32 counties.[36]

The day after the festival ended the Fine Gael spokesperson on industry, commerce and energy, John Kelly, called for an independent public inquiry and said that anti-nuclear groups should have the right to cross-examine officials of the department and the ESB.[37] Christy Moore and a number of other performers brought an anti-nuclear roadshow to Newbridge, Kilkenny, Waterford, Wexford, Cork, Tralee, Limerick, Galway, Sligo, Derry, Belfast, Dundalk and Dublin. Objections notwithstanding, it seemed probable that the Carnsore Point plan, like the building of the Dublin civic offices, would go ahead.

The equally controversial Loughan House project was, after all, operational before the end of the year, despite the many objections from those who disagreed with the provision of a detention facility for twelve to sixteen-year-olds staffed by prison officers. Senator Mary Robinson stated:

> Don't start a public relations tourist brochure description of Loughan House. I know what it is—a place where prison officers will control children in need of special care and support.[38]

This view was shared by twenty-three organisations that opposed what was described as 'the first children's prison in Europe,'[39] including Care, Children First, the Irish Association of Social Workers, the Irish Council for Civil Liberties, the Irish Association for the Prevention of Cruelty to Children, Women's Aid, Cherish, the Mental Health Association of Ireland and the Psychological Association of Ireland.[40]

Patrick MacEntee SC pointed out that the site of Loughan House, near Blacklion, Co. Cavan, would mean that anyone visiting from Dublin—where most of the inmates were likely to be from—faced

> a bus to Enniskillen, a promenade there for two and a half hours, another bus. Then having visited your loved one in Loughan House and stayed in Blacklion overnight you must return, 48 hours after you left Dublin, to your average of seven other children at home. This showed the quality of thought, love and care in the thinking about Loughan House.[41]

And at a protest meeting chaired by Seán MacBride, Pat Carroll of the Labour Party wondered, 'what kind of crazy society do we live in that lets a child grow up in poverty, in a jumbo size class with no job prospects and then spends £10,000 a year to lock him up when his actions become intolerable.'[42]

The Minister for Justice, Gerry Collins, who had attended UCD for seven years before succeeding to his father's Dáil seat at the age of twenty-nine, was unmoved by such arguments.[43] On 26 October, Loughan House, originally a novitiate for the White Fathers Missionary Congregation and bought by the Department of Justice in 1972 for use as a prison, received its first inmate, a fourteen-year-old boy given a two-year sentence in the Children's Court for 'breaking into cars, stealing from them and picking pockets.'[44] By December news had filtered out of one boy stabbing another with a table knife and a mini-riot during which staff members were forced out of a room and furniture was broken.[45]

The minister was supported by Michael Madigan, chairperson of the Dublin City Centre Business Organisation, who wanted 'the professional bodies with an interest in child care to stop criticising Loughan House.'[46] The president of Dún Laoghaire Chamber of Commerce, Jack Corr, said that

> 'do-gooders' should support the Gardaí. The introduction of birching would act as a deterrent and the ignominy of the birch would have far more effect than the pain involved.[47]

Such comments reflected the fact that the opening of Loughan House took place against the backdrop of a scare about juvenile criminality in Dublin, epitomised by the infamous 'Bugsy Malone' story, which found its way into the national newspapers in September.

It began with a front-page story in the *Sunday Press* under the headline 'Dublin Bugsies fly to the sun: City gardaí know them but can't touch them.' It informed readers that 'members of a gang which has terrorised Dublin city centre are sunning themselves in a Mediterranean holiday resort on their ill-gotten gains, angry Gardaí claimed yesterday.'[48] It included quotations from an anonymous garda who fumed, 'When they turn round and practically thumb their noses at us in this way, what can you do?'[49] The story was picked up by the *Irish Independent*, which described the gang as coming from 'the Dublin terror ghetto of Seán McDermott Street.'[50] A week later the *Evening Press* was printing the front-page headline 'Suntanned Bugsie boys back in town.'[51] There was another quotation from an unnamed garda: 'They're back alright with great suntans and sporting sombreros . . . Maybe they're back to see what pickings there are for a winter holiday in the Alps.'[52]

There could hardly have been anything better designed to exacerbate a situation where, in the words of Senator John A. Murphy, 'the voice of

Middle Ireland said "juvenile thugs" should not only be locked up but beaten up.'[53] But an investigation into the stories by the news magazine *Magill* painted a quite different picture of the trip to Benidorm that had provoked them. It discovered that

> no group of 20, or 12, 'Bugsies' flew to Spain. Of the 19 people who did, only five were under 17: this is, 'under-age,' eligible for Loughan House, possible 'Bugsies'. The others were adults. Of the five under 17s, two have no criminal record. Which leaves three who could meaningfully be called, 'Bugsy Malones,' or 'mini-mobsters' or 'teenage hoodlums' or any of the other phrases used to describe the group. This trip was organised by adults in the area. Among those involved in the organisation were a local priest and a local publican. The publican was among the adults who travelled with the group. The mother of one of the three 'Bugsies' was also on the trip. The three 'Bugsies' travelled with their parents' consent. The fares of all three were subsidised by their parents. There was nothing sinister or secretive about their coming or going. The effect of the stories ... was further to inflame newspaper readers against the Seán McDermott Street-Summerhill area. The significance of the timing—a few weeks before Loughan House is scheduled to open is obvious.[54]

The idea that the north inner city was something of a crime hot-spot was not entirely without foundation. In a notorious incident on 27 August a girl in her early teens was abducted from Cathal Brugha Street to Seán McDermott Street, where she was badly beaten and repeatedly raped by a gang of eight youths.[55] And Father Peter McVerry, who set up a hostel for homeless boys the following year and would become one of the most tireless campaigners for the people in the area through his work with the Jesuit Centre for Faith and Justice in Upper Sherrard Street, noted

> an epidemic of joyriding and handbag snatching in Dublin's North Inner City. The intersection of Summerhill and Gardiner Street became known as, 'Handbag Junction.' The Diamond—a large playground area between Summerhill and Seán McDermott Street—could match Mondello for thrills and spills most nights of the week.[56]

But McVerry, who had moved into a tenement in Summerhill along with two other Jesuits in 1974, also observed that

> the place was crawling with rats, rats the size of little kittens, immune to every poison that had been invented ... As we lay in bed at night, you could hear the rats, all night long, crawling in the ceiling, fighting one another, dragging bits of food, sometimes

gnawing through the electric wires. But families on the ground floor would often talk about waking up in the morning and finding a rat on the baby's cot.[57]

Similarly Dickensian conditions came to light when Garret FitzGerald, on the invitation of the newly elected Fine Gael TD for the area, Michael Keating, visited the inner city in July. In Gardiner Street the chairperson of the local community association, Frank Maguire, told FitzGerald about 'the condition of the roofs, which can all be broken into as they are made from an asbestos material which a foot can go through.'[58] There was a woman living with eight children in one room, and eight families sharing two toilets.[59] One woman showed him the open sewer near which her children had to play.[60] In Foley Street he met 'a widow, living in a flat with her married son and his two children. They have no gas and for a long time no water.'[61] Superintendent John Robinson of Store Street Garda Station, rather than agreeing with the nostrums of the law-and-order lobby, suggested that what the area needed most was more social workers. 'Not nine to five people but social workers who are on call at night when most social problems come to light.'[62]

As often happens, the crime wave had focused some overdue attention on conditions within the affected area. James Downey's largely optimistic article, for example, pointed out that

> it was in the inner city—and in some of the soulless anonymous new estates and high-rise flats—that the greatest problems were to be seen and to be seen to be worsening: squalor, poverty, unemployment, alienation, hopelessness, juvenile crime, rape, petty racketeering accompanied by violence, drug abuse, small-scale pimping ... The predictable, and futile, action of the authorities had been Loughan House.[63]

The awful irony was that within a couple of years the introduction of heroin to these areas would almost make the late seventies in the inner city seem like an era of prelapsarian innocence.

———

If it was crime that had brought the problems of the inner city to prominence it was largely the work of one remarkable man that propelled into the public spotlight a form of poverty whose extent and perhaps very existence had been largely unsuspected. Willie Bermingham was a Dublin firefighter who was moved to action by the discovery of the body of a man in his seventies who lived in two rooms in Charlemont Street. In his book

Alone, written with the *Evening Press* journalist Liam Ó Cuanaigh, he wrote:

> He returned from the rain so wet that his clothes were soaked right through and his body very cold. He was able only to take off his jacket and hang it on the door that led to his bedroom. He lay on his bed and must have gained enough strength to pull some old blankets over him to keep warm. Some time later he felt he wanted to get up, but he was able only to grip the bedclothes in his left hand. He succeeded in moving the blankets about eight inches to his left and in drawing his right leg up in an effort to leave the now wet bed. How long it took him to die, I don't know. But die he did and in the most horrible way possible . . . Like many old men and women he had been cast away on the scrap heap. He was left to face loneliness, cold, hunger and depression behind the closed doors of a capital city. He had been sentenced to death, alone and in misery.[64]

In *Alone* (1978) and *Alone Again* (1982) he portrayed, in a matter-of-fact but extraordinarily moving way, the shocking conditions in which some of the city's old people lived. There was the old man

> found living in a plastic dustbin at the public toilets in Drumcondra . . . he hid the receptacle every morning in a laneway and twisted himself into it at nightfall,

and a man

> sleeping in the outside basement of a deserted house in North Great George's Street . . . the shopkeeper frequently noticed rat bites on his face.[65]

An old widow on the North Circular Road

> froze to death on the floor of her rat-infested flat on New Year's Day 1979. A blocked chimney had prevented her from lighting a fire and there was no other safe means of heating her damp basement.[66]

Another widow, in her eighties, was

> found unconscious on the stone floor of her disused shop in Ballsbridge in October 1979. She had an internal haemorrhage and was suffering from hypothermia and malnutrition. A fortnight after her discovery, she died at St Vincent's Hospital.[67]

Alone Again, with its photographs of almost unimaginably squalid living conditions, may be the most harrowing document from this period. Bermingham had brought to light a national scandal. A report by the Society of St Vincent de Paul in 1980 revealed that 59 per cent of old people living alone in the Republic had no hot water and 57 per cent had neither a bath nor a shower.[68] Only 48 per cent even had a hand basin, while one in three were without a flush toilet.[69] A study by the National Prices Commission in 1978 found that the majority of pensioners seem to live on a fairly monotonous series of meals ... There were even instances of pensioners having two meals a day consisting solely of bread, butter and tea ... Inevitably this lack of variety is in part due to the fact that limited income restricts the choice of foodstuffs available to the pensioner.[70]

While continuing to work as a firefighter, Bermingham established the charity and campaigning organisation called Alone. By 1982 he was able to report that, in response to a four-year campaign, £1 million had been allocated to rescuing helpless old people from 'unfit or unsanitary accommodation.' Using this fund, the Department of the Environment began a pilot scheme in the greater Dublin area, with considerable success. Funds were then spread to health authorities throughout the country.[71] By this time

around 3,000 A.L.O.N.E. volunteers were visiting approximately 3,500 old people on a regular basis ... The organisation purchased 10 small dwellings in Dublin from funds accumulated over a three year period. These were given rent free to old people in desperate need who might not have survived a long wait on the housing list.[72]

In 1990, two weeks before his death from cancer at the age of 48, Bermingham opened a complex of twenty-three flats for old people in Kilmainham, Dublin, now called Willie Bermingham Place.[73]

Threshold, another organisation that would play a major part in dealing with housing problems, was formed in 1978. Father Dónal O'Mahony, a Cork priest, was prompted to found the organisation by his experience as a flatdwellers' chaplain in Dublin.[74] By 1981 Threshold had dealt with more than five thousand cases, the majority of them originating in private rented accommodation.[75] Originally funded by the Catholic peace organisation Pax Christi, it continues to provide information and advice to people with housing problems. Its establishment can be seen as reflecting a new radicalism and interest in social and political issues among certain members of the Irish clergy at the time. Between 1977 and 1979, for example, the award-winning 'Radharc' series on RTE television, produced and presented by a group of Dublin priests, included programmes on the plight of Mexican immigrant workers in the United States, human rights abuses in Argentina, prostitution in Thailand, the ideas of the radical Brazilian archbishop Hélder Câmara and the torture of church workers in the Philippines.[76]

Compared with the issues at stake at Carnsore Point, Wood Quay and Loughan House, the furore over pirate radio may seem somewhat trivial. But it illustrated the growing generation gap more clearly than anything else. And, trivial or not, it did also manage to bring people onto the streets on Saturday 21 January, when

> several thousand teenagers marched in a demo of support for Radio Dublin, the pirate radio station whose headquarters was raided by Gardaí last week . . . Placards demanding that Radio Dublin be given a broadcasting licence were carried by the teenagers, who swayed to the music as they surged through the streets. Gardaí accompanied the march, but the atmosphere was good humoured and enthusiastic throughout, and there were no incidents . . .[77]

The appeal of pirate radio lay in the fact that,

> apart from Pat Kenny's Nightbus, RTE radio is bereft of programmes presented by the young, for the young, with music of the kind that the young not only could like, but patently do like (and the young, in this context, includes all of those whose musical tastes have been formed in the twenty years since Presley emerged from Memphis— a sizeable number).[78]

Despite the success of Rory Gallagher, Thin Lizzy and the Boomtown Rats, pop music was almost entirely absent from the air waves of the national broadcaster. The vacuum was filled by the pirates.

Radio Dublin was the original of the species. It broadcast from the home of its founder and head, Eamonn Cooke, in Inchicore, Dublin. (In 2007, he would be jailed for ten years for sexual assaults on young girls in the mid to late seventies.)[79] Cooke benefited from the fact that the Broadcasting (Offences) Act (1968) was clearly aimed at pirate radio ships in the Radio Caroline mould. The act was designed to 'suppress broadcasting from ships, aircraft and marine structures . . . The weakness is that 3 Sarsfield Road is not a marine structure.'[80] By February, Radio Dublin was claiming 'a listenership in the Dublin area estimated at 100,000.'[81]

By then a second Dublin station, ARD (Alternative Radio Dublin), had come into existence, run by Bernard Llewellyn and Don Moore.[82] And in April a third station, Big D, was founded when some members of the staff 'walked out of Radio Dublin because of irreconcilable personal differences with the station leader, "Captain" Eamonn Cooke.'[83]

The pirate craze was not confined to Dublin. By September, Cork had three stations—Cork Broadcasting Company, Alternative Broadcasting Cork and Commercial Cork Radio—while in Limerick, Radio Limerick Weekly Echo battled it out with Radio Capitol Limerick.[84]

Raids by the Gardaí and officials of the Department of Posts and Telegraphs cost the pirates thousands of pounds' worth of forfeited equipment, but they were generally back on the air the following day. Cooke admitted that

> sooner or later the Department of Posts and Telegraphs will find a way through the legal complexities that now protect pirate radio and close him down. He is gambling that by the time this happens the minister, Mr Faulkner, will have legalised commercial radio.[85]

RTE's attitude to the pirates was perhaps epitomised by what happened when the reporter Cian Ó hÉigeartaigh interviewed Bernard Llewellyn. 'Mr Ó hÉigeartaigh was not allowed to broadcast the interview and afterwards received a letter from RTE management reprimanding him and restricting his exercise of editorial responsibility.'[86] The minister, Pádraig Faulkner, was no more impressed, and in November there was news that 'collaborators with pirate radio stations—and that is thought to include advertisers, journalists, disc jockeys, guests etc., can be prosecuted under a bill to be introduced to the Dáil before Christmas.'[87] Senator John A. Murphy accused the pirates of

> appealing to the lowest common denominator of popular taste, itself the product of commercial manipulation ... If the pirates are legalised, the national broadcasting service will be under pressure to lower its standards ... when Mr Bernard Llewellyn of ARD asks for a chance to 'compete' with RTE, does he propose to vary sonic slush with symphony concerts and Thomas Davis lectures.[88]

While no-one would deny that the pirates were driven by the profit motive, the reality of RTE Radio was somewhat more middlebrow than the Reithian ideal suggested by Senator Murphy. It wasn't all symphony concerts and Thomas Davis Lectures on the national channel. A typical weekday's broadcasting could include 'Morning Call', presented by Mike Murphy ('It is imitative of Terry Wogan's BBC2 style, but Murphy's inanities are all his own,' observed the radio critic Mary Leland), Donncha Ó Dúlaing's 'Highways and Byways' and a number of programmes that did in fact lean heavily on pop music.[89] The pop music RTE favoured, however, was of the show tune variety, written by 'some of the century's leading popular composers, people like Jule Styne and Burton Lane,' who featured in a programme entitled 'The Songwriters'.[90] The assumption that Messrs Styne and Lane (the creator of *Finian's Rainbow*) represent a higher pinnacle of the songwriter's art than Messrs Springsteen, Costello, Morrison and Marley, who all released albums in 1978, may not be as common today as it was then. And a weekend schedule that included three hours of 'Airs and Races' ('music between races from Leopardstown'), 'Showstoppers' with Arthur Murphy, 'Hospitals Requests' and 'The Diary of a Nobody' by George and Weedon Grossmith, read by George Green, could probably have borne a couple of hours of punk and new wave.[91]

Pirate radio was not devoid of presenters who saw themselves as more than merely human jukeboxes. Dave Fanning of Big D presented 'a chaotic late-night rock show ... on which you might as easily tune in to four hours of Tom Waits as an all-Irish rock night.'[92] Fanning wanted to play records made by Irish bands as well as those from the hit parades in Britain and the United States.

> He brought new Dublin bands into the studio, interviewed them and played the demo discs. Soon his show was compulsive listening for those who'd had to tune in to foreign stations before Big D. When the *Hot Press* DJ poll was published in the spring of 1978, Dave Fanning came second to the BBC's John Peel.[93]

Though he was very much a public-service broadcaster, Fanning was the kind of presenter who would never have been given a chance by RTE had he not first broadcast with the pirates.

RTE's suggestion that local community radio, run by the national broadcaster, would be a preferable option to the pirates rang somewhat hollow, given the situation in Limerick, which had been waiting six years for a local station. Four days after RLWE went on the air RTE finally opened Radio Shannonside. RLWE broadcast for fifteen hours and received three hundred requests a day from 'listeners as far afield as Milltown Malbay and Cashel.'[94] Shannonside broadcast for two hours daily and had been on the air four days before it received its first request.[95]

In October RTE bowed to the inevitable and announced that the following year it would launch a second national station, with 'a lighter type of programmes, not exclusively pop, though its emphasis will be on the needs of younger people.'[96]

———

After the non-stop sense of drama and crisis that seemed to attend the coalition's years in power, Fianna Fáil's first full year back in power was relatively tranquil. The year did, however, start with fireworks when it was announced on 19 January that the Government had sacked the Garda Commissioner, Edmund Garvey, who became only the second Commissioner to be so removed. (The first had been Eoin O'Duffy, who, after being fired by Éamon de Valera in 1933, went on to form the Blueshirts.) A Government spokesperson said, 'It was important that the government have full confidence in the Garda Commissioner.'[97]

While Garvey's dismissal may have come as a bombshell to the general public, it had been in the pipeline ever since the Commissioner had attempted to prosecute the editorial board of *Garda Review* and subsequently placed them under surveillance. This

> showed the intensity of the conflict between the Commissioner and the leaders of the rank and file Gardaí. It is no surprise that this conflict should have culminated with leaders of the representative bodies demanding Garvey's dismissal. The Garda leaders marshalled their case in two documents presented to the Minister for Justice Gerry Collins before Christmas. They cited at least twelve specific reasons why Garvey should be asked to resign or be dismissed.[98]

The leaders of the representative bodies, including Sergeant Derek Nally, general secretary of the Association of Garda Sergeants and Inspectors (who would stand as an independent candidate for President of Ireland in 1997), found themselves pushing an open door. Garvey was regarded as being so unpopular with the rank and file that,

> as part of the vote-currying exercise during the 1977 campaign, certain Fianna Fáil canvassers seeking the votes of members of the force and their families—an important bloc in its own right— allowed it to be known that if Fianna Fáil were returned Garvey would depart.[99]

The reaction of Máire Geoghegan-Quinn, Parliamentary Secretary at the Department of Industry, Commerce and Energy, was:

> I'm delighted that Jack and Collins got the message. The rest of us have been telling them for months that he should be sacked.[100]

Geoghegan-Quinn told the Government press secretary, Frank Dunlop, that TDs 'were fed up with guards coming into their clinics every weekend complaining about Garvey and his modus operandi and asking the government to do something about him.'[101]

The Government may also have been influenced by revelations that Garvey had ordered secret surveillance of the Director of Public Prosecutions, Éamonn Barnes, and senior officials in the Department of the Taoiseach.[102] There was also his involvement in the Fingerprint Scandal, when he had failed

> to inform the coalition government of a wrong identification of a suspect for the assassination of the British Ambassador. He had told the government of an original identification but did not correct it

after it was proved to be wrong. Garvey knew of the inaccurate identification for about three months before the coalition learned of it in a newspaper article.[103]

Patrick McLaughlin, Assistant Commissioner with responsibility for the Dublin Metropolitan Area, was appointed in Garvey's stead. But the sacked Commissioner took the Government to the High Court, which 'ruled that his dismissal was null and void. The Supreme Court upheld the decision in March 1979 and Garvey was awarded costs and damages. He resigned with dignity the following month.'[104]

———

Garvey could perhaps be seen as another victim of 'the atmosphere of distrust and suspicion created by the coalition government's security policy.'[105] That description might also be applied to the four defendants in what turned out to be the longest criminal trial in the country's history up to that time. Almost two years after the Sallins mail train robbery, Nicky Kelly, Mick Plunkett, Osgur Breatnach and Brian McNally went on trial in the Special Criminal Court. The evidence against them consisted of a questionable eye-witness identification of Plunkett by a man whose house had been taken over by the robbers on the night and signed confessions by Kelly, Plunkett and Breatnach, which they claimed had been beaten out of them.

The trial began on 19 January and had lasted a record sixty-five days when it was abandoned on 6 June. Long before then the proceedings had been reduced to farce by the case of the sleeping judge. It was a journalist with the news magazine *Hibernia*, Niall Kiely, who first brought it to public attention in February.

> Judge John O'Connor seemed to fall asleep on Wednesday last . . . at 2.42 p.m. his head was only inches above the bench but three minutes later he sat up and began to write; at 3.10 p.m., his head seems to be actually resting on the bench but two minutes later he again sits up.[106]

On another occasion,

> Judge O'Connor seemed to be having difficulties staying upright in his chair, his eyes were closing and his head was slumped forward . . . by 2.24 p.m. when MacEntee [counsel for Breatnach and Plunkett] diplomatically requested a two minute break for 'toilet purposes,' someone tugged at Judge O'Connor's robe.[107]

Eventually,

> on 26 April, the fiftieth day of the trial, defence lawyers asked that the court discharge itself. The three judges of the Special Criminal Court, including Judge O'Connor ruled on the matter, deciding that Judge O'Connor was awake all the time ... The High Court backed the decision of the Special Criminal Court. The defence appealed to the Supreme Court, which also backed the decision of the Special Criminal Court. Nine judges had now ruled that Judge O'Connor was wide awake and fulfilling his constitutional responsibilities.[108]

Unfortunately the judge (a former Fine Gael candidate in the old Mayo South constituency) made a good case for the trial to be abandoned when he dropped dead on 6 June. A new trial began on 10 October, and on the following day the charges against Plunkett were dropped when the court heard that the man who had identified him had subsequently

> been face to face with Mick Plunkett in an identification parade and had failed to recognise him. He had then at another line-up identified an innocent man as one of the raiders.[109]

This left Kelly, Breatnach and McNally and their confessions. Noel McDonald sc, prosecuting, said that if Breatnach was to be believed

> you have got to accept the proposition that this was a massive conspiracy by all persons connected with the Garda Síochána, including the matrons, the jailers, the prison officers, the interviewing Gardaí and so on to cover up and to come here and solemnly take oaths and swear falsely that nothing of the sort that is alleged by the accused occurred.[110]

(The parallels with Lord Denning's 'appalling vista' comments on the Birmingham Six case are obvious.) Such a proposition was not entertained by Mr Justice Liam Hamilton, who ruled that 'the injuries found by doctors on the accused men in the mail train robbery were either self-inflicted or inflicted in collaboration with others, but were not caused by members of the Gardaí.'[111] Patrick MacEntee wondered,

> if a solicitor got to a prisoner, found him injured, got a doctor who has him dispatched to hospital; if the injuries were consistent with the allegations of beatings and there was no evidence that they were self-inflicted; if access to a solicitor was refused to the prisoner; if all these things arose from the prosecution case, what more must a prisoner have to give rise to a reasonable doubt? Must we wait for a corpse before a reasonable doubt emanates?—because that seems to be the logic of the situation in which we find ourselves. Is the situation that in Ireland in 1978 we have to solemnly sit around and

wait for a dead body in the police station before a reasonable doubt is raised?[112]

On 14 December, Breatnach and McNally were sentenced to twelve and nine years' imprisonment, respectively. The following day Kelly was given a twelve-year sentence. He had jumped bail earlier that week, however, and gone into hiding. But the criminal justice system had not finished with him or his fellow-defendants.

It was somewhat ironic that in the same year that the claims of Kelly, Breatnach and McNally were being dismissed by the legal system, a case taken by the Irish Government against the British Government on behalf of fourteen internees who claimed to have been tortured by the British army in 1971 at Palace Barracks, Holywood, Co. Down, finally came to a conclusion. Two years previously

> the European Commission on Human Rights had been unanimous in finding that the use of the interrogation techniques (wall standing, hooding, subjection to 'white' noise and deprivation of food and sleep) constituted torture. The United Kingdom had not contested that finding.[113]

But on 17 January, Britain was

> found not guilty of torture in the use of 'in depth' interrogation techniques on fourteen internees in Northern Ireland in 1971 . . . The European Court of Human Rights ruled in Strasbourg, however, that the United Kingdom government had been guilty of inhuman and degrading treatment, contrary to Article three of the European Human Rights Convention, in the use of the interrogation techniques. The 'not guilty' of torture verdicts—by a majority of thirteen to four of the European judges—came as a surprise to the British and Irish legal teams in Strasbourg for the delivery of the judgement.[114]

After the ruling the Attorney-General, Declan Costello, had requested that the British Government 'be asked to institute criminal or disciplinary proceedings against security force members guilty of inhuman and degrading treatment.'[115] There would be no such proceedings. In June 1980 Bernard O'Connor, a schoolteacher from Enniskillen, was awarded £5,000 in exemplary damages against the Chief Constable of the RUC, Kenneth Newman, in the High Court, Belfast.[116] O'Connor had been beaten up by members of the RUC in Castlereagh in January 1977.[117]

Relations between the two governments took a turn for the worse in January when the Secretary of State for Northern Ireland, Roy Mason, accused Jack Lynch of being responsible for the latest breakdown of political talks by speaking of his wish for Irish unity and of the possibility of an amnesty in the event of a political settlement, though Lynch's Government were not even involved in the talks. The attitude of constitutional nationalists in the North to Mason can be summed up the comment of the SDLP leader, Gerry Fitt, whose party voted in favour of British withdrawal at its conference that year.

> Roy Mason acted as a Colonial Secretary in that situation. He wore safari jackets in Royal Avenue in Belfast. He acted as if he were in Leopoldville rather than Belfast.[118]

Buoyed by a decrease in IRA violence in 1977, Mason boasted that he would roll up the IRA 'like a tube of toothpaste.'[119] He was praised by the *Daily Express* as 'the best, toughest, least tractable and most effective Secretary of State ever' in an article that described Northern Ireland as 'that wretched, God-stricken back alley of Europe.'[120] When Mason, in the aftermath of the La Mon bombing on 17 February, blamed the security policy of the Irish Government, Enoch Powell, the former Tory minister who was now Unionist MP for South Down, said that 'the words which fell from the Secretary of State this afternoon were the most impressive which have ever been used from the government front bench on this subject.'[121]

Reaction in the Republic was different. The *Irish Times* wrote:

> 'I have 'em on the run', Mr Roy Mason reported at the end of 1977 with the modesty you might expect of a professional wrestler returning to his corner after a decisive round. But the Barnsley Brawler was wrong. It is he who is on the run, since the day he made it, from the consequences of that boast. If Mr Mason were not warned by his security advisers of the stupidity of his claim, and it's said that he was, the Chief Constable of the RUC, Sir Kenneth Newman, certainly disassociated himself from it on the night of the La Mon bombing.[122]

Mason was accused of seeing the Republic as 'the source of his problems, the comfort of his enemies, the explanation of his failures.'[123]

The deputy leader of the SDLP, John Hume, was equally scathing when he told the party's Armagh Constituency Council in Lurgan:

> For the total wreckage that is an Irish policy we are invited to blame the Republic of Ireland. In the past few weeks we have had a vicious chorus led by the Secretary of State, who should know better, followed by the more jingoistic sections of the British press, accentuated by the shrill and dangerous, almost racial anti-Irishness of Mr Airey Neave.[124]

Lynch was also supported by Garret FitzGerald, who dismissed Mason's claims as

> unprincipled and less than honest. I was infuriated by Roy Mason's remarks because there was so much in them that wasn't true.[125]

Despite the predictions, by FitzGerald himself among other people, that Fianna Fáil in government might adopt a considerably more republican policy than the coalition had, FitzGerald believed that

> Mr Lynch had moved back towards a bipartisan position and that the differences which had temporarily existed between the parties, between 1975 and 1977—'because of the unfortunate commitment to withdraw statement'—had been largely bridged at this stage.[126]

Traditional republican rhetoric was certainly conspicuous by its absence in Fianna Fáil. The La Mon bombing, like Claudy before it and Enniskillen after it, one of those atrocities that showed that nobody made better propaganda against the IRA's cause than the organisation itself, may have had something to do with this, as it was undoubtedly 'a political and public relations disaster for the IRA ... the outrage caused by the death toll and the horrible manner in which the victims met their end was intense and widespread.[127] On the night in question

> three Provisionals from Ballymurphy, all experienced operators, fixed an incendiary [bomb] to a window of the La Mon House hotel, in the heart of Unionist North Down, about ten miles from Belfast. It was a Friday and the bars and restaurants were packed with members of a cycle club and a dog club who were having a night out. The volunteers primed the bomb, drove away and stopped at a call-box to telephone a warning. The phone had been vandalised. They drove on and were stopped by a UDR patrol. It was some time before they were waved on. By the time they reached another phone and rang the RUC, there were only nine minutes to spare. The bomb went off, flinging a sheet of blazing petrol across a crowded room and engulfing the hotel in flames in seconds. Twelve people were burned to death.[128]

All the dead were Protestants. A former Ulster Unionist member of the Constitutional Convention, Jean Coulter, said that 'the republican ghettoes should be bombed from the air. There were no innocent people in them'; but there was no loyalist backlash.[129] In fact only eight people were killed by Protestant paramilitaries in 1978, a year in which 60 of the 88 killings in the conflict were carried out by the IRA.[130] Though this was the lowest number of IRA killings since 1970, it was also the first time since that year that it had been responsible for more than half the deaths, something that would be the case every year from 1978 to 1990 with the exception of 1982.[131] With political progress apparently parked for good, the idea that IRA violence was the major problem that needed to be addressed in the North gained credence. Voices like that of the journalist Kevin Myers, who pointed out that 'the Provisionals, let us not forget, were not the cause of this war but the consequence . . . It would be hard to say that Northern Ireland is not run by a colonial administration through the services of something like a police state,' were increasingly rare.[132]

———

Few people in the Republic would have been aware that IRA inmates in the H-blocks of Long Kesh prison had been protesting against the ending of political status since September 1976 by refusing to wear prison clothing and spending their days wrapped in a blanket. The protest took a new turn a couple of months after the La Mon bombing when, in the words of one H-block prisoner,

> what started off as our refusal to 'slop out' . . . escalated rapidly . . .
> We refused to slop out, and the screws refused to come into our cells
> to empty the pisspots. We then threw our piss and shit out of the
> windows, and the screws hosed down the yard and soaked our cells.
> Then we smeared our shit on the cell walls and poured our piss
> under our cell doors. They would then brush the piss back into our
> cells and hose the inside of the wings, soaking our bedding. In the
> end the screws introduced wing shifts, so that they could clean our
> cells with power hoses. These wing shifts became a source of dread
> because the screws used the occasion to beat us, even going so far as
> to randomly anal search some Blanketman.[133]

The 'dirty protest' might have remained relatively obscure had it not been for the statement issued on 1 August by Archbishop Tomás Ó Fiaich, who had replaced Cardinal William Conway as Catholic Primate of All Ireland the previous year, following his second visit to the H-blocks. Ó Fiaich proclaimed himself

> shocked by the inhuman conditions prevailing in H Blocks 3, 4 and
> 5 where over 300 prisoners are incarcerated. One would hardly allow
> an animal to remain in such conditions let alone a human being.
> The nearest approach to it I have seen was the spectacle of hundreds
> of homeless people living in sewer pipes in the slums of Calcutta.
> The stench and filth in some of the cells, with the remains of rotten

food and human excreta scattered around the walls, was almost unbearable. In two of them I was unable to speak for fear of vomiting.[134]

Ó Fiaich was criticised by the *Church of Ireland Gazette,* while the Governing Committee of the Presbyterian Church accused him of 'grave moral confusion . . . Excuses offered give an appearance as if not only the ultimate aims but even the immediate tactics of the IRA are being blessed.'[135] In response to a Dáil question by Neil Blaney the Minister for Foreign Affairs, Michael O'Kennedy, said that the Government had made representations to the British Government concerning conditions in the prison. However, his comment that 'since the prisoners have been convicted of criminal offences, many of them very serious, he could not accept that they were political prisoners,' implicitly supported the British position, as the withdrawal of political status was what had sparked the protests in the first place.[136]

———

The main economic question worrying the Government was whether to join the European Monetary System, which would link the various currencies of the EEC member-states through an exchange rate mechanism that prevented currencies from moving against each other by more than a certain margin. The negotiations were described by the Minister for Finance, George Colley, as 'among the most important undertaken by an Irish leader since independence.'[137] The chief argument in favour of joining the EMS was that

> the association with the hard currency, the German mark, instead of the soft currency, sterling, would reduce inflation . . . A monetary policy similar to the German one should help impose the discipline on incomes that the government felt was needed but did not have the courage to impose directly.[138]

But there were also arguments that

> much of Ireland's recent upsurge in output, exports and employment was due to sterling depreciation and the consequent improvement in Irish competitiveness. This would cease with membership of the EMS.[139]

Were Ireland to enter the EMS and Britain, as seemed likely, to stay out, the Irish currency would break the parity with the British currency it had maintained since 1826, something of considerable symbolic as well as economic significance. Joining the EMS would mean 'an effective switch of economic masters from Britain to Germany.'[140]

The negotiations did not go well. In October, Colley said that the Government was seeking the transfer of '£650 million of resources to Ireland during the first five years of the new monetary regime.'[141] He 'reported that the Germans and French had indicated that they would be generous with their help. He confidently predicted that Ireland would get the £650 million at least.'[142] His confidence was misplaced. At the EEC summit meeting in Brussels in December 'Ireland was offered a total of £225 million in loans over five years, which one Irish official described as a "derisory" sum.'[143] A humiliated Lynch said that Ireland would join Britain and Italy in remaining outside the EMS. Ten days later

> Lynch announced in the Dáil that Ireland would, after all, join the EMS, because he had received an assurance that the money from the Brussels summit would not be wholly restricted to use for infrastructural projects, like roads and telecommunications. It could also be pumped into the capital and economic programmes for the following year, enabling the government to avoid the extra-tight strictures of spending that they had been faced with as a result of over-spending that year . . . The concessions were really a face-saver, as they amounted to little more than a clarification of what had actually been offered by Brussels.[144]

Whatever about the economic consequences, Ireland's entry had been overshadowed by the unrealistic expectations raised by Colley, who had been surprisingly maladroit for such an experienced politician. A similar lack of nous would cost both him and Lynch dear in the future.

Industrial relations also hinted at forthcoming catastrophe. There were strikes at the Automobile Association, FIAT, Lombard and Ulster Bank, Glaxo Laboratories, RTE, the B&I Line terminal in Dublin, British Leyland in Dublin and Nítrigin Éireann in Arklow.[145]

> Premier Dairies milk roundsmen and helpers struck for five days for improvements in pay and conditions and there were queues for milk in Dublin . . . Local government engineers began a work to rule which, taken in conjunction with action by Dublin Corporation pipe jointers, was soon being blamed for water shortages . . . Irish Shell clerical workers with the support of lorry driver colleagues cut the country's supply of oil and petrol by 25% . . . Strikes in Cement Ltd and Roadstone threatened the supply of raw materials for the building industry . . . For long periods in the year the phone wasn't working or the ESB was warning of power cuts or Dublin Corporation was turning off water supplies.[146]

Even the previously quiescent Irish Nurses' Organisation

> agreed to delete from the rules of their organisation a clause which, until that time, had prohibited their collective strike action. They also decided—goaded on by what they reckoned to be a derisory salary increase of 15 per cent—to demand an across the board increase of 50 per cent on their inadequate salaries.[147]

The most bitter dispute of all was in the Department of Posts and Telegraphs, when a strike by technicians in the Dublin exchanges led to 'a peak being reached during one weekend in March when the country was virtually cut off from the outside world, with telex and phone lines out of order, and businessmen and hoteliers screaming for government intervention.'[148] One of the points at issue was a computer that had been brought in to help with trunk calls. Computerisation must have seemed highly desirable to the Minister for Posts and Telegraphs, Pádraig Faulkner, who found himself presiding over a situation where only 15 per cent of the population had a phone.

> New connections were at a premium and cabling was inadequate. Subscribers had difficulty even making and, indeed, sustaining local calls. A heavy downpour of rain in Sligo could cut Donegal off from the rest of the world.[149]

It was a time of 'the single phone in the freezing hallway, the crisis aura that surrounded every trunk call.[150]

Boom and strikes were intimately connected, as the new prosperity

> led many workers to believe that the economy could bear substantially higher pay increases than the wage agreement allowed. In many cases they were right and employers were happy to settle for quiet private deals rather than face disruption. And in many other cases employers tried to insist on the national agreement terms and the result was confrontation and dispute. It was this same disillusionment with the limiting aspects of successive national agreements, coupled with some political footwork, which also led the trade union movement to take the unprecedented step in November of refusing to even talk about the agreement.[151]

The year ended with the news that 2,300 members of the National Busmen's Union would strike on 2 January. The stage was set for a year of industrial chaos.

———

The disputes, whether industrial, social or cultural, that had marked the year indicated a society in a state of flux, one in which everything suddenly seemed up for grabs, as old certainties were challenged and new tensions were uncovered. It was not surprising that RTE set out to produce a television series that tried to 'raise public consciousness on public issues of considerable public importance.'[152]

'The Spike' was written by Patrick Gilligan and set in a Dublin vocational school. (Gilligan was himself a vocational school teacher.) It would examine

> many problems rooted in class inequality: poverty, prostitution, illiteracy, anti-social behaviour in social institutions, domestic violence, child labour, lack of study time for students with bread winning responsibilities, lack of career opportunities, political hypocrisy and power struggles within the system. Running through it all was an unmistakable indictment of those in power in both church and state from the inconsistencies and injustices pervading the status quo.[153]

The series, however, had one major problem, which became immediately apparent. 'As a production *The Spike* was pretty horrific.'[154] 'This much publicised drama series has turned out to be so bad it must not be taken seriously.'[155]

> There was little ground for anyone to stand on to defend it. Those who would have been willing to accept a critical perspective on the education system and explicit references to human sexuality were undercut by the clumsiness of the treatment of the issues, the superficiality of the characterisation and the immaturity of the underlying point of view.[156]

'Its heart was in the right place but its scripts were awful.'[157] Yet it was not its multifarious dramatic deficiencies that did for the unfortunate series but the moment in the fifth episode, broadcast on 24 February, when a character played by Madeleine Erskine posed nude for an artist in an adult education life class.

On 2 March the Director-General of RTE, Oliver Maloney, announced that 'The Spike' was being cancelled, with five episodes still to be transmitted, because it 'had failed to achieve its programming objectives.'[158] The decision had been aided by the programme's ability to offend a wide spectrum of viewers.

> Rarely can RTE have performed anything so popular as the axing of *The Spike*. Hardly a voice was raised in its defence and such rare and incongruous bedfellows as Eddie Collins [Fine Gael's spokesperson on education], the League of Decency, the teaching unions,

Limerick County Council, the *Irish Times* television critic and *Hibernia* vied with one another in the vehemence of their opposition.[159]

Yet there were dissenting voices who felt that the programme's shortcomings were incidental to a craven willingness by RTE to succumb to outside pressure. Christina Murphy wrote in the *Irish Times*:

> I have a sneaking suspicion that if it had been the sleekest and most sophisticated job that RTE had ever put in the can, the cries of horror would have been only marginally less vocal. I doubt if the League of Decency would have accepted a nude scene however tastefully and relevantly presented. I equally doubt the ability of many teachers to accept an honest look at Vocational Schools, written by Shakespeare and produced by Lew Grade.[160]

And RTE's Controller of Television Programmes, Muiris Mac Conghail, who had openly disagreed with the Director-General's decision, warned that 'the deferment will be seen as a victory for and by those whose criticisms of the series are provoked by prudish or illiberal and censorious considerations: should a pre-emption be effected there is little prospect of RTE ever undertaking a project like this again.'[161] His vision of emboldened pressure groups and future RTE timidity proved prescient.

Yet while the good intentions of 'The Spike' were marred by the ineptitude of its execution, there were artists who were able to put on screen new visions of Ireland that were both dramatically effective and thought-provoking. Three remarkable films with a combined running time of two-and-a-half hours raised hopes that a meaningful native cinema might be developing in a country that for too long had merely provided picturesque backdrops for foreign directors.

The individuality of Bob Quinn's vision was enhanced by the fact that his films were in Irish. Quinn had been an RTE producer before departing in typically flamboyant fashion in 1969.

> He was taking a film crew to Belfast when, at the border, he told the driver to turn left and drove to Mayo and sailed across to Clare Island. The crew returned to Montrose with film of Quinn on a boat, giving the two finger sign ... that was his resignation.[162]

A Dubliner, Quinn moved to An Cheathrú Rua in Connemara, where he converted a former knitting factory into the Cinegael film studio. He argued:

> The whole process is decentralisation. I want to point out that Dublin is not the centre of the universe—or if it is, it's a very mediocre centre. I'm also trying to show that we can, indeed have to,

rely on our own resources to make films and not be dependent on second hand habits from America and Britain.[163]

Poitín was a brilliant illustration of Quinn's thesis. Set in present-day Connemara, it was a bracingly austere and unsentimental tale of the interaction between a poitín-maker, his daughter and his two venal agents, with terrific performances from Cyril Cusack, Dónal McCann and, in particular, Niall Tóibín, as well as the local actors Mairéad Ní Chonghaile and Tomás Ó Fatharta. Tóibín's remarkable mixture of insolence, aggression and barely repressed despair, married to the unblinking eye that enables Quinn to deromanticise one of the most mythologised locations in Ireland, combine to make *Poitín* a film which holds up very well.

Down the Corner was set in Ballyfermot, Dublin, at first glance a polar opposite to Connemara. Yet Joe Comerford, an equally tough-minded film-maker, shared with Quinn the desire to put on screen an Irish reality hitherto ignored. *Down the Corner* was 'the first film to represent working-class Dubliners . . . the film foregrounded work for the first time as a central activity in the lives of working-class people.'[164] It was 'a naturalistic and sympathetic portrayal of the community and its institutions: school, hospital and homes, where pressures of space and money confine the inhabitants.' It announced the arrival of a director who would become one of the most interesting artists of the era.[165]

Exposure was made by Kieran Hickey, a director whose territory was as different from that of Quinn and Comerford as theirs was from each other's. Hickey was an experienced documentary film-maker, whose *Faithful Departed* and *The Light of Other Days* were based on the Lawrence Collection of late nineteenth and early twentieth-century photographs in the National Library. From a script by the novelist Philip Davison, *Exposure* is a tale of male friendship and sexual rivalry set in a provincial hotel, featuring T. P. McKenna, Niall O'Brien and Bosco Hogan, with Catherine Schell as the liberated French photographer whose presence brings the trio's sexual tensions to the surface. It was hailed as

> one of the finest, if not the finest, film ever to emerge from an Irish milieu. It is a calm, perceptive and unblinking look at the Irish condition, or part of it, that resonates pleasurably and disturbingly in the mind long after the film has been seen. It is also hugely enjoyable.[166]

Hickey's achievement, a critic observed, 'has been not only to survive in an inimical environment but also to produce work of sensitivity and high professional competence.'[167]

The environment may have been inimical, and it was by no means certain that the excellence of the three films would make the financing of future work any easier for the directors, but the upsurge in creativity was no coincidence. Both Quinn's and Hickey's films had benefited from the film script award recently instituted by the Arts Council, while there had also been

> the rise of the Irish Film Theatre, the setting up of the Irish Federation of Film Societies, the formation of the Dublin Film Society and, lately, the appearance of *Dimensions*, a film magazine made possible by the co-operation between the Arts Council in the South and the Arts Council in Northern Ireland.[168]

Much of the activity centred around Dublin, where the Irish Film Theatre had

> set out to provide films that would not normally receive a commercial release here . . . Within six months membership had reached 3,300; at the end of last year it stood at 5,800, and it has now risen to more than 6,600.[169]

And the fact that a small town like Carrickmacross could hold a one-day film festival in March, which featured *The Lacemaker, Sunday Bloody Sunday* and *Lenny* spoke volumes about 'the dedicated work of local film societies, who manage frequently against daunting odds, to provide material that their members would not otherwise see.'[170]

Such societies can perhaps be seen as the manifestation of an Irish counter-culture, most visibly epitomised by the big outdoor music festivals of the late seventies, which seemed to provide the missing link between the Fleá Cheoil and Woodstock. There was the Macroom Castle Festival, the 'Boys of Ballisodare' and, above all, Lisdoonvarna. The first Lisdoonvarna Festival proceeded on a July weekend, despite local opposition. 'The owners of most of the 18 hotels and bars as well as the local curate, the Rev. Malachy Hanlon, opposed the festival and contested the application for a licence,' while the ESB refused to provide electricity to the site, despite being offered £2,200 to do so.[171] Undaunted, the organisers

> created a multi-coloured tent village on the 24 acres of bogland a mile below the town which are known as Aughiska. And enterprising salesmen did a brisk business selling sheets of polythene at 40p each for the fans to sit on or rest their sleeping bags on at night.[172]

The festival-goers saw fifty-three acts over three days, including the Chieftains, Dé Danann, the Furey Brothers, Christy and Barry Moore, Paul Brady, Micho Russell and Andy Irvine. 'We would get more trouble on a normal Saturday night in September than we did during the whole weekend,' said a local Garda spokesperson.[173]

Perhaps the defining counter-cultural moment of the year was the news that the Boomtown Rats had made the top of the British singles charts with 'Rat Trap' in November. For all its musical debts to Bruce Springsteen, 'Rat Trap' still had an unmistakable Dublin flavour, most notably in its reference to the Five Lamps, the well-known landmark in Amiens Street.

Yet it is easy to overstate the impact of the Rats, and of the counter-culture in general. For 'Rat Trap' never made it to number 1 in its own country, being kept off the top by the single that to this day holds the record for the number of weeks (ninety) in the Irish charts. 'One Day at a Time', written by Kris Kristofferson and Marijohn Wilkins, was a pretty hackneyed song given a relatively pedestrian treatment by Gloria.

For all the cultural significance of the Irish punk and traditional bands, there were large swathes of Ireland where the musical *lingua franca* was a genre disparaged by music critics and rock fans alike.

> From the mid sixties onwards the musical seeds blown in from Nashville found a particularly fertile ground in and around Ireland's countless Drumshanbos. Posses of *hombres* who had never been further west than Clew Bay began singing in accents that would do credit to John Wayne. And, inevitably, there was a spin-off. The banal music and platitudinous lyrics of the worst of Country and Western music were only too adaptable to the needs of our own cowboys. Country and Irish was born.[174]

This was the province of Gloria, Margo, Philomena Begley, Ray Lynam, Brian Coll, Ian Corrigan, Gene Stuart, Susan McCann, T. R. Dallas and, above all, Big Tom.

> While the rest of the world was rolling with the Stones, creaming with Clapton, crooning with James Taylor or pogoing with the punks, thousands of Irish fans continued listening to Big Tom eulogising his mother. 'Gentle Mother,' 'Flowers for Mama,' 'I Have an Aged Mother.' His deep, sad, earnest voice won him the crown of Country and Irish.[175]

Critical disdain did not worry the stars. In the words of one of them, Jim Tobin, 'My voice comes out very flat on tape, but singing's a lot better than shovelling gravel for a living.'[176]

———

Just as there were those who remained unimpressed by the brave new musical world, there were sceptics who believed that the economic boom was built on shaky foundations. The Fine Gael spokesperson on economic affairs, Peter Barry, warned:

It would be difficult to impose wage restraints in view of the government's policy since coming to office. They said a wage limit of 5% was essential to their policies but that had become 8% and, in some cases in the private sector, as high as 16%.[177]

Equally ominously, 'Government borrowing, which was £506 million in 1976, the last full year of the coalition, rose to £546 million in 1977, followed by a massive jump to £810 million in 1978, the first full year of the new Fianna Fáil government.'[178]

The Trinity College economist Terence Ryan warned that

unemployment, at around 100,000, is historically very high; external government debt amounts to more than £1,400 million and substantially exceeds our total external reserves of £1,042 million; the balance of payments has been running at a deficit on current account of over £220 million; and, on top of all that, the government's borrowing requirement for this year amounts to over 13% of GNP, a figure unprecedented anywhere else in Europe. This is not a picture of a healthy economy.[179]

And the year ended with news that

thousands of people have died in the course of peaceful demonstrations in Iran during the last year, as one of the world's most brutal and corrupt regimes attempts desperately to hang on to power. The indications are, however, that Shah Mohammed Reza Pahlavi will be overthrown, in spite of a succession of 'concessions' to the protesters accompanied by the widespread massacre of demonstrators and that Iran will be plunged into further upheaval with critical consequences for Western capitalism.[180]

Ireland would not escape the repercussions.

| THINGS FALL APART

1979

The memory of the 1932 Eucharistic Congress, that moment when Irish Catholicism proclaimed itself triumphant in the new independent state, was frequently invoked during the visit of Pope John Paul II, notably when he told the largest crowd ever assembled in Ireland: 'We are one in faith and spirit with the vast throng which filled the Phoenix Park on the occasion of the last great Eucharist hosting held on this spot, held at the Eucharistic Congress in 1932.'[1]

That the Irelands of 1932 and 1979 were animated by an identical faith and spirit seemed to be taken as a given during the three-day visit, which began on 29 September. Who could argue with the awesome figures?

The gathering in the Phoenix Park, officially 1,300,000, was probably according to some commentators the largest single crowd of people to come together anywhere in Europe since the War. Add to that the 250,000 at Drogheda, the 20,000 at Clonmacnoise, the 250,000 at the Youth Mass in Galway, the 450,000 at Knock, the 50,000 at Maynooth, the 400,000 at Limerick and the smaller crowds that greeted the Pope on his motorcade through Dublin, at Dublin and Shannon Airports and at the nunciature and it could be concluded that 2,500,000, or half the population of the island have seen Pope John Paul.[2]

The figures and the fervour were enough to persuade most observers that nothing had changed and that the Republic remained as solidly and traditionally Catholic as ever. The visit, said one newspaper, 'made children of us all.'[3] This was not intended as a criticism.

The youth mass in Galway seemed to suggest a successful passing of the torch to the next generation while proving a personal triumph for one member of the hierarchy in particular.

Wearing his purple biretta and episcopal regalia Éamonn Casey played Master of Ceremonies, taking the mike and whipping up enthusiasm . . . To deafening applause the man in white alighted waving and blessing. Casey stood beside him in the limelight; it was as if he had magically plucked the pope out of the Galway sky . . . For a man of Casey's beliefs and loyalty to the Roman Catholic Church, the papal visit was equivalent to a vote of confidence from none other than the Vicar of Christ on Earth.[4]

There was even an expectation that the Pope's plea at Drogheda—'Now I wish to speak to all men and women engaged in violence. I appeal to you, in language of passionate pleading. On my knees, I beg you to turn away from the paths of violence and to return to the ways of peace'—might lead to a profound change in the Northern situation.[5] The following day came a report that

> Provisional IRA members had been so affected by the Pope's call for peace that they must now lay down their arms. A considerable stir was caused by a story distributed by the United Press International news agency which quoted a high-ranking Provisional IRA officer as saying that active service units had been affected by the Pope's plea for peace.[6]

There had been, it seemed, 'no greater or more intense communal religious experience in Irish history.'[7] Nell McCafferty noted the steps that had been taken to facilitate this experience. 'All airports were closed, so that no man but John Paul could come down from above; all traffic had been banned in Dublin city, so the pilgrims must walk to meet him; all workplaces closed to greet he who symbolized spiritual freedom. No other place in the world had made such arrangements.'[8]

The visit even spawned a number of hit records, Jim Tobin and the Firehouse scoring with 'Welcome, John Paul' and Caitríona Walsh weighing in with 'Viva il Papa' before the former Eurovision Song Contest winner Dana released the biggest hit of them all, 'Totus Tuus' ('totally yours'), which went straight to the top of the Irish charts.[9]

With so much communal exultation going on, it remains striking that the Pope's sermons often seemed defensive rather than celebratory. The astute Dónal Foley, one of the few writers who did not lapse into hagiographic mode, felt that

> his sermon, however, on the theme of the Eucharist and Penance and the evil trend of modern influences in Ireland, was traditional. I heard it myself, almost word for word from the Parish Priest in Ferrybank, Canon Brennan, when I was a young boy.[10]

In the Phoenix Park the Pope spoke of how 'Ireland, that has overcome so many difficult moments in her history, is being challenged in a new way today, for she is not immune from the influence of ideologies and trends which present-day civilisation and progress carry with them.'[11] In Galway he warned that 'the desire to be free from external restraints manifests itself very strongly in the sexual domain, since this is an area that is so closely tied to a human personality.'[12] And in Limerick 'he denounced birth control and divorce, and pleaded with Irish women to stay in their places at home, bringing up families.'[13]

The employment of such rhetoric lends credence to the view that the goal of the Pope's visit was not merely, as he claimed, to visit the Shrine of Our Lady at Knock. It was also a visit that 'the Irish hierarchy had organised with the purpose of stemming what it perceived as the rising tide of materialism and secularism.'[14]

When it came to the battles over divorce, contraception and abortion that would dominate the political landscape over the following decade the Pope came to bring not peace but a sword. His lamentation at the Phoenix Park mass that 'the most sacred principles, which were the sure guides for the behaviour of individuals and society, are being hollowed out by false pretences concerning freedom, the sacredness of life, the indissolubility of marriage, the true sense of human sexuality, the right attitude towards the material goods that progress had to offer,' could be seen as a pointed criticism of those who thought it desirable for Ireland to follow the lead of Italy, where divorce had been legalised in 1974 and abortion in 1978.[15] Perhaps the most significant result of the visit was that it 'exacerbated a tendency towards triumphalism in certain Catholic circles. That, in turn, bred an assertiveness, even an arrogance, among lay elements determined to return the country to the pristine purity of 1932.'[16]

There is no event from this era that looks so different in hindsight, no event that is so diminished by hindsight. The Galway mass, for example, looks very different now that we know that Bishop Casey was the father of a son when it took place, as indeed was Father Michael Cleary, who joined him on the altar to perform a kind of warm-up act for the Pope.

There is a tendency to suggest that the fervour that attended the visit was a product of a more innocent time. 'Those were days of innocence, still some years away from the harsh realities which have since caused us so much pain,' suggested Bishop Willie Walsh of Killaloe in a book that elicited memories of the visit twenty-five years later.[17] Many of the scandals that would rob the Catholic Church of much credibility were still to be uncovered. Only a handful of people would have known of Bishop Casey's and Father Cleary's offences against the code of celibacy. And the sexual abuse being carried out by members of the clergy, and in Irish society in general, remained a taboo subject. Yet the existence in previous decades of a network of orphanages, reformatories and industrial schools that incarcerated large numbers of children in conditions of extreme cruelty and deprivation, should be enough to remind us that the idea of an Ireland innocent through ignorance of offences carried out in the name of the church does not hold water. Many people at the various masses probably at least suspected what had happened inside such institutions. Mary Raftery and Eoin O'Sullivan in their great book *Suffer the Little Children* suggest that 'the thousands of victims of industrial schools bear witness to a society unwilling to question its own comfortable certainties out of a fear that those beliefs might have turned out to be built on sand.'[18]

The famed national innocence owed a great deal to self-delusion and wishful thinking.

> Even if the unthinkable were true, and revered nuns, priests and Brothers were treating the child inmates with cruelty, the population lacked any mechanism for dealing with this. All attempts to denigrate the Catholic Church were viewed with extreme hostility, and those few individuals who did so often paid a heavy price ... Irish and German society shared a similar pattern of denial. Both were afraid to acknowledge that terrible events were occurring within their communities.[19]

The contention of Prof. John Bonner, a leading light in the fringe Catholic movements that campaigned against contraception and were massively encouraged by the papal visit, that 'Ireland stands alone in her fight to defend the Judeo-Christian moral code of sexual behaviour and the sanctity of life,' is one of those statements so divergent from reality as to almost elicit admiration for its sheer chutzpah.[20]

Perhaps it was a knowledge of the gap between image and reality that prompted RTE to indulge in some pre-visit censorship. A 'Late Late Show' special was scheduled to deal with the issue of contraception, focusing on the best-selling book *On Our Backs* by Rosita Sweetman. However, it was cancelled as 'inappropriate', as it would have coincided with the Pope's visit.[21] Had the discussion gone ahead, the audience for RTE's most popular programme might well have heard about Vera, who had spent sixteen years in an orphanage run by nuns ('They used beat us with straps ... They beat us till the blood ran out of our backs'), or David, a former inmate of Artane Industrial School ('One Brother used to raise his hands and say, "Lord! Send me a hurley!" You'd have to go and get a hurley then. The base was covered in steel hoops so you can imagine what a belt of that was like').[22] Thirty years before the report of the Ryan Commission and twenty years before the television series 'States of Fear', the nature of these institutions was set down in black and white in Sweetman's book, which also included interviews with homosexuals, prostitutes, a survivor of incest, sexually active young people and others airbrushed from the picture of piety presented to the Pope. Still noteworthy for the frankness with which its twenty-seven interviewees spoke to Sweetman, *On Our Backs* is a remarkable work, which achieves its aim: 'to burst through the curtain of silence about sexuality maintained by the Church and the State.'[23]

Excitable, and quickly discounted, newspaper reports notwithstanding, the Pope's Drogheda message proved largely ineffectual. On 2 October the IRA 'bluntly rejected the plea by Pope John Paul II for an end to violence in the North and claims it has "widespread support" for its operations.' It stated: 'In all conscience we believe that force is by far the only means of removing the evil of the British presence in Ireland.'[24]

There have been claims that the Pope's plea in some circuitous way led to the peace process that came to fruition a decade later; but this seems to be another example of how the process, like all successes, has a hundred fathers. The attitude of senior republican Danny Morrison, looking back on the sermon twenty-five years later, is instructive.

> The British men of violence were allowed off the hook, were not asked to account for the children, women and men they had killed, for the prisoners they had tortured. Papal excoriation was for one side only, the weaker side, the oppressed. I would never listen to the Pope again . . . An opportunity was squandered to put pressure on the British government to resolve the prison crisis and encourage republicans to view an alternative to armed struggle.[25]

In the month following the Pope's appeal the Provisionals killed three members and one former member of the Ulster Defence Regiment, two civilians, two British soldiers and a member of the RUC.[26] There could have been no more unambiguous dismissal of the plea from the altar.

It may be that the event the papal visit most resembles is not the Eucharistic Congress but the celebrations of Queen Elizabeth's Silver Jubilee, which had taken place two years earlier. The late Philip Whitehead, at the time Labour MP for Derby North, described the jubilee as an event where 'the British and two-thirds of the Northern Irish decided that one way to confront a future that might not work was with the trappings of a past which had worked.'[27] That description also applied to Ireland during the papal visit as a nation attempted to find solace in difficult times by harking back to an era when life had seemed much less complex and much less threatening.

——

The fact is that the impression of national unity created during the Pope's three-day tour was largely spurious. Even leaving the Troubles aside, 1979 was a year of dissension and division. One source of tension was the obvious inequity of the taxation system. 'The share of national income paid by those conventionally taxed at source went up from 71.4% to 86.5% in the years 1975–8; by the last year they were providing £1,800 million of the tax take, the self-employed £320 million and the farmers a modest £20 million.'[28] One contributor to this imbalance was the failure to find an effective method of taxing farmers. It was perhaps not surprising that 'those enchained by the Pay As You Earn tax code are baying for the farmers' blood.'[29] The fact that farming incomes had been seen to rise substantially since Ireland joined the EEC led to a situation where the Government could no longer ignore the demand for some kind of comprehensive taxation system for farmers.

Its proposed solution was unveiled by the Minister for Finance, George Colley, in his budget in February. It came as an unpleasant surprise for farmers. 'Bringing more farmers into the tax net was to be expected even if wasn't welcomed by farmers. But a 2% levy on farm produce, which it appears will apply to about 90% of farm production was something which had never crept into the wildest nightmares of either Mr Paddy Lane or Mr Anthony Leddy.'[30] The Irish Farmers' Association and Irish Creamery Milk Suppliers' Association proclaimed themselves 'appalled and horrified at the savage treatment applied to Irish farm families.'[31] Battle was joined.

The Government had picked a particularly inopportune time to look for money from farmers. 1979, it turned out, was the year when reality intruded harshly on the agricultural industry after several years of spectacular rises in income derived from the policies of the EEC. The problem was that

> the reduction in the rapid rate of increase in agricultural prices under the CAP [common agricultural policy] as the EEC finally took fright at the runaway over-production stimulated by prices far above the world average ushered in a slump in agriculture in 1979. FEOGA [European agricultural guarantee fund] payments rose only slightly, from £365.1 million to £381.1 million . . . Many farmers

heavily in debt now found themselves caught on a falling market. As land prices first stabilised, and then fell from their inflated levels, borrowers and purchasers found their security worth less than they and the banks had assumed. The banks did not intend to suffer. They began putting pressure on borrowers who could not meet repayments . . . Rural resentment festered during 1979.[32]

At first Fianna Fáil seemed willing to defy the protests of the farming organisations. On 23 February it was reported that

the government is unimpressed by the argument of farmers' leaders that it should withdraw the proposal to introduce a 2% agricultural levy—despite the explicit threat of commodity strikes and the implicit suggestions of an anti-Fianna Fáil campaign during the European and local elections. Senior members of the government were beginning last night to boil the issue down to one bluntly stated: Who runs the country?[33]

Four days later there seemed to be an answer to this question as the Government 'hammered out a bargain with farm leaders which would make the agricultural levy redundant while causing no loss of revenue to the exchequer this year and paving the way for an income tax yield from farmers in future "in line with the other sectors of the community."'[34] Despite Colley's insistence that the Government had not backed down, the implications seemed clear. The general secretary of the ICTU, Ruaidhrí Roberts, pointed out that 'the deal with the farmers seemed to give their organisations a negotiating role in their own taxation which was something no-one else in the community enjoyed.'[35]

If the outraged response of the PAYE workers to Colley's volte-face was predictable, the scale of it surprised almost everyone. 'On 11 March some 50,000 people marched at a rally organised in Dublin by the Irish Transport and General Workers' Union, and there were other marches in Ballina, Carlow, Cavan, Galway, Limerick, Sligo and Tralee. George Colley compounded the anger of the taxpayers by saying that he did not think anyone was seriously suggesting that such action would produce a government response.'[36] But these protests were only the warm-up act.

On 20 March 'upwards of 150,000 PAYE workers took to the streets of Dublin to demand tax reform in the largest demonstration in the history of the state and in Cork, Galway, Limerick, Waterford, Dundalk and other centres throughout the Republic, tens of thousands of workers also downed tools and joined in protest over the tax system.'[37] The turnout was all the more remarkable given that 'the Irish Congress of Trade Unions opposed the idea of a work stoppage and had earlier asked the Dublin Council of Trade Unions to postpone yesterday's strike.'[38] Yet, following the big March demonstrations, the protest movement began to lose momentum for the time being, with the opposition of the trade union leadership crucial to this process. An all-out strike planned for May Day was fatally compromised when the ITGWU decided against recommending participation to its members.

There was a feeling that the higher echelons of the labour movement had been made uneasy by the energies released during the PAYE protest, something epitomised by the statement of the president of the ICTU, Harold O'Sullivan, that 'taxation is fundamentally a job for parliament and government and I don't accept that mass democracy on the streets is the answer to our problems.'[39] Instead the unions pinned their hopes on the 'National Understanding for Economic and Social Development' worked out between themselves, the Government and the employers after a tripartite negotiating process. This, it was announced in a joint statement on 24 April,

> provides a framework for economic and social progress. It embraces policies on employment, pay and taxation as well as education and social welfare. It represents a practical recognition by government, employers and industry organisations and the trade union movement of the value of an integrated programme of action which will provide the maximum opportunities for increasing employment, support continuing economic growth and social improvement and provide that the resultant benefits are distributed fairly throughout the community.[40]

The agreement aimed at 'full employment within five years ... it can be achieved given the necessary response and sustained commitment from all sections of the community.'[41]

The vice-chairperson of the ICTU, John Carroll, said that 'the breakthrough we had achieved was historic, in that for the first time in this country, and indeed in any country—and I include the Socialist countries—we now had an acknowledgement that the trade union movement not only had a voice to be listened to but had to be brought into the circle where the decisions are made.'[42]

But although the agreement provided £39 million worth of tax allowances for PAYE workers, there were many trade unionists who agreed with Kevin Duffy, secretary of the Building Workers' Union, that

> there was no indication that the government was prepared to bring about realistic reform of the tax system. If the proposals were

accepted, 1979 would be remembered as the year in which the trade union movement lost its nerve.[43]

A growing conviction that the tax system was rigged against the PAYE worker, and the rising inflation that gave Ireland the second-highest rate in the EEC, contributed to a wave of industrial unrest. 1979 would be the second-worst year for strikes, after 1937, with 1.47 million working days lost.[44]

The year's biggest dispute was the national postal strike, the first such strike for more than fifty years, which began on 18 February and ended nineteen weeks later on 25 June. It began when thirteen thousand postmen, telephonists and counter clerks took industrial action. 'Although the Post Office Workers' Union was seeking increases of up to 37%, it is understood that the highest claim the Department was prepared to concede was in the region of 9% and this clearly was insufficient to have the strike deferred.'[45] The secretary of the POWU, Terry Quinlan, suggested that 'the government would have to rethink its attitude to its workers' pay, just as the government had shown its willingness to rethink the 2% levy on the farmers.'[46] On this issue, however, the Government had determined to take a stand. The POWU had 'come up against a firm decision by the Department of the Public Service to hold the line on public sector pay for fear that wage concessions for these workers would spark off a series of parity claims.'[47]

It was an immensely disruptive dispute, which left 'all parts of the country without postal collection or deliveries, operator assisted telephone and telex calls and the wide range of services normally provided by the Post Office.'[48] This was the pre-fax, pre-internet, pre-mobiles era, when the most advanced form of communication was telex—a system of cumbersome text printers connected over the telephone network. The dispute was also a bitter one, described by the Fine Gael spokesperson on labour, Jim Mitchell, as 'the most malevolent strike the country has ever known.'[49] This bitterness reached a peak on 9 May, when

> thirty one Post Office strikers were arrested during violent scenes ...
> A striking Dublin postman, Mr Paddy Brown, was taken to hospital with a suspected broken leg after violence flared between Gardaí and men on the picket line. The disturbances broke out about midday when about 50 postal workers—who were conducting what was described as an 'intimidatory' picket to prevent alleged strikebreaking by CIE's 'Fastrack' service—were confronted by as many Gardaí.[50]

The strike ended with the POWU agreeing to accept an increase of 15 per cent for postmen and telephonists and 12 per cent for clerks. It seemed as though

> the Fianna Fáil government wore down the workers and they were forced back to work. The defeat of the strike was later to have powerful repercussions in dampening public sector militancy and convinced many to look again at the option of social partnership.[51]

But if it seemed like a victory for the Government, it had been of the pyrrhic variety.

> Businesses, from small shops to large hotels, lost thousands of pounds and those outside the STD [direct dialling of long-distance calls] telephone service were virtually cut off for the duration of the dispute. The Inland Revenue was unable to collect taxes, vast numbers of ESB and gas company bills were unpaid, exports and investment were down, the loss to tourism was immense and the inconvenience to the public, particularly those on the Western seaboard and outside the direct dial telephone system was large.[52]

Other strikes also had dramatic consequences. In May more than five thousand tons of refuse had accumulated in the Dublin suburbs because of a dispute involving maintenance fitters, which immobilised three-quarters of the city council's refuse lorries. Refuse collection concentrated on the inner-city areas, on flats complexes and hospitals. As a result, thousands of households in the suburbs had no refuse collected for up to three weeks, and there were fears of health hazards as the warm weather approached.[53]

On 22 November a ban on sterling transactions by the Irish Bank Officials' Association led to a spectacular run on the four main banks, which forced them to close for five-and-a-half days before they gave IBOA members a one-off payment of 12 per cent of salary for extra work incurred by Ireland's joining the European Monetary System. The withdrawals during the run were

> equivalent to the loss of a quarter of total available liquid resources. If sustained for a few days, it would have meant that the four banks would have had no alternative but to call in outstanding loans. Such a development would not have been feasible, especially as the banks have already called in all available outstanding loans as a result of the credit squeeze.[54]

There were bus strikes, strikes at the state fertiliser plant in Arklow, at the Agricultural Credit Corporation, at McDonald's fast food outlets in Dublin, at Dublin Port, Verolme dockyard in Cork and the Chrysler plant in Santry, Dublin. In November, with the onset of the recent cold weather . . . supplies of coal and bottled gas have been hit by unofficial disputes at the Dublin headquarters of Coal Distributors Ltd and Calor Kosangas. The strike at the Ringsend depot of Coal Distributors is the fourth this month, and has halted coal delivery to wide areas of the Dublin and Leinster region where the company is the monopoly importer of coal.[55]

And in December refuse was once more left uncollected in the streets as binmen in west Dublin 'picketed tip heads and depots in defiance of an interim injunction.'[56] In the High Court strikers told Mr Justice McMahon that they would 'defy the injunction and continue to picket.'[57] One of them informed the judge: 'I am a married man with five children. I will stand and I don't give a granny's about anyone. If I am told to strike tomorrow, I will strike.'[58]

The strikes may have contributed to a replacement of the optimism of the previous year with a sense of malaise that would grow over the next decade. But the real problem was that 'the secret of the Hibernian miracle began to emerge in 1979 . . . Net foreign debt jumped from £297 million at the end of 1978 to £1089 million a year later. The deficit in the balance of payments soared from 2.1% of GNP in 1978 to 10.1% in 1979.'[59] The actual deficit of £522 million exceeded the projected budget deficit of £289 million by 81 per cent.[60]

A central factor in this was the oil crisis resulting from the Iranian revolution, which resulted in a reduction in world oil production by 6 million barrels per day in January and February. This led to a 30 per cent rise in oil prices, which damaged the Irish economy by lowering domestic demand, increasing the rate of inflation and reducing export opportunities. The oil crisis was 'a crippling blow to a small economy completely dependent for its competitiveness on the erroneous doctrine of low fuel prices.'[61]

There was also the small matter of a petrol shortage. In May 'a spokesman for Irish Shell said that, in the present quarter, distributors would receive 90% of the amount ordered in the corresponding period of 1978. However, petrol consumption has risen by 10 to 11% in the interim, with the boom in car sales.' The actual shortfall was about 21 per cent.[62] By the end of the month there were reports of motorists camping overnight in queues outside petrol stations.[63]

The petrol situation returned to normal before the end of the summer; but the sense of crisis would fatally undermine Jack Lynch, who the previous year had seemed so impregnable.

It began with two men, two disenchanted men who happened to be staying in the same hotel. Jury's Hotel in Ballsbridge had a special rate for members of the Oireachtas, something that appealed to Tom McEllistrim TD of Kerry North and Jackie Fahey TD of Waterford. They would meet in the hotel at night and talk about politics. Things went on from there.

McEllistrim, whose father (also Tom) had proposed Jack Lynch for the leadership of Fianna Fáil in 1966, remembered:

> We started to have meetings. Fahey and myself had the meetings first. We initiated the thing and then we invited different people to our meetings . . . and all those meetings took place in one or other of our rooms: we might invite Paddy Power and Ray MacSharry tonight, and we might invite Seán Keegan and Seán Doherty the next night. And the way we got the big group together was by inviting them to small meetings first, getting their feelings as to how they felt about the change of leader in Fianna Fáil.[64]

Other TDs became involved, among them Tom Meaney, Eileen Lemass, Albert Reynolds, Pádraig Flynn, Charlie McCreevy, Vincent Brady and Mark Killilea. Reynolds, Doherty and Killilea would join McEllistrim and Fahey in what became known as the Gang of Five, the most important grouping among the TDs who sought to replace Lynch with Charles Haughey.

The Fianna Fáil leadership had lost a great deal of credibility with the party's backbenchers after a series of uncharacteristic political misjudgements.

> The series began with the budget, continued with the attempts to recover from the initial response to the farm levy, leading directly to confrontation with those who pay tax as they earn, and culminating with Mr Colley's reportedly dismissive remarks about the results that could be expected from yesterday's demonstration. Added to the list, the Garvey [Garda Commissioner] and Wood Quay affairs increase the impression of a government that has allowed itself to be wrong-footed or dependent on the luxury of its historic majority.[65]

Yet it was not economic issues that provided the focus for the heave against Lynch. Instead he was assailed for allegedly betraying Fianna Fáil's traditional republican values. The observation that 'a victory for Haughey was not fundamentally because of his manipulation of nationalist sentiment in Fianna Fáil, but rather because it helped to amplify an attack prompted by the failure of Lynch's economic policy' is an astute one.[66]

Haughey would be the beneficiary of the movement against Lynch rather than a participant in it. As the one member of the Government who was an obvious opponent, he was the only option for those who wanted to oust Lynch. But, McEllistrim insisted,

> we were never led by Haughey. We were never encouraged by Haughey or anything like that. I'd meet Haughey in the corridor or something like that and we might just talk about what was happening within the party. But I can say definitely that we were never encouraged by Haughey to do what we were doing or to try and change the leadership of Fianna Fáil.[67]

The boldest challenge to Lynch's authority would not come from Haughey but from the youngest Fianna Fáil TD, who also happened to be one of the party's few women representatives. Then again, Síle de Valera's pedigree as granddaughter of the man who founded the party and led it for thirty-three years probably helped to make her bolder than the average political tyro. Her speech at the Liam Lynch Commemoration in Fermoy on 9 September was a thinly veiled attack on Fianna Fáil's Northern policy under Lynch. 'I look to our party,' she said, 'and particularly our leader to demonstrate his republicanism and bring these beliefs to fruition in our people.'[68] The assertion that 'so many nowadays, who only have material interests at heart, would tempt us to dilute our political aim and goal— namely the achievement of a United Ireland. These opponents are dangerous, as they so often cloak their views under such guises as reconciliation and peace' could also be read as a criticism of her leader.[69] But the passage that drew most notice was the one in which she observed that

> because of British propaganda, some Irish people are now afraid to even use the words, Republicanism, Patriotism, Idealism, Nationalism, whatever about believing in them and acting in their name. It is sad to think that British propaganda in the early 1920s referred to men like Liam Lynch as rebels. Today they would use the words men of violence or terrorists and a generation or two before would have referred to them as felons.[70]

That the members of the Provisional IRA were the heirs of those who had won independence might be the only thing Ruairí Ó Brádaigh and Conor Cruise O'Brien would ever agree upon; but Síle de Valera's implied agreement with this viewpoint placed her outside the political pale.

Lynch responded immediately.

> Deputy de Valera suggests that today British propaganda would refer to men like Liam Lynch as terrorists. This could be interpreted by some as identifying the Provisional IRA with the men of sixty

years ago who genuinely fought for our freedoms, political and economic.[71]

Like a judo player, he attempted to turn the turbulent young TD's strength against her.

> Éamon de Valera, her grandfather, whom she invoked in her statement, had unequivocally renounced physical force when he founded Fianna Fáil in 1926. In the 1940s and 1950s, he took strong action as is now being taken to combat the activities and atrocities of the IRA. Then as now the objective of these subversives was to destroy democratic government which was won for us by men like Liam Lynch.[72]

The claiming for the side of democracy of his namesake, who in fact had died fighting in the Civil War in an attempt to overturn the decision of the Dáil to accept the Treaty, suggested that Lynch was not particularly comfortable on this territory.

Three days after her speech a spectacularly unabashed de Valera implied that Lynch agreed with everything she said but couldn't say so in public.

> It would be difficult, of course, for the prime minister of the country to make the kind of statement I made while in delicate negotiations with the British government, but that does not mean that he disagrees with what I have said, because he is not contesting any of the issues I raised.[73]

Lynch retaliated by letting it be known that two days before de Valera's speech, which she had already circulated to the newspapers, he had told her it was 'contrary to government policy, wrong, unhelpful and untimely. She had left Government Buildings fully aware that the speech was not acceptable.'[74] He moved to impose party discipline by calling a meeting on 28 September, at which 'a motion supporting party policy as expressed by the Taoiseach, was unanimously adopted by over a hundred TDs and senators.'[75] A statement said that 'Miss de Valera withdrew any criticism of party policy on Northern Ireland or of the Fianna Fáil leadership, expressed or implied, in her speech at Fermoy on September 9.'[76] But she saw things differently, insisting after the meeting that 'there is no question of me backing down, no question of that at all. I am happy with the outcome of the meeting.'[77] She pointed out that the 1975 party policy on the North, which included the controversial demand for a British declaration of intention to withdraw, remained party policy, 'and that is the policy I agree with.'[78] Given that Fianna Fáil had never changed the 1975 policy—though its leader seemed determined to let it wither on the vine—she had a point. She had also further weakened a Taoiseach who was coming under increasing pressure.

The damage inflicted on Lynch's leadership by the farm levy and PAYE controversies was added to by a disastrous result in the first direct elections to the European Parliament in June. The Fianna Fáil vote dropped from the 51 per cent gained in the 1977 general election to 35 per cent, and the party that had predicted it would win eight of the fifteen seats won five. There were two stunning victories for independent candidates. Neil Blaney topped the poll in Connacht-Ulster, while in Munster T. J. Maher, chairperson of the Irish Agricultural Organisation Society, which represented the country's agricultural co-ops, won the highest vote in the country.

There was also a bizarre distraction involving Lynch's old political ally Patrick Hillery. For several months there had been rumours in political and media circles that 'the President of Ireland would resign because his wife was about to end their marriage because of his extra-marital affairs with two unnamed women.'[79] It has been suggested that this was 'not a case of malicious gossip but a deliberate invention designed to smear a leading public figure.'[80] In any case, the whispering campaign reached a height at the end of September, when 'the Government Information Service was deluged by queries from journalists about the President's impending resignation.'[81]

The result was that on 3 October, Hillery gave to seven political journalists what has been described as 'the most dramatic and sensational media briefing ever given by an Irish head of state.'[82] This may have been counter-productive, as most people were probably unaware of the story until Seán Duignan's report on the RTE television news.[83] Hillery himself had 'a strong suspicion' that Haughey was behind the rumours, as part of some Machiavellian plot, but no proof for this has ever been forthcoming.[84] The apparently false rumours fizzled out; but they can only have added to Lynch's growing siege mentality.

He was also greatly upset by the killing on 27 August of 79-year-old Lord Louis Mountbatten, a former Viceroy of India and uncle of Queen Elizabeth's husband. Since the early 1970s he had holidayed every summer at Classiebawn Castle in Mullaghmore, Co. Sligo, close to Bundoran on Donegal Bay. He, and the Gardaí, were well aware of the risks. 'Bundoran was a popular resort with Derry folk, and inevitably the summer crowd enjoying a vacation break would include IRA members and sympathisers who would be bound to hear of Mountbatten's presence and might be tempted to strike a spectacular blow against the British Royal Family.'[85]

But, though repeatedly warned, 'he adopted a fairly cavalier approach to his own personal security.'[86] On the fatal Monday morning, with a number of family members, he boarded his 27-foot fishing boat. As it pulled out, observed by a Garda car, a bomb concealed on board was detonated by remote control. Mountbatten was killed instantly, as were his fourteen-year-old grandson Nicholas Knatchbull and fifteen-year-old Paul Maxwell from Enniskillen, who had been working on the boat as a summer job. A fourth victim, Mountbatten's daughter's 83-year-old mother-in-law, died in hospital.[87]

Lynch issued a statement that described Mountbatten as 'a man of great courage' with 'a remarkable record of service to mankind.' He described the perpetrators as 'relentlessly and invidiously proving to be the real enemies of Ireland.'[88]

> The killing caused a wave of disgust, anger and disbelief. Mountbatten was 79 years old and universally honoured. His long military career had never brought him near Ireland. As a symbol of colonial oppression he was hopelessly inappropriate, having presided over India's secession from the empire.[89]

Nevertheless the IRA saw the killing as a propaganda victory, particularly as later the same day two bombs killed eighteen British soldiers near Warrenpoint, Co. Down. From their point of view the assassination of Mountbatten 'was designed to drag the world's attention back to the Irish problem. It was also intended to give heart to the movement, recovering from a morale-draining period of arrests and convictions.'[90] An IRA statement said that 'the British Army acknowledge that after 10 years of war it cannot defeat us but yet the British government continue with the oppression of our people and the torture of our comrades in the H Blocks. Well, for that we will tear out their sentimental, imperialist heart.'[91]

On 23 November, Thomas McMahon, a carpenter from Carrickmacross, Co. Monaghan, was given a life sentence at the Special Criminal Court for his part in the Mullaghmore bombing. He had been arrested when Garda James Lohan had considered him to be acting suspiciously when stopped at a roadblock in Granard, and was in custody when the bomb went off.[92] Francis McGirl from Ballinamore, Co. Leitrim (a nephew of the senior IRA figure and former Sinn Féin TD John Joe McGirl), who had been driving the car, was acquitted.

The bombing led to demands from the new British Government, led by Margaret Thatcher, for increased security concessions by the Irish Government. The Taoiseach attended the state funeral for Mountbatten at Westminster Abbey after which TV pictures showed him visibly moved and borne down by a welter of accusatory ceremonial occasioned by assassins from his own country. He later attended a difficult meeting with Mrs Thatcher, at which increased Anglo-Irish security co-operation was agreed.[93]

Given the context in which the meeting occurred, Lynch was in a difficult position. The Government press secretary, Frank Dunlop, recalled that Thatcher

> was incensed that Ireland was doing nothing, in her view, to police the border ... that we were refusing to extradite terrorists for crimes committed in other jurisdictions . . . and that we were in effect harbouring and providing safe haven for murderers. Nobody in the Irish delegation was expecting a tirade of such vehemence, and Lynch, who at this stage had lost the fire in his stomach on matters of this sort, was slow to reply. Thatcher saw his silence as agreement, tacit or otherwise, with her point of view.[94]

The perception that Lynch had made security concessions to the British would further damage his standing among his party's backbenchers, and would lead to another disciplinary crisis. Things finally unravelled during a few disastrous days in November. On the 7th he went to the United States. On the same day voting took place in two by-elections, one in his own constituency of Cork City, the other just up the road in Cork North-East. The result scarcely seemed in doubt, as there were 'hardly two other constituencies in the entire country more favourably disposed towards Fianna Fáil than these two. Almost certainly the Fianna Fáil vote will drop but hardly to the extent of endangering either seat.'[95] At the general election two years previously Lynch alone had amassed more votes than all the other parties put together in the Cork City constituency.

The results were startling. In Cork North-East, Myra Barry, a daughter of the sitting Fine Gael TD, Dick Barry, topped the poll, as Fianna Fáil's vote dropped by 12 per cent. In the Taoiseach's own constituency the Fianna Fáil vote fell by 23 per cent, and Liam Burke of Fine Gael took the seat.

To this rejection by the voters Lynch added a self-inflicted wound. In Washington he told journalists that 'an air corridor along the border between Ireland and Northern Ireland was part of the improved security arrangements that he had worked out with Mrs Thatcher following the murder of Lord Mountbatten.'[96] This was political dynamite. The British had been seeking permission to 'overfly the border in an air corridor extending five kilometres on either side of the border while in pursuit of suspected terrorists.'[97] Some of Lynch's opponents suspected that he had granted this permission, though this was 'alien to Fianna Fáil's republican tenets and unsavoury in the eyes of the Irish public generally.'[98] At a meeting of the parliamentary party on 24 October, Tom McEllistrim had asked 'if the Taoiseach and the government had given permission to the British to overfly the border, and he moved that if this was so that the permission should be withdrawn.'[99] Lynch told him that, 'as of now, the British have not permission to overfly the border.'[100]

Dr Bill Loughnane of Co. Clare pressed Lynch further. 'Do you mean when you say that there will be no infringement of sovereignty that the Irish government will not allow the British Army to cross the border either on land or in the air?'[101] 'The British Army will not be allowed across the border,' Lynch replied, and McEllistrim withdrew his motion.[102]

Lynch's comments in Washington appeared to show that he had misled the party. Loughnane told the *Irish Independent*:

> If he said what he is reported to have said in the U.S., then that was a false statement to us. When he returns, I am going to demand that he comes clean and tells us the truth. Will the British Army be allowed to cross the border into the Republic, or will they not?[103]

Lynch rang George Colley and demanded that he call a meeting to remove the party whip from Loughnane. Colley called the meeting but was unable to push through the disciplinary measure. It was at this meeting that 'it became clear that Lynch had lost the confidence of a large minority of the Fianna Fáil Parliamentary Party.'[104] The endgame had begun.

> When Lynch returned from the U.S. there was an atmosphere of incredible tension in Fianna Fáil. He went to one parliamentary party meeting saying that he had heard stories of caucus meetings and asked who was involved. Only Pádraig Flynn stood up publicly to admit his role.[105]

It didn't matter. Lynch's position had become untenable.

At first he planned to resign in the new year, but he stepped down on 5 December, apparently because he thought this might benefit Colley in the inevitable leadership contest. Lynch had led the party for thirteen years and been Taoiseach in all but three of them. One of the ironies of his departure was that it left Fianna Fáil exactly where it had been when he came in: facing a leadership contest between Haughey and Colley. In 1966 'the rivalry threatened to tear the party apart, so much so that Lemass stepped in to persuade Jack Lynch to stand as a compromise candidate.'[106]

This time the possible compromise candidates, Desmond O'Malley and Michael O'Kennedy, decided against standing and left the field clear for a contest between two men whose destinies seemed linked ever since they had been classmates at St Joseph's Christian Brothers' School in Fairview, Dublin. In their twenties the men had been friends, and it was Colley who introduced Haughey to Fianna Fáil. When Haughey won a Dáil seat at the fourth attempt, in Dublin North-East in 1957, it was at the expense of George's father, Harry. At the following election, in 1961, Colley joined Haughey as a TD for the same constituency, which they would share until 1969, when Colley moved to Dublin North-Central. When Haughey was sacked from the Government in May 1970 it was his old classmate who replaced him as Minister for Finance.[107]

Colley's image was more patrician than that of his driven rival, but in reality his 'political ambitions were, if anything, even more intense than those of Haughey.'[108] That he was still seen as a possible leader in 1979 spoke volumes about the degree to which Haughey was distrusted, particularly within the Government. After all, it was Colley who was largely responsible for botching the farm levy and alienating the PAYE workers, severely exacerbating the backbench dissent that would drive Lynch from office. At the time of the tax protests it was felt that 'one of the most obvious casualties of all this must be Mr Colley's ambition to lead Fianna Fáil in succession to Jack Lynch'[109] An opinion poll in May showed him with a 53 per cent disapproval rating.

Haughey, on the other hand, had an approval rating of 75 per cent, 2 points higher than Lynch.[110] And this was despite his unimpressive performance in piloting through the Dáil the Health (Family Planning) Bill, which made Ireland 'the only country in Western Europe where condoms were a prescription item.'[111] If the bill 'was a great disappointment to those who felt Haughey was a liberal on social issues,' there were cynical reasons of political calculation for this.[112] Before bringing in legislation he engaged in a lengthy process of consultation with interested groups, some of them of the fundamentalist persuasion. Haughey told the Dáil that

> it is clear to me from my consultations that majority opinion in this country does not favour [the] widespread uncontrolled availability of contraceptives. It emerged clearly that the majority view of those consulted was that any legislation to be introduced should provide for a more restrictive situation in relation to the availability of contraceptives than that which exists by law at present.[113]

The very existence of the family planning clinics that had sprung up in response to the Supreme Court decision in the McGee case would be placed in jeopardy by an amendment to the bill tabled by Haughey himself, which 'would require the presence of a pharmacist and the provision of a full-scale chemist's shop in any clinic that was to sell contraception'—an extremely difficult provision for the cash-starved clinics to observe.[114] The central section of the bill

> required that those seeking to purchase any kind of contraceptive, even condoms and spermicides, had to get a prescription from a doctor, who in turn had to ensure, 'when giving the prescription or authorisation, that the person required the contraceptives for the purpose, *bona fide*, of family planning or for adequate medical reasons or in appropriate circumstances.'[115]

The Irish Medical Association was not particularly pleased to see its members appointed as keepers of national morality and insisted that 'the prescription or authorisation of condoms is not a medical function.'[116] The minister's response was a masterpiece of unctuousness. He did not, he said, 'want a situation in which the means of artificial contraception would be widely available throughout the community without any form of control. Doctors are in the best position to exercise that control.' If they did so 'it would be a historic decision, an altruistic one for which they will merit the gratitude of future generations.'[117]

Haughey famously described the bill as 'an Irish solution to an Irish problem,' a perhaps unconscious echo of the religious right's belief that the country was a shining exception in a godless world.[118] How else could family planning be seen as a specifically Irish problem?

The solution did not impress everyone. The Labour Party TD John Horgan described the bill as 'a piece of political hypocrisy, second only to Pontius Pilate . . . a monument to the Nervous Nellie in Irish society.'[119] *Hibernia* thundered: 'This is a sectarian bill with sectarian intent. It is the product of weak politicians bending in front of the most reactionary element in Irish society today.'[120] The minister would not have been particularly worried about these criticisms. Under Haughey, Fianna Fáil would court the Nervous Nellies and the 'reactionary element' by positioning itself as the party of Catholic morality, in contrast to Garret FitzGerald's mildly liberal Fine Gael, especially when that party found itself in coalition with the Labour Party. The Health (Family Planning) Bill not only sought to restrict contraception but made favourable mention of 'natural family planning', a pet cause of the likes of Prof. John Bonner, who, 'along with members of the National Association of the Ovulation Method of Ireland (yet another organisation with strong links to the

Knights, founded in 1978),' met Haughey 'to impress upon him the deadly characteristics of the Pill and IUD and the tremendous success of the Billings Method.'[121]

'Natural family planning', which included systems based on abstinence and the measurement of fertility indicators such as the level of cervical mucus and the length of menstrual cycles, was enjoying something of a vogue, particularly among the Catholic clergy, following the Pope's reaffirmation of the church's ban on 'artificial contraception' in the encyclical *Humanae Vitae* in 1968. At this remove we may be inclined to agree with the observation of Dr Patrick Leahy, a Ballyfermot GP who would find himself in frequent conflict with the likes of Prof. Bonner.

> All this fucking nonsense about control, self-control, the rhythm method, well it's ridiculous. If the sexual act means anything it's a mutual thing, between two people with an emotional content in the here and now. Christ, the thought of sitting down with thermometers and charts and mucus samples saying 'we'll have sex next Tuesday', it's ridiculous. A crazy situation. The 'Natural' family planning method has me boggled. How sticking a thermometer up your rectum can be natural I don't know.[122]

Even after all the pandering, the bill remained too liberal for the Minister for Agriculture, Jim Gibbons, who left the Dáil chamber rather than vote for it. To the chagrin of many within Fianna Fáil who had supported the legislation, Lynch refused to discipline Gibbons. Gibbons was a social conservative, but his decision had extra political resonance, as he had been the chief prosecution witness at the Arms Trial, where his evidence had conflicted with that of Haughey.

The race to succeed Lynch seemed too close to predict. Both men were confident, in fact over-confident. Haughey 'totted up his likely support and concluded that he would get 58 votes to Colley's 24.' Colley, Séamus Brennan remembered, 'informed Jack Lynch that he had the votes and all would be well. The impression he gave me was that if you wanted to lead Fianna Fáil, you didn't canvass backbenchers.'[123]

Michael O'Kennedy and Brian Lenihan were the only members of the Cabinet to vote for Haughey; but the support of the backbenchers saw him home by 44 votes to 38. A mere nine years after being sacked from the Government, and put on trial, the 54-year-old Haughey became Fianna Fáil's fourth leader.

The mood in the Colley camp was one of shock. Séamus Brennan, the mastermind of the general election landslide two years previously, was 'devastated, actually. I just couldn't believe it.'[124] After the count, Frank

Dunlop met Senator Des Hanafin. Hanafin 'would not believe me when I told him that Charlie had won. He kept saying, "Oh, my God, the party is ruined. Ruined."'[125]

There was even a momentary possibility that the Colley supporters might break completely with precedent and refuse to vote for Haughey in the Dáil as Taoiseach. Bobby Molloy recalled:

> Quite a large number were seriously upset at the notion that they were going to have to serve in a party led by Charlie Haughey. There was a meeting held after the Parliamentary Party election attended by a large number of people, TDs and ministers, and a number supported the notion of voting against Haughey as Taoiseach when it came to the vote in the house. But I argued very strongly against that. I argued on the basis of party loyalty that, as democrats, we had to accept the result.[126]

Instead the fireworks on 11 December were provided by Garret FitzGerald, who launched an extraordinary attack on Haughey.

> I must speak not only for the opposition but for many in Fianna Fáil who may not be free to say what they believe in or express their deep fears for the future of this country under the proposed leadership. People who are not free to reveal what they know and what led them to oppose this man . . . He comes with a flawed pedigree. His motives can be judged ultimately only by God, but we cannot ignore the fact that he differs from all his predecessors in that those motives have been and are widely impugned, most notably, but by no means exclusively, by people within his own party . . . They and others, both in and out of public life, have attributed to him an overweening ambition, which they do not see as a simple emanation of a desire to serve but rather as a wish to dominate, even to own, the state.[127]

There was similar fevered language from Noël Browne, who described Haughey as a cross between the former Portuguese dictator António Salazar and Richard Nixon. The wild language, with its invocations of danger, fear and prison camps, heralded a new era in Irish party politics, where the questionable nature of Haughey's character would become the opposition's most potent electoral weapon.

Haughey's first Government saw demotions for Martin O'Donoghue, Bobby Molloy, Denis Gallagher and Jim Gibbons. In came Albert Reynolds as Minister for Posts and Telegraphs, Ray MacSharry as Minister for Agriculture, Dr Michael Woods as Minister for Health, Paddy Power as Minister for Fisheries and Máire Geoghegan-Quinn as Minister for the

Gaeltacht. Not only did O'Donoghue, whose reputation as an economic mastermind had been a casualty of the 1979 downturn, lose his job as Minister for Economic Planning but the department itself was abolished. A couple of days after his sacking

> Haughey's Garda driver arrived at the ex-minister's home in Rathgar and handed in a strange parcel. When O'Donoghue and his wife opened the parcel they found two dead ducks inside, along with a short message from Haughey, 'shot on my estate this morning.'[128]

Colley remained in the Government, having 'informed Haughey that he would serve only under certain conditions; that he would have to remain as Tánaiste, that he would have to be satisfied with who were to be appointed Ministers for Justice and Defence and that he would have to be satisfied with the overall structure of the government. Haughey agreed on all points.'[129] Gerry Collins remained Minister for Justice, Pádraig Faulkner became Minister for Defence, and Colley became Minister for Energy.

There would be no honeymoon for Haughey. On 21 December, at a Fianna Fáil function in Dublin, Colley laid bare the tensions within the party when he contradicted Haughey's statement that he had promised him loyalty and support. Haughey

> called Colley in and exacted a qualified loyalty pledge from him. The Tánaiste gave Haughey loyalty as Taoiseach but not as leader of Fianna Fáil. An uneasy truce prevailed.[130]

———

Even if there still seemed something slightly provisional about his leadership of Fianna Fáil, Haughey would be one of the few Irish people who could look back on 1979 with satisfaction. Another would be Josie Airey, whose quest for justice ended on 9 October in Strasbourg, when 'for the first time in the history of the state Ireland was judged guilty before an international court of having violated the human rights of one of its citizens.'[131] The European Court of Human Rights ruled that 'Ireland had violated article six of the convention by depriving Mrs Airey, a mother of four, of an effective right of access to the High Court to seek a judicial separation from her husband.'[132] It further decided that 'Ireland was also in breach of article eight to the convention by not guaranteeing Mrs Airey her right to respect for private and family life. Not having been put in a position in which she could apply to the High Court, she was unable to seek recognition in law for her *de facto* separation from her husband.'[133]

The legal battle had lasted seven years, but Josie Airey, who died in 2002 at the age of 70, is recognised as 'undoubtedly the most influential figure in securing the introduction of a civil legal aid scheme in Ireland.'[134] She had been a victim of the refusal of Irish society, and in particular of the Government, to recognise the complex realities of personal life. It could be argued that, although the civil legal aid system remains far from ideal, more good flowed from the fight for justice of this former market trader from Cork than from the visit that had enraptured the country in the year she finally won her case.

Chapter 9 ⟶

THE TOTALITY OF RELATIONSHIPS

1980

The new decade was only nine days old when Charles Haughey appeared on television to tender a grim warning to the country.

> I wish to talk to you this evening about the state of the nation's affairs, and the picture I have to paint is not, unfortunately a happy one. The figures which are now becoming available to us show one thing very clearly. As a community we are living way beyond our means. I do not mean that everyone in the community is living too well. Clearly many are not and have barely enough to get by. But taking us all together, we have been living at a rate which is simply not justified by the amount of goods and services we are producing. To make up the difference, we have been borrowing enormous amounts of money, borrowing at a rate which just cannot continue.[1]

What is striking, in retrospect, is how confident Haughey looks. Subsequent political pressures would mean that his most routine pronouncements took on an embattled air. But at this stage, mere months into his reign as Taoiseach, he could still manage to look like the able and decisive leader his supporters felt was needed to supplant Jack Lynch. 'Mr Haughey did a superb job within the scope of the medium, and came across as big brother—not Big Brother—with elegance and charm,' wrote the *Irish Times* television critic, Fergus Pyle, who astutely noted that with the broadcast

> Mr Haughey was establishing himself as the leader of the nation—the first time it had been done in the post-television era in Ireland—in exactly the same way as Mr de Valera did at countless street corners over interminable years, Mr Lemass did by standing in the Shadow for an unconscionable period of time, and Mr Lynch by mild manners and patience, none of which Mr Haughey has time

or disposition for. It was a personal political broadcast in which the binding of the wounds within Fianna Fáil was at least as important as winning the hearts and minds of the FUE and ICTU.[2]

The personal tone of Haughey's speech set the tone for the year, when taking a political position seemed to become a matter of making a judgement on Haughey's integrity rather than that of the Government. 1980 was,

> beyond a shadow of a doubt, Mr Charles J. Haughey's year. From start to finish, he was, more than most holders of his office have been, at the centre of things: the economy and industrial relations, Anglo-Irish intrigue and the Northern conflict, political controversy. He succeeded in having politicians and observers . . . judge every event by reference to its impact on him, his career and, specifically, his chances of re-election.[3]

This cult of personality was obvious at the Fianna Fáil ard-fheis in February, when Haughey

> was given an ecstatic welcome by more than 5,000 delegates. He was piped into the RDS by the ITGWU brass band to the strains of 'A Nation Once Again.' In the front row, people expressed their devotion with an almost religious intensity, erecting little shrines to Haughey and displaying photographs on posters and tables they had pillaged from the press area.[4]

He even found time to make an appearance on stage at the Siamsa Cois Laoi music festival in Cork, where he sang 'Monto' with the Dubliners.

Haughey has subsequently been indicted on two charges in connection with his television address: that of personal hypocrisy and that of political inconsistency.

There isn't really a defence against the first charge now that we know that the man who explained that the nation 'must undertake only the things which we can afford' owed Allied Irish Bank more than £1 million at the time.

> By the middle of January 1980, with Haughey now Taoiseach, he authorised his crooked accountant Des Traynor to finalise a settlement . . . the debt was now £1.143 million. AIB agreed to take £750,000 in settlement. Haughey was getting a £390,000 gift. The bank left a notional debt of £110,000 on the books, to which interest would not apply, which Haughey was to clear as 'a matter of honour.' This, of course, was never paid off. The bank, however, didn't bear the brunt . . . The £390,000 could be written off as a bad debt and claimed against tax liabilities. As ever, the taxpayer would

pick up the tab. The £750,000 to settle the debt was channelled through Guinness Mahon, the private bank of which Haughey's crooked accountant friend Des Traynor was a de facto chief executive and in which Haughey now opened an account.[5]

It's intriguing to ponder what effect Haughey's own financial position might have had on the economic policies he followed during his first term. Could it be that he felt hypocritical prescribing fiscal rectitude, given his own personal position, and that this lessened his resolve in taking tough financial measures? Could it even be that a man who had proved so adept at dodging a day of reckoning with the banks thought there might be some way in which the country too could wriggle out of paying its bills in full?

Dermot Nally, secretary to the Government from 1980 to 1993, noted that

> if you want a prescription for what should have been done I think you would find it in the speech that was made by Charlie Haughey in January 1980. What happened afterwards was a direct contradiction of what he said in the speech which always puzzled me.[6]

Perhaps the explanation may lie in the fact that cutting public spending might not have been Haughey's political priority. While it is the section urging financial restraint that is best remembered, most of the speech was about the vexed question of labour relations. After the industrial chaos of 1979, Haughey declared that there was

> one thing above all else which we can do to help get the situation right and which is entirely within our control. I refer to industrial relations. Any further serious interruption in production, or in the provision of essential services, in 1980 would be a major disaster. Strikes, go slows, works to rule, stoppages in key industries and essential services, were too often a feature of life in 1979. They caused suffering and hardship: at times it looked as if we were becoming one of those countries where basic services could not be relied upon to operate as part of normal life. Immediately following my election as Taoiseach, I received countless messages from all over the country from people in all walks of life, appealing to me to do something about this situation.[7]

He went so far as to suggest that improved industrial relations might hold the key to economic recovery.

> I am asking for a universal commitment to industrial peace in 1980. I am asking every worker and employer, every trade union, every employers' organisation, every farmer and farming organisation,

every housewife, in fact every individual citizen, to play a part in ending this humiliating, destructive industrial strife and putting in its place discussion, negotiation and peaceful settlements.[8]

A Taoiseach preoccupied with the restoration of peace on the labour front was never going to approve the kind of harsh cutbacks and wage restrictions that would have seen more rather than less industrial trouble. His strategy did seem to bear fruit as regards labour relations. The number of days lost through strikes fell from 1.47 million the previous year to 412,000, the lowest since 1975.[9] The only problem was that this outbreak of relative peace had no effect on a worsening economic situation, one that set the tone for the depressed decade to follow. 1980 was, put simply,

> a year of recession . . . the stark facts of the year stand out clearly. Unemployment, rising relentlessly, has become perhaps the biggest single social and economic problem that this country faces . . . However the state of the economy rises and falls, the number of people out of work—and more seriously the number of young people who have never known what it is to have a job—goes on growing.[10]

It was the year in which a dream died.

> The hopes raised by EEC entry in 1973 that the Irish economy had embarked on an ever expanding growth path began to appear decidedly tarnished during 1980, a year in which those heady aspirations ran up against the cold hard facts of reality. For the first time since Ireland's take-off in the 1960s, the steam began to run out of the economy.[11]

By October 'there were 111,000 officially out of work, a rise of some 28,000 on the unemployment figures for October 1979.'[12] But the Irish economy was like

> a bathtub where the tap has been left on, but the plug has not been inserted. At the tap end the Industrial Development Authority continues to pump in new jobs at a rapid pace. But its efforts are dissipated by the even greater number of existing jobs that are disappearing down the plughole.[13]

One of the reasons was an increase in export penetration, from 29 per cent in 1977 to 38 per cent in 1980, which led to a lack of competitiveness for native firms in the home market.[14] It was also a disastrous year for farmers, who suffered

> the biggest crash for decades in Irish agriculture . . . farm incomes dropped seriously, the livestock population was reduced by 5%, milk production dropped for the first time in 15 years, the cost of inputs rose and the rate of product price increases stayed static or fell.[15]

There was even a return of that old seventies favourite, rampant inflation. By June it had risen above 20 per cent for the first time since 1979.

> The impact of higher oil prices is evident in the rise of 12.9% in the price of fuel and light to the consumer in the quarter ending in May. In the past year fuel and light costs have jumped by 51.1%, the fastest rising component of the Consumer Price Index. Oil prices resulted also in a jump in the cost of transport of 9.6% between February and May. The cost of transport has gone up by 29.6% in the past 12 months.[16]

There had been speculation that Haughey might be inclined towards the kind of monetarist policies employed by Margaret Thatcher's Government to bring down inflation in Britain. But in the month before his Government's first budget he received a timely reminder of trade union power. On 22 January

> an estimated 700,000 people in 37 centres throughout the Republic took to the streets to impress on the government their demands for reform of the PAYE tax system. In Dublin alone the Gardaí estimated that 300,000 took part in the march . . . Stewards said that between 350,000 and 400,000 had joined the demonstration. The march organisers claimed a turnout of 60,000 in Cork; 50–60,000 in Limerick; 30,000 in Galway and smaller attendances at the other demonstrations which were held in venues in every county in the Republic.[17]

This time the ICTU had called the march rather than opposed it, apparently agreeing with the contention of Sam Nolan, secretary of Dublin Council of Trade Unions, that Haughey 'must choose between justice and equality for the PAYE wage and salary earners and the protection of the wealthy in our society.'[18]

The size and fervour of the demonstrations left Haughey with little choice, and the budget of the new Minister for Finance, Michael O'Kennedy, on 27 February finally offered some respite to PAYE workers, with an increase in allowances and a widening of tax bands. Allowances were increased from £1,115 to £1,515 for a single person and from £2,230 to £3,030 for a married couple, while a single person now had to earn £9,000 per annum before they paid the top rate.[19] For once, at budget time,

> farmers and self-employed fared less well than PAYE employees. The notional tax system has been dropped. Farmers must now pay tax on the basis of their accounts. An additional 9,000 farmers have been brought into the tax net . . . The self-employed will not receive

the increase in tax allowances afforded to PAYE employees. In addition, they will have to pay their tax more promptly, in one instalment rather than two.[20]

These reforms took the heat out of the PAYE protest movement and placated the unions, as did another 'national understanding', which the Federated Union of Employers accepted 'with deep reluctance and only after much cajoling and persuasion.'[21]

Much of the economic malaise was not the Taoiseach's fault but rather the consequences of Martin O'Donoghue's policy failures and such external factors as the rise in oil prices. But Haughey's growing tendency towards indecision was most clearly illustrated by what the *Washington Post* called the Donlon Affair. Seán Donlon, Ireland's ambassador to the United States, was

> an immensely impressive diplomat, with an astonishing network of contacts. A book purporting to list those with the greatest influence in Washington placed the President (first Jimmy Carter, then Ronald Reagan) at number one and Donlon at number twelve . . . He was on intimate terms with the chief Irish-American politicians, led by the 'Four Horsemen,' Senator Edward Kennedy, Senator Daniel Patrick Moynihan, Representative Tip O'Neill and Governor Hugh Carey of New York.[22]

Yet for all their power and influence the Four Horsemen were not the only representatives of Irish-American opinion. There was a gaping divide between the Four Horsemen on the one hand and Noraid, the Irish National Caucus and other republican groups rejecting Dublin policy. Donlon and his officials in Washington

> divided their time between cultivating and encouraging one part of Irish-America and discouraging or circumventing another part of Irish-America. They found themselves in particular conflict with Congressman Biaggi and his adhoc committee on Capitol Hill, a group close to Noraid, which had been explicitly denounced by Mr Lynch when Taoiseach.[23]

Congressman Mario Biaggi had been *persona non grata* with the Lynch Government, but there was an indication that attitudes were changing.[24] In July came news that the Government was planning to move Donlon to the ambassadorship to the United Nations. Haughey apparently believed that

> Donlon had exceeded his brief in his exertions against the Irish National Caucus and that it was no part of the duties of an Irish diplomat to be frustrating the efforts of an American congressman

to enquire into the iniquities of the British administration in Northern Ireland.'[25]

This drew a furious reaction from the Four Horsemen, who

privately condemned Mr Haughey for his reported decision and are scathing in their criticism of his motives . . . In the past these four very powerful Irish American politicians sat down with members of the Irish government and attempted to determine the best course to pursue with the eventual hope of Irish unity. They sought to cut the flow of arms and money from the u.s. to Ireland . . . now it appears to them that their efforts are not being tolerated.[26]

The quartet had in effect delivered an ultimatum to Mr Haughey.

They would withdraw their support of the Irish government's policy on Northern Ireland if it seemed that Mr Haughey was relying on forces they consider antagonistic to them. Mr Donlon became the test case.[27]

A spooked Haughey reversed his decision and issued a denial that there had ever been plans to move Donlon. Nobody believed him. It had been 'the most pathetic collapse of leadership that has occurred in living memory.'[28]

In their glee over the humiliation of Haughey and their gratitude for the blow dealt to republican supporters in the United States, the leader of Fine Gael, Garret FitzGerald, and the leader of the Labour Party, Frank Cluskey, seemed to have missed the important point that there was

one aspect of the 'Donlon Affair' more than any other that may disturb Irish citizens concerned about their country's right to run its own affairs. That is the apparent veto power exerted by the 'Four Horsemen' over a decision that strictly speaking, belongs to the Irish government and no-one else, about who should represent Ireland in Washington.[29]

The Donlon affair was perhaps the principal cause of a ferocious attack on the new Taoiseach by Vincent Browne, then editor of *Magill.*

Those who waited for ten years for the new beginning with Charlie Haughey must have begun to wonder by now what the long wait was all about. In the seven months since he has become Taoiseach, Charles Haughey has failed to make any significant impact on any of the issues on which he was most looked to for leadership and change; the economy, the North and security. But worse than that, he has revealed himself as a weak leader who mistakes public relations gimmicks for decisiveness and courage.[30]

Browne made life more uncomfortable still for Haughey when he marked the tenth anniversary of the Arms Crisis by printing a series of articles that shed new light on the old controversy. The articles grew out of meetings between Browne and Peter Berry, Secretary of the Department of Justice at the time of the Arms Trial, whose papers were used by *Magill*. Browne explained that, after he had written articles on the Arms Crisis for the *Sunday Independent* in 1975,

> Mr Berry was anxious to talk about the events of those years, 1969 and 1970, and I visited him subsequently and had a series of discussions about the Arms Crisis with him.[31]

Browne found that the crisis was as sensitive a subject as it had ever been when

> only one of about twenty printers approached in connection with the printing of the section containing the Arms Crisis article agreed to print and this printer hadn't the capacity to do it. Eventually we arranged to have the section printed in England and our intention was to ship that section back here and have it bound and collated with the two sections printed by our usual printers ... The company which was engaged to do the collating opted out at the last minute and we had to ship the two sections from here to London, collate them with the third section printed in Oxfordshire and then ship the lot back to Ireland. Both our regular distributors refused to handle the issue and we were forced to make ad hoc distribution arrangements with freelance distributors which proved chaotic.[32]

These obstacles notwithstanding, the articles were a journalistic sensation and established *Magill* as the leading current affairs magazine of the day. Among the conclusions were that 'Mr Haughey was involved in the attempted importation of arms from the outset,' that 'Mr Lynch was first informed of the arms plot on October 17 1969 by Mr Peter Berry, Secretary of the Department of Justice—not six months later as he has repeatedly stated,' and that 'Mr Neil Blaney was the instigator and motivator of the entire enterprise.'[33] The articles were not unsympathetic to Haughey, declaring that 'the real scandal of the arms crisis was not what Haughey did but what was done to him and the other defendants' and suggesting that 'a series of decisions ... seem to suggest that the provision of arms for the defence of the Catholic community in Northern Ireland would not have been inconsistent with government policy.'[34] There were harsher judgements on Lynch:

> Having had the attempted arms importation fully investigated and having approached the two ministers involved, he informed the Government that the affair was closed and he let it be known that

he was not going to fire the two men. Then, solely on the basis of a threat by Liam Cosgrave to raise the matter in the Dáil, he fired the two men and, worse than that, he allowed them to be prosecuted in the courts.[35]

And on Blaney:

> You organised and co-ordinated the entire enterprise from the outset but when the crunch came you saved your own hide and refused to come out and defend the operation as a whole when the people you involved were dragged through the courts.[36]

Haughey was described as 'silly', 'reckless' and 'callous'. The articles added to the whiff of sulphur that surrounded him, and they would be expertly capitalised upon by Fine Gael in elections to come.[37]

With so little going right for him on the domestic front, Haughey pinned all his political hopes on the possibility of the political breakthrough on the North that had evaded his predecessors. He hewed to a traditional republican line at the ard-fheis when describing Northern Ireland as 'a failed political entity, artificially sustained,' where 'violence and repression were inevitable.' But he surprised his political opponents with his success in apparently building a good working relationship with Margaret Thatcher.[38]

Haughey famously presented Thatcher with a Georgian silver teapot when they met in London on 21 May. Perhaps it helped set the tone for a meeting that he called 'one of the friendliest and most open of my political career.'[39] He declared himself happy that Thatcher 'is now prepared to give the problem of Northern Ireland the kind of attention once devoted to reaching a settlement in Zimbabwe.'[40] They agreed to develop 'new and closer political co-operation between their governments and to hold regular meetings to review progress,' which would be held twice a year.[41] The unexpected success of the meeting meant that an aura of high expectation would surround the meeting between the two Governments later in the year.

One obstacle to this was the worsening situation in the H-blocks and in Armagh Prison, where twenty-two women had launched their own no-wash protest after alleged mistreatment at the hands of male prison officers. The plight of the prisoners was brought dramatically home by *On the Blanket,* a book written by Tim Pat Coogan, editor of the *Irish Press,* containing interviews with prisoners, their families and prison officers and first-hand accounts of the conditions in Long Kesh and Armagh. The book was described by James Downey as an

> extraordinary account of an extraordinary thing . . . From the very

first sentence, itself a model of the genre, it grips as it horrifies. One would have to be extremely insensitive or extremely prejudiced to fail to be moved by it.[42]

The book was a best-seller, and it remains one of the finest books written by an Irish journalist. Coogan's descriptions of the prisoners are jolting.

> They were aged 21 or 22 . . . when the cell door opened they both looked frightened and looked anxiously at us for a moment. They were pale and naked except for a blanket draped over their shoulders. They stood silently, fear hardening into defiance, I felt, as we looked at the cell. It was covered in excrement almost to the ceiling on all four walls. In one corner there was a pile of rotting, blue moulded food and excrement.[43]

The poet Paul Durcan, an outspoken critic of the IRA, described his shock at 'the irrefutable evidence of the Nazi-like behaviour of the British government in Northern Ireland in general and in Long Kesh in particular . . . Their behaviour is bereft of any morality whatsoever.'[44] But the National H-Block Armagh Committee found it difficult to garner support for the prisoners

> from sectors of public life located outside the prisoners' family network and the narrow Sinn Féin base. Most organisations or public bodies with a relevant local or national focus were offered the opportunity to support the five demands . . . The list of refusals included all the main political parties in Ireland, the ICTU, the GAA and the Catholic Church . . . Those who got involved were of the Left: H-Block demonstrations were not noted for the attendance of the well-heeled and professional classes.[45]

The women's movement found itself divided over the issue of the prisoners after Nell McCafferty wrote an article in the *Irish Times* headed 'It is my belief that Armagh is a feminist issue.' Even by McCafferty's standards it was a hugely passionate piece of polemic, right from its famous opening sentence: 'There is menstrual blood on the walls of Armagh Jail in Northern Ireland.'[46] It continued:

> The 32 women on dirt strike there have not washed their bodies since February 8th 1980; they have used their cells as toilets; for over 200 days now they have lived amid their own excreta, urine and blood. The windows and spy-holes are boarded up. Flies and slugs grow fat as they grow thin. They eat, and sleep and sit in this dim electrically-lit filth . . . The consequences for these women, under these conditions, will be, at the least, urinary, pelvic and skin

infections. At worst, they face sterility and death.[47]

McCafferty concluded that 'it is my belief that Armagh is a feminist issue that demands our support.'[48]

The paper printed replies from several feminists who strongly disagreed with this conclusion. One claimed that 'the Provisionals are now turning the full weight of their publicity machine on the women in Armagh in the chauvinistic expectation that the plight of members of "the weaker sex" will produce a greater public outcry than is forthcoming for the men of H-Block.'[49]

———

National H-Block Armagh Committee member Miriam Daly was at first glance an unlikely republican figurehead. She is thanked in the preface to the magnificent *Ireland Since the Famine* by F. S. L. Lyons, who has since become a kind of patron saint of revisionist historians.

> She became a committee member of the Irish Labour History Society when it was founded in 1973 and organised its first symposium the following year in Belfast. She set up an extra-mural course in Labour History at Queen's which attracted (mainly Protestant) trade unionists.[50]

She had also been chairperson of the IRSP, though she left the party in 1979.[51] On 26 June she was in her house on the Andersonstown Road in Belfast when gunmen gained entry.

> Once inside, they cut the telephone wires and tied Miriam Daly hand and foot ... Putting a cushion to Miriam Daly's head they shot her five times with a 9mm semi-automatic pistol. The cushion deadened the sound of the shots. A short time later, her 10 year old daughter, back from school, found her mother lying dead in the hallway of their home.[52]

Daly's funeral in Swords, Co. Dublin, demonstrated her connections outside the world of republicanism. Among the mourners were Dónal Barrington, a High Court judge, Father F. X. Martin of UCD, and Rev. James McEvoy, professor of scholastic philosophy at Queen's University.[53]

Two other members of the IRSP, Ronald Bunting Junior and Noel Lyttle, and Councillor John Turnly of the Irish Independence Party (all three of them Protestants) were also murdered in 1980. In January the following year Bernadette McAliskey was severely wounded in an attack on her home by the UDA.

The systematic murdering of some of the H-Block Committee's most able members has led to speculation that

> their campaign led directly to the major hunger strikes of 1981 which galvanised support on an unprecedented scale. Could the British government have foreseen that and attempted to prevent it by encouraging one of its agencies, the UDA, to assassinate the political activists on the National H-Blocks Committee?[54]

The oration at Miriam Daly's graveside was given by her old IRSP colleague Osgur Breatnach, who had his conviction for allegedly taking part in the Sallins train robbery overturned by the Court of Criminal Appeal on 22 May, along with that of Brian McNally.

> The court found that, having steadfastly refused to speak and having made no admission, Breatnach allegedly suddenly confessed to the crime. The court also said that Breatnach's interrogation took place in 'what must be considered as the possibly menacing environment in an underground passageway in a Garda station . . . The court concluded that Breatnach's statements were not made voluntarily and that even if they were the circumstances in which they were taken did not pass the test of fairness. As there was no other evidence against Breatnach the Court quashed his 12 year sentence.[55]

In the case of McNally the court noted that

> at the time of McNally's alleged verbal statement he had been in custody for 44 hours and had denied any involvement in the robbery up to that point. Then, following very lengthy periods of interrogation in the small hours of the morning, the verbal statements were allegedly made. The court said that there were no circumstances that justified the Special Criminal Court in accepting such statements as evidence, that what McNally had undergone amounted to 'oppressive questioning.'[56]

News of the successful appeal prompted the men's fugitive co-defendant, Nicky Kelly, to return from America. Kelly 'was convinced I'd either be freed immediately or at worst be detained in custody until an appeal would be heard.'[57] The latter is what happened; but when the Court of Criminal Appeal heard his case

> they rejected the application, saying that Kelly had 'failed to show even the contemplation of dissatisfaction with his trial or the intention to challenge the verdict of any court at any time prior to 29th of May 1980.' Of his application, they said 'he has failed to adduce evidence of facts or circumstances to which his inaction can be attributed.' Basically the court was challenging his lawyers for not

presenting them with all the facts, as though they were attending an appeal hearing rather than making application for a right to appeal. The judgement was widely regarded as strange.[58]

Kelly would spend Christmas in Port Laoise. It would not be the last time he did so.

Public sympathy for jailed republicans, never high, was probably reduced further by the deaths of three gardaí in two separate incidents during the year. The first one was particularly shocking, as it involved the first multiple killing of members of the force since the IRA shot two gardaí dead in Rathgar, Dublin, on 16 August 1940.

On 7 August 1980 four gardaí from the Castlerea station, Derek O'Kelly, Michael O'Malley, John Morley and Henry Byrne, were responding to reports of a bank robbery in Ballaghaderreen, Co. Roscommon, when their car collided with that of the robbers at Shannon's Cross, near Loughglynn.

> The getaway car smashed into the patrol car on the right front side. The left door . . . opened and a tall, hooded man in a combat jacket got out. He was holding a shotgun . . . He pointed the gun at O'Kelly's head and the Garda ducked under the steering wheel. Without any warning, the gunman opened fire . . . Another gunman fired a burst of shots from the revolver into the patrol car, shattering the front windscreen and rear windows . . . The volley of bullets hit Garda Henry Byrne, who was sitting on the back seat.[59]

Byrne would die from his wounds. When Morley, armed with a submachine gun, set off in pursuit of the gunmen he was shot in the leg and bled to death. His last words were 'Say goodbye to my wife and kids for me.'[60] His status as a former football star added to the effect the killings had on the public.

Colm O'Shea and Patrick McCann were convicted of murder. A third man, Peter Pringle, was also convicted but was later freed on appeal. Their lack of verifiable republican connections prevented the two men from being freed under the Belfast Agreement, and at the time of writing they remain in prison.

There were no doubts about the republican connections of the man responsible for the third garda killing of the year. Peter Rogers was a Belfast IRA man who had participated in a famous escape from the prison ship *Maidstone* in Belfast Harbour in 1972. After his escape he moved to Co. Wexford, where he came into contact with Detective-Garda James Quaid, a former hurling star who had won an all-Ireland medal with Wexford in 1960.

One of Quaid's detective duties was to monitor the movements of known republicans. One of them was Peter Rogers . . . Detective James Quaid knew Peter Rogers well . . . On numerous occasions, detectives had taken Rogers in for questioning about paramilitary activities.[61]

On 13 October an armed gang robbed both the Allied Irish Bank and Bank of Ireland in Callan, Co. Kilkenny. At 10:30 p.m. Quaid and Garda Dónal Lyttleton were investigating the crime when they came across Rogers on a by-road between Wexford and Duncannon. Rogers had nothing to do with the robbery, but in his van were 83 pounds of gelignite, electronic detonators, four guns, decoders, mercury switches and delayed-action units. When the gardaí confronted Rogers he

> ordered the two detectives out of the van and into the nearby quarry at gunpoint, firing a shot over the heads. He asked the detectives to let him go so that way 'no-one would get hurt.' Quaid responded by pulling out his gun and ordering Rogers to give himself up. When he refused, Quaid opened fire.[62]

In the ensuing gun battle Quaid was struck by a bullet that severed an artery in his leg. He bled to death at the scene. Rogers, who had also been wounded, gave himself up to gardaí a few hours later. Like O'Shea, McCann and Pringle, he was sentenced to death, but the sentence was commuted to life imprisonment. On 22 December 1998 he was freed under the Belfast Agreement.

It wasn't just the Garda Síochána that suffered losses in 1980. Three members of the Defence Forces were killed while on peacekeeping duty in Lebanon. On 16 April, Private Stephen Griffin, who had been shot nine days earlier, died. Two days later Private Thomas Barrett, Private Derek Smallhorne and Private John O'Mahony 'were escorting two unarmed UN military observers from the Irish Battalion area to Ras, close to the Israeli border, when they were ambushed by eight militia men.'[63] O'Mahony was wounded, but Smallhorne and Barrett were captured and murdered by members of the 'Free Lebanon Army', a Christian militia financed and trained by Israel.

The Irish reaction was one of fury. The embassy in Beirut said that 'this outrage was perpetrated by Israeli backed forces and we attribute the murder of the two Irish soldiers to the Israeli government because they are arming the de facto forces.'[64] The public's outrage might have been even more pronounced had they been privy to 'intelligence information which suggested that a Shin Bet [Israeli Security Agency] officer had actually been present at the murders and had stood by to witness the shots being fired into the necks of Barrett and Smallhorne.'[65]

There was an extraordinary response from the Israeli ambassador, Shlomo Argov, who seemed shocked that the Irish had the temerity to complain about the deaths of their soldiers.

> You sit there all so smugly up in Dublin and just pass judgement on things that are happening on the other side of the moon, without any real feel for the situation. The situation is a much more complicated one than that, and I don't really know where you muster the moral courage to decide that Major Haddad [head of the Free Lebanon Army] should be eliminated along with his forces . . . I find it really incredulous that people in Dublin, of all places, should be so insensitive to the plight of a Christian minority. What is the world coming to? I think you should show a little understanding for the Christians. I think you should show a little understanding for us.[66]

Argov's ire may have been provoked by the Irish embassy statement; but what really angered the Israeli government was a statement made in Bahrain in February 1980 by the Minister for Foreign Affairs, Brian Lenihan,

> acknowledging 'the role of the Palestinian Liberation Organisation in representing the Palestinian people.' From that moment on the Irish had been singled out for vilification by the Israelis.[67]

Lenihan 'was proud of the Bahrain declaration, preceding as it did by a few months the Venice Declaration on similar lines by the European Council of Ministers.'[68]

Two years later an assassination attempt on Argov would provide the pretext for the Israeli invasion of Lebanon, which would end with the massacres in the Sabra and Shatila refugee camps perpetrated by Christian militiamen.

———

Senseless death was also the subject of the inquiry into the Whiddy Island disaster the previous year, which reported on 25 July 1980. On 9 January 1979 an explosion occurred when the French tanker *Betelgeuse* was unloading its cargo at Whiddy Island in Bantry Bay, Co. Cork, killing all forty-three crew members and seven local workers at the Gulf Oil terminal. In his 488-page report Mr Justice Declan Costello held two transnational oil companies, Gulf and Total, responsible for the disaster. The report stated that 'the major share of responsibility for the disaster must lie with Total, as the tanker's owners, for failing to keep the vessel properly maintained even though they were aware that it was in a dangerous condition.'[69] But it also blamed Gulf Oil

> for failing to take adequate measures to ensure the safety of the men on the offshore jetty at Whiddy and the crew of the tankers berthed alongside. And it finds that active steps were taken by some Gulf personnel—including senior management—to suppress the fact that the dispatcher, Mr John Connolly, was not in the control room when the disaster began. False entries were made in logs, false accounts were given of the disaster, both to the tribunal and in investigations held before the public hearings and efforts were made to avoid making statements to the Gardaí.[70]

In October 1974, 650,000 tons of crude oil had been accidentally pumped into Bantry Bay from the tanker *Universe Leader*. 'This was the largest oil spill in the history of the multi-national Gulf Corporation, and it resulted in new, more stringent safety precautions being introduced at Gulf installations around the world.'[71] Yet only three months later the tanker *Afran Zodiac* leaked 115,000 tons of heavy fuel oil into the bay.[72]

Unease over Whiddy Island may have played its part in reducing the Government's enthusiasm for building a nuclear power station. A song by Mick Hanly, 'The Workers Are Being Fooled Again', drew a parallel between Whiddy and Carnsore, and it provoked an angry phone call to RTE from Máirín Lynch, wife of the former Taoiseach, when sung by Christy Moore on the 'Late Late Show'.[73] The Three Mile Island accident the previous year, in which a nuclear power station in Pennsylvania suffered a partial meltdown of its core that necessitated the evacuation of the surrounding area, also seemed to affect the Government's attitude, as did the replacement of Desmond O'Malley by George Colley as the minister responsible. It was a triumph for the activists of the anti-nuclear movement that

> the government is likely to abandon its plans for a nuclear power station at Carnsore Point, Co. Wexford, at least for the time being. [The] main reasons for the delay are fears raised by the leak at the U.S. nuclear plant in Harrisburg and the possibility that alternative sources of energy could become available. Mr Colley has recently repeated that he is still to be convinced that nuclear power is the best answer to the problem of providing energy supplies.[74]

———

The National Gay Federation chose to go the legal route in its challenge to the status quo when in the High Court in June its best-known member, David Norris, challenged the legal ban on homosexuality on the grounds that it was an unconstitutional infringement of personal privacy. For the state, Rory O'Hanlon sc argued that

> sexual relations outside marriage constituted a violation of bodily integrity, and homosexuality did so in a particularly grave manner as being against the order of nature and a perversion of the biological function of the sexual organs ... It was important that the state should do all in its power to discourage the spread of homosexuality and in particular should not appear by the laws to condone sexual practices calculated to undermine the institutions of marriage and the family.[75]

Among those testifying on behalf of Norris was the author of *Prejudice and Tolerance in Ireland*, Father Mícheál Mac Gréil, who said 'he would like to see homosexuality decriminalised and he would hope that the attitude of the people become more tolerant.'[76]

Giving his judgement in October, Mr Justice Herbert McWilliam said that 'there was no foundation for any of the common beliefs that male homosexuals were mentally unbalanced, effeminate, vicious, unreliable, less intelligent or more likely to assault or seduce children, or young people, than were heterosexual males.'[77] Nevertheless he ruled against Norris, because 'it is reasonably clear that current Christian morality in this country does not approve of buggery, or of any sexual activity between persons of the same sex.'[78]

The National Gay Federation would take its case to the Supreme Court, but it had gained something even in defeat, as for the first time in Ireland

> homosexuality was dragged out from under the carpet. Puny mentions in newspapers gave way to large-scale, largely positive, media coverage; furtive, knowing nods and winks were replaced with frank discussion; the belief, or wish, that homosexuality was non-existent could no longer be accepted. At last, the realities of life for gay people were made known.[79]

Another landmark was the appearance of Joni Crone, the lesbian rights activist, on the country's most popular television programme, 'The Late Late Show'. She was the first 'out' gay woman to appear on Irish television.

> The newsroom at RTE contacted me on the Monday following the interview to find out if I had lost my job. I was able to tell them that the managing director of the small computer firm where I had worked had called me into his office and assured me that my job was

secure and that as far as he was concerned my sexuality was irrelevant in relation to my work . . . On a personal level, I suffered rejection from my family, received threats of violence and experienced ostracism.[80]

The eighties would see social issues moving to the forefront of the political agenda in the way that the Northern conflict had in the early seventies and industrial relations had later in that decade. It was appropriate, therefore, that 1980 saw the appearance of perhaps the two most influential organisations in the coming battles, the Divorce Action Group and the Irish branch of the Society for the Protection of Unborn Children.

The Divorce Action Group was founded by Máire Bates, a solicitor at the Coolock Law Centre in Dublin, set up by the Free Legal Advice Centres, Lylie Doyle, a member of Gingerbread, the organisation for one-parent families, and Dave Ellis, also of the Coolock Law Centre.[81] In April, Éamonn O'Farrell of the DAG said that there were at least twenty thousand separated people and that

> this figure is increasing by at least 700 per year. These figures are based on the 717 successful applications for Deserted Wives' Allowance in 1976, or the roughly similar number of people who appeal for annulments of their Catholic marriages. Divorce must, therefore, be granted, not merely because it is universally recognised as a basic civil right but because it is a social necessity for those directly affected by martial instability.[82]

The *Crane Bag* published an interview with Senator Mary Robinson and her successor in Trinity, Mary McAleese. Both women came out strongly in favour of divorce legislation. McAleese said:

> The fallacy of not allowing divorce but allowing legal separation is based on some sort of erroneous and silly notion that the legal concept of divorce is some sort of social evil. I think William Duncan's recently published book, *A Case for Divorce,* makes the point that the notions which give rise to the constitutional ban on divorce, i.e. that it's a social evil, that where one has divorce more marriages break down, that people won't take their commitments responsibly or, the even more fallacious one, that divorce damages children, are all built on myth and not fact.[83]

There have been suggestions that the Pro-Life Amendment Campaign was guilty of a gratuitous display of power, given that there was no possibility of abortion being introduced in Ireland. Yet it seems clear that there was genuine concern among some of those who would join SPUC and PLAC that abortion might well find its way onto the statute book. This fear was stoked by an article in the February issue of *Hibernia* by Paddy Prendiville that suggested that the constitutional right to privacy 'could pave the way for abortion rights' and revealed that

> a group of determined feminists in Dublin are planning a programme of demands and agitation under the heading of a woman's right to choose. Their demands include the decriminalisation of abortion, open referral for abortions at hospitals and health centres and the removal of all social and economic discrimination against single mothers.[84]

Prendiville, a pro-feminist journalist, proved to be prescient, as on 8 August

> the first feminist organisation in Ireland to advocate abortion on demand was launched in Dublin ... 'The Woman's Right to Choose' started off with eight members, the majority of whom had been involved in family planning and the distribution of contraceptives from ad hoc clinics throughout the city in the past few years.[85]

The crucial events in the forming of anti-abortion groups were two conferences in Dublin in September, one of which, at Trinity College, is often cited as the origin of the Pro-Life Amendment Campaign.[86] The conference was organised by Prof. John Bonner under the auspices of the World Federation of Doctors Who Respect Human Life.

> About 200 doctors attended, including [the] Dublin gynaecologist Dr Julia Vaughan, soon to emerge as the main front person for the Pro-Life Amendment Campaign. Vaughan, a former nun, was a highly respected gynaecologist with a practice at the Catholic Mount Carmel private hospital in Dublin.[87]

The other conference, at Carysfort College, Blackrock, Co. Dublin, was addressed by Dr C. Everett Koop, joint author with the Evangelical theologian Francis Schaeffer of *Whatever Happened to the Human Race?*, a hugely influential book for pro-life campaigners in America. Koop (who two years later would be appointed Surgeon-General of the United States by Ronald Reagan) predicted that 'within five years the American constitution will be amended to guarantee the right of every unborn child to live.'[88] Dr Margaret White, president of SPUC in Britain, asked the delegates, 'Why do you not do something in Ireland about the agencies that are sending young girls to Birmingham for abortion? I am surprised that nobody is doing anything about it.'[89]

The message seemed to strike home. On 28 December, Loreto Browne, a UCD student and one of the founders of the Dublin Branch of SPUC, called at a meeting outside Leinster House for the closure of 'two abortion referral clinics operating here under the law.' Her call was later repeated at a meeting at the Central Bank by the Lord Mayor and Fine Gael TD, Mr Fergus O'Brien. Several hundred people had marched from Parnell Square carrying lamps inscribed 'Our Lady of Knock,' crucifixes entwined with rosary beads and white flowers and banners with such messages as 'abortion kills babies.'[90]

When the annual conference of the National Union of Journalists reaffirmed its support for abortion rights there were several resignations. Four journalists with the *Limerick Leader* said in their letter of resignation, 'We the undersigned regard abortion as murder.'[91] However, Brendan O'Brien of the Dublin Broadcasting Branch asserted that 'the majority of Irish journalists would wholeheartedly support most of the motion ... The abortion debate was at a very primitive and early stage in Ireland.'[92]

At the Fine Gael ard-fheis, which passed a unanimous motion against abortion, there was an impassioned intervention from a young female delegate, Finola Gill, who said

> she was not for abortion. She deplored it. But if she found herself pregnant in the morning, her first thought would be how to get rid of the baby. 'And don't tell me this same thought doesn't cross the mind of practically every single pregnant girl in this country ... because everyone here is part and parcel of a society that offers no Christian love and charity to unmarried mothers. You have helped to create and maintain the stigma of illegitimacy. How many of you would be proud to walk into Mass with your unmarried pregnant daughter?'[93]

The following year Finola Gill would marry John Bruton, who would be Taoiseach when divorce was finally legalised, in 1996. SPUC would achieve its objective much sooner.

———

One result of the battles over the 'pro-life' amendment was that RTE would have been far more cautious about showing certain scenes of the drama series 'Strumpet City' about life in Dublin in 1907–14, based on the best-selling novel by James Plunkett. In one scene a group of children of the strikers in the 1913 Dublin Lock-out are being escorted to a ship that will take them to England and the homes of well-wishing trade union members who wish to relieve their parents, themselves on the verge of starvation, of the burden of looking after them. They are ambushed by a group of Catholic zealots, led by a priest, inflamed by the notion that the children may be going to non-Catholic homes. The escorts are beaten up and the terrified children are taken into custody by the demonstrators while hymns are sung. The scene is historically accurate, but its offence to religious piety was perhaps something RTE would not have hazarded in the changed climate of the coming years.

A good case can be made that 'Strumpet City', scripted by Hugh Leonard and directed by Tony Barry, is RTE's finest achievement. For all its popularity, it is remarkably discomforting. It is a politically engaged drama but one done on an epic scale. Its like has not been seen since.

'Strumpet City' was not alone in its ability to strike a hugely resonant contemporary chord by looking at the past. In October, Brian Friel's play *Translations* created a sensation when it came to the Gate Theatre for the Dublin Theatre Festival. The verdict was that '*Translations* simply has to return to Dublin ... Two weeks in the Gate cannot possibly accommodate all the people who want to see it.'[94] It is the story of an attempt by an English survey team to map an area of Co. Donegal in 1833. Its themes of cultural imperialism, misunderstanding and resistance, which owe something to the work of the critics George Steiner, Edward Said and Seamus Deane, had an obvious bearing on the situation in the North.

Translations was the first production by the Field Day Theatre Company, a group founded in Derry by Brian Friel and Stephen Rea to produce the play. It subsequently became an important cultural group that, in addition to producing plays, published a series of pamphlets and a three-volume *Anthology of Irish Writing*, an enormous achievement that proved to be the cause of one of the bitterest controversies in Irish cultural life since the riots at the opening of *The Playboy of the Western World*. Its aim was

> to create a shared consciousness which might make possible communication across Ireland's border; to give all Irishmen an artistic 'Fifth Province' rising above and covering the whole island, an hypothetical province which would neither accept the North/South division, nor ignore the separate traditional strengths of those on either side ... The intention is to create an awareness, a sense of the whole country, North and South together, and to examine predominant attitudes to the island as a whole.[95]

The writer Thomas Kilroy, who would write the outstanding play *Double Cross* for Field Day in 1986, described the company as 'the most important movement of its kind in Ireland since the beginning of the century.'[96]

———

The Field Day *Anthology* would include a brief paean to Charles Haughey, described as a politician who 'skilfully combines de Valera's meticulously crafted republicanism with Seán Lemass's best possible blend of cosmopolitan modernity and ancestral loyalty for present-day Ireland.'[97] Haughey was also keen to transcend the North-South division and may have felt that such a consummation might be possible when, on 8 December, Margaret Thatcher and a team including the Foreign Secretary, Lord Carrington, the Chancellor of the Exchequer, Geoffrey Howe, and the Secretary of State for Northern Ireland, Humphrey Atkins, arrived in Dublin for a meeting attended by great expectations. The meeting

> had all the trappings of a historic occasion: the imposing setting of Dublin Castle, heads of government meeting behind closed and highly guarded doors, senior ministers and their advisers, and teams of lesser officials. The presence of Lord Carrington added to the atmosphere of expectation. Had he not already achieved the impossible in Zimbabwe? And had he not, in the process, persuaded Mrs Thatcher to reverse her position on fundamental issues?[98]

Afterwards Haughey did nothing to dispel the idea that a historic breakthrough might be in the offing, describing the summit as

> highly significant, indeed historic, raising to a new plane discussions between Dublin and London on Northern affairs and offering the prospect of debating 'the totality of relationships within these islands' . . .[99]

The term 'totality of relationships' was taken to mean that everything was on the table, supporting Haughey's claim that 'no limits were being placed on the arrangements that might be agreed.'[100] The days after the meeting saw 'the encouragement of the perception that a process had been established that would eventually bring about unification.'[101]

Thatcher did little, at first, to dispel such speculation. Asked in the House of Commons by the Labour Party leader Michael Foot to grant an emergency debate and disclose what had been discussed, she demurred, saying, 'These were matters which had all to be explored and no decisions had yet been made.'[102] Enoch Powell's description of the Dublin meeting as a 'mini-Munich' added to the impression that Haughey's optimism was not without foundation.[103]

In the Dáil, Haughey described the British delegation as 'the most important to visit this country since the foundation of this state or indeed for a long time before then,' while Garret FitzGerald warned that 'London and Dublin could not achieve a settlement over the heads of the people of Northern Ireland. That was the route to war, not to peace.'[104] But when FitzGerald suggested that 'the talks had not been concerned with the constitutional position of Northern Ireland but with improved relations,' Haughey replied, 'I am not accepting what Deputy FitzGerald said.'[105] Yet it would have been obvious to anyone who resisted the temptations of euphoria that

> the joint communiqué issued at the close of the summit was significant not for what it said but for the multiplicity of possible meanings the marvellously evasive wording allowed . . . The British government's earlier reiteration of the constitutional guarantee to the Protestant majority in Ulster should have sufficed to banish thoughts of constitutional breakthroughs . . . but in the heady days following the summit there was no mention of the unity by consent declaration.[106]

The biggest blot on the landscape of Anglo-Irish relations was the worsening situation in the H-blocks. The day the Dublin meeting was held was also the forty-third day of hunger strike for seven men in Long Kesh—Raymond McCartney, John Nixon, Seán McKenna, Brendan Hughes, Leo Green, Thomas McFeeley and Thomas McKearney—who had been refusing food since 27 October in pursuit of five demands: the right to wear their own clothes; the right not to do work dictated by the prison authorities; the right to free association; the right to receive weekly letters, visits and parcels; and the restoration of all remission lost as a result of the prison protests.

The republican leadership outside the prison was against the idea of a hunger strike. Gerry Adams wrote to the prisoners that 'we are tactically, strategically, politically and morally opposed to the hunger strike.'[107] The leadership

> were against the hunger strike for several reasons. They feared it might dissipate resources and energies from the 'war'; they did not believe there would be sufficient mass support to sustain a long and traumatic campaign; and they were not convinced it was a battle they could win. There was always the fear that if the British broke the men within they would break the men without.[108]

Yet such was the desperation of the prisoners that one of them,

Lawrence McKeown, who would later spend seventy days on hunger strike, recalled that if the IRA had expressly forbidden the hunger strike 'it would have been an absolute disaster because people would have gone on hunger strike anyway, and it would have caused a major split within the IRA.'[109]

Thatcher immediately stated: 'I want this to be utterly clear. The Government will never concede political status to the hunger strikers or to any others convicted of criminal offences.'[110] Yet there were still those who feared that the British Government might strike a deal with the hunger-strikers, and urged them not to. The five leaders of the North's Unionist parties—James Molyneaux of the Official Unionist Party, Ian Paisley of the Democratic Unionist Party, James Kilfedder of the Independent Unionists, Ernest Baird of the United Unionists and Ann Dickson of the Unionist Party of Northern Ireland—signed a statement condemning any such deal. 'The government must learn that the Unionist family, whatever their internal differences, are one in their determination to defend and maintain the union and to see the IRA defeated . . . They cannot and will not tolerate any deals with Ulster's enemies.'[111]

Garret FitzGerald seemed equally determined to strengthen Thatcher's resolve and 'urged the British government not to yield to the H-Block hunger strikers' demand for political status.'[112] He claimed that the British 'put lives in danger by leading people to think that by hunger strike they could achieve their objective. That put lives in danger and this was unfair.'[113] He also expressed concern for the Catholic community in the North, as they had

> withstood tremendous pressure and intimidation to get them to participate in these protests. They stood up to that pressure and now they are to be put in danger by the hunger strike and the possible reaction to it.[114]

In connection with resolutions supporting the hunger-strikers, he had asked Fine Gael councillors

> not to support such resolutions and if there was support for them from Fianna Fáil to let him know. There was no question of asking for names of Fianna Fáil councillors but it would be something useful to know which could be discussed with the government.[115]

History would not be kind to FitzGerald's belief that intransigence is the best way to save the lives of hunger-strikers, or indeed his assertion that there was little support for the H-block protests among Catholics in the North. On the day he expressed these sentiments a crowd estimated by organisers as being over twenty thousand attended a H-block march in

Coalisland, Co. Tyrone, something that hinted at the political upheaval of the coming year.[116]

As indeed did some of the protests on the southern side of the border during the H-Block Day of Action held on 10 December, three days after the Anglo-Irish summit meeting in Dublin.

> In Dundalk many workers left their employment to join in a march and rally attended by an estimated 2,500 people. Pubs and shops also closed . . . In Monaghan workers from most of the local factories stopped work for an hour, and shops and pubs also closed while a demonstration was held in the town in support of the hunger strikers . . . A rally at Letterkenny involved 2,500 to 3,000 people. Industry, shops and pubs closed in Letterkenny, Buncrana and Ballyshannon . . . In Clones there was a complete shut-down of the town.[117]

But the most significant intervention was made by Síle de Valera during the Donegal South-West by-election. On 1 November, from a platform in Letterkenny that she was sharing with the Taoiseach and eight Government ministers, she launched a stinging attack on Thatcher's handling of the crisis. She criticised

> bungling by the British government when it comes to Irish affairs, this time in relation to their insensitive handling of the delicate issue of the H-Blocks . . . Not once, but twice, this week in the Commons the British Prime Minister issued callous, unfeeling and self-righteous statements on the stance which the British government are taking in regard to the position of the H-Block prisoners . . . The Iron Lady image of which the British Prime Minister seems so proud, is little less than a mask for an inflexible and insensitive lack of common humanity.[118]

Much of this is now close to orthodoxy as regards the British Government's handling of the hunger strikes, but the response from Fianna Fáil could best be described as panic-stricken.

> From the platform in the square 30 top Fianna Fáil people . . . went at the instruction of the Taoiseach . . . for a hastily convened meeting where a statement was prepared that was issued one hour later in the name of [the] Director of Elections Ray MacSharry. It was made clear in this statement, which Haughey himself went through line by line . . . that Síle de Valera's speech did not reflect the views of the government.[119]

The following day a source close to Haughey said that 'if she continues on this road she is out of the party.'[120]

The *Kilkenny People* described the speech as an 'emotionally charged argument . . . which could do little except stir up antagonism and create further division,' while the *Tuam Herald* suggested that de Valera 'had opened her republican mouth a little too wide again.'[121] There was a dissenting view from the *Longford News,* which said that 'De Valera told Margaret Thatcher some home truths in her speech and spitted out, fair and straight, what most republican people are thinking.'[122]

Garret FitzGerald accused the young deputy of 'incitement to violence' for her comment that 'if the situation is allowed to continue or deteriorate the British government must shoulder the responsibility for further deaths, whether it be in H-Block, on the streets, or elsewhere throughout the six counties.'[123]

Meanwhile the condition of the hunger-strikers worsened. Tommy McKearney would recall:

> I was in extreme pain. I'd been vomiting. I was running a temperature and I had a severe headache. I hoped that a solution would be arrived at which would not end in death, but in some ways there was a feeling going through me that if this pain were to continue, death would be a welcome arrival. If I could only remove the pain, I would die happy.[124]

But Seán McKenna was in the worst state, and by the fifty-third day he had slipped into a coma.

> It was certain that he had only hours to live. Just at this psychological crux, a British government document appeared, presented to Brendan Hughes via a Catholic Church intermediary. It offered what seemed to be a compromise on the prisoners' demands and the protest was called off. But even on a superficial reading the document was full of imprecision. Hughes and his five semiconscious comrades knew that rejecting the document meant that Seán McKenna would die. There was really no choice.[125]

The end of the hunger strike came as a huge relief to both governments. Yet it quickly became obvious that the protest had failed.

> Despite that, the Sinn Féin leaders attempted to present the document as a victory, but their efforts were less than convincing. A celebratory march held in West Belfast attracted only a paltry crowd. Morale at grassroots level was low and confusion was widespread.[126]

Journalists who saw the document given to the prisoners thought it showed

> that no concession of substance has been made by the British government. The documents make it clear that prisoners will be

expected to wear prison-issue clothes during working hours, though one repeats Mr Atkins' statement of October 23rd that civilian-type clothes will be issued rather than the old style denim prison uniform. Prisoners will be expected to do prison work.[127]

The struggle in the H-blocks had, it seemed, run its course. But the IRA commanding officer in the prison was not prepared to leave it at that. His name was Bobby Sands.

In his heart Sands knew that they had lost, and the loss had devastated him. He held himself responsible, blaming himself for being wrong-footed and outwitted by the authorities, for being too trusting of their gestures of good faith, for being duped by their willingness to deal with him, for trusting promises made by the British when he should have known better, for the breakdown in communications between the hunger strikers and the prison command. He was the first to raise the question of a second hunger strike. Within a day of the hunger strike's end he was importuning the IRA leadership to be allowed to restart the protest himself immediately.[128]

Sands would be the central figure the following year as the North exerted an unexpected influence on politics south of the border, even directly affecting the result of the election between Haughey and FitzGerald as they fought the first of their four battles for power.

Chapter 10 ∾

| DEATH TRAPS

1981

It is for its deaths that 1981 will be remembered.

One set of deaths was sudden, the other lingering. One was unexpected, the other, by the end, horribly predictable. One set of victims became largely forgotten by all except family and friends; the others remain political icons, commemorated by countless books, murals and ballads. In both cases blame is disputed, and the families of the dead remain embittered by their treatment at the hands of the political establishment. And what both the forty-eight victims of the Stardust fire and the ten men who died in the H-block hunger strike also have in common is that they probably cost Charlie Haughey a victory in that year's general election.

First came the fire. 'There's a fire in the Stardust,' said the caller to Dublin Fire Brigade. 'Where is the Stardust?' asked George Glover in Tara Street Station. 'In Artane . . . The whole place is on fire,' said the caller.

The call came at 1:43 a.m. on 14 February, and although six fire tenders were on the scene within minutes, by the time the rescue operation began most if not all of the forty-eight young people had died.[1]

The Stardust was one of the premier entertainment venues for young people in Dublin. It regularly presented some of the biggest names in popular music, including Joe Dolan, who performed at the gala opening night.[2] It was part of a complex in Kilmore Road also containing a pub, the Silver Swan, and a restaurant, the Lantern Rooms, owned by Patrick Butterly and managed by his son Eamon.[3]

On 13 February, 841 patrons attended a disco in the Stardust.[4] At 1:40 a.m. a nineteen-year-old waiter, Liz Marley, looked through a gap in the curtains screening off an unused part of the club and saw two seats on fire. Members of the kitchen staff and security men were alerted, and one man tried to put the flames out with a fire extinguisher. Three minutes later dancers saw smoke drifting from beneath the screen. The DJ appealed for calm, but almost immediately the music stopped and the microphone went dead. People began to stampede towards the exit.[5]

At 1:45 security men pushed up the screen that divided the area where the fire was now blazing from the disco area. Flames 'shoot up and up almost instantly, setting fire to seats, walls and the ceiling.'[6] At 1:47

> all the lights go out, including the exit signs. The entire room is now full of thick black smoke, cutting visibility to nil. Many collapse from the choking fumes.[7]

Four minutes later the fire brigade and ambulances arrived. By 2:20 the fire had been put out. It had lasted only forty minutes but had killed forty-eight young people. The next day reporters saw

> the steel shutters covering the windows of the men's lavatories in which so many people had sought refuge from the flames only to find themselves in a terrible trap. The tempered steel of the shutters bore the futile marks of firemen's axes, like the peck marks of birds' beaks. That steel did the job it was designed to—to stop people getting through the window. In one corner there survived just one fragment of the polystyrene roof tiling, which had showered the panic-stricken youngsters below with liquid, burning plastic like napalm.[8]

Eighteen-year-old Geraldine Lynch said it was 'just like a sheet of wallpaper, like the wall itself was burning.'[9] The state pathologist, Dr John Harbison, would conclude that the victims 'died directly from shock due to extensive burns or from inhalation of smoke or fumes.'[10]

Most of the dead and injured came from the housing estates of Bonnybrook, Kilmore, Edenmore, Coolock and Artane.[11] They were shockingly young: Marcella McDermott from Raheny was seventeen; her brothers George and William were nineteen and twenty. Sixteen-year-old Martina Keegan died with her nineteen-year-old sister Mary. Paula Lewis was nineteen, Michael Barrett seventeen, Liam Dunne eighteen.[12]

The number of deaths could have been even greater but for some acts of heroism. Michael Kelly, who lived nearby, went into the blazing building and

> shone a torch he was carrying with him around and saw people lying on the ground in front of the men's toilet. He managed to bring one of them out of the building and made two further journeys into the ballroom, clearly at considerable risk to himself and brought others out.[13]

One firefighter, Noel Hosback,

braved the intense heat around one of the toilets to save a number of people. He kicked open the door of one of the toilets and ascertained that there were still people in there. He then went back to the spirit store and called for breathing apparatus, which was handed to Fireman Bernard O'Rourke from outside the building and then to Fireman Hosback. He then succeeded in getting people out of the toilet and into the spirit store, where they were helped out of the window by Fireman O'Rourke and Sub-Officer Brian Parkes.[14]

But why had a minor fire spread so quickly and killed so many people? The tribunal of inquiry under Mr Justice Ronan Keane, which sat for 122 days and published its 633-page report the following June, found that

> the rapid spread of the fire throughout the Stardust was due to a combination of factors: (1) The presence of a tier of seats containing quantities of combustible material abutting a wall lined with combustible carpet tiles; (2) The presence of a low ceiling; and (3) The presence of a large area of combustible seating to which the fire could, and did, eventually spread ... The tables and carpet on the floor probably played a secondary role in the spreading of flames. The combustion of furnishings in the alcove produced quantities of carbon monoxide sufficient to cause or contribute to many of the deaths.[15]

The fire was a disaster waiting to happen, because of the extraordinarily lax attitude to fire safety at the time. The tribunal found, for example, that

> there was no inspection whatever of this building by any member of the Fire Brigade, either in the Fire Prevention Department or fire-fighting service, from the day it opened until the fire ... [This] was one of the most disquieting facts to emerge at the inquiry.[16]

Lack of political will had also contributed to a situation in which

> most of the recommendations in a major report on the Fire Service in 1975, including the establishment of a comprehensive system of fire safety inspection, have yet to be implemented. Draft building regulations which would ban the use of highly combustible material in building construction are still 'under discussion' after more than four years.[17]

The Stardust fire brought an end to the softly-softly approach. By 1 May thirty-three discos and dance halls had been closed after fire inspections.[18]

The tribunal also had specific criticisms of Eamon Butterly's attitude towards fire safety. Most notably it found that his policy of keeping the exit doors chained and locked until at least midnight led to one exit being actually locked and chained while the fire was in progress; and that this policy was pursued by Mr Butterly with a reckless disregard for the safety of the people in the premises. Mr Butterly's legitimate objective of preventing unauthorised persons from gaining access to the Stardust could have been readily achieved by the stationing of doormen at each of the exits, but he deliberately elected to pursue a policy which was more economical in the use of doormen and was manifestly dangerous.[19]

As a result of this finding, the Stardust Relatives' Committee asked the Director of Public Prosecutions, Éamonn Barnes, for the owners of the Stardust to be prosecuted. They argued that 'reckless negligence leading to death' was a basis for a charge of manslaughter.[20] However, Barnes decided in August that

there were 'insufficient grounds' to take criminal proceedings against the owners of the Stardust alleging negligence resulting in manslaughter . . . The reaction to Mr Barnes' decision from the Stardust relatives was one of disbelief. A statement issued by the committee said: 'nothing has been done and nothing has been learned. It's a great shock to learn that nobody is accountable or responsible for the deaths of these children.' The victims condemned the D.P.P.'s decision as 'contradictory and dismissive,' of the tribunal's findings.[21]

Before the end of the year Eamon Butterly had applied for, and was granted, a renewal of the licence for the Silver Swan. And in 1983 he received £581,946 after winning a malicious damages claim against Dublin City Council, as Judge Seán O'Hanrahan in Dublin Circuit Court ruled that the fire was started maliciously.[22] To this day the Stardust relatives dispute that finding and continue to call for a new public inquiry.

The Stardust lay in the heart of Charles Haughey's constituency of Dublin North-Central. His immediate reaction was to cancel the Fianna Fáil ard-fheis, which had been due to begin on the Saturday. It had been expected that Haughey would use it as the platform for a general election campaign, but the cancellation meant that these plans had to be scrapped. The delay would cost him dearly.

Firstly, the economy came in for exposure and punishment: it was revealed to be in far more dubious health than the January budget had led people to believe. Secondly, the 'special relationship' between Haughey and Margaret Thatcher, which had been acclaimed to be close enough to lead the Irish people 'down the road to unity' was exposed to sustained examination which undermined its seriousness. Furthermore, when the Maze [Long Kesh] hunger strike, which began on the first of March, produced the grim reality of sacrificial starvation, that 'special relationship' failed to come up with any answers. Thirdly, Fine Gael and Labour, with ample warning that an election was in the offing, had plenty of time to prepare reasonably convincing campaigns.[23]

One of the ironies of the time is that it was the self-proclaimed republican Charlie Haughey who more or less sat idly by as Bobby Sands starved to death, without the Taoiseach aiming one word of public protest at Margaret Thatcher. A year later he had no hesitation in ruffling British feathers during the Falklands War; but during the hunger strike he was careful not to denounce the actions of the Tory Government, despite repeated requests from the families. This may have been because the diplomatic triumph of the previous year's Anglo-Irish summit meeting was seen by Haughey as his most potent weapon in the coming election. Essential to that triumph had been the supposed special relationship with Thatcher. To have publicly upbraided her over her government's approach to the crisis would have been to risk the kind of rebuff that made it clear how illusory that relationship really was. Considerations of electoral advantage trapped Haughey into silence at a time when even those not normally sympathetic to the Provisional IRA expressed concerns about the British Government's intransigence.

The second H-block mass hunger strike within a year was heralded by an IRA statement on 5 February.

> It needs to be asked openly of the Irish bishops, of Cardinal Ó Fiaich and of politicians like John Hume: what did your recommended ending of the last hunger strike gain for us, where is the peace in the prisons which, like a promise, we held before dying men's eyes?[24]

Four days later came the news that the new strike would begin on 1 March. On this occasion it would be staggered, so that the prisoners would not all be approaching death at the same time. The five demands were as before.

The first hunger-striker would be Bobby Sands, commanding officer of the IRA prisoners in Long Kesh. It was believed that Sands was

> critical of the circumstances surrounding the ending of the last strike and is aware that the chances of exerting new concessions from the British government by repeating the exercise are remote. He is said to have accepted that a new fast may end in his death and

that of the other hunger-strikers. The view is widely shared in republican and H-Block activist circles.[25]

On 25 March came an incident that suggested a threatening new departure south of the border. Geoffrey Armstrong, director of employee relations at the British Leyland car plant in Coventry, was addressing a seminar on industrial relations in Trinity College organised by the Dublin Junior Chamber of Commerce when three men,

> two of whom were armed, burst in through the back door of the lecture room. The three, who were of slight build and in their early twenties, were wearing military-style jackets and balaclava helmets. One stayed near the door, while the others advanced towards Mr Armstrong carrying revolvers. One turned to the audience and shouted in a nondescript accent, 'Everybody freeze, nobody move. This action is in support of the H-Blocks.' They then brandished their weapons as if to shoot a woman sitting in the front row. The gunmen turned, however, on Mr Armstrong, who had moved back from the podium, and shot him three times.[26]

Armstrong received leg wounds that required minor surgery. The attack was disowned by the National H-Block Armagh Committee and denied by the Provisional IRA. Reports that 'former members of a Red Brigades cell known to have been active in Trinity College were responsible for the attack' might have seemed fanciful had they not been confirmed by the conviction two years later of Giovanni Mariotti for the shooting.[27] Mariotti had been sentenced in absentia to eight-and-a-half years' imprisonment in Italy in December 1980 'for subversive association and possession of "war weapons".[28] He was given a twelve-year sentence on 16 February 1983. Gardaí said that Mariotti had

> close links with Revolutionary Struggle, a thirty-strong group spawned, they say, in Trinity College in the mid seventies . . . Detectives say that there are close links between Revolutionary Struggle and the Red Brigades, and other organisations such as the German Red Army Faction (Baader Meinhof) and the Grapo organisation in Spain. They are based mainly in Dublin, but may also have small cells in Cork and Limerick. In a recent issue of their newspaper 'Rebel' they openly called on the unemployed to rob banks and post offices, instead of mounting protest marches. Most of them come from middle and upper class backgrounds and are considered by Gardaí as 'extremely dangerous'.[29]

Despite these fears, Revolutionary Struggle, some of whose members would later make their mark in journalism and academia, faded from the scene, and they remain merely an intriguing footnote in the history of Irish radicalism in the seventies and its links with militant anarchist groups in Europe.

Bobby Sands's unexpected victory in the Fermanagh-South Tyrone by-election on 10 April was

> a serious embarrassment to the British government. It also represents a body blow for those representatives of the minority, including the SDLP and the Catholic Church, who had maintained that the vast majority of anti-unionists do not in any way wish to be associated with violence or violent organisations.[30]

It was perhaps the effects of that body blow that drew from the SDLP leader, John Hume, the following immortal entry in the annals of sophistry:

> I would contend that Mr Sands now has political status and the only sort of political status I think any Irishman would want, which is that conferred by Irish people going out and voting . . . This is very much preferable to any Irish republican than any status conferred by a British government.

He expected that Sands, having achieved this political status, would have declared that he had achieved it and then given up his hunger strike.[31]

The new MP did not give up his hunger strike, and ten days later he was visited by three members of the Dáil: Neil Blaney, John O'Connell and Síle de Valera. He had been fifty-one days on hunger strike. Dr O'Connell predicted that Sands had

> about six days to live. I get the impression that he was fully resigned to die . . . I saw in that man more determination than I've ever seen in any man before. I asked him if he was prepared to make a compromise. He pointed out that compromise had already been made on the prisoners' side by the ending of last year's hunger strike.[32]

Haughey's main effort to resolve the hunger strike came two days later when he invited the Sands family to his home, reversing an earlier refusal to meet any relatives. Marcella Sands, the hunger-striker's sister, would recall that Haughey

> had the papers for a formal application to the European Commission of Human Rights on the table before him. The Taoiseach gave her the impression that an application would be a mere formula, allowing Britain off the hook and most probably resulting in the acceptance of the essence of the five demands in time to save her brother's life.[33]

When a delegation from the Commission met Marcella Sands, the hunger-strikers' legal adviser, Pat Finucane, and the officer commanding the republican prisoners in the H-block, Brendan 'Bik' McFarlane, the position turned out to be very different.

> Rather than investigating on the spot the Commissioners wanted Sands to take over Marcella's application and then to start proceedings with a special meeting in five days' time. The bottom line was that if Sands was to survive to pursue his application he would have to abandon his hunger strike . . . The prisoners' worst suspicions of a re-run of December 1980 appeared to be confirmed and in a statement from Owen Carron the Provisionals made it clear that, as they saw it, the blame lay with Haughey alone who, they said, had 'misled' the family.[34]

McFarlane was scathing about Haughey's intervention.

> Haughey, the ultimate survivor, slipped quietly out of the firing line, satisfied that he had thrown the ball into someone else's court . . . Nothing was achieved from their intervention, save to expose Haughey for the conniving self-seeking politician he has always been.[35]

On 4 May came news that Haughey

> is not expected to respond to demands that he should publicly ask the British government to concede the five demands of the hunger-strikers in Long Kesh. Ever since the first hunger strike in the H-Blocks six months ago, Mr Haughey has declined to endorse the full demands of the Provisional IRA prisoners in relation to clothing, work and free association, although he has urged the British government to make unspecified concessions on humanitarian grounds.

At the weekend Owen Carron, Sands's election agent, said that his last request had been that 'Charles Haughey should publicly demand that the British move on the prisoners' five demands.'[36] The following morning a statement from the Northern Ireland Office said that 'Mr Robert Sands, a prisoner in The Maze, died today at 1.17 a.m. He took his own life by refusing food and medical intervention for sixty-six days.'[37]

Sands's death led to widespread displays of sympathy and anger in the Republic. In Dundalk images of Haughey and Thatcher were burnt at a march attended by three thousand people'[38] In Monaghan

> three volleys of shots were fired over a black coffin draped with a tricolour, which was carried flanked by a colour party in

paramilitary uniform through the town . . . Sligo saw one of the biggest demonstrations in years, with 8,000 marchers and a complete closedown of the town centre. All local factories closed except for one on continuous production. Hundreds of workers left the giant Snia factory to join the march. The centre of Tralee closed down for several hours and workers attended a midday vigil. In Limerick, after a door to door appeal from H-Block committee members asking businesses to close, the city came to a standstill for more than an hour, and all premises closed for two hours. Hundreds of workers came into the city from the Alumina site on the Shannon Estuary, joining the parade of 2,500.[39]

It also provoked a political reaction. The Lord Mayor of Limerick, Clement Casey (Fianna Fáil), said that it was

> tragic to see that the British have not moved an inch in the sixty-one years since the death of Terence MacSwiney after seventy-four days' hunger strike. Will they ever learn?[40]

His party's leader in the European Parliament, Paddy Lalor, said that Sands's death was 'again the supreme sacrifice by an Irishman in an effort to achieve simple humanitarian prison conditions denied by the United Kingdom.'[41] And on 8 May both Haughey and Garret FitzGerald 'called for the urgent intervention of the European Commission of Human Rights in the Long Kesh hunger strike.'[42]

The provincial papers struck an atypically republican note. 'It does not matter a damn to the British government if every Irish prisoner—IRA or UVF—in every Irish prison died tomorrow morning,' wrote one. 'Not a rib of hair would be stirred on Mrs Thatcher's well groomed head.'

'A stupid principle must remain unchanged,' thundered the *Roscommon Herald*. 'Bobby triumphed without violence; the intransigent Iron Lady, through the violence of discriminatory incarceration, has gathered a thick indelible coat of rust in the eyes of peace-loving humanitarian people throughout the world,' commented the *Connacht Telegraph*. The *Clonmel Nationalist* suggested that 'Britain still possesses a happy and smug infallibility that does not brook compassion.'[43]

Yet there were signs that this passion would not be sustained. On 15 May, when Francis Hughes, the second hunger-striker to die, was buried in Letterkenny

> almost every shop stayed open—in contrast with the day of the Sands funeral. In Sligo, where 8,000 had marched on the day of the Sands funeral, only 700 marched in memory of Hughes.[44]

In Dublin the march in memory of Sands had been marked by violence, as missiles were thrown at gardaí

> by youths who rampaged along O'Connell Street, across O'Connell Bridge, past Trinity College, into Grafton Street and Dawson Street and up to St Stephen's Green. Most shop windows in Dawson Street were broken and six cars overturned and set alight . . . A squad car from Pearse Street station parked outside the University Club was rolled over before being set on fire.[45]

There was more trouble after Hughes's death, when at least eight petrol bombs

> were thrown at Gardaí in the O'Connell Street area of Dublin following a meeting and march protesting [at] the death of the two hunger strikers . . . A provincial bus going to Busáras from the Broadstone depot was burned and destroyed at Killarney Street . . . A bus was hijacked near Mountjoy Square and rammed into the Hill 16 public house . . . Another bus was hijacked . . . and set on fire with a petrol bomb.[46]

Yet even these explosions gave no hint of what would happen when demonstrators marched to the British Embassy in Merrion Road on the afternoon of Saturday 18 July. What did happen was 'the most serious street violence ever to break out in the Republic' as a result of the Northern conflict. More than two hundred people, including 120 gardaí, were injured.[47] Trouble broke out almost as soon as the marchers were forced to halt two hundred yards short of the embassy

> by barricades manned by 500 Gardaí in full riot gear positioned at the junction of Merrion Road and Simmonscourt Road. Scores of youths forced their way past the march stewards and seized the barricades. Hundreds more in the march pushed forward, supported by many more behind who hurled stones and bottles at the Gardaí. Within minutes the situation had deteriorated into a pitched battle.

It looked as though the marchers might break through to the embassy, but the gardaí held firm and

> eventually mounted a powerful baton charge which pushed the main body of the march back up Merrion Road. Gardaí swept into the gardens in pursuit of the people who had been stoning them. It was the incidents from this stage onwards that gave rise to the widespread allegations of Gardaí brutality made by marchers and many reporters . . . Reporters in the area saw numerous cases of what they believed to be excessive use of force.[48]

Big Tom, the king of Country and Irish, struts his stuff. Critically reviled, the music played by the likes of Big Tom, Margo and Philomena Begley nevertheless commanded the loyalty of a huge swathe of the Irish population. (*Derek Speirs, Report Ltd*)

Giving Holy Communion to more than a million people requires a bit of planning. The Sacrament is lined up and ready to go as the Pope says Mass at the Phoenix Park in September 1979. (*Press Association Images*)

David Kelly (*left*) as Rashers Tierney, the best-loved character in what was probably the finest series ever produced by RTE, 'Strumpet City'. Brendan Cauldwell (*right*) played Hennessy, the ne'er-do-well friend of Rashers, just one of a gallery of vivid characters created by the novelist James Plunkett. (*RTE Stills Library*)

Marchers protesting against the decision of Dublin Corporation to build civic offices at Wood Quay, Dublin, where a Viking site of huge historical importance had been unearthed. The protests did ensure that much valuable archaeological work was carried out, but the offices were built on the site all the same. (*Irish Times*)

Charles O'Connor (*left*) and Barry Devlin of Horslips rock out at Studio 54, New York. The group were, 'the rock and roll version of the rural electrification scheme, bringing light and sound to places which had previously only seen men in mohair suits playing country music.' (*Rex Features*)

Charles Haughey, surrounded by supporters after he had been elected leader of Fianna Fáil in 1979. Haughey's victory owed a great deal to Síle de Valera (*immediately behind him*). Her criticisms of Jack Lynch's Northern policy greatly weakened the then Taoiseach, whose resignation paved the way for Haughey to take over. (*Irish Times*)

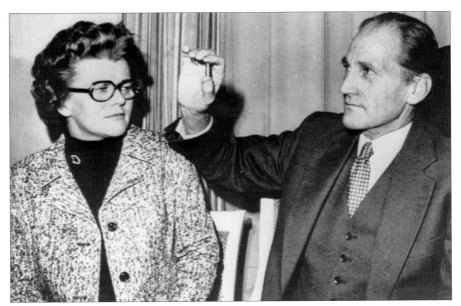

Dr Tiede Herrema, managing director of the Ferenka factory in Limerick, holds up a bullet given to him by his kidnappers, Eddie Gallagher and Marion Coyle. Herrema was taken from outside his home in Limerick on 3 October 1975 and released on 6 November after a seventeen-day siege of a house in Monasterevin. The kidnappers were trying to secure the release of IRA prisoners, including Rose Dugdale, Gallagher's then girl-friend. (*Keystone/Getty Images*)

Soldiers carry the coffin of the former Taoiseach and President Éamon de Valera at Glasnevin Cemetery. De Valera died on 29 August 1975, aged ninety-two. (RTE *Stills Library*)

A young girl holds up a banner during a 1984 anti-drugs march in Dublin. The heroin epidemic in Dublin's inner city led to the formation of Concerned Parents Against Drugs, a remarkable response by some of the most marginalised communities in the country. (*Irish Times*)

Ronald Reagan takes to the podium on 3 June 1984 as he returns to the putative village of his ancestors, Ballyporeen, Co. Tipperary. Elsewhere the welcome was somewhat less fulsome, with the rare sight of left-wing protestors making common cause with the Catholic Church, which effectually boycotted the visit because of its disagreement with US policies in Central America. (*Corbis*)

Margaret Thatcher and Garret FitzGerald together as the Anglo-Irish Agreement is signed on 15 November 1985. The agreement was a triumph for FitzGerald, who a year before had been publicly humiliated by Thatcher's 'out, out, out' comments in response to the New Ireland Forum report. (*Press Association Images*)

U2 lead singer Bono in familiar messianic mode at the 1985 Live Aid concert in Wembley Stadium, London, the brainchild of his predecessor as iconic Irish rock star *du jour*, Bob Geldof. (*Dave Hogan/Getty Images*)

Spectacular the riot may have been, but it was something of a last gasp from the H-block protest movement.

Charlie Haughey was no longer Taoiseach, but Garret FitzGerald proved no more effectual in dealing with the crisis. On 6 August certain relatives of the hunger-strikers were allowed to meet FitzGerald, though others, including Seán Sands, brother of Bobby Sands, and Theresa McCreesh, sister of Raymond McCreesh, who had died on 21 May, were denied admission. Mary and Nora McElwee, sisters of Thomas McElwee, who would die two days later,

> broke down and ran out of the meeting in tears. 'He's doing nothing, he's asking for suggestions,' Ms Mary McElwee told the other relatives waiting in the foyer. The government was going to let her brother die, she said.[49]

It was the relatives' fifth meeting with FitzGerald, and it would be their last.

> 'We will not meet with FitzGerald or his representatives again until he will talk constructively with us about a solution,' they said in a statement. Five of the relatives remained in the ground floor room where the meeting had taken place. When they refused to leave, they were carried out by Gardaí.[50]

The response of FitzGerald and the acting Minister for Foreign Affairs, John Kelly, was to lay all the blame for the hunger strikes on the republican movement and to suggest an immediate unilateral end to their military campaign.

> A completely different climate would be readily created in which the whole problem would be readily resolved, if the IRA and INLA declared an end to their campaign of violence in Northern Ireland which was incompatible with the humanitarian basis upon which the problem of protesting prisoners was being approached.[51]

Until recently it was believed that the closest the strike came to being settled was on 29 July, when Gerry Adams met six of the hunger-strikers

> to outline what he knew to be available from the British should the strike be brought to an end: a package that fell short of the full demands, but one that indicated substantial movement—the abolition of prison uniforms, with prisoners to wear their own clothes; the unofficial segregation of prisoners; free association at weekends and for part of each day; the granting of the strikers' demands concerning parcels and visits. But the prisoners rejected this set of offers and persevered for their full demands. There was to be no compromise this time around.[52]

However, in his book *Blanketman* (2005), Richard O'Rawe, a H-block prisoner and PRO for the hunger-strikers, claimed that the prisoners accepted a similar compromise on 5 July, only for the IRA Army Council to veto it. O'Rawe's claim is disputed by Brendan McFarlane and Lawrence McKeown, who had spent seventy days on hunger strike when it ended on 20 August

> without the prisoners securing their aims, although on October 6th the Secretary of State James Prior made significant concessions to their position in regard to clothing, remission, association and visits.[53]

Ten men were dead. One of them had been, for a little under two months, a member of Dáil Éireann.

Kieran Doherty was one of two H-block prisoners who caused a seismic shock by being elected to the Dáil in the general election of 11 June. The decision of the National H-Block Armagh Committee to put forward nine candidates in that election had not been without controversy. One committee member, Bernadette McAliskey,

> took the view that well-known people should stand. They argued that attitudes in the South were different from those in the North and the situation in Fermanagh/South Tyrone could not simply be translated to the Republic.[54]

It appeared that McAliskey was correct. Less than a week before the election it was reported that

> Doherty's candidature is causing surprisingly little stir in the constituency—neither the party workers or the ordinary voters appear to be paying him much attention. The view of both Fianna Fáil and Fine Gael election workers is that Doherty will pick up between 1,000 and 1,500 of [Captain James] Kelly's votes and will add a few hundred more on his own account.[55]

In fact Doherty would receive 9,121 votes, only 303 less than the poll-topping Minister for Education, John Wilson, and would win the fourth of five seats in Cavan-Monaghan with almost two thousand votes to spare. In Louth, Paddy Agnew, a H-block prisoner from Dundalk, topped the poll with 8,368 votes, more than 2,500 ahead of his nearest rival. The hunger-striker Joe McDonnell, standing in Sligo-Leitrim, received 5,639 votes and was only 315 votes behind Mattie Brennan of Fianna Fáil when he was eliminated on the fourth count. Had he stayed ahead of Brennan he could well have taken the final seat.[56]

In Dublin West, Tony O'Hara, brother of the INLA hunger-striker Patsy O'Hara, outpolled Mary Robinson (Labour Party) and Tomás Mac Giolla

(Sinn Féin the Workers' Party) and on the first count was only two hundred votes behind the sitting Fianna Fáil TD, Liam Lawlor, despite Sinn Féin members refusing to work for him because he was not an abstentionist.[57] Seán McKenna, who had almost died in the 1980 hunger strike, won 11 per cent of the vote in Kerry South, and Martin Hurson, who would die in the 1981 strike, won 10 per cent in Longford-Westmeath. In Waterford another hunger-striker, Kevin Lynch, won 7½ per cent. Altogether, H-block candidates averaged 15 per cent of the first-preference vote in the constituencies they contested. This was a remarkable performance, given that they had been 'without money, a national organisation, television exposure (thanks to the censorship laws), or any sympathetic media.'[58] It was probably beyond the wildest dreams of even their director of elections, Dáithí Ó Conaill, who said the day before the election that 'if the H-Block prisoner candidates in the general election post between 2,500 and 3,000 votes they will have put up a creditable performance.'[59]

The taking of two Fianna Fáil seats, by Doherty and Agnew, would have significant repercussions. At the time, Doherty's victory came as a source of fresh hope to the prisoners. One of them, Tom Holland, recalled that

> the strong feeling in our wing was that Kieran Doherty's success could be the source of a conclusion to the H-Block tragedy. The view centred on the opinion that the 26 counties establishment could not sit idly by as one of its TDs slowly neared death in the H-Blocks ... Our general impression was that, if Doherty was allowed to die, then our strategy had failed; if a sitting TD couldn't move them then nothing would.[60]

In fact Doherty's status as a democratically elected member of Dáil Éireann made no difference. On 2 August the 25-year-old Doherty died after seventy-three days on hunger strike, the longest of any of the 1981 hunger-strikers. In Monaghan

> the news of his death brought growing numbers of people out banging bin lids in Church Square and Park Street. Bonfires were set alight at one end of Park Street and on Pound Hill. As tension grew in the town, well over 100 people marched on the Garda station in North Road and began hurling stones and bottles at it and a number of Garda cars parked outside the station.[61]

Doherty's death drew a response from Michael O'Leary, leader of the Labour Party and Tánaiste in the new coalition Government, that contradicted the Taoiseach's view of the hunger strike as solely the fault of the republican movement.

The British government has the major responsibility in finding a solution to the Maze hunger-strike. This latest death, like the other deaths, could have been avoided, given flexibility on the part of the British government and the Provisional IRA leadership.[62]

Niall Andrews of Fianna Fáil was the only member of the Dáil to attend the funeral of his fellow-TD in Milltown Cemetery, Belfast. The march in Dublin to commemorate Doherty's death drew only three hundred people.[63]

Magill's judgement of the role of successive Governments in dealing with the hunger strike was that

> the last Fianna Fáil government made very little effort to pressurise the British into reaching a settlement of the crisis and attempted to use the crisis for its own electoral purposes. Furthermore . . . the present government was motivated primarily by a desire to sabotage the Provisional IRA and in doing so to divide the families of the hunger strikers in order to pressurise the latter into breaking their fast. It also emerges, however, that the present government has shown a remarkable commitment towards solving the crisis—a factor greatly underestimated by the relatives of the hunger strikers—and that in its dealings with the British government it has encountered prevarications, disingenuousness and downright lies.[64]

What is most striking today about the ten men who died is their youth. 'They were mostly ardent but inexperienced guerrilla soldiers; they were in prison too long to gain more experience.'[65] And although it was customary for Conservative and Unionist politicians to refer to the men as 'murderers', the reality was that only one of them, Francis Hughes, had been convicted of murder.[66] Thomas McElwee had been convicted of manslaughter and Raymond McCreesh of attempted murder. Sands, O'Hara, McDonnell and Doherty were all serving long sentences for the possession of weapons. In the case of Sands and McDonnell, one revolver, found in a car in which they were travelling, earned them fourteen years each.[67]

The political journalist Dick Walsh, a persistent critic of republican violence, said that the majority of voters in the Republic did not support the IRA yet were

> angered by the inflexibility of the British government and see no reason why what they would regard as a sensible approach to prison conditions could not provide a solution. They find themselves impressed by the argument that many—perhaps most—of the prisoners in Long Kesh have grown to manhood in an atmosphere

of strife, that their conditioning has helped to recruit them into the ranks of the Provos or the INLA, that they have been tried in highly unusual circumstances, to say the least, and in many cases have been convicted on little evidence.[68]

There is little doubt that most people in the Republic would have welcomed a compromise by the British Government. Yet this recognition, that on this issue the IRA had a case, was largely irrelevant, because the hunger strikes' brutally laid bare the total impotence of the Government in dealing with the North only months after claims of an imminent historic breakthrough. As late as 24 May, after four prisoners had already died, when asked if he should not express his concern more forcefully to the British over the H-block protests and the deaths of the hunger-strikers,

> Mr Haughey told reporters that such an approach would create 'a confrontational situation' and there would be no benefit from confrontation. Asked what he would do if a dozen or two dozen hunger strikers died, he said every death was a tragedy, that he hoped for a solution through the European Commission or through flexibility on the part of the prison administration and added that the solution of the Northern Ireland problem was a firm priority.[69]

Jack Lynch, severely criticised because he was adjudged to be insufficiently republican, must have allowed himself a wry smile at this less than combative showing by his successor. Haughey undoubtedly felt that

> even if he had wanted to do so, it would have been impossible for him to clash with a British prime minister with whom he was claiming to have made a historic breakthrough on partition.[70]

For all the good it did him, Haughey might as well have thrown diplomatic caution to the winds. Because even before the hunger strike it becam.e apparent that there had been much less to the Dublin Castle meeting than had met the eye. The truth had been out since 18 March, when the Minister for Foreign Affairs, Brian Lenihan, was forced to admit that 'there was no question of the constitutional structure of the North being included in the joint studies set up after the Anglo-Irish summit last December.'

> Mr Lenihan had been asked by the Labour leader, Mr Cluskey, on the RTE television programme Today Tonight if the British Prime Minister Mrs Thatcher and her Northern Secretary Humphrey Atkins were lying when they denied that the constitutional position of the North was under discussion. Mr Lenihan replied that 'there is

no question of constitutional—it is institutional structures we are talking about.[71]

Five days later the limits of the 'special relationship' became even more apparent when it emerged that 'a brief five minute meeting between the Prime Minister and the Taoiseach in the course of the European Council had been almost entirely taken up by a "very annoyed" Mrs Thatcher.'[72] Thatcher, it seems, had severely upbraided Haughey over what she perceived as the Irish Government's misrepresentation of what had been agreed. Garret FitzGerald observed:

> It is odd and most unfortunate that Mr Haughey's Northern policy is based exclusively on his relations with the British Prime Minister. We have never been gullible about the British. We have always known that Britain will put her interests before Irish interests. We do not and we shall not place an exclusive or inordinate reliance on Britain in our approach to Northern Ireland.[73]

When, on 29 June, Haughey finally stated that the primary responsibility for the hunger strike lay with the British Government, Sinn Féin observed that the 'initiative was four months and four days late.'[74] Haughey's statement, the day before the Dáil met to elect a new Government, seemed nothing more than 'an indication that the Fianna Fáil leader is preparing to adopt a more republican position in opposition.'[75] Opposition had never been part of the Haughey plan. He had been

> obsessional about this election since he became Taoiseach in December 1979. A persistent refrain among his entourage since then has been, 'when he gets a mandate of his own' . . . Thus equipped, we were assured, he would sort out a recalcitrant party and cabinet, the hard decisions would be taken on the economy, industrial relations would be reformed, his much vaunted decisiveness, toughness and shrewdness would emerge.[76]

An opinion poll published four days into the campaign seemed to indicate that this mandate would be forthcoming. Excluding the 14 per cent of undecided voters, it showed 52 per cent intending to vote for Fianna Fáil, 32 per cent for Fine Gael and 11 per cent for the Labour Party. Haughey led FitzGerald as preferred Taoiseach by 43 to 40 per cent.[77] The survey also showed that despite Fianna Fáil's attempts to make the North an issue it ranked a distant third, at 14 per cent, when respondents were asked to rate the most important issue of the elections. Unemployment was at the top, followed by prices and inflation.[78]

The big difference this time was that Fine Gael ran a far more professional campaign. Perhaps more importantly, it caught the public imagination with what was billed as a weekly payment of £9.60 to women working in the home. This was in reality a proposal that women working in the home would be entitled to half the married tax credit directly; but it did move Fianna Fáil to produce sexist advertising that drew protests from women's groups. One warned that

> Fine Gael is making advances to your wife and they propose doing it with your money ... Avoid the cost and the complications. Vote Fianna Fáil on June 11.

The other stated:

> Fine Gael wants to rob Peter to pay Paula ... and they propose to make it legal! The £500 per annum Fine Gael say they would pay to some housewives would be deducted from their husband's tax relief. Think, Paula ... would Peter like that?[79]

Fine Gael also drew attention to the poor economic performance of the Government, contrasting the predictions made in the white paper in January 1978 with how things had turned out. Instead of the promised 5 per cent inflation the 1980 figure had been 18 per cent; instead of unemployment dropping by 30,000 it had risen by 34,000; borrowing was not the hoped-for 8 per cent of GNP but 14 per cent; and the expected increase in national output of 7 per cent had turned out to be 0.25 per cent.[80]

Fianna Fáil was also made uncomfortable on the campaign trail by the attention of republicans. In Ballyshannon, Co. Donegal, 'Mr Haughey and his supporters were pushed up and down the streets by a crowd of about fifty pushing, shouting protesters while the Gardaí vainly tried to form a cordon.'[81] And things took a further turn when

> a bomb was discovered in the Fianna Fáil election headquarters in Castleblayney, Co. Monaghan, only hours before the Taoiseach ... was due to visit the premises ... The INLA claimed responsibility for the bomb and said that the device had been planted as a warning to Mr Haughey for allegedly collaborating with the British government and refusing to take action while hunger strikers died.[82]

Bernadette McAliskey attacked Fianna Fáil's republican credentials, asking

> How can the people of the Southern side of the border take the hand of friendship offered by Mrs Thatcher when the other hand is on the throat of our people in the North? How can you allow a government acting in your name to claim a 'unique relationship' with such a hard-necked, spiteful reactionary woman?[83]

In the election campaign Fianna Fáil sought an advantage by portraying itself as the protector of Catholic morality—a role it would pursue with increasing avidity in the coming decade. 'The campaign for abortion is the vilest threat of all,' warned Kit Ahern TD.

> That is why Fianna Fáil will introduce a Pro-Life constitutional amendment when we win this election. Contrast the attitude of the Labour party. They are dragging their feet on the most important moral issue to confront our people since their independence. Why? Because they have made their bed with left-wing intellectuals and Marxist elements.[84]

Rory O'Hanlon TD declared that it was 'frightening to see abortion being discussed at the highest level in Fine Gael notwithstanding the censure of the party leader.'[85] Albert Reynolds worried that the Labour Party 'seek to bring in divorce and abortion which is totally against the wishes and values of Irish people. Abortion is murder—and the people want no part of it.'[86] A vote for the Labour Party, said Councillor Michael Finneran, was 'not a vote for marriage at all, but for living in sin.'[87]

This orgy of self-righteousness makes it almost a relief to turn to the more traditional form of scaremongering practised by Tom McEllistrim, who told constituents that

> if you don't vote Fianna Fáil Garret FitzGerald will be the next Minister for Finance and Frank Cluskey will be the next Minister for Agriculture. And farmers of Abbeydorney, you know what that means. The Labour party is committed to a policy of nationalising all farming land. Vote for a coalition and they will move in and take your land.[88]

Fianna Fáil's use of the abortion issue as an electoral weapon probably had its roots in an interview given to the *Evening Herald* on 30 March by Maria Stack, a medical student from Listowel and one of the four vice-presidents of Fine Gael, in which she said that

> if a woman wants to terminate an unwanted pregnancy there is nothing the law can do to stop her. Many of those who oppose abortion do so without giving any thought to the problem. On medical grounds I would support the right of a woman to choose abortion as a last resort.

This led to her being immediately disowned by the party,[89] which illustrated the tensions between the young liberals attracted to Fine Gael by FitzGerald's leadership and the old guard of the party, who hewed to a traditional line on moral issues.

FitzGerald prevented Fianna Fáil from making political capital by

agreeing, as did Haughey, to hold the referendum proposed by the Pro-
Life Amendment Campaign. The groups that made up the PLAC included
the Congress of Catholic Secondary School Parents' Associations, the Irish
Catholic Doctors' Guild, the Guild of Catholic Nurses, the Guild of
Catholic Pharmacists, the Catholic Young Men's Society, the St Thomas
More Society, St Joseph's Young Priests' Society and the Christian
Brothers' Schools Parents' Federation. The draft amendment they
proposed read: 'The state recognises the absolute right to life of every
unborn child from conception and accordingly guarantees to respect and
protect such right by law.'[90] Opponents noted that the word 'absolute'

> would deny all rights to the woman even in cases where her life was
> threatened by continuing pregnancy. That such a wording would
> emanate from practising gynaecologists was deeply disturbing. It
> did not, however, raise an alarm bell in the minds of the leaders of
> the two largest political parties . . . It seems extraordinary that a man
> of FitzGerald's intelligence, with his pluralist outlook, his much-
> vaunted academic interest in theology and other religions, his
> antipathy to the sectarian nature of much of the state's laws and
> constitutional procedures, should have bowed the knee so quickly
> and so unthinkingly to those people.[91]

The bowing of the knee, whether motivated by heedlessness or
cynicism, would cause FitzGerald serious problems in the future. For the
moment, though, his campaign continued to gather momentum. The
new-found dynamism of the Fine Gael campaign was epitomised by his
tour of the country by special train.

> Each venue had the local party faithful in attendance and local
> candidates on their best behaviour. Garret hats, T-shirts and posters
> were everywhere. FitzGerald held press conferences on the train for
> the local media, explaining the party's programme and ensuring
> invaluable print and picture publicity from the provincial
> newspapers . . . In the vital business of electoral razzmatazz, Fine
> Gael had not just matched Fianna Fáil. They were eclipsing them.[92]

Things were not going so well for the Labour Party leader, Frank
Cluskey, whose chances of becoming Minister for Agriculture and
dispossessing the farmers of Co. Kerry were endangered by his clash with
the party's great vote-getter, John O'Connell. The problem was that both
men

> wanted to stand in Dublin South-Central. So obvious was the
> impending clash and so potentially destructive that the failure to
> head it off by quiet consultation points to negligence amounting to

a political death wish. The party hierarchy, instead of trying to compromise or inspecting O'Connell's claim that there was room in South Central for two labour seats, backed Cluskey's surgical removal of O'Connell. O'Connell's branch was shifted into Dublin West, without consultation with the members or with O'Connell.[93]

The result was that O'Connell decided to defy the Administrative Council and run in Dublin South-Central anyway, effectually exiling himself from the party.

As the campaign drew to a close, FitzGerald gave a speech in Roscommon that began with a statement that 'it is irresponsible to seek to make political capital out of the tragedy of Northern Ireland' and then went on to do exactly that.

> When we are told, however, that by the next Fianna Fáil ard-fheis we will be able to see the way forward to Irish unity without any indication of how this is to be achieved, two entirely predictable but disastrous results follow. The men of violence and the intimidators North and South are encouraged by the evident irresponsibility of government to pursue their evil campaign. Secondly, the Unionists of Northern Ireland, those who should be reconciled by Dublin to considering a common future with us, are provoked to further intransigence. Irish unity is once again postponed.[94]

All the stops had been pulled out. Fianna Fáil held a final press conference with celebrities who supported the party, among them Paddy Moloney of the Chieftains, the show-jumper Eddie Macken, the Dublin footballer Gay O'Driscoll and Donncha Ó Dúlaing of RTE.[95] In Galway West, Michael D. Higgins was backed by the actor Peter O'Toole, who 'posed with Alderman Higgins for pictures at the Labour election rooms [and] spoke to election workers.'[96]

The problem facing Haughey was that this would be only the third election held when real income per capita had dropped since the previous one.[97] On the previous two occasions, in 1957 and 1977, the incumbent Government had been trounced. It would defy all recent experience, one commentator wrote in *Magill*,

> if Fianna Fáil were not to suffer electorally from an inflation rate edging towards 20 per cent, unemployment now well over 100,000 again, a fifty per cent drop in farmers' incomes, industrial relations disruption in key social service areas and a general feeling of drift and indecisiveness.[98]

Yet even when all the first counts were in the result remained up in the air. Máire Geoghegan-Quinn conceded defeat when she found herself behind her party colleagues Bobby Molloy, Mark Killilea and Frank Fahey on the first count.[99] In the event, huge transfers from Molloy and Nicky O'Connor saw her home ahead of Fahey with 1,500 votes to spare.

When the dust settled, Fianna Fáil had 78 seats out of 166, Fine Gael 65 and the Labour Party 15, with others, including two H-block candidates, obtaining 8. The Labour Party suffered a crushing blow when its leader lost his seat in Dublin South-Central, where John O'Connell topped the poll and the Fine Gael newcomer Gay Mitchell beat Cluskey for the final seat by more than a thousand votes. That Fine Gael received almost three times as many transfers from O'Connell's surplus as Cluskey did sums up the bitterness of the falling out between the two men.[100]

There was the highest number of successful candidates from outside the two main parties since 1961. They included Jim Kemmy, a former member of the Labour Party's Administrative Council, who had left the party in 1972 after clashes with the sitting TD, Stephen Coughlan, and formed his own socialist organisation in Limerick East. There was also a first seat for Sinn Féin the Workers' Party, with Joe Sherlock beating Fianna Fáil to a seat in Cork East. In his victory speech he told his supporters that 'we have only begun the real fight on the road to a socialist republic.'[101]

Fianna Fáil's total vote had dropped by 5½ per cent to 45 per cent, its lowest since 1961, Fine Gael's rose by 6 per cent to 37 per cent, the highest in the party's history, while the Labour Party's dropped 1½ per cent to 10 per cent, the party's worst result since 1957.[102] Michael O'Leary, unanimously elected leader to replace Cluskey, was faced with a huge task. Fine Gael had done notably well in Dublin, where it increased its vote by 8½ per cent, with both the Labour Party and Fianna Fáil dropping by 5½ per cent. With the coalition three seats short of an absolute majority and Fianna Fáil five seats short, the identity of the new Taoiseach was far from certain, though FitzGerald was clearly the favourite.

For a while it looked as though there might be a quite different alternative when it was suggested that a view was gaining ground in the Labour Party that it should support a minority Fianna Fáil Government.[103] However, a special conference on 28 June voted by 737 votes to 477 to approve coalition with Fine Gael. The ITGWU and FWUI had both come out against coalition, and 'it was generally believed that most of the 320 Dublin delegates and of the 150 trade union delegates had voted against coalition, with rural delegates heavily in favour.'[104] But the coalition still 'needed support or benign abstention from the six independent and minor-party TDs if it was to enter government.'[105]

Two days later FitzGerald was elected Taoiseach by 81 votes to 78. John O'Connell, who had been appointed Ceann Comhairle at the beginning of the day's business, could not vote, while Neil Blaney, Seán Loftus, Joe Sherlock and Noël Browne all abstained. Jim Kemmy voted for FitzGerald, who had been proposed by Oliver Flanagan, whose unbroken tenure since 1943 made him the longest-serving member of the Dáil.

The motion to re-elect Haughey as Taoiseach had been lost by 83 to 79. Of the independents, Blaney had voted for his old friend, while Sherlock, Kemmy and Browne voted against him, and Loftus abstained.

FitzGerald set about naming his Government. His selection was not without surprises. The surprises were unpleasant for the leading members of the party's old guard, as the former ministers Dick Burke, Richie Ryan and Tom O'Donnell found themselves passed over. There were also raised eyebrows at the omission of Michael Keating (Fine Gael) and Barry Desmond (Labour Party). And even the most perspicacious of political pundits could not have predicted that FitzGerald would name James Dooge, a close friend and adviser who was not a member of either house of the Oireachtas, as Minister for Foreign Affairs. The choice of Alan Dukes, formerly an agricultural economist with the Irish Farmers' Association, as Minister for Agriculture was also a surprise.

The incoming Government was greeted with a nasty surprise when it discovered that 90 per cent of the year's budget deficit

> was already spent, and it was only 1 July. It was plain that Fianna Fáil had grossly under-provided for various departments in the 1981 estimates. Without more funds, government services would run out of money by September or October.[106]

It was a baptism of fire for the Minister for Finance, John Bruton, in his first senior Government position. He opted to bring in a supplementary budget on 21 July, which ensured that 'the new deficit would be £787 million, £160 million less than it would otherwise have been.'[107] The budget included

> increased charges on various services (postal, electricity, telephone and mortgage interest rates) that had been postponed in the later stages of the Haughey administration. Increases in excise duties (on alcohol, tobacco and oil products) and in VAT were announced.[108]

There was also a 1 per cent levy on all incomes, which would go into a Youth Employment Fund.

The eye-catching £9.60 a week stay-at-home allowance never really got off the ground. The architect of the plan, the economist Brendan Dowling, had wanted it implemented automatically, with an opt-out clause ... But Finance maintained [that] this was not feasible. What resulted was an opt-in scheme. Families had to apply for the £9.60, which was, after all, a deduction from the husband's earnings. Inevitably, only a highly motivated minority of women pursued it.[109]

Coalition ministers defended the harsh supplementary budget on the grounds that

its predecessor's high level of foreign borrowing had left the country at the mercy of foreign bankers. Should they recall their loans, Ireland would have to seek assistance from the IMF, which would be forthcoming only if the government of the day agreed to draconian politics that would bear hardest on the weaker sections of society. To obviate this danger, the government argued, it was necessary to put the economy in order, by phasing out the current budget deficit and reducing reliance on foreign borrowing.[110]

Yet there was severe disgruntlement among members of the Labour Party, whose Administrative Council declared that

the Labour ministers had exceeded their mandate from the June special conference when they agreed to the provisions of the July budget, and there were constant calls from individual members, and from the party's youth wing, for a withdrawal from government.[111]

A report by the Economic and Social Research Institute in June revealed that

the net direct tax burden (income tax and PSRI contributions, less children's allowance) on the average industrial worker has increased 2.5% since June 1979. On the other hand, the net direct tax burden on the well-off taxpayer, earning four times industrial earnings (£27,000 per annum) has fallen by 4.6%.

This may explain why working-class voters in particular resented austerity measures.[112]

Yet the economic auguries were undeniably grim. The Organisation for Economic Cooperation and Development

forecast that among its 24 member countries, Ireland would have the lowest rate of growth in 1982, the fourth highest rate of unemployment, the second highest rate of inflation, the worst balance of payments deficit and the highest level of debt repayment.[113]

The person charged with solving these economic problems caused a stir when, in a radio interview, he announced his intention

to lead a crusade, a republican crusade, to make this a genuine republic ... We expect the Northern Unionists to join a state which, in 1979, was bringing in laws based on the theology of one church. Now that has to change and what I want to do is lead public opinion towards that change. And if eventually it transpires that the Irish people don't want this, if the people in the state want to remain fundamentally a 26 county state based on a majority ethos and are not prepared to work with the people of Northern Ireland towards unity on a basis that could be common to both, well then I will accept defeat and leave politics at that stage if necessary.[114]

The 'constitutional crusade' interview was immensely significant as 'the first time in the history of the Irish state that a Taoiseach had stated that there were sectarian aspects to Southern society and dedicated himself to eliminating these.'[115] Haughey responded by criticising

too much wishy washy talk of appeasing unionists and all that ... Why doesn't Dr FitzGerald refer to the fact that the Unionists in Northern Ireland won't permit children in Northern Ireland to have swings on a Sunday? Why do we have to do all the reparation and the self-abasement and excusing for our existence?[116]

He expanded on this theme on 11 October when telling the crowd at the unveiling of a memorial to Éamon de Valera in Ennis that there was no reason

to apologise to anyone for being what we are or for holding the beliefs that we do: we angrily reject accusations of either inferiority or sectarianism. Once again we are asked to believe that somewhere else things are ordered much better than they are here and that there exists a superior form of society which we must imitate.[117]

Haughey may have had a point, however, when he said that changes in the Constitution 'should be undertaken on their merit, not with a view to impressing Northern Unionists, the British or anyone else.'[118] His view was echoed by Martin Mansergh, a former civil servant who had recently become head of research in Fianna Fáil, who commented that

we can't centre national development around whether or not it pleases the Unionists. Nor do I see that one has to go to extreme lengths to accommodate those who totally refuse to participate.[119]

Time and again, progressive social legislation would be defended on the grounds that it would send useful smoke signals over the border. Yet a liberalisation of the family planning laws and an end to the constitutional prohibition on divorce were surely necessary in their own right for a more tolerant and less repressive Republic. To argue for their necessity on the grounds that they gave a good impression to Unionists was to leave oneself open to the riposte of social conservatives that the fact of unmarried people being able to buy condoms in the Republic would not make the OUP or DUP one whit more responsive to the idea of a united Ireland.

Nevertheless, FitzGerald's intervention was a courageous and timely one. Or rather it would have been had his actions lived up to his rhetoric. The problem was that at the time he gave the 'constitutional crusade' interview he had already given a commitment to PLAC to hold a referendum that would be seen by the Protestant churches as sectarian. He would repeat this commitment before the following year's second general election, and he would be in Government the year after that when the 'pro-life' amendment, the ultimate expression of 'laws based on the theology of one church,' was passed. And he did not 'accept defeat and leave politics at that stage if necessary.' This avowedly pluralist politician would in fact bequeath the country a Constitution more sectarian than the one he inherited. His pluralism, like his opposite number's republicanism, proved utterly ineffectual when faced with political reality.

The dire financial position inherited by the Government owed a great deal to the situation described by Seán Barrett, a lecturer in economics in Trinity College, in which

> politicians treat public expenditure as their personal gift to the populace. They boast at Ard Fheiseanna of the amount of public money they have been able to spend on their pet projects and they get cheered and applauded. The whole thing is quite crazy. Nobody asks how is the thing financed, if we can afford it or the money effectively used and if the programme is achieving the objective it was intended to achieve.[120]

One project in particular came to be seen as epitomising this tendency. It had its roots in the papal visit to Knock, Co. Mayo, when Monsignor James Horan, the parish priest,

> sought an airport for Knock to cope with pilgrims, who were expected to come in tens of thousands, if not more . . . Government officials were highly sceptical of this, and of the advisability of any airport at all; but when it eventually came to [the] government, appropriately in Holy Week 1981, and with a Department of Finance recommendation for deferral of [a] decision, the project was approved, the state to bear the cost. What had been visualised initially as a small airstrip escalated rapidly into one capable of intercontinental jets . . . Beside a comment in the memorandum for government saying of the request 'this is irreversible,' a senior Finance spokesman had written: 'It is outrageous.' Nevertheless, the

project was approved and once state contracts were signed it became irreversible.[121]

The approval owed much to the political nous of Horan, who used Haughey's trip to Castlebar to unveil a memorial plaque at the site of his own birthplace to extract

> a minimal promise of an airport and put his organisational talents to work. Expenditure of £567,000 had been incurred before the project got formal government approval and Horan hurried things along towards his own goal of an international airport, arranging for work to begin on drainage and access roads in the run-up to the general election—a period in which politicians would be highly unlikely to challenge the actions of a popular figure who was merely doing his bit for the West.[122]

Such considerations cut no ice with Barry Desmond, who became Minister of State at the Department of Finance after the election; and in December, largely at Desmond's instigation, 'the government announced that it would not be providing any further funds for a proposed airport at Knock . . . which according to independent assessment would be an expensive white elephant.'[123]

Yet the decision played very differently in Co. Mayo, where the go-ahead for the airport was seen in the context of local economic depression.

> Travenol in Belmullet, 250 jobs gone: Travenol in Castlebar down from 1,500 to just over a thousand jobs. In January Roadstone will put half of its 60 workers on a three day week; Ryan's Hotel in Westport, closed for the winter, 30 jobs gone. Castlebar bacon factory down from 320 to 140 in two years. Innumerable small firms making six or seven workers redundant.[124]

The budgetary case for halting the project may have been unanswerable, but the symbolism suggested a disdain for the west of Ireland on the part of the coalition, which would help the province remain Fianna Fáil's electoral heartland for the rest of the decade.

The further adventures of Knock airport will be dealt with in the second volume.

———

Yet even the social problems of the west paled into insignificance when compared with those of an area like St Teresa's Gardens, a flats complex off Donore Avenue in Dublin.

Local employment had fallen away, the younger generation was being rehoused in the new suburbs on the city's outskirts, in satellite towns like Tallaght and Clondalkin and Dublin Corporation was downgrading the Gardens to a low priority area—with a maintenance and servicing policy to match . . . The fact that many young couples wanted to stay in the area where they were reared, not to mention the socially disruptive effect of transplanting families haphazardly from one side of Dublin's growing urban sprawl to the other was blithely ignored by the planners. The implication of allowing traditional inner city employers like the rag trade and meat processing business to run down, while attracting new employers to the mushrooming satellite towns were also ignored. City Hall seemed wilfully determined to create blackspots in Dublin's core, where layer after layer of deprivation would be piled on the inhabitants.[125]

To this cocktail of misery was added a final deadly ingredient: heroin. The Iranian Revolution in 1979 led to the West being flooded with cheap heroin as fleeing émigrés converted their money into drugs that could be sold on the European and American market. The south inner city was the first area to be affected, with St Teresa's Gardens becoming a particular black spot. 'Within three years there were an estimated 200 abusers living in or calling daily to pushers in the complex. All efforts to rebuild the community had collapsed.'[126]

The family who largely controlled the drug trade in the area, and who would become the public face of the heroin epidemic in Dublin, were the Dunnes. They were the sons of Christopher 'Bronco' Dunne, a labourer who had once served time in prison for manslaughter after killing a man with a single punch. Ten of the family had amassed more than 150 convictions between them. The Dunnes were brought up in the New Street area of the inner city and then in Crumlin, and they had endured lives of considerable deprivation, even by the standards of the time. In 1958 ten-year-old Larry, nine-year-old Robert, eight-year-old Vianney and seven-year-old Henry had slept rough in the Wicklow Mountains for three months, surviving by stealing from local farms before they were captured. In 1960 Larry and Henry travelled to London in search of their father and slept rough in the city for five days. Eight Dunne brothers had served time in the notorious industrial school system, at Daingean, Upton, Artane and Letterfrack. In 1955 one brother, Hubert, drowned while trying to rescue a fellow-inmate at Upton. Seven years later Vianney, better known as Boyo, was beaten so severely by the Christian Brothers in Artane that he spent time in the National Children's Hospital.[127]

Henry Dunne had been one of the country's most infamous armed robbers; but it was his brother Larry who would be seen as the head of the family's drug-dealing enterprise as the problem began to spread and as heroin hit the north inner city in the summer of 1981. 'In a matter of a few weeks it had devastated the area.'[128]

In the Liberty House flats off Railway Street local residents saw 'increasing numbers of youngsters, including schoolgirls, injecting themselves on the stairways and leaving the blood-splattered syringes behind them for the toddlers to pick up.'[129] The problem was exacerbated by the fact that a campaign by city-centre businesses against illegal street trading meant that 'thousands of garda hours were wasted in an unnecessary battle to suppress illegal trading while a few hundred yards away pushers slipped unhampered through the flat complexes of the North Inner City.'[130]

Tony Gregory, the local independent socialist councillor,

> didn't believe initial reports and thought they were grossly exaggerated until he visited a local pub, the Jetfoil on the North Wall, one of the venues used by pushers, and saw the problem for himself. Pubs in the Talbot Street area were also used extensively for drug trafficking. One of them, Kelly's, was called 'The Chemists Shop', by local wags. So was Foley Street Park, which became known locally as 'Needle Park.'[131]

The sudden increase of heroin abuse is obvious from the growing number of people with opiate problems attending the National Drug Advisory and Treatment Centre at Jervis Street Hospital. (Opiates include synthetic opiates such as Diconal.) In 1979 the number was 148, but by 1981 it had jumped to 400; by 1983 it would be 790. 64 per cent of the opiate abusers in 1981 were under twenty-four; all but 10 per cent of them were under thirty.[132]

The scale of the problem threatened to destroy communities that were already struggling. In St Teresa's Gardens

> there was a serious squatting problem; a third of the 350 flats were changing hands each year, and a survey disclosed that almost sixty per cent of residents were unemployed. Not one local youngster was attending a third level college. The cul-de-sac from Donore Avenue into the Gardens was a dead end in every sense for the 1,250 tenants trapped inside.[133]

Yet such areas would still manage a community response even as the drug problem grew worse in the coming years.

That community response would eventually be the subject of a song, 'Whacker Humphries', by Christy Moore, who by 1981 was functioning as a kind of bard of republican and radical causes. He did so at the head of a sublime band, Moving Hearts, which married musical and political radicalism on an eponymous debut album that is one of the finest ever released by an Irish band. Moore's bandmates included his former Planxty colleague Dónal Lunny and Davy Spillane, a brilliant uilleann piper in the mould of Liam Óg Ó Floinn.

But it was the other members of the group who made Moving Hearts a new departure in Irish traditional music. The likes of the guitarist Declan Sinnott, formerly of Horslips, the alto saxophonist Keith Donald and the bassist Eoghan O'Neill came from backgrounds in rock and jazz rather than folk music. Moving Hearts possessed a unique voice that combined great musical complexity and delicacy with an angry and passionate political stance, described by Keith Donald as 'republican socialist or socialist republican.'[134] In the words of one critic, 'Moving Hearts stand for something, they react to the world around them, they refuse to remain silent in the face of the manifold injustices of the modern world.'[135]

Above all, the group was defined by the vocals of Christy Moore, the closest thing there was to a musical spirit of the age. Four years later he would write a song for his album *Ordinary Man* about the Stardust fire, 'They Never Came Home', which cut so close to the bone that Eamon Butterly obtained a High Court injunction that caused the album to be withdrawn from the shops until it could be reissued without the song. In 1986 he performed at the funeral of the chairperson of the Stardust Relatives' Committee, John Keegan, whose teenage daughters Mary and Martina had died in the fire. Seven years later he sang 'They Never Came Home' at the opening of a memorial park to the victims.[136]

Moore would also provide the most memorable musical memorials for the 1981 hunger strike, recording two songs written by Bobby Sands, 'McIlhatton' and 'I Wish I Was Back Home in Derry', and a song inspired by the final days of Patsy O'Hara, 'The Time Has Come'. Moore would remain haunted by the memory of the hunger strikes, writing in his autobiography:

> I remember recording 'On the Blanket' in Collooney, Co. Sligo the night that young Martin Hurson died on hunger strike. Moving Hearts were playing in the Community Hall. Mick Hanly and I shared the vocals. Some days later we were performing at an open-air festival in Castlebar, Co. Mayo. I heard on the radio that Kieran

Doherty had succumbed to the Hunger. I remember going into the Artists' Bar feeling numbed by the news, and I was taken aback at the total lack of interest amongst the liggers and giggers. Something stirred inside me that day. I began to realise that the showbiz community was not where I belonged.[137]

Chapter 11 ~

| GUBU ROI

1982

Pa Ubu: There's only one solution: I'll take over command myself.
Ready about. 'Bout ship. Let go the anchor. Go about in stays, wear
ship, hoist more sail, haul down sail, put the tiller hard over, up with
the helm, down with the helm, full speed astern, give her more lee,
splice the top gallant. How am I doing?
—Alfred Jarry, *Ubu Roi* (1896)

Where to start with 1982? A cursory glance would show that Garret
FitzGerald was Taoiseach on 1 January and held the same office
on 31 December. But what an abundance of incident in
between!—two general elections, a Government falling unexpectedly on a
budget vote, another losing a vote of confidence, two separate heaves
against the leader of the country's biggest party, political scandals
involving personation, interference with the Gardaí, the use of police in
another state to falsely imprison a witness, the arrest of a murderer in the
Attorney-General's flat, an attempt to thwart the plans of our next-door
neighbours in a foreign war, a post-election deal that worked, a by-
election stroke that didn't, and a general feeling that political life was being
scripted by a satirist of genius.

Above all it was the year of GUBU. When Charlie Haughey described the
events surrounding the resignation of the Attorney-General, Patrick
Connolly, as 'an unprecedented situation . . . a grotesque situation . . . a
bizarre happening . . . an unbelievable situation,' his old adversary Conor
Cruise O'Brien coined the acronym GUBU to describe Haughey himself
and his Government.[1] 'You've got to hand it to the man, you really have,'
wrote Cruise O'Brien: 'he is grotesque, unbelievable, bizarre and
unprecedented.'[2] The term stuck.

It's tempting to think of Haughey in 1982 as Gubu Roi. In Alfred Jarry's farcical play *Ubu Roi,* Pa Ubu is a power-mad courtier who ruthlessly seizes power from the king, only to be overthrown by his enemies. It's not a bad description of Haughey's *annus horribilis.*

And yet it had all started so well. He had, for instance, the pleasure of watching in the Dáil on 27 January as

> Garret FitzGerald knelt up on the bench in front of Kemmy, asking, gesticulating, probably pleading. Kemmy looked steadfastly down at the paper in front of him, his thick glasses casting shadows on the gloomy face. The Fianna Fáilers sniggered at FitzGerald and he jumped back to a sitting position, grinning like a guilty schoolboy. The game was up.[3]

FitzGerald was attempting to persuade Kemmy to support the coalition Government's budget, which needed the votes of two independents to get it through the Dáil. The problem was that the budget was

> more severe than even the most pessimistic critics had feared. Reduced food subsidies, new taxes on clothing and footwear, together with general increases in VAT, excise duties, income tax and social insurance contributions, as well as restrictions on mortgage tax relief and personal loans were among the main provisions . . . The most controversial item in the budget . . . was the decision to subject clothing and footwear to the newly increased VAT rate of 18%. Up to now these 'necessities of life', in Mr John Bruton's words, had a zero VAT rating, but he made it clear that this exemption could no longer be justified.[4]

When asked why children's clothing and footwear could not be exempted from VAT, FitzGerald explained that 'this could have led to a situation where some women with small feet could have bought their shoes cheaper than their children who had larger feet.'[5]

Noël Browne was able to stomach the budget, but his fellow-socialist Kemmy was not. The votes of Kemmy, Seán Loftus (independent) and Joe Sherlock (Sinn Féin the Workers' Party) ensured that the budget was defeated, 82 votes to 81. Kemmy felt that Fine Gael had displayed

> a take it or leave it attitude at the crucial moment. I got the impression that they thought I was only bluffing, that I would back down at the last second and cast my vote with the government as I had done in every key division since the previous July.[6]

Loftus also detected an unbending attitude on the part of Fine Gael.

> I had been prepared to compromise to vote with the government if the 18% VAT on children's clothing and footwear had been dropped . . . I went into the lobbies with Fianna Fáil . . . It was Fine Gael's

ineptitude that brought down the government.[7]

It is hard to disagree with this analysis, given that the coalition actually dropped the proposed tax on clothing and footwear in the subsequent election campaign. Now, facing the country with the most austere of budgets as a campaign platform, it appeared set for electoral defeat. Haughey should have relished the opportunity to score a convincing victory; instead he tried to avoid an election altogether by trying to pull the kind of stroke that would disfigure the political landscape in the coming year.

> After a meeting of the Fianna Fáil front bench immediately after the government had lost the vote, Haughey issued a statement: 'It is a matter for the president to consider the situation which has arisen now that the Taoiseach has ceased to retain the support of the majority in Dáil Éireann. I am available for consultation by the President should he so wish.[8]

This was a reference to the power of the President not to grant a dissolution of the Dáil. If that were to happen, Haughey would take power without any election.

Haughey was not simply available for consultation, he was apparently keen to influence Hillery's decision as well. By the time FitzGerald reached Áras an Uachtaráin to request the dissolution

> seven phone calls had been made to the president's official residence by members of the Fianna Fáil front bench, in an effort to persuade President Hillery to . . . refuse Garret FitzGerald a dissolution and call on Charlie Haughey to form a government.[9]

The President was

> disturbed and angered by what he regarded as quite unwarranted efforts, repeatedly made, to interfere with his office. In addition, one of the calls, received by the President's Aide de Camp . . . included threatening language concerning that officer's future if he did not put the call through . . .[10]

Hillery resisted the pressure, but the episode 'revealed among those responsible little or no respect for the institutions of the state.'[11]

This attempted coup having failed, Fianna Fáil nevertheless began the election campaign as favourites. The manner in which the Government had fallen could have made the result a foregone conclusion; but Fianna Fáil was forced onto the back foot early in the campaign by an article in *Magill* headed 'How Haughey cooked the books in 1981,' which claimed that

> a confidential document from the Department of Finance leaked

anonymously to *Magill* suggests that prior to the last election the government of Charles Haughey effectively falsified budgetary finances, before engaging in a massive splurge of public expenditure financed by foreign borrowing ... The affair raises serious questions about the credibility of Charles Haughey and his suitability as Taoiseach ...[12]

The budget deficit for the year was £802 million and, without Bruton's supplementary budget, could have reached £971 million. Under-estimation of budget deficits had become something of a tradition: in 1979 the excess of the actual over the projected deficit was 81 per cent and in 1980 was 58 per cent. (In 1981 it turned out to be 56 per cent, though without Bruton's intervention it would have reached a record 89 per cent).[13] *Magill's* contention was that 'there was an element of deliberation in the under-estimation of public expenditure for 1981 on a vast scale,' and that this happened so that Fianna Fáil could engage in

> a massive binge of public expenditure to be paid for entirely out of foreign borrowing in an attempt to win the election. More than anything else, it was this ... that has caused such a serious crisis in the nation's public finances.[14]

Fianna Fáil reacted by calling *Magill's* editor, Vincent Browne, 'somewhat insane. He's on a constant ego trip. He promotes gutter journalism and is a totally discredited journalist.'[15] This bluster, however, did not disguise the fact that there was no serious attempt to challenge the truth of a story that was particularly damaging to Fianna Fáil on the two fronts where it was most vulnerable: financial competence and the leader's credibility. These weaknesses gave the coalition a fighting chance in an election in which it might have expected a trouncing. At first Haughey

> rejected not only the detail but also the whole economic strategy of the budget. That night and on the following day at his press conference ... he dismissed what he called the 'obsession' with foreign borrowing: repeatedly he spoke of government and commentators 'hypnotised' with the subject.[16]

But under pressure from senior front-bench members, such as Martin O'Donoghue and Desmond O'Malley, he rowed back on that attitude, and Fianna Fáil broadly accepted the argument for fiscal rectitude during the campaign as the state of the public finances became a general election issue for the first time.

Even Sinn Féin the Workers' Party, the most left-wing party in the Dáil, accepted the need for a reduction in the deficit; it just felt that the

Government was going about it the wrong way. The party's TD, Joe Sherlock,

> did not disagree with the overall strategy of the budget—reducing the deficit on the balance of payments. He had put a submission to the government that this should be done by increasing capital taxation rather than by increasing the price of petrol, milk, butter and other things bought by ordinary people.[17]

FitzGerald went so far as to make financial austerity a point of national pride, suggesting that if the coalition won, Ireland's credit would stand high

> because the people would have supported very tough measures to provide a basis to expand the economy in a sound way in the future. Foreign journalists now asked about the economy, not Northern Ireland. When they had done so, Irish credibility would be very high. Ireland would be seen in a new light and this would have a practical effect on investment.

As so often with FitzGerald, one eye was trained across the water.

> Our image which for historical reasons was poor in Britain would change radically. Our own view of ourselves would also change. We would change. We would have greater self-respect and self-confidence.[18]

FitzGerald set the election agenda, and the opposition did not greatly dispute it. Fianna Fáil even produced an alternative budget, largely the work of Martin O'Donoghue, which was not greatly different from the one that had failed to get through the Dáil. The main difference was that it would drop VAT on clothing and footwear and replace the lost revenue by 'bringing forward the date of payment of corporation tax; and by applying VAT on imports at the point of import rather than the point of sale.'[19] The outgoing Minister for Finance, John Bruton, pointed out that these changes would be a one-off measure that would merely postpone the problems until 1983.

O'Donoghue's return to favour was an attempt by Haughey to dispel the aura of amateurism that had come to surround the party on matters of economic policy. Yet an opinion poll showed the coalition with a lead of 55 to 23 per cent over Fianna Fáil among voters asked who they thought would best tackle Government spending and foreign borrowing.[20] The same survey showed FitzGerald leading Haughey by 56 to 33 per cent as preferred Taoiseach. Given that only nine months had passed since the men had been neck and neck, and that Haughey had not been in a position of power in which he could have alienated voters, this precipitous drop was something of a mystery. The best explanation may be that Haughey's popularity problems were the result of

> criticism of his leadership within his own party. The argument would be that the public expects swingeing attacks by one party on the leadership or policies of another and discounts them accordingly. When, however, serious dissent and criticism surfaces within a party, public opinion takes the matter more seriously and is more likely to be affected by it.[21]

The dissent and criticism had come from a backbencher from Co. Kildare named Charlie McCreevy, who on 27 December the previous year had complained that Fianna Fáil

> seem to be against everything and for nothing. There is a considerable number of the Fianna Fáil Parliamentary Party, representing the views of the organisation throughout the country, who are less than satisfied with Fianna Fáil in opposition.[22]

McCreevy, previously little known,

> became a celebrity overnight and handled his criticisms of the party well. He let his outspoken challenge come to a Parliamentary Party meeting and then used the occasion to repeat his criticisms, confining them to party uncertainty and lack of direction, caused principally by the failure to discuss issues. Then he resigned the party whip and left the meeting, pledging his continued loyalty to Fianna Fáil.[23]

The Haughey factor notwithstanding, the coalition still faced an uphill struggle. In the previous election it had won a combined eighty seats to Fianna Fáil's seventy-eight. With no H-block candidates this time, Fianna Fáil was virtually certain to regain seats in Louth and Cavan-Monaghan, for a start. And its claim that 'the coalition's deflationary policies are responsible for the highest level of unemployment in decades' could not be dismissed out of hand.[24] The previous six months had been disastrous in relation to unemployment, with about a thousand people a week joining the dole queue. Half way through the campaign came the news that unemployment had reached a new record of 146,592, with a quarter of those under the age of twenty-five.[25]

Fianna Fáil had a further boost when Haughey performed well in the first live televised election debate between the two main party leaders. Haughey unsettled FitzGerald when defending Fianna Fáil's refusal to join the all-party committee on marital breakdown. For Haughey,

> my personal view is that I don't believe that divorce answers the problem of marital breakdown. I believe that we should concentrate

our efforts on legislation and action to protect the family first of all, and then to help the families where there is a marital breakdown situation.[26]

He added that the Labour Party

said that it wanted divorce no matter what the arguments were. He thought Dr FitzGerald also wanted divorce, although perhaps not with the same urgency and emphasis as the Labour Party.[27]

An angry FitzGerald described Haughey's arguments as 'codswallop'.[28] Given that Haughey, so deftly posing as the defender of family values, was at the time several years into an extramarital affair with a well-known journalist, FitzGerald may have erred on the side of kindness.[29]

The election was another close-run thing, and the results were strikingly similar to the previous one. Fianna Fáil's vote rose by 2 per cent to 47 per cent, and the party gained four seats to give it a total of 81. Fine Gael's vote went up by 0.8 per cent to 37 per cent, but it actually went down two seats to 65. The Labour Party went down 0.8 per cent to 9 per cent but held its 15 seats. Sinn Féin the Workers' Party won 2¼ per cent of the vote and 3 seats, while there were four independents: Neil Blaney, Jim Kemmy, John O'Connell and a new face in Dublin Central, the independent socialist Tony Gregory.[30]

The H-block vote the previous year had been 3 per cent, but only 1 per cent accrued to Sinn Féin in this election. Given that the 2 per cent difference was almost exactly the same as the increase in the Fianna Fáil vote, the support of all three main parties could be said to have remained almost static.

Had Fianna Fáil won 129 additional votes in Cork East, 154 more in Wicklow and 411 extra in Cork North-West it would have obtained an absolute majority. Instead it was the second hung Dáil in a row. The horse-trading was about to begin, and it would make Tony Gregory a household name.

Before that could happen there were a couple of other events that would set the tone for a dysfunctional year. One marginal seat Fianna Fáil had not managed to capture was Dublin North, where it had been only 166 votes short of a second seat in 1981. It was the kind of constituency where every vote would be crucial. The day after the election it was reported that

Gardaí are investigating an allegation that the election agent for the Fianna Fáil leader, Mr Haughey, voted twice during yesterday's poll. It is alleged that the agent, Mr Patrick O'Connor, a solicitor, his wife Joan and their daughter Niamh, voted twice in the Dublin North constituency—first at Malahide polling booth and shortly afterwards at Kinsealy polling booth.[31]

It was fair to say that 'nobody was closer to Haughey than Pat O'Connor.'[32] He was his neighbour, his election agent, his solicitor in property dealings and a member of his defence team during the Arms Trial. The allegation that O'Connor had asked for and received ballot papers twice had the potential to do enormous damage to Haughey. However, on 20 April the charges were dismissed in Swords District Court by Judge Dónal Kearney, who said

> there was no way of proving that any particular person had voted at all. This might be deemed to be a loophole in the law, but it was a loophole that could only be cured by amending legislation.[33]

The most intriguing part of the affair, however, was the Garda investigation. In charge of this was Superintendent William Byrne, a former classmate of Haughey's, who had been head of the Fingerprint Section before being transferred to Coolock Garda Station in the wake of the scandal concerning the improper identification of fingerprints after the assassination of the British ambassador, Christopher Ewart-Biggs. Although neither the head of the District Court Section in the Chief State Solicitor's office, Kevin Matthews, nor anyone from the office of the Director of Public Prosecutions asked him to do so, Superintendent Byrne took it upon himself to interview again the key witnesses in the case. These new interviews produced changed statements. The presiding officer at the Kinsealy polling booth, Michael Morgan, now said: 'I cannot recall being presented with a voting card or taking off and handing a ballot to Mr Pat O'Connor.' The polling clerk at Kinsealy, Ann Craddock, said she was

> now satisfied that I could easily have made an error in striking off names, including Patrick and Niamh O'Connor from the register of electors. I did not realise what I was really saying in my statement to the guards at Coolock on the night of the elections as I was too tired and hungry from work and newspaper men and all I wanted was to get out of the station and go home.[34]

The Director of Public Prosecutions

> asked commissioner Patrick McLaughlin to institute an inquiry into the handling of the investigation of the allegations against the O'Connors. One of the main points of concern was the reason why Michael Morgan changed his statement.[35]

In 1983 an inquiry was carried out by the head of the Community Affairs Section in Garda Headquarters, Superintendent Owen Giblin. His report

> included an account of an interview in which he asked Super-

intendent Byrne why he had returned to three of the witnesses who had already given statements to the Gardaí. Superintendent Byrne told him that he had gone back to Ann Craddock and Dearbhla Egan because of the second statement from Michael Morgan. In fact, the dates on the document produced at the time showed that Morgan was the last of the three to give a second statement.[36]

Yet again a Garda investigation had given grounds for public disquiet.

———

> *Pa Ubu:* Well, citizen, you're in a fine pickle, aren't you? You wanted me to pay what I owed you, and when I refused you rebelled and plotted against me, and where did that land you? In jug!

The votes were still being counted when Jim Gibbons, who had regained his seat in Carlow-Kilkenny, fired a shot across his old enemy's bows by saying that 'he expected the question of the leadership to be raised at the first meeting of the parliamentary party.'[37] Haughey's opponents were emboldened by the fact that some of his staunchest supporters—Eileen Lemass, Flor Crowley, Seán Moore, Carrie Acheson, Paudge Brennan and Mark Killilea—had lost their seats and that

> during the election campaign Mr Haughey was generally regarded as a liability within the party and this was reflected in the decision to remove his face from their advertisements for most of the three weeks.[38]

It looked as though battle had been joined on 25 February

> with the declaration by Mr Desmond O'Malley that he would contest the position of nominee for Taoiseach at the Parliamentary Party meeting this morning. The timing of Mr O'Malley's announcement, made just after midnight, put an end to speculation that there would be no contest because of the possible effect it might have on the formation of the next government. The statement from Mr O'Malley said, 'in response to demands from many people within the Fianna Fáil organisation I have decided to let my name go forward for consideration when the position of Fianna Fáil nominee for Taoiseach comes up for decision at the parliamentary party meeting today.'[39]

The O'Malley camp 'privately estimated that he would gain 46 of the 81 votes that would be cast.'[40] Haughey appeared to be feeling the pressure. When he was approached by a reporter from a Dublin daily newspaper and asked if he intended to resign, Mr Haughey replied forcefully, 'You can fuck off,' and then spelt the word out letter by letter.[41]

O'Malley's chief supporters were Martin O'Donoghue, George Colley, Bobby Molloy, Charlie McCreevy, Jim Gibbons and Séamus Brennan, who held a series of meetings after the election. One problem was that they disagreed about how Haughey should be removed.

> Colley argued that there should be two votes at the parliamentary party meeting: one to get rid of Haughey, the other to select his successor. Despite his protestations that he neither wanted to be party leader or Taoiseach, this procedure would have left the way open for Colley to put himself forward . . . O'Malley favoured a single vote . . . O'Donoghue favoured no vote at all. He wanted to speak to other senior party members to see if a meeting would decide Haughey's departure plus an agreed replacement. A delegation would then go to Haughey and present him with a *fait accompli.* The others felt that O'Donoghue saw himself as the agreed replacement but allowed him to proceed with his plan; they felt it had no chance of success.[42]

The disunity among the conspirators played its part as the challenge began to melt away when the Haughey loyalists Ray Burke, Brian Lenihan, Seán Doherty, Pádraig Flynn and Ray MacSharry began to contact those named as O'Malley supporters by Bruce Arnold in the *Irish Independent.*

> Some backed off their support for O'Malley and expressed annoyance that they had been exposed. More significant . . . was the disappearance of a number of TDs on whose support they were counting. Suddenly, it seemed, there were people who did not want to know them.[43]

The campaign by Haughey's supporters

> relied to a large extent on a combination of promise and fear: the promise of positions in Mr Haughey's government and the fear that if Mr O'Malley won there would be no Fianna Fáil administration.[44]

By the morning of the meeting the plan had unravelled, and O'Donoghue

> told O'Malley he should withdraw the challenge to avoid splitting the party. O'Malley said he was going ahead. Bobby Molloy was also questioning the wisdom of going ahead and Seamus Brennan was beginning to wonder how O'Malley could back down without losing face.[45]

As the meeting began, O'Malley and Brennan

sat beside each other, O'Malley apparently unaware of the confusion among his supporters. As the room filled with TDs, there was no great rush to sit beside them; Brennan and he were alone in the crowd . . . Ray Burke strode in, clapping his hands as he went and declaring: 'Deputies and senators, I give you the next Taoiseach, Charles J. Haughey.' Everyone leapt to their feet clapping. It was all over bar the shouting. Haughey had won an enormous psychological victory.[46]

There was worse to come for O'Malley, whose supporters

> were shocked when Dr Martin O'Donoghue—who has himself been mentioned as a possible future leader of Fianna Fáil—spoke out against any move to displace Mr Haughey at this time. It was after hearing Dr O'Donoghue's speech that Mr O'Malley decided to withdraw.[47]

O'Malley would not speak to O'Donoghue for seven months. Haughey's rivals had been shown that it would require an enormous effort to shift the man from his position. It could be argued that they would never properly learn this lesson.

All the while, the courtship of Tony Gregory had been proceeding. Gregory, a history teacher at Coláiste Eoin in Booterstown, Co. Dublin, was a former member of the Ard-Chomhairle of Official Sinn Féin who had left the party 'primarily because he felt they had moved away from republican policies.'[48] After a brief association with the IRSP and then Noël Browne's Socialist Labour Party he had stood successfully as an independent candidate for the North Inner City ward in the 1979 local elections before being elected to the Dáil at the second attempt in February 1982, beating the Labour Party leader, Michael O'Leary, into fifth place in Dublin Central. Gregory was

> part of a group of social workers and political activists who organised one project after another, fought one corporation plan after another, always seemed to be on the winning side of arguments—and still saw the centre city crumble into degradation and poverty.[49]

The son of a dock labourer and a small farmer's daughter from Co. Offaly who had come to Dublin at a young age to work, Gregory had done 'more to highlight the drug problem in working class communities than all the other TDs combined.'[50] The central area of Dublin, between the canals, was the most deprived in the country, having

> lost 2,000 jobs per year since the mid 1970s . . . The inner city housing stock is old, overcrowded and dilapidated. Most of the

residents of the worst dwellings are old people ... One third of the households in the inner city have no bath or shower ... Almost three quarters of inner city residents have completed their education by the time they are 15. A particularly strong correlation between the lack of education and unemployment exists, according to the NESC survey, in the North City Centre area where it was found that nearly 80% of those aged between 15 and 18 had left school, nearly all (86%) with no educational qualifications. Almost all were unemployed.[51]

The outgoing Taoiseach had been alerted to the problems during the campaign when his Dublin Central walkabout was interrupted by a man who exclaimed:

> There's no newsagents here, there's no chemist and no barber shop, there's no police station and no public telephone. How can anyone assist the Gardaí, how can anyone report a crime in a place like this?

Gregory's vote for Taoiseach would be vital, and he took advantage of this to seek a deal that would improve the lot of his constituents. Haughey and FitzGerald both wooed Gregory. He and his negotiating team, his brother Noel and the social workers Mick Rafferty and Fergus McCabe, did not warm to FitzGerald and were

> less than impressed by his grasp of what they were after. Haughey seemed to have an overview of the inner city problems and the solutions which would be agreeable to the team. He announced that he would borrow the money necessary to meet the points agreed. It was productive investment and that was what he was about. FitzGerald asked where they thought he could get the money from. The team didn't think it was their job to write his budget. They argued with both leaders that if they didn't invest in housing and employment now they would have to invest in the Department of Justice later on.[52]

Haughey pursued the negotiations with a certain theatrical brio. On meeting Gregory for the first time on 23 February he greeted him with the words: 'You know what I want. What do you want?' After signing an agreement between the two sides on 5 March he quipped: 'As Al Capone said, I like doing business with you.'[53]

Haughey came away with the promise of Gregory's vote. Gregory bagged a deal that included an inner-city employment scheme to create 3,674 new jobs, the building of 1,350 new homes in 1982, rising to 2,000 by 1984, training and placement for three hundred to five hundred young people from the inner city, the establishment of an inner-city development authority (the chairperson and five members to be nominated by Gregory), a 5 per cent tax on derelict sites, increasing by 1 per cent per annum, and a tax on existing and future office development and rental of 2 per cent of rental income.[54] In addition

> the massive 27 acre Port and Docks Board site near the Custom House which was to have been utilised for office blocks is now to be divided between houses, industry, recreational space and office blocks. Money is also to be found to provide 3,000 Corporation flats with bathrooms and showers. About 500 will be provided per annum and £1 million is to be provided this year.[55]

Gregory was taking no chances: he had the deal witnessed by the general secretary of the ITGWU, Michael Mullen, and brought it to the Dáil with him.

The kibosh was conclusively placed on Fine Gael's hopes when the Labour Party voted against going back into coalition with their erstwhile colleagues. The vote of the Administrative Council was tied, with the chairperson, Michael D. Higgins, giving the casting vote against. The decision 'left the party bitterly divided, with anti-coalitionists triumphant and frustrated coalitionists complaining about the lack of realism of their colleagues.'[56]

Sinn Féin the Workers' Party also decided to vote for Haughey after Fianna Fáil promised to find

> a new owner for the threatened Clondalkin Paper Mills and if necessary to nationalise them. They also agreed to ensure [that] laid-off Clover Meats workers in Waterford would be allowed their social welfare benefits and promised to build a comprehensive social and economic plan which SFWP could judge on its merits.

But their plans to do so almost came unstuck when the Dáil met on 9 March.[57] The three SFWP deputies, having stepped out of the chamber when Paddy Gallagher fancied a smoke and Joe Sherlock wanted to go to the toilet, found themselves locked out when the vote began. Cometh the hour, cometh Mark Killilea of Fianna Fáil, who had recently lost his seat in Galway West. 'I caught 'em by the seat of the trousers,' said Killilea, 'and pushed 'em towards the press area and told 'em in quick, hard to your left, up on top of the Irish box and jump for your lives.'[58] They took his advice and, with Proinsias de Rossa,

> burst through the press gallery and vaulted into the distinguished visitors' area to reach the Fianna Fáil lobby. Among the people they had to climb over to get to the floor of the house were Mrs Maureen Haughey and her daughter Eimear.[59]

Dramatic as this was, it wasn't strictly necessary. Haughey was elected Taoiseach for the second time, by 86 to 79. But the acrobatic escapades of Sherlock, De Rossa and Gallagher did provide a suitably GUBU prelude to the GUBU Dáil. On the day, their party leader, Tomás Mac Giolla, predicted that the Government would last a year.[60] He would turn out to have been hopelessly optimistic.

There was much adverse comment about the Gregory deal, which was variously estimated as costing from £80 million to £500 million over four years.[61] And there were disdainful sniffs when the new TD appeared in the Dáil wearing a jacket and pullover but no tie. The outgoing Cathaoirleach of the Seanad, Charlie McDonald, complained:

> If people can walk into the Dáil as they walk into a pub, democracy must be on the slide in this country. I maintain that deputies should be soberly dressed for such an important occasion.[62]

Gregory, who witnessed much worse affronts to democracy every day in his constituency, was hardly perturbed by such sentiments. And it is hard to disagree with the words of one of Ireland's most esteemed historians, Joe Lee, who commented that

> critics denounced the idea of a special deal as disgraceful, allegedly debasing the coinage. What was disgraceful in this case was less the deal than the fact that it needed a deal to win some attention for one of the most deprived areas of the country, an inner city constituency ravaged by poverty and neglect, and their concomitants, unemployment, bad housing and a vicious drugs problem.[63]

Having secured Gregory's vote, Haughey immediately set about trying to divest himself of the need for it. With eighty-one seats and the guaranteed support of the independent Fianna Fáiler Neil Blaney, Fianna Fáil needed only one more seat to remove its dependence on Gregory (given that convention would oblige the Ceann Comhairle, John O'Connell, to give a casting vote to the Government in the event of a tie). The need for a new EEC Commissioner appeared to give Haughey his opportunity.

One was needed because Michael O'Kennedy had selflessly resigned from the post to return and try to win a second seat for Fianna Fáil in the marginal Tipperary North constituency. But David Molony of Fine Gael held on, and O'Kennedy succeeded merely in displacing his party colleague Michael Smith.

The man Haughey had in mind as O'Kennedy's replacement also had a Tipperary connection. A Thurles CBS past pupil, Dick Burke, had been the Commissioner before O'Kennedy and was known to be disillusioned by

FitzGerald's failure to give him a ministerial post after he had been elected in Dublin West in 1981. Normally such a plum position would have been kept within the party, but Haughey wanted to use the job as a way of removing a coalition TD from the Dáil, to be replaced with a Fianna Fáil one in the subsequent by-election. Burke at first refused the job, which Haughey then offered to Ted Nealon, who also turned it down.[64]

The second time around, Burke took the bait, ringing Haughey's adviser, Pádraig Ó hAnnracháin, to accept. Ó hAnnracháin was ecstatic.

> He asked Burke to hang on a moment, and dashed down the corridor to Haughey's room with the good news. Haughey came up to hear himself. He spoke to Burke and heard the confirmation again. 'Let me be the first to congratulate you,' the Taoiseach said in grave tones. When he put down the phone, he was beaming. 'We've got it,' he told Ó hAnnracháin. And with that Haughey danced a little jig on the floor.[65]

Haughey's elation was understandable. The two main parties had run neck and neck in the general election; but Fianna Fáil had a ready-made candidate in Eileen Lemass, who had lost her seat by a narrow margin to her party colleague Liam Lawlor. The best Fine Gael could offer was Liam Skelly, who had gone to national school in Inchicore with Jim Mitchell, the party's poll-topper in the constituency. The party had to hold an emergency meeting of its Castleknock Branch to make Skelly a member just before the election.[66]

But on 25 May, Skelly won. He was just behind after the first count, and he was elected by the transfers of Tomás Mac Giolla of SFWP, who wiped out the Labour Party candidate. Mac Giolla's transfers went to Skelly by a margin of more than two to one over Lemass, dealing a crushing blow to the confidence of the fledgling Government. Garret FitzGerald would pinpoint the by-election as

> one of the most significant in recent times. It severely damaged Fine Gael morale and weakened Charlie Haughey's position in the party, which was already under challenge. The Workers' Party learned that its support for Fianna Fáil was extremely unpopular with the voters and this encouraged it to 'ditch' the Fianna Fáil government at the first opportunity six months later.[67]

After Dublin West there would always be a sense that this Government's days were numbered.

The by-election had taken place in the shadow of controversy about Fianna Fáil's attitude towards the Falklands War. Argentina had taken over the islands on 2 April. Margaret Thatcher despatched a task force in response, and on 1 May the British offensive against the Argentine forces began. At first Ireland joined in EEC sanctions against Argentina. The sinking of the Argentine cruiser *General Belgrano* on 2 May, which was outside the 200-mile exclusion zone around the islands declared by the British, with the loss of 323 lives, heralded a change of attitude by the Government. The following night the Minister for Defence, Paddy Power, described the sinking of the *General Belgrano* as the action of 'a hit and run driver.' Britain did not deserve much sympathy, said Power, and this cast doubt on its honesty and credibility. 'We felt that Argentina were the first aggressors. Obviously Britain themselves are very much the aggressors now.'[68]

The Taoiseach denied that Power's comments reflected Government policy, but the following day came news that 'the government has asked for a meeting of the UN Security Council to call for the ending of hostilities in the South Atlantic and intends to propose the withdrawal of EEC sanctions against Argentina.'[69]

Meanwhile the deputy leader of Fine Gael, Peter Barry, demanded the resignation of the Minister for Defence. Haughey defended the Government's change of tack by stating that

> as a neutral nation that has always refrained from military alliance of any kind, we have to take a very clear view of any action, economic or otherwise, that would appear supportive of military action. We were never very enthusiastic about the imposition of sanctions but the argument was persuasive that they could be instrumental in applying pressure to achieve the implementation of resolution 502 and so lead to a diplomatic solution ... but sanctions complementing military action are not acceptable to us as a neutral country.[70]

Haughey's Government was not alone in opposing the continuation of trade sanctions: the Italian government took the same line. And on 24 May, Ireland bought a motion to the Security Council that called for the 'suspension of hostilities for 72 hours ... negotiations for a continuing ceasefire by the Secretary-General with UN observers to ensure compliance ... and an interim report to the Security Council by the Secretary-General at the end of the 72 hours.'[71] An amended resolution, omitting the ceasefire, was passed unanimously but had no practical effect. The British forces were well on their way to victory by then and by 14 June had recaptured the islands.

Both at the time and since, the Government's actions over the Falklands have been widely held to be to its great discredit.'[72] Haughey was accused of 'a desire to achieve temporary popularity at the expense of our international credibility.'[73] And Gerry Fitt, now the independent MP for Belfast West, accused Haughey of causing anti-Irish sentiment in Britain, because 'by running off to the United Nations Ireland was undermining the British position.'[74] Yet there was a legitimate argument for saying that

> the EEC sanctions were imposed in order to prevent conflict, not to be allied with it . . . The argument surfacing in the EEC was that Britain moved too quickly and therefore 'forfeited' the right to EEC sanctions.[75]

And Fitt's argument was faintly ludicrous, there having been no particularly compelling reason why the Irish Government, or the United Nations, should have been concerned with strengthening the position of one side in the conflict vis-à-vis the other rather than attempting to bring about a negotiated solution.

It is a matter of record that the *General Belgrano* 'had not been sailing towards the Falklands but away from them, towards a position where none of the task force had been deployed,' and the British government's action in sinking the cruiser has been widely criticised as being 'ordered, whether recklessly or with malice aforethought, at a time when it was certain to destroy the last best hope for a negotiated peace, which had been tabled that very day by President Belaúnde of Peru.' The fiercest critics, notably the Labour MP Tam Dalyell, argued that the prime purpose of the sinking was to sabotage the Peruvian peace plan. He contends that, if the Prime Minister had accepted the plan, 'she knew that she would be deprived of the military victory, which is what the Falklands War was all about.'[76]

The Government's behaviour at the time looks far from dishonourable. It now seems an eminently sensible argument that

> Charlie Haughey was quite right to withdraw Ireland's support for EEC sanctions against Argentina . . . Given our own history, it is quite right that we should be unashamedly suspicious of any British assertions of sovereignty anywhere in the world, most of all over islands 8,000 miles away. In the light of the persistent moralising we have had to listen to from London over the years about IRA violence, it would be quite unpardonable for us to do anything, for that reason alone, but oppose the gratuitous murder of several hundred Argentinians by the sinking of the *Belgrano* outside the 'Total Exclusion Zone' which Britain itself composed. Murder is murder is murder.[77]

There were plenty of real reasons to be doleful about the Haughey Government, in particular those connected with the new Minister for Justice, Seán Doherty, a former member of the Special Detective Unit, who was opposed to divorce and in favour of the death penalty. Doherty had been one of the main beneficiaries of Haughey's decision for the first time to name a Government without allowing his opponents in the party a veto over appointments. The Taoiseach refused, for example, to name George Colley as Tánaiste. When the Government was announced, a disgruntled Colley complained: 'Mr Haughey offered me a post in the cabinet but refused to appoint me Tánaiste. He had offered the appointment as Tánaiste on Sunday February 21 but yesterday he said he could do not do so because of my recent activity in the party.'[78]

Given that Colley had been to the fore in the efforts to oust the party leader, Haughey would need to have been something of a saint to offer his rival the job of Tánaiste. Not being a saint, he opted for Ray MacSharry.

> When Haughey called him to his office and told him he was going to be Tánaiste and Minister for Finance, MacSharry replied, 'I will in my fuck.' The two of them argued for a while until Haughey simply stood up and walked out of the room.[79]

Of the other main ministries, Industry and Energy went to Albert Reynolds, Education to Martin O'Donoghue, Foreign Affairs to Gerry Collins, Labour and the Public Service to Gene Fitzgerald, Agriculture to Brian Lenihan, and Trade, Commerce and Tourism to Desmond O'Malley. But Doherty's appointment as Minister for Justice was

> the biggest surprise, even among Haughey's supporters . . . This appointment surprised O'Malley and shocked Colley. A number of Haughey's supporters were also disturbed.[80]

Doherty's approach to his new job is nicely illustrated by his party colleague David Andrews, who recalled that

> although he was Minister for Justice, he said that because he was also a TD he was perfectly entitled in his capacity as a TD, to make representations to the Department of Justice—in other words, to himself. So he was entitled to lobby himself on behalf of his constituents; otherwise they would be disadvantaged because they would not have a public representative to act on their behalf. It was an interesting point of view.[81]

The Dowra Affair was the most striking example of political interference with the Gardaí during Doherty's term. The trouble began on 21 December 1981 when Jimmy McGovern was assaulted in the Bush Bar, Blacklion, Co. Cavan, by Garda Tom Nangle. The significant thing about the case was that Tom Nangle's sister Maura was married to Seán Doherty. On becoming Minister for Justice, Doherty had asked the head of the Security Section of the Department of Justice, Jim Kirby,

> to instigate an enquiry through the Gardaí with the RUC about James McGovern ... Kirby telephoned Chief Superintendent Tom Kelly, one of the senior officers in the Intelligence and Security Branch of the Gardaí. He asked Kelly to contact the RUC and enquire about James McGovern. Kelly did so and was told by the RUC that McGovern was clean. He relayed the information back to Kirby.[82]

This was improper enough, but worse was to follow. McGovern was due to give evidence against Nangle at the District Court in Dowra on Monday 27 September. As a result,

> on Friday September 24 or Saturday September 25 the RUC was contacted again by a senior Garda officer—not Chief Superintendent Tom Kelly—about Jimmy McGovern ... The RUC HQ in Belfast ordered that McGovern be taken into custody but a Special Branch officer in the Fermanagh area, D.I. [Detective-Inspector] Ian Carter, questioned the order. His views were over-ruled, however, and the order was confirmed by Assistant Chief Constable Trevor Forbes.[83]

On Monday 27 September, McGovern did not turn up at the court, where Nangle was claiming self-defence and bringing up the fact that the man he'd struck had been involved in the election campaign of the hunger-striker Kieran Doherty. 'It was extraordinary that every time there was a question of assault connected with guards there was the question of so-called patriots,' tut-tutted District Justice John H. Barry before he threw out the case in the absence of the main prosecution witness.[84]

That absence was the result of the fact that at 6:30 that morning McGovern, who had spent the night in his cousin's house, had been 'woken up by an armed and uniformed constable pulling at the blankets on the bed and telling him that he was under arrest as a suspected terrorist.'[85] McGovern was brought to Gough Barracks in Armagh. As he was being interrogated,

> a senior officer in the RUC telephoned a counterpart in the Intelligence and Security Branch at Garda Headquarters. The special request from the South, which they had spoken of a few days previously, was being looked after, he said.[86]

McGovern was released at 7:30 that night and driven home by the RUC.

It seemed obvious that 'Doherty had been involved in using both the Garda Síochána and the RUC to interfere with the court case.'[87]

That an ordinary law-abiding citizen had been harassed to this extent merely because he had the misfortune to be assaulted by the Minister for Justice's brother-in-law was bad enough, but that a member of a Government that never tired of paying lip service to the plight of Northern nationalists had apparently arranged for one of them to be taken into custody by the RUC for purely personal reasons was downright sinister. The 'Republican Party' Minister for Justice had apparently perpetrated

> 'the ultimate 'fix,' but at what cost? For a Fianna Fáil minister to allow the RUC to have such a favour to hold over the Gardaí and the Irish government demonstrated an extraordinary lack of concern for the political circumstances, and an extreme insensitivity to the traditions of his own party.[88]

There were other examples of Doherty using the Department of Justice as his own fiefdom, most notably the case of Sergeant Tom Tully of Boyle Garda Station. Sergeant Tully was outraged by a situation in which

> Doherty, or officials under his control in the Department of Justice regularly contacted the station and asked for charges against constituents to be dropped. Sometimes Doherty would make the call himself and give a direct order to the guards.[89]

After Doherty's intervention had secured the quashing of a case against Keaney's pub, near Boyle, for being open after hours, Tully

> had been pushed far enough and he made a vow: the next time Keaney's had to be raided, he would do it himself and he would ensure personally that charges were brought if the law was being broken.[90]

At the end of May, Sergeant Tully found six people drinking after hours at Keaney's. On 28 July, thirteen days after the summons had been served on the publican, Michael Keaney, Tully 'was told that he was being shifted to a garda station on the border, Ballyconnell, County Cavan.'[91] Tully appealed to the Commissioner, Patrick McLaughlin, but 'was told that his request for a meeting had been rejected and that his appeal had failed; he was to go to Ballyconnell two days later.'[92] He then appealed to the review body within the force that adjudicated on internal disputes. His case seemed hopeless, as the Association of Garda Sergeants and Inspectors had never won a case before this body. This time, however, the review body, made up of the Deputy Commissioner, Larry Wren, the Assistant Secretary of the Department of Justice, Liam Breathnach, and a member of the Executive Committee of the AGSI, Michael Boyle, made a unanimous decision to

overturn the order instructing Tully to move to Ballyconnell . . .
Doherty was furious. That night he phoned Wren and Breathnach
at their homes to castigate them. Next day he summoned both to his
office separately to reinforce his complaints about their decision . . .
Against all the odds the local sergeant from Boyle had bested the
Minister.[93]

Doherty's mood was not improved when the Tully case, like the Dowra
affair, was picked up by the media and became the subject of public
outcry. Tully's statement, that he was

> the victim of a vicious piece of victimisation at the hands of the
> Minister for Justice and some Garda officers because I would not
> yield to political pressure to square serious violations of the law,

seemed to paint a picture of a minister and a Government out of
control.[94]

———

The scandal that would do most damage to the Government and would
live longest in the public memory had nothing to do with Doherty, though
it too concerned matters of crime and punishment. Its calamitous effect
on the career of a member of the Government was the result more of
freakish bad luck and a lapse of judgement than of any political
corruption; but it would give rise to the term 'GUBU' and, fairly or not,
massively exacerbate the notion that the political system was in chaos.

It began on 22 July with one of the most brutal murders in the history
of the country. Bridie Gargan, a nurse, was on her way home from St
James's Hospital to her flat in Castleknock when she stopped to sunbathe
in the Phoenix Park. She was approached by a man carrying an imitation
pistol and a lump hammer who told her to get into her car. He ordered her
to lie on the back seat. 'She got into the car but then she panicked. He took
out his lump hammer and hit her several times on the side of the head.' As
her attacker drove out of the park,

> an ambulance driver noticed the injured woman on the back seat,
> blood on the window and the parking permit for St James's Hospital
> on the windscreen. He concluded that the driver was a doctor taking
> the injured person to hospital so he signalled the car to follow him
> while he led the way through the traffic, with siren and flashing
> lights, to St James's.[95]

The killer eventually abandoned the car, and his victim, in Rialto.

Bridie Gargan was taken to the Richmond Hospital, where she died four days later.

Three days later the murderer of Bridie Gargan met Dónal Dunne in Edenderry. Dunne had advertised a shotgun for sale, but the man who had answered his advertisement took the shotgun and shot him in the face. 'He left Donal Dunne's body in the bog, partially hidden by undergrowth, and stole his car to drive back to Dublin.'[96]

The killer was Malcolm McArthur, a 36-year-old from Trim who had lived in the United States with his uncle after his parents separated, then returned to Ireland in the late sixties. McArthur lived off an inheritance derived from the sale of his family's 180-acre farm. By 1982 he was running short of funds and had begun to fantasise about becoming an armed robber.

His next move after murdering Dunne was to try to rob a former American diplomat named Harry Bieling who lived in Killiney, Co. Dublin. The man escaped from the house after being held prisoner by McArthur for several hours. That evening McArthur decided to see if an old friend would put him up for a few days. That old friend was the Attorney-General, Patrick Connolly.

Connolly had been friends for several years with McArthur's girl-friend, Brenda Little, and had no inkling that anything was wrong. McArthur enjoyed a relaxing few days in the Attorney-General's apartment in Dalkey, travelling with Connolly in his state car to a match in Croke Park. Meanwhile the Gardaí began to close in on him, aided by a phone call McArthur had made to Dalkey Garda Station after the Killiney incident, during which he

> gave his name and a false address in the centre of Dublin and mentioned the incident at Bieling's house. It hadn't happened, he told the Garda who answered the telephone, there was no need for them to worry. It was just a joke, he said.[97]

On Friday 13 August, Connolly arrived home from work at Government Buildings to find Superintendent John Courtney, who was heading the investigation into the Gargan and Dunne murders, outside his apartment with two other gardaí. They entered the flat and arrested McArthur.

What happened next sealed Patrick Connolly's political fate. The following morning Superintendent Courtney and Detective-Inspector Noel Conroy called to Connolly's apartment to interview him. When asked to make a statement, Connolly

> refused and a row ensued, peppered with sharp language. Connolly

argued that he was an innocent party to the affair, that he was Attorney General, about to leave on his holidays, and could just as well make a statement when he returned.[98]

Courtney and Conroy argued that

> they had to treat him like any other citizen: they said they needed to question him as to why a man about to be charged with double murder had been living in his flat. Connolly was unmoved, and eventually Courtney and Conroy were forced to accept that he would make a statement when he returned.[99]

That the principal law officer of the state thought it was acceptable to leave the jurisdiction, and that the Gardaí allowed him to do so, may be charitably ascribed to the shock produced by the awfulness of the murders and the unusual circumstances surrounding the arrest. On Saturday night the Taoiseach spoke on the phone to Connolly, who was staying overnight in London before flying to New York, and asked him to return. Connolly refused. But when his plane landed in New York on Sunday, Connolly found himself 'besieged by reporters,' because the *Sunday Tribune* that morning had broken the story of his flight from Dublin. When Haughey telephoned him at his hotel and ordered him back, Connolly bowed to the inevitable. When he arrived in London on Monday night

> the story had grown to such dimensions that BBC television had an Outside Broadcast unit filming Connolly's arrival at Heathrow live on its main evening news ... By the time that Connolly's car drove through the gates of Kinsealy [Haughey's home] his every movement was being relayed around the world by news agencies, radios and TV stations.[100]

Connolly spoke to Haughey for half an hour, and they agreed that there was only one possible course of action. 'Because of his unique position under the constitution and the law, and the embarrassment caused to the government, it was his public duty to tender his resignation. The Taoiseach accepted it.'[101] The stage was set for Haughey to bemoan the strange circumstances of the case, and for Conor Cruise O'Brien to coin the term that would forever dog Haughey's steps. Malcolm McArthur would be sentenced to life imprisonment for the murder of Bridie Gargan, and he remains in prison to this day. He was never charged with the murder of Dónal Dunne.

———

Pa Ubu: Woe betide any of you who step out of line, because I'll give him the full treatment, including a session of nose and tooth twisting and tongue pulling.

The general air of catastrophe surrounding the Government emboldened Haughey's opponents within Fianna Fáil to make yet another effort to unseat him. On 1 October, Charlie McCreevy tabled a motion of no confidence in Haughey's leadership for the next meeting of the parliamentary party. Haughey retaliated by seeking a public pledge of support from the members of his Government and by insisting that any vote would have to be of the open roll-call variety. McCreevy objected.

If the Taoiseach is so sure of the overwhelming support of the Fianna Fáil TDS, surely he is not afraid to face the challenge in a secret ballot. Mr Haughey himself was elected leader by secret vote. I have called for a secret ballot in accordance with the rules of the Fianna Fáil organisation. His attempt to change the rules is an attempt to intimidate TDS.[102]

He went on to perfectly encapsulate the spirit of 1982 by observing that never before in the history of the state have politicians and the political system been held in such low esteem. It is us politicians and our parties that have contributed to such disillusionment and disappointment ... Reckless and daft economic proposals have been made for electoral gain. The public financial morass threatens our financial independence. The economy, looked at from any angle, is an appalling mess. Unemployment is rising to unprecedented levels ... The Irish people are no longer looking to politicians to solve our problems. The electorate do not believe us any more.[103]

McCreevy did not manage to get his secret ballot, but this time the challenge to Haughey did not evaporate. O'Malley and O'Donoghue refused to pledge loyalty and resigned from the Government, and twenty-two TDS backed the motion of no confidence in a roll-call vote, among them the junior minister Sylvester Barrett, George Colley, Pádraig Faulkner, Séamus Brennan, Bobby Molloy and David Andrews. The aftermath of the vote added to the whiff of sulphur surrounding Haughey. Andrews recalls that

the mood among some Haughey supporters waiting outside was ugly. Some of them had been drinking for most of the day, so much so that Gardaí tried to persuade Charlie McCreevy to leave Leinster House by a side entrance. He bravely told them that he was going out the same way he had come in. For his pains, he was followed across the car park, kicked and jostled and called a 'bastard' and a 'blueshirt.' When Gardaí finally managed to get him into his car, the crowd surrounded it and banged on the roof, continuing to hurl insults at him . . .[104]

A month later the Government finally fell. On 18 October Bill Loughnane died, and the following day Jim Gibbons suffered a heart attack that severely incapacitated him and prevented him from attending the Dáil. This reduced Fianna Fáil's effective Dáil strength to 78. On 4 November the Government lost a confidence motion, 82 to 80, the Workers' Party deciding that it was finally time to bring the whole sorry saga to a conclusion.

No other Government was ever quite the same as the Fianna Fáil one of 1982. To this day 'Haughey's GUBU government is now part of the folklore of Irish life. Everything it touched seemed to turn to ashes.'[105] It would be immortalised the following year by *The Boss*, written by Peter Murtagh and Joe Joyce, the two best investigative reporters of the time, which has lost none of its power to shock and enthral.

The events of the previous months seemed to ensure that, after a second hung Dáil, the contest between FitzGerald and Haughey would finally produce a decisive result. In keeping with the tenor of the year, Fianna Fáil decided to fight an almost entirely negative campaign, based largely on the notion that FitzGerald was the instrument of British interests in Ireland.

> In Meath and Westmeath, a leaflet with Fianna Fáil's name took its theme from a famous World War One recruiting poster depicting Lord Kitchener, declaring: 'Your country needs you.' It showed Kitchener pointing at the reader, declaring: 'Thatcher wants Garret. Do you?'[106]

Haughey said that collaboration by Fine Gael with the British Government posed 'the most serious threat to Ireland's independence since the second world war.'[107] And on the Saturday before the election he accused FitzGerald of

> colluding with 'a trained British spy,' a reference to the elderly Duke of Norfolk—the former head of British intelligence—who in a recent speech had referred to having lunched with FitzGerald.[108]

Fianna Fáil had been given its opening by FitzGerald's suggestion, originally made in the BBC Dimbleby Lecture in May, that 'an All-Ireland policing and judicial system would help the British and ourselves to ensure that members of the IRA could not evade arrest and conviction by passing rapidly from one jurisdiction to another.'[109] When the Secretary of State for Northern Ireland, James Prior, forecast that FitzGerald would probably make the same suggestions during the election campaign, Fianna Fáil used this as a plank in its argument that

> the Fine Gael leader was an instrument of British policy, in collusion and collaboration with the British government and that both the British government and the media were interfering in the election because they wanted Charles Haughey out.[110]

In his campaign speech on the North, FitzGerald proposed

> a federal solution to the problem of cross-border security. These included the establishment of an All-Ireland Security Council and court and prison system with a new police force separate from the Gardaí and the Royal Ulster Constabulary that could operate on either side of the border.[111]

Fianna Fáil represented these proposals as implying that, in the words of the Minister for Foreign Affairs, Gerry Collins, RUC men would 'turn up in the company of the Gardaí on the doorsteps in Kerry, Donegal, indeed anywhere in the country.'[112]

FitzGerald's proposals were characteristically insensitive to the feelings of those who thought that the problems in the North were not solely a result of IRA violence, and they were criticised as 'ludicrous' by the *Irish Press* and 'vague, improbable and likely to undermine the effectiveness and independence of the forces of law and order' by the new Attorney-General, John Murray.[113] But it is hard not to agree with the contention of the *Irish Independent* that 'the campaign barrel has been scraped.'[114]

And it was ironic to see FitzGerald being attacked as the candidate favoured by Thatcher, when the previous year Haughey had been making political capital out of the claim that he enjoyed a special relationship with her. Fianna Fáil's supposed fears about an all-Ireland police force also rang hollow, considering the Government's unconcern about the level of cross-border co-operation during the Dowra Affair. Given that Fianna Fáil had suggested consistently that there was an organised smear campaign against Haughey, it did it little credit to fight an election almost solely on the basis of a smear campaign of its own.

At times Fianna Fáil spokespersons almost seemed to be suggesting that FitzGerald himself was a British spy. Its campaign was based on 'a political conspiracy theory, rationalised out of circumstantial rather than rational evidence and relying on minor political figures like the Duke of Norfolk.'[115] Most tellingly, in the course of losing his televised debate with FitzGerald, Haughey declined the opportunity to repeat the allegations to his face.

It has been suggested that 'the All-Ireland court and police proposals had been the lifeline that saved Fianna Fáil from a greater collapse,' but in fact the election results, on 15 November, were remarkably similar to those predicted by the opinion polls at the start of the campaign.[116] Fianna Fáil's vote dropped 2 per cent, to 45 per cent, its worst performance since 1961, and it lost six seats, to achieve a total of 75. Fine Gael reached another record with 39 per cent of the vote and 70 seats—a gain of 7 that put it within touching distance of its rivals. The Labour Party increased its vote for the first time since 1969 and gained one seat, for a total of 16, its vote of 9½ per cent a minor triumph for the new leader, Dick Spring, who had been forced to take over when Michael O'Leary resigned a month before the election.

O'Leary had quit when the party conference voted to leave the decision on joining a coalition Government to a special post-election conference.

> I have reluctantly concluded that I cannot contest the next general election guided by an electoral strategy in which I have no confidence. This is the most difficult decision I have made in my public career.

He promptly joined Fine Gael.[117]

Dick Spring had been in the Dáil for only eighteen months but was immediately charged with negotiating a joint programme for Government with Fine Gael that would find favour with his party's rank and file. Vincent Browne pointed out that 'prior to these talks the biggest thing Spring had ever negotiated was his mortgage.'[118] The thirty-page agreement was approved, and on 14 December, FitzGerald was elected Taoiseach for the second time. The reign of Gubu Roi was over—though there would be one final postscript, one that would almost lead him to the political guillotine.

It had been a bad year for Haughey and an even worse one for one of his closest friends and allies. On Thursday 29 April, Patrick Gallagher

> received a phone call summoning him to the headquarters of the Northern Bank Finance Company. He was told to bring his solicitor. Gallagher drove the 18 miles from Straffan House to Dublin with his brother Paul. The siblings stopped at Ryan's pub in Parkgate Street, not far from the Phoenix Park and its racecourse, one of the projects that were threatening to destroy his business empire. They arrived at the Northern Bank's boardroom . . . to meet their fate . . . The bankers told the Gallaghers that the family's business could no longer survive with more than £28 million in debts and collapsing property deals. This was the end, the bankers said.[119]

It was Gallagher who had helped out when Haughey had needed

money to settle his debt with Allied Irish Bank. He had become head of the Gallagher Group eight years earlier when his father, Matt, died. The beginnings of the Gallagher empire had been humble: Matt Gallagher's 'first contract at the age of 17 had been a two-mile stretch of road between Tubbercurry and Collooney, Co. Sligo, on which the first profit was £17.'[120] He had moved to England, where he made his fortune in the building trade before returning to Ireland, taking over Paramount Builders Ltd in 1958. He would later rename it the Gallagher Group.

After their father's death, Patrick and Paul Gallagher, as joint managing directors,

> introduced policy changes which appeared to be heading the group for even greater success and profit. Instead of continuing to build houses for all and sundry, they took a deliberate decision during the recession years of the mid seventies to go for the upper end of the market. And, even more significantly, the group increasingly became involved in property deals in the centre of Dublin.[121]

The new strategy seemed to pay dividends. Patrick Gallagher lived in Straffan House, Co. Kildare, while Paul bought Castle Howard at Avoca, Co. Wicklow.

In November 1979 came Patrick's greatest coup when he sold Seán Lemass House, St Stephen's Green, to the Irish Permanent Building Society for £7.5 million five days after he had bought it for £5.4 million.[122]

His downfall came because 'he gambled on a boom at a time when the economy was submitting to ever deeper recession. He staked all on the belief in a never-ending growth in the property market, a growth that has continued since the early 1960s.'[123] He was unable to offload the Slazenger site in St Stephen's Green, which was 'yielding little or no income and financed by extensive borrowing on which he was paying interest at well over 20 per cent a year.'[124] His attempt to sell it to Irish Life for £15¾ million fell through when he

> could not offer full vacant possession . . . The final move to acquire the H. Williams Group can be seen as the last throw of the dice. A supermarket chain was seen as a potential source of liquid cash for the hard-pressed group.[125]

The day after Gallagher announced that the H. Williams purchase had fallen through, the banks swooped to place the group into receivership. Gallagher owed Northern Bank Finance £15 million and Allied Irish Investment Bank and Bank of Ireland £6 million each. The young millionaire, it appeared, was

> the last of the great property tycoons who dominated the Irish

business scene in the nineteen seventies. His demise will serve as a warning to other property developers as well as the more humble dabblers in bricks and mortar that the recession has come home to roost in the Irish property sector.[126]

All over the country people were learning the same lesson: that their best-laid plans could be upset by the parlous state of the economy. In 1982 unemployment had moved into double figures, where it would remain until 1998. From 1982 it would rise every year until reaching a peak of 17 per cent in 1986. Only twice between 1984 and 1993 would it dip below 15 per cent.[127]

June 1982 offered a preview of this future, where the dole queue and the economic emigrant became increasingly familiar symbols of Irish life. It was a month in which

> unemployment took a serious turn for the worse . . . as a new spate of redundancies added over 3,000 people to the dole queues, pushing the national total to the highest ever figure of 150,859 . . . The underlying level of unemployment has now risen by 16,500 in the past six months, and by 27,400 over the past year.[128]

A prominent economist described the increase in employment as 'atrocious' and forecast that unemployment might reach 170,000 the following year.[129] He was wrong: it would reach 180,000.[130]

With Ubu Roi gone, the ball was in Garret FitzGerald's court.

Chapter 12 ↝

| THE MORALS OF A TOMCAT

1983

One Sunday morning in August 1983 the congregation at Mass in Fethard, Co. Wexford, were greeted by the sight of

> a woven cradle and in it a life-sized baby doll tucked beneath a blanket, its plastic arms outstretched. A sign attached to the cradle bore the words: 'Thou Shalt Not Kill' ... After Mass altar boys stood by the church exits and handed out pro-amendment leaflets.[1]

This was the year of the 'pro-life' amendment, a year in which the Catholic Church 'demoted legislative democracy by endeavouring to inject a theocratic dimension to the 1937 Constitution.'[2]

The referendum demonstrated the renewed bullishness of both the church hierarchy and certain members of the laity who unapologetically sought to ensure that society conformed to a traditional Catholic notion of morality. Those responsible for the amendment were described as

> using the emotive issue of abortion as a symbolic issue for other purposes. They want to row back the liberal tide which has resulted in a relaxation in the laws on contraception and a greater willingness to consider the removal of the constitutional prohibition on divorce.[3]

The amendment had 'very little to do with the actual issue of abortion but a great deal to do with re-asserting the Catholic nature of this state and reversing recent trends towards a pluralist society.'[4] This fundamentalist backlash was obvious from incidents such as one in Wexford in which, when a group of people held a meeting to discuss setting up a family planning centre, about twenty members of SPUC descended on the meeting, in White's Hotel, with such slogans as 'Instead of women controlling their fertility men should control their virility.' The priest who organised the protest was the same one who had arranged for the cradle to be placed on the altar in Fethard. His name was Seán Fortune.

The fact that while Fortune was campaigning for the amendment he was raping young boys in his parish illustrates the most problematic feature of the campaign. Its fundamentalist zeal to enshrine a sectarian amendment in the Constitution was bad enough; but almost nobody at the time could have guessed just how hypocritical it was for the Catholic Church to be engaging in moral warfare.

Father Michael Cleary, perhaps the most fervent clerical supporter of the amendment, was keeping secret the fact that his housekeeper, Phyllis Hamilton, had given birth to two children by him, one of whom had been given up for adoption. One member of the hierarchy, Bishop Éamonn Casey, was also the father of a son born nine years previously and safely tucked away with the mother, Annie Murphy, in the United States.

In 2009 the report into the handling by church and state authorities of allegations against clerics of the Archdiocese of Dublin found that its

> pre-occupations when dealing with cases of sexual abuse, at least until the mid 1990s, were the maintenance of secrecy, the avoidance of scandal, the protection of the reputation of the church, and the preservation of its assets. All other considerations, including the welfare of children and justice for the victims, were subordinated to these priorities.[5]

Of the 325 cases of child abuse examined, 14 took place in the sixties and seventies and 64 in the eighties.

The Archbishop of Dublin at the time of the referendum, Dermot Ryan, was aware of complaints of child abuse, as was his predecessor, John Charles McQuaid, and his successor, Kevin McNamara. Ryan and McNamara, who were vocal supporters of the amendment, both covered up the scandal within the diocese, and it was not until 1995 that the church began to inform the civil authorities of complaints about sexual abuse by priests. As for rank-and-file priests, 'the vast majority simply chose to turn a blind eye.'[6] When complaints were made to the church authorities

> complainants were often met with denial, arrogance, cover-up and with incompetence and incomprehension in some cases . . . The attitude towards individual complainants was overbearing and in some cases underhand.[7]

Archbishop Ryan

> ignored the advice given by a psychiatrist in the case of Fr Moore that he should not be placed in a parish setting. Fr Moore was subsequently convicted of a serious sexual assault on a young teenager while working as a parish curate. As problems emerged Archbishop Ryan got different people to deal with them. This seems

to have been a deliberate policy to ensure that the knowledge of the problems was as restricted as possible.[8]

James Kavanagh, who served as auxiliary bishop from 1972 to 1988,

> tried to influence the Garda handling of the criminal complaints they had made against Fr Carney. He persuaded a family to drop a complaint they had made to the Gardaí.[9]

In 1987, when not a single complaint of child abuse had been passed on by Archbishop McNamara to the Gardaí, the archdiocese took out insurance against claims that might be made by victims of child abuse. This was an act

> proving knowledge of child sexual abuse as a major cost to the archdiocese and is inconsistent with the view that Archdiocesan officials were still on 'a learning curve' at a much later date, or were lacking in an appreciation of the phenomenon of clerical child sex abuse.[10]

In 2005 the report of the inquiry into the Diocese of Ferns (covering most of Co. Wexford and parts of Cos. Carlow and Wicklow) identified more than a hundred complaints of child sexual abuse against priests and found that both Bishop Dónal Herlihy and his successor, Brendan Comiskey, 'placed the interests of individual priests ahead of those of the community in which they served.'[11] Here were the moral watchdogs whose writ would run in 1983, when 'the campaign proved to be one of the most vitriolic and divisive in the history of the state.'[12]

The campaign had its roots in the promise given by both Charlie Haughey and Garret FitzGerald in 1981 to the Pro-Life Amendment Campaign to hold a referendum. The following year Fianna Fáil published the text of its proposed amendment shortly before the November general election. It read:

> The State acknowledges the right to life of the unborn and, with due regard to the equal right to life of the mother, guarantees in its laws to respect and, as far as practicable, by its laws to defend and vindicate that right.[13]

This text appeared to possess a miraculous unifying quality, because, despite 1982's uniquely bad-tempered political atmosphere, it won immediate fulsome praise from the leader of the opposition, who announced that

> he was relieved at the wording. It was along the lines that he had pressed for and Fine Gael and himself would be able to give it their total support . . . There was no possible disagreement with the government.[14]

In reality FitzGerald's instant thumbs-up

> was inspired by political opportunism. Confident that they were about to topple the government, most Fine Gael politicians did not want to risk a single vote being lost. Suggestions that they were soft on abortion would lose quite a few.[15]

Yet the contradiction between FitzGerald's talk of pluralism and constitutional crusades and his support for the referendum was immediately apparent to Conor Cruise O'Brien, who observed that

> Garret's crusade commits him to removing specifically Catholic provisions in the constitution. He can't now start shoving new specifically Catholic provisions in it. In terms of crusading (secular style) he would look like Richard the Lionheart embracing Islam.[16]

The *Church of Ireland Gazette* pointedly commented: 'What a pity that those who talk of constitutional campaigns and raise the hope of better days to come prove to be as empty as the rest of them when words come to deeds.'[17]

Even within FitzGerald's own party there were those who saw that backing the amendment didn't really fit with his image as a politician of principle. Said one member of Young Fine Gael, Barbara Cahalane, 'It is the sort of spinelessness that I would normally associate with another party. It is leading from behind.'[18] In the final analysis

> it boiled down to a question of honesty and courage—the honesty to admit that when forced to confront the complexities of the abortion issue some people did see a justification for it in cases of rape, incest and other tragic situations.[19]

It was a test that FitzGerald failed.

There was significant opposition to the referendum as early as December 1982, when the Executive Council of the ICTU came out against it and pointed out that it would not 'help to resolve the dilemma faced by many thousands of women annually in this sensitive matter.'[20] Such namby-pamby talk cut no ice with the likes of the prominent campaigner William Binchy, who suggested that

> if abortion is a criminal offence in Ireland, it should also be a crime for an Irish woman to procure an abortion elsewhere.[21]

By February, Government unease about the referendum had grown to the extent that

> as many as 15 members of the Fine Gael Parliamentary Party have reservations about the forthcoming abortion referendum.[22]

The new Attorney-General, Peter Sutherland, had been a referendum sceptic since the idea had been mooted, and at the end of January he advised FitzGerald that the Fianna Fáil wording

> was likely to be interpreted by the Supreme Court as excluding the
> kind of intervention that takes place in hospitals in accordance with
> the existing law so as to save the life of a mother who has cancer of
> the womb or has an ectopic pregnancy. This was because if such
> operations were to be put to the test in the courts after the
> enactment of this amendment, a surgeon who had carried out such
> an operation with fatal consequences for the child could not
> reasonably be said to have upheld the right to life of the unborn
> child equally with that of the mother.[23]

Instead of prompting the Government to abandon the referendum,
this intervention resulted in the coalition putting forward its own
amendment, which stated: 'Nothing in this Constitution shall be invoked
to invalidate or to deprive of force or effect a provision of the law on the
grounds that it prohibits abortion.'[24] The problem with this proposed
amendment was that both the PLAC and the Catholic Church stated their
preference for the original one. SPUC described the new amendment as
'totally and completely unacceptable and a complete abnegation of the
government's solemn commitment,' which was fair enough, given
FitzGerald's previously expressed love of the Fianna Fáil amendment.[25]
The Catholic hierarchy took the same view and expressed an

> earnest hope that at the end of the debate, our legislators will put
> before the people a form of amendment which will give them an
> opportunity to decide whether or not they wish to give to unborn
> human life the full constitutional protection already guaranteed to
> every citizen.[26]

To add to the Government's difficulties the Fine Gael TDs Alice Glenn,
Tom O'Donnell, Michael Joe Cosgrave and Liam Cosgrave (junior) issued
a statement that said that they could not accept

> the fact of the total omission of any reference to the right of life to
> the unborn. We cannot accept the situation whereby the door would
> be left open to the Oireachtas to legalise abortion at some future
> date. This could be extremely dangerous in the event of a hung Dáil
> similar to the last two Dáils.[27]

With other members of Fine Gael and the Labour Party unhappy with
the amendment, and with some Labour TDs opposed to the idea of a
referendum altogether, the coalition parties were hopelessly divided. The
result was that, on 27 April,

> the government was defeated heavily when Fianna Fáil's choice of
> wording for the constitutional amendment on abortion was

overwhelmingly accepted by the Dáil. In a series of discussions on
the Referendum Bill, the Fine Gael wording was rejected by 88 votes
to 65, the Fianna Fáil wording was accepted by 87 votes to 13 and the
Bill was passed 85 votes to 11.[28]

It is worth recording the names of the ten TDs who voted against both
amendments, thereby taking the decision that there was no need for any
referendum at all. They were Ruairí Quinn, Toddy O'Sullivan, Mervyn
Taylor, Barry Desmond, Joe Bermingham, Frank Cluskey and Eileen
Desmond of the Labour Party, the two Workers' Party TDs, Tomás Mac
Giolla and Proinsias de Rossa, and Tony Gregory. It is striking that while
Alan Shatter and Monica Barnes, perhaps the two most liberal Fine Gael
TDs, were praised for breaking ranks, they still voted for their own party's
proposed amendment. In contrast, Bermingham, O'Sullivan and Eileen
Desmond made a far more radical gesture, which is worth remembering,
given the perceived conservatism of the Labour Party outside Dublin.

The decks were now cleared for 'the whole dismal saga of the abortion
referendum with its mixture of ignorance, bigotry, hysteria and farce.'[29]
FitzGerald said that 'he would issue a simple statement saying why the
formula which had now been passed by the Dáil was unacceptable because
of its inherent dangers, but he would not campaign against the
amendment.'[30] Why the head of the Government would not campaign
against something he considered dangerous was not explained.

Those who did wish to take part in the campaign set about their task
with gusto. Typical of its tenor was an anti-amendment meeting at which
Mina Uí Chribín, a frequent campaigner for the Catholic right, and
supporters tried 'to shout down the speakers and to break up the meeting.'
When Senator Mary Robinson spoke, Uí Chribín shouted: 'What would
you know about morals anyway? You've the morals of a tomcat.'[31] The
contribution of a Methodist clergyman she greeted with roars of 'Who
cares about Protestants anyway? The wording should read, "Get all the
Protestants out."'[32] Gene Kerrigan of *Magill* observed that

> the ambidextrous Garret FitzGerald has something in each hand for
> the Irish people. A crusade in one hand and an amendment in the
> other. Tone and Davis in one hand, Mina Uí Chribín in the other.[33]

The campaign would become 'a moral civil war', in which pro-
amendment forces sought a return to traditional values of censorship and
authoritarianism.[34] Gay Byrne, the host of 'The Late Late Show', who
'more than any other individual symbolised the openness of the new
values and the willingness to discuss all issues and points of view, was
successfully shouldered onto the sideline'[35] when he was prevented from

holding a discussion on the referendum by the chairperson of the RTE Authority, Fred O'Donovan.

A kind of moral McCarthyism took hold, so that

> a member of the INTO running for the senate this year was asked one question by his Executive: not on education but where he stood on the amendment. When he said he opposed it he was refused his union's backing and withdrew from the election. On several RTE programmes, notably an interview with June Levine, there was censorship which precluded discussion of abortion. One producer was reprimanded and effectively banned from working on certain programmes after arranging an interview with Anne Connolly of the Well Woman Centre.[36]

The climate was such that eleven members of the IFA who spoke out against the amendment were suspended, along with Dónal Cashman, president of the organisation, who proposed his own suspension.[37] The journalist Mary Holland, chairperson of the Anti-Amendment Campaign, who had spoken about having had an abortion, was 'called a murderer at public meetings.'[38]

> The Catholic Church intervened at every opportunity, as when a letter from the Archbishop of Dublin, Dr Ryan, was read out at all Catholic masses in Dublin on the Sunday preceding the referendum, stating that a rejection of the amendment would leave a possibility of abortion becoming legal sooner or later in Ireland. The letter concluded by advising the electorate to vote 'yes.'[39]

Bishop Joseph Cassidy of Clonfert declared that 'the most dangerous place in the world is in a woman's womb.'[40] Father Michael Cleary appeared on 'The Late Late Show' to present

> a collection of gravely disabled people to illustrate his point that if the unborn were not protected by the constitution women would choose not to have disabled babies and the wheelchair users surrounding him in the television studio would have been murdered in the womb.[41]

The feminist Ursula Barry thought the referendum

> represented a new era characterised by outright confrontation ... The success of the PLAC's campaign saw the demoralisation and partial defeat of a movement that had achieved so much in the previous decade.[42]

The campaign was also disheartening for the Protestant churches, all of which opposed the amendment. Dr John Ward Armstrong, Church of Ireland Archbishop of Armagh and Primate of All Ireland, described it as 'the Mother and Child scheme all over again' and an attempt to 'force a moral theology on a whole people which is symptomatic of only one church.'[43]

The referendum in September saw a turn-out of 55 per cent and a Yes vote of 67 per cent. An examination of the votes reveals the rough location of the Irish Bible Belt. Of the eight constituencies that returned a Yes vote greater than 80 per cent, six were in Connacht-Ulster and another on the west coast in Munster. The highest Yes votes came in the conservative bastions of Roscommon and Mayo East (both 83 per cent), followed by Donegal North-East, Donegal South-West, Kerry South, Cavan-Monaghan, Cork North-West and Mayo West. The east coast was the liberal stronghold, with five constituencies in the greater Dublin area—Dún Laoghaire (58 per cent), Dublin South (54 per cent), Dublin North-East (51 per cent), Dublin South-East and Dublin South-West (both 50 per cent)—rejecting the amendment.[44]

Meanwhile the number of Irish women travelling to Britain for abortions continued to increase. In 1983 it was a new record: 3,677. In 1984 it rose to 3,946.[45]

To Garret FitzGerald's credit, he would admit being

> seriously at fault in accepting without adequate consideration or legal advice—however much in good faith—the proposed wording when it was put forward by Fianna Fáil in early November 1982. The fact that, given the scale of the Fine Gael and Labour defections in the eventual Dáil division on the issue, the amendment would clearly have been put through the Dáil by Fianna Fáil in opposition, even if I had rejected it from the outset, is a poor excuse for my error of judgement.[46]

It was a costly error. The effect of the campaign was to embolden 'a regressive and somewhat sinister force in Irish society.'[47] When FitzGerald made genuine moves towards a pluralist society, that force would be lying in wait.

Fianna Fáil, meanwhile, would continue to deride any attempts at liberalisation. In September the party's chief whip, Bertie Ahern, sneered: 'One could be forgiven, listening to some politicians and commentators, for thinking the whole Republican idea consisted in the liberalisation of laws on contraception, divorce and abortion.'[48] Unencumbered by any doubts about the value of eternal moral conservatism, Fianna Fáil had been boosted by the sight of the coalition tying itself in knots. Haughey must have derived particular pleasure from the floundering of his opposite number. Yet three months before the Government's proposed amendment was defeated in the Dáil it seemed that he had finally run out of road. On that day one of his party colleagues remembered Haughey saying that

> he would take his own decision in his own time. I think most of us present understood this to mean that he intended to step down within a few days. Ray Burke argued strongly that Haughey should not suffer the humiliation of being told to go straight away and should be allowed the dignity of choosing his own time. His opponents allowed him this breathing space—a charitable but naïve reaction.[49]

Haughey had been brought to the brink of defeat by the last—and most serious—incident of the GUBU era. On the evening of 19 January the new Minister for Justice, Michael Noonan, summoned the Garda Commissioner, Patrick McLaughlin, and the Deputy Commissioner in charge of security, Joe Ainsworth, to his office separately. Noonan told McLaughlin that he would find it

> very difficult, if not impossible, to defend certain of McLaughlin's actions were they to become public. The criticisms included the investigation of the Pat O'Connor incident, the Tully transfer order, the Dowra Affair, his relationship with Ainsworth and his apparent lack of control over him. Fifteen minutes after McLaughlin left, Noonan confronted Ainsworth until 12.30 a.m. He went through the same process, asking him to account for his actions. Before noon on Thursday 20 January Noonan received a short resignation letter from Ainsworth. After lunch McLaughlin's letter arrived. He too was resigning.[50]

The following day it was revealed that

> the telephones of two journalists, Miss Geraldine Kennedy and Mr Bruce Arnold, were officially tapped at the behest of the former Minister for Justice Mr Seán Doherty . . . Mr Ray MacSharry, the former Tánaiste and Minister for Finance in Mr Haughey's government, used a miniature tape recorder to bug a conversation he had with the former Minister for Education Mr Martin O'Donoghue.[51]

The initial reaction from Fianna Fáil was to brazen things out, appealing to the ever-elastic notion of 'security'. A statement from the party's front bench bemoaned the fact that 'the irresponsible activities of the present government in the area of security' had caused the retirement of McLaughlin and Ainsworth.[52]

But this was never really going to fly. Although 'Ministers for Justice have the power to authorise telephone tapping . . . according to precedent, such measures are only taken in connection with Garda investigations into subversion and major crimes.'[53] It was obvious that neither Arnold nor Kennedy had been involved in either subversion or crime. Their only offence was to be 'engaged in writing about the in-fighting within Fianna Fáil . . .'[54] In Arnold's words,

> the action by the Minister for Justice was unquestionably illegal. The reason, in both cases, was to track down the sources for well-informed articles about the future plans of the dissidents within the Fianna Fáil party . . . 'Security' became 'national security'; then it became 'government leaks'; finally it became the tracking down of alleged party 'disloyalty'.[55]

Even Fianna Fáil members found Haughey's attempt to explain away the bugging risible. At a parliamentary party meeting he argued that

> Doherty had acted because 'national security' was being threatened by 'cabinet leaks.' When Pearse Wyse asked what leaks, he replied that, for example, the party's farm plan had appeared in the *Farmer's Journal*. This provoked a chorus of laughter.[56]

For the second time in five years a Garda Commissioner had been forced from office. And though the spotlight would almost immediately shift to Doherty and Haughey, the bugging scandal raised questions about why senior Garda officers had proved so amenable to political pressure. It was not the first time that Ainsworth had hit the headlines, as his career

> had been marked by controversy, culminating in his appointment as a Deputy Garda Commissioner by the previous government . . . The appointment was unprecedented in the history of the Gardaí as it was the first time there had been three deputy commissioners. At the time the Association of Garda Sergeants and Inspectors expressed surprise at the creation of the new post . . . His appointment as a Chief Superintendent in 1968 was also controversial.[57]

Ainsworth's brother Jude was a Fianna Fáil member of Castlebar Urban District Council and a political associate of Haughey's close ally Pádraig Flynn.

The implications of the bugging would be overlooked as everyone became caught up in the drama of Haughey's impending struggle for political survival. It was the *Sunday Independent's* political correspondent, Joseph O'Malley, who described them most succinctly.

> Had Fianna Fáil won the November 1982 general election, would any of what has now emerged publicly be other than rumour, suspicion and private allegations? Would the country be further

down the road towards the setting up of an incipient police state via a covert parallel police force reporting to the Minister for Justice on internal party opponents—through tapping journalists' phones, and all in the name of national security.[58]

The apocalyptic rhetoric on the day Haughey became Taoiseach for the first time suddenly looked much less far-fetched.

Doherty moved to protect Haughey, stating that the party leader 'did not know that I was tapping those journalists,' and Haughey claimed he 'knew absolutely nothing about any activities of this sort and would not countenance any such abuse.'[59] It didn't seem to matter. By 27 January, the day Haughey hinted to his colleagues that all he wanted was a dignified exit, there was a media consensus that

> the resignation of Mr Charles J. Haughey as leader of Fianna Fáil seems imminent . . . Several former supporters told Mr Haughey yesterday that with the latest in a series of scandals damaging the party the pressure for a change in leadership had become irresistible.[60]

Speculation now switched from the question of whether Haughey would step down to that of who would replace him.

> There was open canvassing for support for such candidates as Mr Michael O'Kennedy and Mr Des O'Malley in the corridors of Leinster House last night although some deputies still cling to the hope that an agreed candidate could be found and a contest avoided. Mr John Wilson and Mr Gerry Collins were the men on whom this hope was pinned.[61]

In fact Haughey had no intention of stepping down, having 'already decided to hang on and fight it out if necessary.'[62] This caused 'considerable confusion and embarrassment . . . when Mr Haughey refused to submit his resignation and Mr O'Kennedy and Mr O'Malley found that they had been canvassing for a position which wasn't vacant.'[63]

It would take a tragic accident to save Haughey. The irony was that it would involve one of his opponents. Clem Coughlan was travelling to Dublin for the meeting in which he was expected to vote against Haughey. His car collided with an articulated lorry, and he was killed instantly. The following day's meeting was adjourned as a mark of respect; but what happened after that infuriated Haughey's opponents, who 'had let it be known that they would be seeking a short adjournment until Friday, rather than to next Wednesday so as to minimise Mr Haughey's room for manoeuvre.'[64] Instead, after a minute's silence, the chairperson of the parliamentary party, Jim Tunney, announced that the meeting would be adjourned till the following week and then ran out the door. 'Mr Tunney ignored Miss Mary Harney, who was on her feet demanding his attention at the time and he did not return to the meeting despite demands that he do so.'[65]

Tunney's procedural jiggery-pokery gained extra breathing space for Haughey. Forty-one TDs demanded a meeting the following day, but the chairperson decided that there would be no meeting until Monday. 'By then the panic which was engendered by the bugging revelations had abated somewhat.'[66] A reprieved Haughey and his lieutenants set about securing his survival. Haughey now appealed to all members of the party

> to rally behind me as their democratically elected leader and give me that total support that I need to restore unity and stability ... It is my intention that the Ard Fheis should devote itself to a full examination of the state of the organisation and the causes of our present problems and difficulties ...[67]

Haughey's opponents reacted furiously to what they saw as an attempt 'to go above the heads of the parliamentary party to the grassroots ... The spectre was created even more lucidly of Ard Fheis power dictating to the elected deputies.'[68] Charlie McCreevy described him as 'a disgrace to the democratic tradition of Fianna Fáil and of the Irish nation,' whose statement had been 'totally fascist in content and tenor.'[69] Some detected an implication that Haughey did not accept the right of the TDs to vote him out of office, and Gerry Collins warned that 'it has always been the parliamentary party that elects the leader. This is how the party founder ... intended it to be and nobody is going to change the rules at a moment's notice.'[70]

The fraught atmosphere caused some of Haughey's opponents to slightly lose the run of themselves. Ben Briscoe said he was as 'shocked and outraged and fearful as anybody else. I think it will go down in history as one of the most dreadful statements of any parliamentary leader.'[71]

Yet it has been suggested that Haughey, having lost the support of the parliamentary party, 'regained it after he appealed, on Lenihan's advice, to the party activists in the country over the heads of his deputies.'[72] In an interview he denied any intention of subverting the will of the TDs, saying, 'I've never tried to avoid any decision of the parliamentary party. I will, with honour and dignity, accept any decision of the parliamentary party.'[73] He added: 'I am looking forward to tomorrow with confidence ... I never contemplate defeat. I'm not contemplating it now.'[74]

His survival depended on the report of the committee that Fianna Fáil had set up to inquire into the bugging scandal and that would report to the parliamentary party meeting before the vote. It would also depend on how the TDs interpreted the murky tale of Ray MacSharry's meeting with Martin O'Donoghue.

In October, Seán Doherty had asked Joe Ainsworth to supply MacSharry with

> a miniature tape recorder and sensitive microphone. Mr Ainsworth delivered the equipment to Mr MacSharry in his office . . . Mr Doherty again contacted Mr Ainsworth and said he wanted a tape transcribed. The tape was sent by Mr Doherty to Mr Ainsworth's office. Later, Mr Ainsworth delivered two copies of the transcript.[75]

That MacSharry, while still Tánaiste, had bugged a conversation with a party colleague was extraordinary; and when the bugging story broke he had joined Doherty in resigning from the Fianna Fáil front bench.

MacSharry explained that he was concerned about his personal position after being told by Seán Doherty, Albert Reynolds and Pádraig Flynn that Martin O'Donoghue had 'been involved in discussions referring to "unspecified financial arrangements".[76] He also threw in references to

> serious allegations and rumours . . . that he had, for instance, bought farms, had purchased stock for them, that he owned a holiday complex in Donegal and recently that he was sick and even dying. I was told a political scandal was about to break about Ray MacSharry.[77]

The relevance of these rumours to the bugging was not explained, and they were not mentioned again. Aside from anything else, MacSharry must have felt insulted at the implication that his fervent support for Haughey was financial in nature.

The kernel of O'Donoghue's argument seemed to be that

> those who were financially compromised could not act for themselves in any vote on the leadership unless first released from bondage. By releasing them, you were not necessarily telling them to vote against Haughey; you were simply releasing them from the shackles that bound them and then at least they could vote as free men again.[78]

He insisted that he had

> never tried to bribe Mister MacSharry. He had gone into the meeting to see whether Mr MacSharry or anybody else in the party had any financial problems and to see what could be done to help them.[79]

At the very least, O'Donoghue had strayed into ethically dubious territory by being the messenger of those prepared to offer financial inducements. His fellow-dissidents 'expressed their astonishment at Dr O'Donoghue's recklessness in having such an interview with Mr MacSharry who can hardly be described as a political ally.'[80]

MacSharry's justification for recording a private conversation seemed to be that 'he had to protect his own name and integrity from any insinuations that he was in a compromising situation.'[81] And when the parliamentary party met, the committee inquiring into phone-tapping 'placed greater blame on Martin O'Donoghue than it did on either Doherty or MacSharry.'[82] Haughey began the most important meeting of his political life by proposing that the party whip be removed from both O'Donoghue and Doherty. The proposal was accepted.

It has never been satisfactorily explained why MacSharry needed to take the unprecedented step of bugging a party colleague. Raymond Smith, the *Irish Independent* reporter whose book *Charles J. Haughey: The Survivor* covers the year of GUBU admirably, felt that the reason he put forward for taping the conversation with O'Donoghue

> in no way . . . excuses that course of action. He should have had the gumption to come face to face with Martin O'Donoghue and ask him bluntly what was behind the stories . . . To stoop to the act of bugging a private conversation could not be excused on any grounds. It comes into the same category as Seán Doherty instigating a bug on the phones of two journalists.[83]

The transcript of the conversation revealed that even though O'Donoghue was unaware of being bugged, he never made any attempt to bribe MacSharry, even when given an opening by the mention of the money rumours.

Haughey's survival was probably ensured by the report of the party committee investigating the phone-tapping, which found that he had not known about it. It's not clear how it came to this conclusion, given that Haughey *did* know, and would be forced from office when Doherty finally decided to tell the truth nine years later. David Andrews entered a minority opinion, which said that Haughey as party leader 'should take ultimate responsibility for the whole affair,' and he would describe the conclusions reached by the other committee members—Jim Tunney, Bertie Ahern and Michael O'Kennedy—as an 'utter whitewash.'[84]

But the report did the job, and Haughey defied all predictions by defeating the motion of no confidence, 40 votes to 33. It was hailed as a remarkable victory; yet there are few politicians who would have opted to remain as head of a party they had divided in such a manner. Ray Burke, a former Haughey supporter who had turned against him, declared:

> What I cannot understand . . . is why Charlie Haughey himself does not see that the great majority of the party want him to stand aside—not as a matter of disgrace or dishonour but simply to allow someone else to take over.[85]

The reasons for Haughey's refusal to surrender might have been clearer to Burke and others had they been privy to their leader's financial arrangements, then being looked after by his accountant, Des Traynor.

In May that year 'a second residential current account with Guinness and Mahon was opened. During the seven months of its existence, £211,344 was lodged to the account.'[86] Between 1979 and 1987 a total of £1,761,127 was lodged in four Guinness and Mahon accounts held by Haughey, although tracing the origin of all the money has not been possible, because 'much of it travelled through accounts controlled by Traynor before being lodged to Haughey's name. Some of these accounts were in the name of Amiens Securities Limited.'[87]

Some of the money appeared to have come from P. V. Doyle, the owner of the Westbury, Berkeley Court, Burlington, Montrose, Skylon, Tara Tower and Green Isle Hotels. Doyle made lodgements totalling £120,000 to the Amiens account in May and June, with the same sum transferred from the Amiens account to Haughey's loan account. Doyle was only one of the many contributors to Haughey's secret funds.[88] Had Haughey lost the leadership of Fianna Fáil and relinquished the power and influence that came with it, it is doubtful if these contributors would have been so eager to support his flamboyant life-style. When Haughey battled against the dissidents he was trying to stave off not just political but also financial ruin.

His success in keeping his job was in stark contrast to the situation of many of his fellow-citizens. In the same week

> the closure of the Rank's Flour Mills in Dublin meant the loss of 300 jobs. Within the next few weeks a further 200 redundancies are expected . . . Gallagher's tobacco plant in Tallaght is to lay off 93 workers from all sections of the factory . . . Another 59 jobs are going at the Noyek plant in Santry, Dublin. Further redundancies are planned at the Semperit tyre plant at Ballyfermot . . . In the soft drinks trade, Savage Smyth intends to put some of its 160 production workers on a three day week . . . in Dublin Port up to 280 redundancies are being sought . . .[89]

In August came the news that the Dunlop tyre factory in Cork would close the following month, with the loss of 680 jobs. Dissatisfaction with the redundancy terms led to a sit-in that continued until October, when the workers accepted an improved offer from the company.

1983 was the year of the sit-in, as all over the country workers who had been made redundant occupied factories. Fourteen workers at Rank's mill in Dublin were sent to Mountjoy Prison for occupying the factory in protest at the company's failure to offer the levels of redundancy payment recommended by the Labour Court. When they were released they rejoined four of their workmates who had remained inside the plant. There were occupations too at the Kingdom Tubes tyre plant in Tralee (closed with the loss of 295 jobs), the Datsun car assembly plant in Dublin (213 jobs gone), Carrigaline Pottery in Co. Cork (210 jobs), the Lemon's sweet factory in Dublin (75 jobs), and the Ross Shipyard in New Ross (60 jobs), as workers attempted to save their jobs. It seemed possible that these acts of economic desperation would move the Government to action. But in February 1984 it was announced that

> no replacement industries will be sought for those factories where the workforce engages in a sit in under a new industrial policy adopted yesterday by the government. The decision was taken on the advice of the IDA as a result of the poor industrial image created abroad by such occupations . . .[90]

None of these occupied factories would survive.

No workers fought as hard to keep their factory open as those in Clondalkin Paper Mills, where 240 workers had been occupying the plant ever since its closure in January 1982, with the loss of 458 jobs. By February the following year six former employees—Denis Kenny, Brian Nolan, Eugene Charles, Gerry Courtney, John O'Keefe and Niall Nolan—were facing imprisonment 'if they continued to disobey a High Court order that they should stop occupying the factory premises.' Courtney told Judge Mella Carroll that they were looking for their jobs back, and until the Government purchased the mills he was prepared to accept any punishment the court imposed.

> I have worked in Clondalkin Paper Mills for twenty-seven years . . . I have reared seven children. My wife or none of my children have ever been in court. This is the first time I have ever been in a court. All I want is my job back so that I can support my family and live like a man again. I don't consider myself a criminal.[91]

The night before the men were to be jailed a meeting between the Government and the ICTU resulted in the Government agreeing to buy the mills for £1.7 million. The decision followed 'intense pressure from the ICTU which warned that failure to do so would have serious repercussions on industrial relations and on relations between the union and the government.'[92] Peter Keating of the Federated Workers' Union of Ireland hailed it as a victory and declared: 'We have been given every reassurance that the mill will be reopened. We are satisfied that it will.'[93]

But later in the year it emerged that the Government had other ideas, with the Minister for Energy, John Bruton, stating that 'the mills would not be reopened until it could be shown that they could be operated on a viable basis.'[94]

What the workers saw as a betrayal by the coalition resulted in renewed protests, and in November two former employees, Myles Speight and Brian Nolan, began a hunger strike.[95] Seán MacBride said that on reading the evidence he was convinced that the Government was guilty of a 'gross breach of trust' with the workers and the ICTU.[96]

On 16 November a surprise announcement that the Government had accepted a proposal for a paper conversion project at the Dublin mills led to the ending of the hunger strike and the calling off of a 'day of action', involving a work stoppage and demonstration in support of the Clondalkin workers, called by Dublin Council of Trade Unions.[97] Although the factory, renamed Leinster Paper Mills, was back in production by 1984, it closed for good in 1987, despite one final occupation.

The occupations of 1983 can be seen as one of the final flourishes of trade union radicalism, which would greatly diminish in the coming years of persistently high unemployment.

The response of the Minister for Finance, Alan Dukes, to the crisis was to bring in 'the toughest budget for decades,' which included

> VAT increases which raise the standard rate from 30 to 35% and the lower rate from 18 to 23% . . . a one per cent levy, which is described as temporary, that will apply to all income and yield £47 million, or almost twice as much as capital taxation this year.[98]

The budget was heavily criticised for being likely to

> abort the modest recovery in the economy, raise the level of unemployment, put the potential inflation rate this year up to about 12 per cent and ensure a crucifying fall in the living standards of all with the possible exception of those who rely on pensions and unemployment assistance . . .[99]

Yet it could have been harsher still. Dukes went on radio to say that 'the budget deficit for the year would have to be cut from the £900 million in Fianna Fáil's proposed estimates to £750 million.'[100] The Labour Party's reaction was furious, but it was the Taoiseach himself who put the kibosh on the Minister for Finance's plans. FitzGerald decided that officials in the Department of Finance were taking 'a rather apocalyptic view' and 'overstating its case' and that Dukes should abandon his plans.[101]

By September, FitzGerald seemed to have come round to Dukes's position, saying that the following year's budget 'would have to yield spending cuts of half a billion pounds. Some semi-state companies would have to be shut down if they were uneconomic.'[102] This was unacceptable to the Labour Party, and Dick Spring contacted FitzGerald to tell him that the party would pull out of Government if those cuts were implemented. Instead, the Labour Party wanted

> greater capital taxation and a bigger tax yield from farmers and the self-employed. On the other hand, Fine Gael were totally opposed to capital taxation. They saw the business and farming communities as their natural constituencies. The business sector, in particular, had some very discreet but effective ways of conveying their displeasure to Fine Gael politicians and backroom boys.[103]

The Government limped on, even though the Labour Party now knew that Fine Gael 'wanted all the pain of tough decisions to be inflicted on our constituency.'[104] Even home ownership,

> once the security of the working class, turned into a bad joke as Ireland's property market collapsed. [The Society of] St Vincent de Paul, once the helping hand to society's neediest, began receiving its first requests for help with home mortgages, from the very people who used to contribute to the charity.[105]

The Minister for Industry, John Bruton, committed the state to a £126 million rescue package for the Dublin Gas Company, but the Minister for Trade, Commerce and Tourism, Frank Cluskey, 'was opposed to bailing out a private company: he wanted the government to go all the way to nationalise it. Bruton was equally ideologically convinced—against nationalisation.'[106] Cluskey 'could not agree that state money should be used to contribute to [the] private wealth of the individual investors who controlled the company.'[107] He resigned from the Government.

———

The Government also had to deal with a series of IRA kidnappings. The victim of the first one was Shergar, the wonder horse that two years previously had won the Derby at Epsom by a record ten lengths. On the night of 8 February the family of the head groom, Mr John Fitzgerald, was held at gunpoint and locked in a room of their home . . . Mr Fitzgerald, after identifying Shergar to the armed and masked men who arrived at the stud around 8.30p.m. on Tuesday was forced to bridle and load the stallion into a horsebox which was then driven to an unknown hiding place.[108]

The kidnapping had been made easy for the gang, as security at the stud was extremely lax. A ransom demand was received, but the kidnappers were unable to provide proof that the horse was still alive. It soon became apparent that it had perished. Its fate remains a mystery, and its body has never been found, though it has been claimed that 'very soon after the kidnapping, Shergar threw himself into a frenzy in the horsebox, damaged his leg and had to be shot.'[109]

The IRA informer Seán O'Callaghan has alleged that Kevin Mallon planned the kidnap and that the IRA team included Nicky Kehoe, later a Sinn Féin councillor. Kehoe was certainly involved during the next kidnap attempt, which was an even greater disaster for the republican movement.

The IRA planned to kidnap Galen Weston, the Canadian billionaire and owner of the Brown Thomas shop in Grafton Street. However, the Gardaí had been tipped off and lay in wait for the gang inside Weston's house. As they were moving into position, Weston, who had been told about the plot, was playing polo in England with his friend Prince Charles. A gun battle between members of the Special Task Force and the IRA, during which the gardaí fired almost two hundred rounds, ended with four kidnappers being wounded and captured, including Nicky Kehoe, who was unhurt, though he had been one of only two IRA men to exchange shots with the gardaí. Three men were believed to have escaped.[110] Peter Lynch was sentenced to fourteen years in prison, Kehoe to twelve years, and John Hunter, Gerry Fitzgerald and John Stewart to ten years each.[111]

But the IRA was not finished yet. Don Tidey, chief executive of Quinnsworth, had set out from his home in Dublin to drive his daughter to school on 24 November. At a junction he was flagged down by a man in a Garda uniform who then put a machine gun to his head and dragged him from the car.[112]

The hunt for Tidey and his kidnappers began to focus on the Ballinamore area of Co. Leitrim after a tip-off from the RUC Special Branch in December. The pursuers included soldiers with blackened faces mingling with members of the Special Detective Unit, all carrying submachine guns[113]; they also included a number of recruit gardaí. On

16 December one of these, Gary Sheehan, came across a man in combat fatigues holding a rifle. The man failed to answer when Sheehan spoke to him. Sheehan turned to tell Private Patrick Kelly when

> a burst of automatic rifle fire rang through the forest, drowning out his last words . . . There were more loud bangs as the armed members of Garda Sheehan's unit returned fire. The gun battle was brief but fierce. Another recruit garda, Joseph O'Connor, heard a moan or grunt . . . Private Kelly had been hit by the gunfire and was now lying motionless on the ground . . . A few feet to the right lay the body of Gary Sheehan. Both men were dead.[114]

Sheehan's death would lead to criticism of the use of recruit gardaí. Many were not long out of their teens; some were eventually escorted from the scene, 'sobbing, with blankets over their shoulders suffering from trauma and shock. There was panic and confusion everywhere.'[115] It was undoubtedly a disaster for the state. 'Two men were lying dead . . . two others, a detective and a civilian were wounded; and the kidnappers, although heavily outnumbered, had managed to escape.'[116]

Tidey himself managed to escape during the shoot-out, but the kidnappers slipped through the cordon, and five days later they escaped capture again after being tracked to a house in Claremorris, Co. Mayo.

A Cork IRA man, Mick Burke, would later turn himself in and be sentenced to twelve years' imprisonment for his part in the kidnap.[117] He would be the only member of the gang to be convicted.

One of the men the Gardaí wanted to question was Brendan McFarlane, the OC of the IRA prisoners during the hunger strike, who had been one of thirty-eight prisoners to escape from Long Kesh in September. In January 1998 he would be arrested in connection with the kidnapping and charged with falsely imprisoning Tidey and with possession of a firearm with intent to endanger life; but in the High Court in July 2003 Mr Justice Aindrias Ó Caoimh ruled that 'the right to a fair trial had been prejudiced by the delay in prosecuting and the loss of items on which Gardaí claimed his fingerprints were found.' He ordered that the trial should not go ahead.[118]

Yet while the operation had been a fiasco for the Gardaí, the kidnappings had been a propaganda disaster for the IRA. In the words of one republican,

> practically every guard and soldier in the state was on our backs and all for a few quid. Between Shergar and then Tidey you couldn't move a finger that year . . . Then you're taking people who aren't actually involved in the conflict . . . and you've got their wives and

daughters and sons on television, crying their hearts out. It costs you sympathy and support and then it was inevitable that we were going to come into conflict . . . with the Gardaí or the army. It was completely stupid.[119]

One consequence was that Kevin Mallon, the architect of the kidnapping strategy, lost credibility within the IRA, something that helped the younger activists as they took over the reins from the older generation based in the Republic, with whom Mallon had been closely associated. Ruairí Ó Brádaigh resigned as president of Sinn Féin and Dáithí Ó Conaill as vice-president before the party's ard-fheis in November. Ó Brádaigh explained that his

> departure from the office of President of Sinn Féin became inevitable with the defeat in 1981 by a simple majority of the Éire Nua policy of a new four province federal Ireland with maximum decentralisation of power and decision making within a democratic socialist republic.[120]

The 'Éire Nua' policy was not the only bone of contention. Gerry Adams's victory in the West Belfast constituency in the 1983 British general election gave a boost to the arguments of those who suggested that the traditional policy of abstention might be a dead end. At that year's Wolfe Tone commemoration in Bodenstown, Adams, who replaced Ó Brádaigh as president, said that republicans would

> have to realise that ordinary people . . . accept Free State institutions as legitimate. To ignore this reality is to blinker republican politics, to undermine the development of our struggle and . . . to have a basic flaw in our analysis.[121]

This view placed a greater emphasis on the necessity of becoming involved in community issues. It was an approach that found favour with Christy Burke, a party activist who ran a local advice centre in Dublin's inner city. The previous year he had been approached by Father Jim Smyth, a Jesuit who worked in the inner city and lived in a one-bedroom flat. Father Smyth wanted to know if Burke would join a local group of parents who wanted to do something about the heroin problem in the area. Burke agreed.

Hardwicke Street was where what would become known as the Concerned Parents Against Drugs movement began. The organisation

> was born out of the misery and neglect of Dublin's flat complexes. The inner city was a community ravaged by material deprivation and squalor, but it took heroin to break its spirit.[122]

Over the previous couple of years the situation in the inner city had become truly hellish. In Liberty House in the north inner city,

> youngsters who had once spent £40 or £50 a week on heroin packs
> were now spending £100 a day . . . Instead of shooting up in the
> darkness of pub toilets or the privacy of their own bedrooms they
> were doing it openly in the flats. Many were young girls . . .[123]

The problem finally hit the headlines in 1983 when a study found that the addiction rate in the north inner city was 'on a par with the most notorious drug ghettoes in the u.s.'[124] The author of the report, Dr John Bradshaw, concluded his report by stating:

> It is not difficult to think that these young people . . . are the victims
> of society. They live in a dingy, squalid, architecturally dispiriting
> area; education seems to provide no mode of escape;
> unemployment is to be their almost inevitable lot; their parents are
> quite often separated or dead; abuse of alcohol is a common
> problem; crime the societal norm; imprisonment more likely than
> not.[125]

In a confidential letter to Dr Geoffrey Dean, director of the Medico-Social Research Board, Bradshaw wrote that Dublin

> may prove to have taken an unwanted palm in the field of drug
> abuse . . . Addiction to heroin sometimes starts in the youngest
> teenagers, and there is no gradual progression from soft drugs to the
> very dangerous heroin but rather a child's first experience of
> addictive drugs is of a self-administered intravenous injection of
> smack [heroin].[126]

Bradshaw also criticised the condition of the National Drugs Advisory Centre at Jervis Street Hospital, which was

> housed in dark, dingy, drab and wholly dismal surroundings that
> more than match the Seán MacDermott Street ambience which is
> the kind many addicts experience domestically. There can be no
> addict going to the centre but would be depressed by its
> atmosphere, its pokiness, its magnificently unwelcoming and
> almost undetectable entrance.[127]

These inadequacies seemed indicative of an uncaring state response. 'Why', asked one publication, 'has Jervis Street hospital only nine beds for in-patient treatment? Why is the Drugs Advisory Centre there stuck into a tiny portakabin with inadequate facilities and staff and no crèche or anything?'[128] Dr Dean observed that 'in north-central and south-central Dublin, more was done by the church than by the state to deal with heroin addiction.'[129]

Having to rely on their own resources, the affected communities turned to Concerned Parents Against Drugs to provide some kind of solution. In the heroin black-spot of St Teresa's Gardens, one community worker, Willie Martin, recalled that

> it was decided to keep all the junkies off the stairs, and all outsiders who were involved with drugs out of the flats. The feeling was that we had enough junkies of our own without having to contend with outsiders from all over the city. This plan worked out very well. Parents stood on the corner of the flats and politely refused admission . . .[130]

This was followed by the sending of 'a small delegation to each of the pushers' doors to ask them to give up selling heroin in the flats or get out.'[131] After they had been evicted,

> the men were out on patrol all night, every night. The women looked after the days, keeping the junkies out of the flats, explaining to them that there were no longer drugs in St Teresa's Gardens, eventually proclaiming a drug-free zone.[132]

Three hundred residents then

> moved the furniture out of the empty flats. They formed a human chain from the flats, down to the ground floor, handing the items of furniture carefully down the line. The evictions were carried out in this way to ensure that no handful of anti-drugs activists could be singled out for retaliation.[133]

CPAD groups would be criticised for vigilantism, but in a movement that mobilised so many people on such an emotive issue

> the most striking feature was that there wasn't more violence. The tactic of mass protests outside the homes of pushers . . . was in itself usually intimidating enough to stop drug trafficking in an area.[134]

There were also some notable Garda successes against drug dealers, most strikingly by a unit 'originating in the enthusiasm of a few young members of the force.'[135] It was set up by Mick O'Sullivan, a detective in the Security Task Force. O'Sullivan and a small group of other gardaí, including his former school friends Aidan Reid and Tony Lane, would 'pose as drug addicts to observe and move in on the pushers. They won the nickname of the Mockeys . . .'[136] The Mockeys 'broke the grip of the Dunnes on heroin distribution in Dublin's north inner city. In two years, they were to make well over half of the hundred drug busts in . . . the capital's toughest crime area.'[137]

Among their arrests was that of Mickey Dunne, sentenced to seven years' imprisonment. He was the first member of the family to be arrested for drug trafficking. In July 1983 Larry Dunne absconded while on trial for possession of heroin and cocaine. 'The constant pressure of public protests together with the activity of the mockeys in the area had the desired effect on the pushers.'[138] In Hardwicke Street, where it had all begun, the concerned parents' movement led to a rebirth of community confidence, as 'the committee went from strength to strength, organising the reconnection of cable TV, summer projects, Christmas parties for old folks and generally breathing life back into the flats.'[139] The CPAD would move into more problematic territory in 1984, but its achievements in its first year were a remarkable assertion of self-reliance and spirit in the country's most neglected communities.

—

Not far from the north inner city during the summer of 1982 a series of systematic beatings

> had been carried out by the same gang on men in Fairview Park. The Park was used by gay men as a meeting place and cruising area and the gang picked on them as easy targets to beat and rob.[140]

In the early hours of 10 September the gang struck again after one of them, Patrick Kavanagh, sat down on a park bench as bait. The gang members later described how their victim sat down on the bench beside Kavanagh, and they

> 'hid behind the trees with the sticks' . . . Armstrong said he saw the two starting to scuffle on the bench. Kavanagh shouted 'get the bastard.' Declan Flynn began to run . . . He almost made it. They got him just ten yards from the gate and the main road . . . They began to beat and kick him. When they had finished Declan Flynn lay on the path choking on his own blood.[141]

He died on admission to James Connolly Memorial Hospital in Blanchardstown. His attackers were nineteen-year-old Tony Maher and eighteen-year-old Robert Armstrong, both members of the Air Corps, eighteen-year-old Patrick Kavanagh, seventeen-year-old Colm Donovan and a fourteen-year-old who cannot be named. As Flynn lay dying, Maher stole £4 from his pocket and Kavanagh took his watch.[142] 'We were all part of the team to get rid of queers from Fairview Park,' said Armstrong.[143]

When, in March 1983, the quintet were convicted of the murder and sentenced to five years (Armstrong and Maher), four years (Donovan), two years (Kavanagh) and one year (the juvenile), Judge Seán Gannon suspended the sentences and allowed them to walk free. 'This,' he said, 'could never be regarded as murder.'[144]

The verdict caused outrage among the gay community, who felt it sent the message that 'it was OK to kill a queer.'[145] It also proved to be a catalyst for the nascent gay rights movement. A public meeting was held,

> attended by a large number of gay men. There was a lot of anger expressed at the meeting and the idea for the protest march was welcomed and supported. The Dublin Lesbian and Gay Men's Collective set about organising the march. About 800 people supported the march which went from Liberty Hall to Fairview Park, where a rally was held with speakers from DLGC, the Rape Crisis Centre and the National Gay Federation. It was a very significant march for the Irish Lesbian and Gay movement and the largest Gay march ever held in Ireland.[146]

Nine years later the gang leader, Robert Armstrong, broke into a flat in Ballymun with an accomplice and raped a woman who was seven months pregnant. He received a ten-year jail sentence.[147]

———

Seán Gannon wasn't the only judge whose remarks raised eyebrows. In August 1982 a secondary school teacher, Eileen Flynn, was sacked for giving birth to a baby son by Richie Roche, a separated man with whom she was living in New Ross. She took a case for unfair dismissal to the Unemployment Appeals Tribunal, then the Circuit Court and the High Court. Bank of Ireland refused to handle an account set up to raise the money for her appeal; and in the Circuit Court, Judge Noel Ryan dismissed her appeal, commenting:

> Times are changing and we must change with them, but they have not changed that much or in the adjoining jurisdiction with regard to some things. In other places women are being condemned to death for this sort of offence. They are not Christians in the Far East. Here people take a serious view of this and it is idle to shut one's eyes to it.[148]

These cases showed that at the same time as the state congratulated itself on having extended the protection of the Constitution to include the 'unborn child' there were grown members of the community who did not enjoy the full protection of the law. There was no place for either Declan Flynn or Eileen Flynn in the ideal country imagined by those who had campaigned for the 'pro-life' amendment and many of those who had voted for it.

There is the further irony that at the same time that the Sisters of the Holy Faith were sacking Eileen Flynn in New Ross because she (in the words of Sister Rosemary Duffy) 'openly and despite warnings to the contrary continued to live a lifestyle flagrantly in conflict with the norms which the school sought to promote,' Father Seán Fortune continued to rape teenage boys with impunity down the road in Fethard.[149]

Fortune would commit suicide in March 1999, ten days before he was due in Wexford Circuit Court to face sixty-six charges of sexual abuse against twenty-nine boys. He had become an outcast and an emblematic figure of the clerical child abuse scandals that began to engulf the church in the nineties and would continue through the next decade and beyond.

Eileen Flynn had married Richie Roche eleven years previously, and the couple had four more children. In 2000 she had returned to teaching in the Christian Brothers' primary school in New Ross and six years later was offered a permanent post. She died in September 2008, and at her funeral hymns were sung by pupils from the school, who also formed a guard of honour for her. The principal of the school, Brian McMahon, said she was 'much loved and respected by parents, pupils and colleagues in the CBS.'[150]

Chapter 13 ∽

| OUT OUT OUT

1984

On 17 July 1984 a customer at Dunne's Stores in Henry Street, Dublin, attempted to buy South African fruit. Mary Manning, a cashier, refused to carry out the transaction, thus setting in motion a series of events that would see eleven young workers become global symbols of the struggle against apartheid in South Africa.

Mary Manning's gesture had its roots in the decision taken by the annual conference of the Irish Distributive and Administrative Trade Union to instruct its members not to handle South African produce. Employees boycotted South African goods in Clery's, Roche's Stores and Quinnsworth without incident; but the story was different at Dunne's.

Two days after other employees had followed Mary Manning's lead, Dunne's decided to put an end to the boycott. Karen Gearon, the shop steward, recalled that

> Mary was brought upstairs with myself and was given five minutes to reconsider her position. We weren't allowed to talk to each other during the five minutes. She was kept in one room and I was kept in the other. And then we came back in and Mary said, 'No, I'm sticking by my position.'[1]

Dunne's insisted that the workers handle South African goods or be suspended. In retaliation eleven workers from the Henry Street shop— Mary Manning, Karen Gearon, Catherine O'Reilly, Theresa Mooney, Vonnie Munroe, Sandra Griffin, Alma Russell, Michelle Gavin, Liz Deasy, Dorothy Dooley and Tommy Davis—mounted a picket. One worker from the Crumlin branch, Brendan Barron, took similar action. Ben Dunne, the head of the Dunne's Stores group, later said that he had 'made the decision that we couldn't allow people in the organisation to decide which goods to sell and which not to sell.'[2]

The workers would remain on strike for two years and nine months, and their struggle would be described as one that 'stands with the 1913 Lockout as a key moment in the history of trade unionism in Ireland.'[3] Brendan Archbold, the IDATU official most closely associated with the strike, would call it 'probably the finest example of trade union solidarity ever.'[4]

Making the resilience of the strikers all the more remarkable was the fact that they were subjected to severe pressure. Gearon remembered that

> in the early stages of the strike we had a lot of police harassment. On numerous occasions there would be five women on the back door to prevent deliveries. The management inside would call the police, and there would be at least three policemen to every one striker ... Some of the women strikers had to have hospital treatment for injuries caused by management and police violence.[5]

There were also times when

> many of the public spat at them and shouted abuse, calling them 'nigger lovers' and telling them to 'look after their own instead.' It took the ICTU a year to issue a statement of support. In the meantime, two of the strikers had visits from the Special Branch, who told them that they were 'silly little girls', who did not realise that they were small cogs in a big wheel.[6]

Yet the tenacity shown by the young women and their male colleagues paid off when the protest began to attract international support. In December 1984 they

> were invited to meet Bishop Tutu in London, on his way to collect the Nobel Peace Prize. He stated publicly that he supported the strike and asked Ben Dunne to reinstate all strikers and give them the right not to handle South African goods.[7]

The dispute became an international *cause célèbre* in March 1985 when the strikers were invited to South Africa by Bishop Tutu and the South African Council of Churches to see conditions for themselves. On arriving at the airport in Johannesburg they were put under armed guard and held for several hours before being put on the next flight home. As they left they told the soldiers escorting them to the plane: 'We will be back to South Africa when it is free.'[8]

Finally stung into action, the Government discussed the matter with the supermarket chains, which agreed to phase out South African goods. The drawback was that there was no time limit, and the statement by Dunne's Stores that 'they would only phase out South African produce if they could find better quality and cheaper prices' showed that, in effect, nothing had changed.[9]

The duration of the dispute inflicted significant hardship on those involved. Vonnie Munroe, who had a three-year-old daughter, lost her house because she was unable to keep up mortgage payments on her strike pay of £21 a week. But the spirit of the strikers is perhaps best summed up by her comment that, 'even though I was forced to take a one bedroomed flat, we were still better off than the terrible conditions that the blacks were living in in South Africa just because of the colour of their skin.'[10]

There was considerable local as well as foreign support. On the night before the trip to South Africa the strikers were able to raise £6,000 in collections in Dublin. Notable supporters included the Moving Hearts saxophonist Keith Donald, who busked in Henry Street and gave his takings to the strike fund. Bertie Ahern, in opposition, declared that the strikers were

> supported by the trade union movement, by most workers and by people in all sections of Irish society. However, apart from finances, three or four of the people involved have severe health problems as a result of being out in inclement weather. It is within the jurisdiction of the government to force a conclusion in this case. The people concerned have made a stand and they deserve assistance. It is unreasonable to expect them to go back and to handle South African produce. They will not do that.[11]

The dispute was brought to an end in April 1987 when the coalition Government brought in a ban on the importing of South African goods. The proposal of the Minister for Labour and the Public Service, Ruairí Quinn, was supported by his Labour Party colleagues but opposed by a majority of Fine Gael ministers. Garret FitzGerald went against party opinion, and his vote saw the measure through. In the words of Karen Gearon,

> We won ... We didn't start the movement, the movement was there before us, but we certainly brought a new life to it, and we raised its profile. Before this strike there were about six divisions of the Anti-Apartheid movement in Ireland. By the time we finished there was an Anti-Apartheid division in every single county and some had three or four.[12]

The Dunne's Stores strike was one of the most remarkable stories of the decade, but no less remarkable in its way was the story of another Irish involvement in a fight for social justice in a foreign land. On 6 May 1983 three priests and six community workers in the Negros region of the Philippines were arrested and charged with the murder of Pablo Sola, mayor of the town of Kabalankan, and his four bodyguards on 10 March 1982. The priests were accused 'of having organised the killing, accompanying the killer'.[13] One of them was Father Niall O'Brien, a Columban Father who had been a missionary in the Philippines since shortly after his ordination in December 1963. He was in no doubt about the reasons for his arrest.

> We were accused for basically the same reasons the Church had been attacked during the previous 15 years—because the work of the Church for justice rocked the social boat and endangered deep-rooted and long-standing vested interests.[14]

Father O'Brien found the plight of the Filipino people under the US-backed dictatorship of President Ferdinand Marcos intolerable; but the language in which he expressed his dissent would have been unthinkable from an Irish missionary not too many years previously. The problem, he felt, was that

> colonialism was replaced by neo-colonialism. The u.s. discovered that there was no need to have the stars and stripes flying over the Philippines as long as the laws ensured u.s. economic domination and u.s. military bases. Martial law opened the gates to international finance, which marched in with vast self-serving projects and full rights to repatriate their earnings. The two-million dollar nuclear plant built in an earthquake prone area, is a typical example . . . Balked in their push for reform, many idealistic students took to the hills and joined the then minuscule New People's Army . . . Effective reform has been rejected and many people have reluctantly taken up the grim alternative of rebellion.[15]

Niall O'Brien may not have been a revolutionary communist, but his language and his actions were undeniably radical. He was incensed about a situation in which

> only 1.5 per cent of the Negros population owned any land at all. Among a total of 332,000 families in the province, 330 families owned 45 per cent of the sugar land, 30 families controlled 60 per cent of the fishing catch and fourteen families held 150,000 hectares (about 350,000 acres) of lumber concessions. And this translated into extreme poverty for at least 82 per cent of the province's 1.8 million people.[16]

This belief led Father O'Brien and his colleagues to agitate for land reform, to help in the setting up of trade unions and to educate the local population about human rights, while setting up co-operatives and 'basic Christian communities', a non-hierarchical form of grassroots church organisation with much greater lay involvement than the normal model.

Father O'Brien was one of many religious inspired by 'liberation theology', a radical interpretation of Catholic doctrine most famously expounded by the Peruvian theologian Gustavo Guttiérez in *A Theology of Liberation* (1973). Guttiérez urged the clergy to adopt

> a life of solidarity with the poor. The poor must be empowered to become agents of change so that they can fight injustice and transform society.[17]

Liberation theology proved immensely influential, not only in its Latin American birthplace but in other areas of the Third World. That it seemed to find particularly fertile ground among Irish missionaries owed something to its being embraced by Brian McKeown, the former lay missionary who was director of the church's Third World aid agency, Trócaire, and Bishop Éamonn Casey of Galway, the organisation's chairperson. In the bishops' pastoral letter on the foundation of Trócaire in 1973 (written by McKeown) they had promised that the organisation would

> give whatever help lies within its resources, to the areas of greatest need among the developing countries. At home, it will try to make us all the more aware of the needs of these countries and of our duties towards them. These duties are no longer a matter of charity but of simple justice.[18]

Yet the embracing of liberation theology was bound to meet with resistance. Guttiérez himself explained: 'If I say my priority is to evangelise the poor, the rich in Latin America immediately say that this is communism, because questioning structures that keep people poor is considered subversive.'[19] Or, in the words of the Brazilian Archbishop of Olinda and Recife, Dom Hélder Câmara, 'When I give food to the poor they say I am a saint; when I ask why the poor have no food they call me a communist.'[20] The Marcos regime obviously took the same view of the Negros Nine, as O'Brien and his fellow-accused came to be called.

The lay workers were first held in Bacolod Provincial Jail, while the three priests—O'Brien, the Australian Father Brian Gore and the Filipino Father Vicente Dangan—were held under house arrest. But on 26 January 1984 the priests 'broke in' to the jail to join their comrades. Father

O'Brien's captivity attracted huge attention in Ireland, and he described
how

> Ireland had outdone itself with letters. In fact, one class out of one
> school alone, that of Sister Bríd in Killester, organised 500 letters to
> each of many different officials and passed the campaign on to other
> schools ... In all ... there must have been about 15,000 received in
> the cell ... Some were very touching, many were deliberately written
> to cheer us up ...[21]

Conditions in the prison were primitive, and there was a fear that
members of the Nine might be assassinated before or during the trial.
Nevertheless, Father O'Brien refused to accept a pardon, on the grounds that
this would constitute an admission of guilt. But on 3 July, amid mounting
international pressure on the Marcos regime, the charges were dropped.
Father O'Brien told the American television channel NBC that he was

> filled with deep joy to be out of this terrible prison but it is no worse
> than the conditions under which many people must live. We have
> been in prison because we worked to change these conditions—we
> will continue to work to change them because we believe that as
> long as half the world is hungry no-one is free.[22]

Father O'Brien was deported after his trial and returned to Ireland a
hero. Later in the year he published *Seeds of Injustice*, a fascinating diary of
his time in prison, which ended with the questions:

> Who allowed this injustice to continue? Who wrote it in the first
> place into the structures of society? Who turned a blind eye to it?
> Who was too busy about many things to hear the cry of the poor as
> they called out?[23]

He returned to the Philippines when the Marcos regime was
overthrown in 1986, and he would spend the rest of his life there.

It is ironic that the trial of the Negros Nine took place as the Catholic
Church, under Pope John Paul II, was turning against liberation
theology. That year the Congregation for the Doctrine of the Faith, the
church's doctrinal watchdog, headed by Cardinal Joseph Ratzinger,
issued a criticism of aspects of liberation theology. The following year
the prominent Brazilian liberation theologian Leonardo Boff was
silenced by the Congregation, which issued further criticisms of the
movement the following year and censored other theologians. By the
end of the decade, liberation theology was almost completely
marginalised. The church would never again place such an emphasis on
social justice, a change noted by Father O'Brien's fellow-defendant
Father Brian Gore, who observed on returning to Negros in 2008:

I see the same power structure, skewed economic set up, and deplorable conditions afflicting our sugar workers, farmers, fishermen, urban poor . . . Unlike in the 70s and 80s which I considered as the most productive years in the lives of the Negros churches and clerics, today I don't see a lot of them living and working among the poor.[24]

Yet in its heyday a version of liberation theology spread to the Catholic Church in Ireland, as some priests and nuns 'began to work in the inner city, with the homeless, with single parent families, with battered wives, in Ballymun . . . on itinerant [Traveller] encampments around the wastelands of Dublin.'[25] Their number included Father Peter McVerry, who ran the Jesuit Centre for Faith and Justice in Dublin and who believed that

society is run by and for the middle class, against the poor, and that to achieve justice, a fundamental change at the political and cultural level is needed. Working for justice is the only thing worth doing and the church confirms that the gospel is not preached where work for justice is not going on. None of the people I work with go to Mass. They wouldn't dream of going. I don't see why they should, because it's made inaccessible to them.[26]

Some of them, like the Augustinian Father Michael Mernagh, had drawn inspiration from their time as missionaries. Father Mernagh had spent nine years in Nigeria, and after returning he set up a Family Resource Centre in the Liberties of Dublin. He starkly illustrated the differences between the hierarchy and the small group of the radical religious with his observation that

the dominant ideological attitudes in this society have been influenced by the Church through the schools, so that we have an unbalanced understanding of what the gospel values are about, of what morality is about, of what justice is about. There's an Ireland of the rich and an Ireland of the poor, an Ireland of the slums and an Ireland of the Phoenix Park races, and there is nothing being done about that at the teaching and faith level. Take the list of pastorals last year, they were almost all to do with sexual morality.[27]

When, twenty-three years later, former archbishops and auxiliary bishops of the Dublin diocese found their reputations in tatters because of clerical child abuse, the one form of sexual immorality towards which they had felt able to adopt a *laissez-faire* attitude, seventy-year-old Father Michael Mernagh would walk from St Colman's Cathedral in Cóbh to the Pro-Cathedral in Dublin as a gesture of atonement for the church's behaviour.

Another priest to go against the grain was Father Vincent Travers, parish priest of St Mary's parish, Tallaght, where, on 14 June, there were

> bitter protests against the presence of itinerants ... Almost 300 people stood in the middle of the junction between Oldbawn Road and the dual carriageway blocking traffic. Smaller groups held up traffic in other adjacent areas. They are protesting against the continual presence of travelling families on the by-pass. Residents in an area near a proposed temporary site for these travellers have also insisted that they will not be allowed on this.[28]

In the parish newsletter Father Travers wrote about the Travellers' feelings of

> rejection and alienation and the lack of respect for their dignity and rights, their experience of hurt and contempt at being called 'knackers' ... The travelling people are symbolic of the third world people we identify with, stand up for and support, in such faraway places as El Salvador, Nicaragua and the Philippines. However, when the victims are on our doorsteps, we cannot and will not take the necessary steps to end once and for all the inhuman conditions in which hundreds of families ... are forced to live. I wonder how we would feel if Filipinos organised protests and marches in Manila in favour of human rights for Irish travellers? I suggest we would feel both embarrassed and ashamed.[29]

These priests remained a minority, but there was one occasion when the new radical spirit in the church seemed to significantly affect the hierarchy. It is remarkable that during the visit of Ronald Reagan to Ireland in June

> the church hierarchy boycotted a state banquet at Dublin Castle in Reagan's honour in protest against the u.s. government's interventionist policies in Nicaragua and El Salvador ... They supported the Trócaire leadership of Casey and McKeown by showing solidarity with the voiceless people of El Salvador and Nicaragua ... This was an extraordinary, if not revolutionary, gesture ...[30]

The hierarchy's boycott was merely the most unexpected gesture during a visit that was largely dominated by the protests against it. Most of the protests may have come from the left, but the population as a whole

seemed at best ambivalent about Reagan. Bishop Casey fired the opening
salvo of the protest campaign as he

> rejected President Reagan's assertion that his critics were
> misinformed, and said that the President didn't understand what
> was going on in Central America. The Bishop said that it was the
> U.S. government's policy of continuing to give aid to a state which
> had murdered 40,000 of its own people and thus affirming the
> policy of repression, which was at the core of Christian objections.[31]

The day before the visit it emerged that

> three Telecom Éireann employees have been barred from working
> on communications equipment and services connected with
> President Reagan's visit on the grounds that they are allegedly
> 'security risks.' Telecom Éireann was instructed to bar the workers
> by the Garda authorities, acting on the advice of the U.S. Secret
> Service.[32]

On the same day three holders of honorary degrees from the National
University of Ireland—the maritime historian Dr John de Courcy Ireland,
the director of the Meteorological Service, Dr Austin Bourke, and the
former chairperson of Bord na Móna, Dr Aodhogán O'Rahilly—
announced their intention to return them because they regarded

> the presentation of an honorary Doctorate of Law to President
> Reagan as 'outrageous' at a time the President has refused to be
> bound by the decision of the International Court of Justice. The
> three also object to his policies in Central America and his nuclear
> policy in Europe.[33]

Reagan received a traditional Hollywood Irish welcome. When he
arrived to receive his honorary doctorate from University College, Galway,

> a lorry converted into a parade float with a sign: 'we welcome
> Ronald Reagan,' played Irish music at high volume . . . In front of the
> lorry on the motorcade route, a group of teenagers danced Irish jigs
> as the president's car passed. On the float itself, men and women
> dressed in traditional attire sat in a mock Irish cottage living-room
> complete with fireplace and a religious picture.[34]

In Ballyporeen, Co. Tipperary, where Reagan's Irish ancestry had
apparently been discovered during a search of the parish records by the
parish priest, the chairperson of the community council presented Reagan
with a carving in Irish oak representing the local church and the
Templetanny Chalice and a penal cross. 'He told the President, "Now you
are one of our own."'[35] Yet there were only 3,500 people in Ballyporeen, the
low number

attributed to tight security and the bad weather ... Gardaí manned all entry routes from 3 a.m., houses were searched by the u.s. Secret Service and even manholes in the street were sealed ... 500 demonstrators who had marched several miles to Ballyporeen from a nearby rally protesting in favour of nuclear disarmament and against u.s. policy in Central America were kept outside the village boundaries and out of sight of the presidential party.[36]

Thirty-four women who had set up a 'peace camp' in the Phoenix Park were arrested and detained on grounds of dubious legality, while the journalist Frank Kilfeather witnessed an attack on two young men in Capel Street, Dublin, after one of them waved an anti-Reagan poster as the motorcade passed on its way to the state banquet in Dublin.

A Special Branch detective appeared from nowhere, jumped on his back and flung him to the ground, cracking the back of his head off the pavement ... The young man lay stunned and shocked ... He said he was Seosamh Ó Braonáin and he was a student at Trinity College. 'All I did was put up a poster,' he said. 'I didn't think that this could happen in a country like this.' ... His friend said he was John Mulqueen, President of the Trinity College Students' Union. He said he was dragged against the barrier and kicked. 'I was dragged by the neck and kicked in the back. I asked the men to identify themselves but they just kicked me again.'[37]

That night ten thousand people marched through Dublin in the 'Ring around Reagan' demonstration. The crowd included two hundred nuns making common cause with the Workers' Party, some sections of the Labour Party, Jim Kemmy's Democratic Socialist Party, the Communist Party of Ireland, Sinn Féin, People's Democracy, the Irish Post Office Engineering Union, the Irish National Teachers' Organisation, the Amalgamated Union of Engineering Workers, the Campaign for Nuclear Disarmament, students from the Institute of Philosophy and Theology in Milltown, the Green Alliance and the Community Workers' Co-Operative.[38]

The following day the protest took place in the Dáil itself when

the two Workers' Party TDs, Tomás Mac Giolla and Proinsias de Rossa, and an independent deputy, Mr Tony Gregory, walked out of the Dáil chamber in protest at United States foreign policies ... As they stood up in succession announcing their decision to withdraw, other members voiced their opposition to the three deputies' action and there were shouts of 'out, out' at them.[39]

The Government seemed more concerned about what a spokesperson described as Charlie Haughey's 'outrageous gate-crashing' of the farewell

to Reagan at Dublin Airport. Unwilling to be excluded, Haughey stood
with the specially invited guests during the speeches of farewell and
the National Anthems and while President Reagan inspected the
guard of honour. When the official party lined up . . . he made his
way across the tarmac . . . By the time Mr Haughey arrived the
President and Mrs Reagan had already passed along the line but the
Fianna Fáil leader did bid farewell to most of the official American
party.[40]

_____

With Reagan out of the way there was another foreign leader to keep
happy. In November, Garret FitzGerald set off for England to persuade
Margaret Thatcher of the merit of the report of the New Ireland Forum,
which had been set up the previous year with a great deal of ballyhoo. The
idea was that of the SDLP leader, John Hume, who wanted a Council for a
New Ireland in which politicians from the Republic would

join us in abandoning rhetoric and, by placing their cards on the
table, show what sort of role there will be for the Protestant
community, what share of power, what safeguards, what sort of
economic situation and what would be the relations between
church and state.[41]

FitzGerald's response was to propose the New Ireland Forum, 'in which
all constitutional parties . . . including the unionists, would be invited to
participate. Its objectives would be an ending of the violence, reconciling
the two traditions in Ireland and securing peace and stability.'[42]

The Forum opened its doors on 30 May in Dublin Castle and was
described by FitzGerald as 'a unique attempt to bring peace and stability
. . . by facing reality, the reality of the tragic and frightening crisis of
Northern Ireland.'[43] It had nine Fianna Fáil members, eight from Fine
Gael and five each from the Labour Party and the SDLP. It received 317
written submissions and heard thirty-one oral presentations, among them
those of Seán MacBride, the Tory MP Sir John Biggs-Davison (joint author
of a book entitled *Ireland: Our Cuba?*), the Labour MP Clive Soley, the
Church of Ireland and Labhrás Ó Murchú of Comhaltas Ceoltóirí
Éireann.[44]

The Unionist parties, however, boycotted the Forum, though there
were appearances by individual unionists in a personal capacity. Sinn Féin
was not even given the opportunity to boycott it, as it was expressly

excluded because of its support for violence. In these post-Belfast Agreement days it beggars belief that anyone thought that violence could be ended without any engagement with those who were perpetrating it; so there was some justice in Sinn Féin's description of the Forum as

> a last desperate effort to save the face of the SDLP. The parties in the South are trying to ignore the fact that the SDLP are no longer the party representing nationalist opinion. Any discussions which exclude such a substantial proportion of the Irish people are doomed to failure.[45]

This point was graphically illustrated less than two weeks after the launch of the Forum when Gerry Adams gave Sinn Féin its first big electoral win over the SDLP by taking the West Belfast seat formerly held by Gerry Fitt in the British general election.

Another inconsistency was that the Forum sat during the 'pro-life' amendment campaign, which cast a harsh light on all the rhetoric about addressing the fears of Northern Protestants. This inconsistency was noted by the anti-amendment campaign, which, in a letter handed in to the Forum by Senator Catherine McGuinness and the human rights campaigner Brigid Wilkinson, asked the Forum to recommend a No vote. The Forum declined to do so.

Nevertheless, the report was awaited with a certain degree of anticipation. Published on 2 May, it was severely critical of Britain's role in the North, declaring that

> the basic approach of British policy has created negative consequences. It has shown a disregard of the identity and ethos of nationalists. In effect it has underwritten the supremacy . . . of the Unionist identity. Before there can be fundamental progress, Britain must realise its position and responsibility.[46]

The Forum suggested three options: a united Ireland, a confederation of both states, or joint authority between Britain and Ireland, all options to be achieved by consent. However, 'while Dr FitzGerald described a unitary state as the preferred option of the participants, the Fianna Fáil leader, Mr Haughey saw it as their only choice.'[47]

The British Secretary of State for Northern Ireland, James Prior, pointed out the report's main flaw, which was that

> none of the forum's options were likely to win acceptance in the North. There was no reason . . . to expect consent to change, either to a unitary state or to the other suggested forms of a new Ireland— federation or joint sovereignty.[48]

Opinion polls published a couple of weeks later showed that, while

53 per cent of people in the Republic thought the Forum had been a useful exercise, only 26 per cent of those in the North agreed. In the Republic 50 per cent of the electorate thought the unitary state to be the best of the suggested options, with 22 per cent plumping for federation, 15 per cent for joint authority and 13 per cent for none of them. Even among Fine Gael supporters the scarcely novel idea of a united Ireland came top (42 per cent), while it was almost as popular with Labour Party voters (56 per cent) as with Fianna Fáil supporters (58 per cent). In the North the three options received almost the same level of underwhelming support, with a unitary state and joint authority favoured by 14 per cent, and 13 per cent opting for federation; 59 per cent liked none of the options.[49] Against this unpromising background Garret FitzGerald sallied forth in November to meet Margaret Thatcher.

Six weeks earlier, on 12 October, an IRA bomb planted in the Grand Hotel in Brighton during the Conservative Party conference killed five people, including Sir Anthony Berry MP, the Government's deputy chief whip, and severely injured a number of others, including Margaret Tebbit, wife of Norman Tebbit, one of Thatcher's closest political allies. The IRA narrowly failed in its mission of killing the Prime Minister, whose hotel bathroom was severely damaged. There could scarcely have been a less propitious time for persuading Thatcher of the justice of Irish nationalist aspirations, not least because only hours before the Taoiseach arrived at the Prime Minister's country residence, Chequers, she had been visiting the Tebbits in hospital.[50]

Although Thatcher did not say 'Out, out, out,' as commonly believed, at her press conference on 19 November after the meeting with FitzGerald, it is a pretty good summing up of the answer she did give to a question about the Forum report.

> I have made it quite clear—and so did Mr Prior when he was Secretary of State for Northern Ireland—that a unified Ireland was one solution that is out. A second solution was a federation of two states. That is out. A third solution was joint authority. That is out. That is a derogation from sovereignty. We made that quite clear when the report was published.[51]

The revelation that the Forum had been wasting its time was bad enough, but the rhetorical punch of those three 'outs', and the dismissive nature of Thatcher's delivery, was enough to make the press conference seem like a national humiliation. The English political journalist Hugo Young shrewdly observed that 'the headmistress appeared to have been slapping down the product of childish minds.'[52] And Geraldine Kennedy

of the *Sunday Press* caught the mood of national outrage by noting that
when a Taoiseach, any Taoiseach, travels abroad, he speaks for the
Irish people, and the Irish people saw Dr Garret FitzGerald being
walked all over on their television screens on Monday evening. He
was seen as the emperor with no clothes.[53]

A furious *Irish Press* editorial had the headline 'Out! Out! Out!
Damned Forum,' and raged: 'Mrs Thatcher flatly stated that Northern
Ireland was British and that was that. Not a blind bit about the
inadequacies of the Northern state or its awful impacts on our own society
were even hinted at.'[54] The *Irish Times* editorial mused that

> Dr. FitzGerald's own situation must inspire sympathy and even pity.
> Few have worked harder or longer for a settlement, few have so deep
> a commitment or so genuine a care for the people of both the
> Northern communities, trapped in their seemingly permanent
> political impasse. The meagre fruits he has gathered at this meeting
> must induce an emotion close to dismay ... perhaps in his own Fine
> Gael party, in particular.[55]

Sympathy and pity were not on the agenda for Charlie Haughey when
he told FitzGerald in the Dáil:

> You have led this country into the greatest humiliation in recent
> history. You have failed ignominiously in an area of vital national
> interest. Because of your incompetence, misjudgement and
> ineffectiveness, you have done grievous damage to our national
> political interests and our pride. History will record that it would
> have been better if your visit to Chequers had never taken place.[56]

> Thatcher's ministers in the Northern Ireland Office despaired that she
> showed little appreciation of FitzGerald's own delicate political
> position ... When FitzGerald rebuked her in the Dáil, she told a
> group of colleagues that she simply didn't understand what he was
> talking about.[57]

One of them doubted whether she would ever be prepared to do
anything that discomforted the Unionists: 'She is terrified of their
plantation extremism.'[58] When Thatcher visited Dublin in December she
adopted a more conciliatory tone and insisted that

> there is no rift between myself and Dr FitzGerald. We had a very
> constructive summit at Chequers. If you read the whole
> communiqué, you will find the extent of the agreement there, that
> we both abhor violence and we will not accept it as a means of
> pursuing political objectives, that we seek peace and stability in
> Northern Ireland and that we seek a new political framework

acceptable to both communities . . .⁵⁹

The Government might have expected more gratitude for two notable security successes during the year that significantly reduced the ability of republicans to inflict damage on British forces in the North.

There would have been severe repercussions had the IRA managed to get hold of the cargo of arms that was on the trawler *Marita Ann* when it was captured by the Naval Service off the Kerry coast in September. One of the largest consignments of weapons ever destined for the IRA, it included   .

> 91 rifles . . . eight sub-machine guns, 13 shotguns and 51 handguns.
> . . . 1,000 rounds of armour-piercing ammunition . . . hand grenades,
> night sights and electronic debugging equipment. Estimates of the
> value of the consignment ranged from $1 million to $1.7 million.⁶⁰

The money for the seven tons of arms had been put up by a drug dealer from Boston, Joe Murray, and the shipment had been organised by the IRA in conjunction with an infamous Irish-American criminal, Whitey Bulger. The consignment had been brought across the Atlantic in the trawler *Valhalla* from Boston and then transferred to the *Marita Ann* in the Atlantic fishing grounds known as the Porcupine Bank.⁶¹

It was a risky operation and became even more so when the *Valhalla* 'encountered terrible storms, suffered damage and was two days late.'⁶² The transfer of the cargo to the *Marita Ann* proved nightmarishly difficult, because when the two vessels came together

> the seas were running high . . . There were fears that if the steel hull
> of the *Valhalla* continued to collide with the wooden hull of the
> *Marita Ann* in the Atlantic swell, severe damage could be caused . . .
> The two vessels therefore lay off from each other and crewmen
> secured a rope between them. The skippers kept their vessels in
> position by steaming with just enough power to avert a crash. [The]
> *Valhalla* engineer John McIntyre used the rope to haul himself
> along in a punt, making more than a dozen trips to transfer the
> crates of arms . . . It was a difficult, physically demanding and indeed
> hazardous manoeuvre . . .⁶³

Yet all this derring-do was in the service of a lost cause. McIntyre had told the FBI about the shipment. Seán O'Callaghan, a senior IRA figure who knew about the operation, was a Garda informant. Bulger too was an FBI informant.

On 29 September the *Marita Ann* was intercepted by two naval vessels that lay hidden from the trawler's radar behind the bulk of the Skelligs off the Kerry coast.

When the *Marita Ann* failed to stop the 972-ton *Emer* fired four tracer rounds across the trawler's bow. The trawler came to a halt . . . The naval officer in charge of the boarding party was armed only with a pistol . . . but he never had to cock it . . . Armed Gardaí also went on board. There was no resistance from anyone on the trawler.[64]

On board the *Marita Ann* were the skipper, Michael Browne, two crewmen, Gavin Mortimer and John McCarthy, an IRA man, Seán Crowley, who had travelled from Boston on the *Valhalla*, and Martin Ferris, the former Port Laoise hunger-striker. At the Special Criminal Court, Browne, Ferris and Crowley were each sentenced to ten years' imprisonment, while Mortimer and McCarthy received five years each. On 30 November, John McIntyre disappeared. He had been murdered by Bulger, who had discovered McIntyre's involvement with the FBI.

On the day after the *Marita Ann* was seized, Dick Spring happened to be unveiling a statue of Roger Casement in Ballyheigue. There were protests from Kerry Sinn Féin members, and

> as the Tánaiste made his speech a black flag was waved and the group chanted 'traitor.' Placards reading: '1916 The Aud; 1984 The Marita Ann. What has changed?' were raised.[65]

Spring rejected the parallels, saying, 'In 1916 the vast majority of people in this country gave a validity to what was happening; that is not the case in 1984, when they have rejected violence.'[66]

In the 2002 general election Martin Ferris would stand for Sinn Féin in the Kerry North constituency and top the poll. The man losing his seat to Ferris would be Dick Spring.

———

At 6:30 a.m. on 17 March, two miles from Newmarket-on-Fergus, Co. Clare,

> a convoy of 12 Garda cars converged on a cottage, which is at a narrow crossroads . . . When the cottage was surrounded and heavily armed Gardaí had dug themselves in behind ditches, trees and cars, they called on McGlinchey and the three men with him to surrender.[67]

Dominic McGlinchey was chief of staff of the INLA, a post he had held since July 1982. His tenure 'was marked by a high level of terrorist activity and ruthlessness in dealing with the opposition within and without the organisation . . . In several places significant numbers of former Provisionals joined McGlinchey's INLA.'[68] In the previous two years the organisation had killed thirty-eight people, compared with a total of thirty-four victims claimed between its foundation in 1975 and 1982.[69]

McGlinchey had been a wanted man in the Republic since December 1982,

> when the Supreme Court confirmed an extradition order against him to Northern Ireland where he was wanted for the murder of an elderly County Antrim woman, Mrs Hester McMullan. She was murdered in 1977 when several armed men sprayed her . . . home with bullets.[70]

The call on McGlinchey and his three companions to surrender was 'answered by a burst of gunfire from the upper part of the cottage and the shooting continued for about twenty minutes. In all it is estimated that about 100 rounds were fired.'[71] One member of the Garda force, Christopher Power, was wounded in the shoulder. McGlinchey then

> asked for a priest to be called and also that Mrs Bridget Makowski, an IRSP member of the Shannon Town Commissioners should be sent for. Mrs Makowski . . . had been looking after the two McGlinchey boys at her home in Shannon where she and her husband have lived for the past 12 years.[72]

Shortly after the arrival of the priest, McGlinchey, Ciarán Damery, Damien Bird and Séamus McShane surrendered. By the following morning McGlinchey had been extradited to Belfast. It was a landmark in co-operation between the two legal systems, as McGlinchey was the first person to be extradited from the Republic to the North for an offence connected with the Troubles. Previously courts in the Republic

> had refused to order people to Northern Ireland if the people sought claimed that the alleged offence was a political one or an offence connected to one. This compliance with the terms of the Extradition Act provoked Unionist politicians and some British politicians to charge that the Republic was a haven for terrorists. The RUC claimed that hundreds of republican terrorists sought for crimes in the North were walking the streets of the south.[73]

McGlinchey's extradition 'was as widely welcomed in British government circles and in some quarters was seen as a possible breakthrough in the battle against republican groups . . .'[74] The view in London was that, 'despite the judicial nature of the extradition order, the move springs basically from government policy.'[75]

There was better news for Bridget Makowski's party colleague Nicky Kelly, who walked free from custody on 17 July after four years and two months in prison. Over the previous year interest in his plight had snowballed. The Release Nicky Kelly Campaign attracted such disparate supporters as Vincent Browne, the *Evening Press* sports columnist Con Houlihan, the psychiatrist Prof. Ivor Browne, the chairperson of the Irish Anti-Apartheid Movement, Kader Asmal, and the human rights campaigner Father Denis Faul. Kelly himself received letters from Jane Fonda and her husband, Tom Hayden, and the writers Heinrich Böll and Isabel Allende (niece of the late President of Chile, Salvador Allende).[76] Yet the Government remained unbending, even when Kelly embarked on a hunger strike, which lasted from 1 May to 8 June 1983. Visiting him near the end of the hunger strike, his solicitor, Greg O'Neill, found him being

> helped into a wheelchair padded with pillows and wheeled to a hatch in a cage constructed inside a military hospital ward—rather like a bird cage . . . in which some dangerous wild animal might have been housed in a Victorian zoo. The corridor leading to the room was policed by up to 20 armed soldiers, stationed behind no fewer than 20 sandbagged machine gun emplacements. The building itself was ringed by four circuits of rolled barbed wire, patrolled by half a dozen soldiers with guns at the ready . . . there to give emphasis to the lie that Kelly was a dangerous terrorist.[77]

Those arrangements seemed like a visual symbol of Government obduracy, so there was some surprise when Kelly was released a year later. The Government admitted no mistake on the part of the justice system and instead said that the release had been made on 'humanitarian grounds,' because

> during the four years of his imprisonment, he had lived through a whole series of court actions and appeals during which his expectations of achieving freedom were repeatedly raised and dashed. This, combined with the hunger strike which he had undergone, had imposed constant pressure on him and made his custodial sentence more severe than that undergone by anybody else serving a similar length of time.[78]

The spokesperson for the Department of Justice added that the Minister had also taken into account

> the effect on Mr Kelly of the fact that his campaign was being manipulated by all sorts of other people, some of whom 'had the objective of bringing everything into disrepute.'[79]

The comment's combination of self-pity, sanctimony and cynicism has few equals.

In reality the justice system had brought itself into disrepute by its treatment of Kelly, something tacitly acknowledged by Mary Robinson in granting him a presidential pardon in 1992. Kelly's case had attracted so much support in part because he seemed to stand for all the alleged victims of police brutality. He became a symbol as much as an individual.

———

In the same way, a fifteen-year-old schoolgirl from Granard, Co. Longford, would become a symbol of the secrets that lay beneath the puritanical carapace which enabled many people to harbour the delusion that when it came to sexual matters Ireland was a beacon of goodness in a sinful world. The illusion of Irish exceptionalism was a widely cherished one. It was the fate of Ann Lovett to provide one of the revelations that would finally shatter the illusion.

On 31 January, when morning classes ended, she
> left school as usual but didn't go home. After calling briefly to a friend's house, she slipped back through the small streets and disappeared into the grotto by the graveyard on the hill at the top of the town.[80]

At half-past four her schoolmate Jimmy Brady and two other boys
> were walking from school down a lane past the grotto outside the church when they saw a red schoolbag at the grotto. They went around to the grotto and he saw Ann Lovett lying on some stones.[81]

At the inquest Jimmy Brady recalled that he 'went over to her and lifted her hand and said, "Ann, are you all right?" She opened her eyes and closed them again.'[82] An adult who arrived on the scene sent for the parish priest, Father Francis Gilfillan, and a doctor, Thomas Donoghue, who called an ambulance. 'On the way in the ambulance she was critically ill but she was young and he had a little hope for her but not much.'[83] When the girl was brought in to Mullingar Hospital, recalled Dr Máire Skelly, 'her clothes were wet and she was ice cold. Momentarily her lips became pink but almost immediately she stopped breathing.'[84] The pathologist, Dr Kevin Cunnane, would give the cause of death as 'a combination of exposure and blood loss associated with childbirth.' He believed exposure was the main factor. He said that the infant appeared to have been full term and had been born.[85]

It took a few days for the story of Ann Lovett's death to leak out into the wider world. At the *Sunday Tribune* the news editor got an anonymous phone call saying that a girl had died giving birth a few days earlier.[86] He passed the story on to a reporter, Emily O'Reilly, who

> went through the newspapers and found a notice for the death of Ann Lovett in the *Irish Independent* . . . I remember there was a big debate in the newsroom then about whether we should name Ann Lovett in the story. It was the journalist Maggie O'Kane who said that no-one would remember an anonymous child, but that everyone would remember the name Ann Lovett.[87]

The reaction to the *Tribune's* front-page headline, 'Girl, 15, dies after giving birth in a field,' was one of shock. Nuala Fennell, then Minister of State with Responsibility for Women's Affairs and Family Law, described the death as a national tragedy. 'Everyone had known for a long time', she said, 'about the problem of teenage pregnancies, and yet there did not seem to be any clear policy of awareness among schools in dealing with the issue.'[88] She called for an inquiry into Ann Lovett's death, as did the Council for the Status of Women, which said the death was 'a shattering indictment of our society and its Christian principles.'[89]

The *Longford Leader* made a notorious attempt to claim the dead girl as a kind of martyr for those Christian principles in an editorial that wondered:

> Could it be that an intelligent teenager, who presumably was fully aware of all the facilities available to unmarried mothers, deliberately decided that was not for her? Could it be that she decided that the Virgin Mary meant more to her than all these things? Who is to say Ann Lovett did not die happy? Who is to say that she and her son are not in heaven? Who is to say that she has not fulfilled her role in life as her God has decreed? As our Lord said: 'Suffer little children to come unto me.'[90]

This attempt to portray Ann Lovett as a kind of cross between Maria Goretti and Bobby Sands drew the wrath of Conor Cruise O'Brien:

> 'Suffer little children to come unto me.' Yes, but he didn't tell us, did he, to leave them on their own while they are coming for months, with no shred of human help or comfort to seek in the end the company of a painted statue in the rain.[91]

Cruise O'Brien correctly forecast that the breaking of the story would prove to be a watershed and that

> the publicity which has surrounded the deaths of Ann Lovett and her son carries a message into every community in Ireland where

such things have happened and been hushed up. The message is that the good old hush-up system may be beginning to break down.[92]

Few had done as much damage to the hush-up system as Gay Byrne, and in the aftermath of the Lovett case he was responsible for what has been called 'the most devastating piece of broadcasting yet heard in Ireland.'[93] Perhaps only in a country in which so much had gone unsaid for so long could a chat-show host have exerted the kind of influence that Gay Byrne did, both on television with 'The Late Late Show' and on radio with 'The Gay Byrne Hour'. In the words of the novelist Colm Tóibín, he had the vital knack of 'knowing how fast the pulse of the country was beating and knowing whose pulse he should be taking.'[94]

Ever since the death of Ann Lovett, letters had been pouring in to Byrne. He and his producer, John Caden, with the aid of two actors, used the letters to construct 'the most relentless assault which has ever been presented to a mass audience on the accepted version of reality in this country.'[95] The majority of the letters were

> direct accounts of personal experience. Most of the letters came from women who had given birth in rural Ireland outside marriage. Some of them were heartbreaking. One, in particular, an account of how a servant in a house gave birth in a locked room and then murdered the baby was absolutely shocking. Gay had a special tone that morning. He didn't comment on letters, but he spoke a few times . . . There was an intense calm about the way he spoke, a controlled anger almost.[96]

――――

The events in Granard seemed perfectly in keeping with the mood of national malaise, which deepened considerably in 1984. There was evidence, for example, of a crime wave. When the previous year's crime statistics were published in June they revealed that the number of indictable offences (serious crime) had risen by 5 per cent since 1982 to reach a record 102,837. Ten years previously the figure was 40,000. The number of crimes detected by the Gardaí had dropped to 33 per cent, compared with 50 per cent ten years previously. The number of burglaries had risen by 11½ per cent since 1982.[97]

Economically things were no better, with unemployment rising above 15 per cent for the first time, where it would remain for eight of the next ten years. At the beginning of February it was reported that 'since this time last year 28,546 people have joined the dole queues.'[98] So tenacious was unemployment that it defied economic logic, as 'manufacturing output rose 5 per cent in 1983 and 17 per cent in 1984 so that economic recovery, such as it was, had been "all output, no jobs."'[99]

Nothing epitomised those dark days like the fall of Ford. When it opened in 1917 the company's plant on the Marina in Cork had been the first Ford factory outside North America. By May 1930 it was employing more than seven thousand workers. The production of tractors in Cork began in 1919, with the first Model Ts being assembled in 1923. On' the factory's fiftieth anniversary

> a £2 million investment program was announced to re-build, re-equip and re-modernise the assembly plant. As a result the plant was to become the largest and most modern factory of its kind in Ireland.[100]

By 1972 the plant was producing the two most popular cars in Ireland as well as exporting four thousand cars to Britain. However, Ireland's membership of the EEC required that Government protection for car plants had to cease. Employment declined, but it was still a shock when it was announced on 17 January that Ford was closing down its car assembly operation, with the loss of eight hundred jobs.[101]

Ford explained the closure by saying that 'the factory was not competitive' and that 'Europe had more car-producing capacity than it needed.'[102] Only two years previously the company had spent £9 million on modernising the plant for the assembly of one hundred cars a day for export to Britain.[103] The closure was a catastrophe for Cork, as it not only took £11 million out of the local economy but also brought to

> at least 1,800 the number of jobs which have gone in Cork since the Dunlop closure on September 30th last. In 1983, 2,470 jobs were lost in the Cork area and unemployment rose 21%.[104]

Yet perhaps the grimmest economic story of the year was the demise of Irish Shipping Ltd. It had traded profitably every year between 1968 and 1982, there had never been a strike in the company and it would never have closed 'were it not for some tragically bad judgements which led to the signing of the company's disastrous charter commitments.'[105] The company was formed in 1941 to keep Ireland supplied during the Second World War. The dangers faced by its crews were made manifest one year later when thirty-three men were lost after the *Irish Pine* was sunk by a German submarine in the North Atlantic. Such ships as the *Irish Maple*, the *Irish Larch* and the *Irish Oak* were familiar names to schoolchildren, who tracked their progress through the 'Follow the Fleet' scheme, launched in 1967.

In 1979 the company

> entered into the first of nine controversial long-term chartering
> arrangements, which were finally to destroy the company. Neither
> the board of Irish Shipping, nor the relevant department was asked
> to sanction these agreements. There is no evidence [that] they were
> debated at board level.

The problem began in 1979 when one ship was chartered for eight
years, without any prearranged 'back to back' cargoes to keep it earning.
This deal was also was adopted with eight other ships over the next two
years.[106]

The charters were arranged by Celtic Bulk Carriers, a trading company
formed by Irish Shipping with the British shipping company Reardon
Smith. During the two years in which the nine crucial agreements were
signed the chairperson of Celtic Bulk Carriers was Willie O'Neill, general
manager of Irish Shipping.[107] The seeds of the company's destruction had
been sown.

People would wonder 'why experienced executives such as Willie
O'Neill, Derry O'Neill and the financial controller Aubrey McElhatton—
with or without the knowledge of the board—lent their support to these
arrangements.'[108] The answer was that

> in 1979 everyone was talking about growth. After the second oil
> shock ships were queuing up to transport coals around the world.
> In 1979 shipping was booming.[109]

But the company would be undone by a situation in which

> in 1981 the world tramp shipping market started to weaken. In 1982
> it collapsed . . . The profitability of the charter agreements depended
> on the earnings which each of the vessels would bring in to the
> company. The result of this was that the company incurred losses of
> approximately £12 million to March 31st 1983 and approximately £34
> million to March 31st 1984.[110]

The Minister for Transport and Communications, Jim Mitchell, spelt it
out for the Dáil as the Government announced the liquidation of Irish
Shipping Ltd on 14 November.

> Even if the company had confined its activities to operating its fleet
> of four deep sea vessels, the collapse of the freight market would
> have posed serious problems, but the company would have been in
> a position to ride out the recession without insurmountable losses.
> As a result of the agreements entered into in respect of the
> additional ships, the country was left, when the market collapsed,
> with nine chartered vessels earning only a fraction of the cost to the
> company under the charter agreements.[111]

This resulted in 'the destruction of what was up to then a viable and successful state enterprise with a very proud record of financial success.'[112] The Government was simply not prepared to pay the £144½ million it said was needed to keep the company alive for the next five years.

The sudden and seemingly avoidable nature of the demise of Irish Shipping left a bitter taste in many mouths. Fianna Fáil's spokesperson on transport, John Wilson, stated that it was one of the saddest days since he entered the Dáil in 1973.

> The killing off of the company was little short of national sabotage. If the Government had wanted to find a way of sustaining the company, even in a slimmed down operation, they could have done so.[113]

The Government had in fact been presented with an alternative by the board of Irish Shipping, which did not believe that liquidation was the only option. It suggested that the Government could

> renegotiate the seven long-term charters . . . This would have amounted to between £20 and £30 million over and above the cost of liquidation . . . Under this deal the borrowings of the company would be greatly reduced, there would be significant shareholders' funds and Irish Continental Lines, a subsidiary through Ocean Bank Developments, would be in a better position than if Irish Shipping was wound up.[114]

This option was not pursued, and, as the Government had guaranteed only part of the money owed by the company, there was the spectacle of the country's ships being arrested as they put into port. Within a week of Jim Mitchell's announcement the *Celtic Venture* was arrested in Savannah, Georgia, and the *Irish Spruce* was arrested in Marseille.

During the 1987 general election leaflets were circulated calling for a vote against Fine Gael and the Labour Party. Under the heading 'Lest we forget,' they pointed out that since the liquidation of Irish Shipping

> 1. The staff of that company received nothing over and above the statutory amount paid by the Department of Labour to staff of insolvent companies. Even wages and holiday pay earned by them prior to liquidation is unpaid. 2. The outgoing government has paid out over £100 million of Irish taxpayers' money, mainly to foreign banks and finance houses in settlement of commitments arising out of this liquidation.[115]

———

It was a grim year all round. The fight of Concerned Parents Against Drugs came close to triggering 'open war, a war that could have involved organised crime, the Provisional IRA and the Gardaí.'[116] The confrontation resulted from clashes between members of the movement and criminals from the Crumlin area in Dublin, who formed a group called the Concerned Criminals' Action Committee and 'warned that the Concerned Parents would not be allowed to jeopardise the livelihoods of local criminals engaged in illegal activities which were not related to drugs.'[117] With the successes of the Concerned Parents in the inner city, Crumlin was now 'the centre of the Dublin heroin trade, the various groups distribute heroin in £10 packs to their pushers by means of a network of small boys living in the area.'[118] But the situation in Crumlin was complicated, because

> a large number of the city's serious criminals live there, or retain links with the community if they move. This factor made any communal challenge to the pushers more difficult, as local people didn't know how many of the individual dealers had links with organised crime.[119]

On 20 February gunmen shot and wounded a Concerned Parents activist, Joey Flynn, in St Teresa's Gardens. On 11 March, Tommy Gaffney was kidnapped from the Park Inn in Harold's Cross. Gaffney was an alleged associate of a man 'widely regarded by detectives in Dublin as the cleverest and most dangerous criminal in the country.'[120] The man was Martin Cahill, dubbed 'the General' by journalists. The previous year Cahill and his gang had carried out the largest robbery in the country's history, getting away with £2 million worth of jewellery from a jewellery manufacturing company, Thomas O'Connor and Sons, in Harold's Cross.

Gaffney's associates blamed the Concerned Parents for his kidnapping, and three days later they marched on St Teresa's Gardens, where they were confronted by local activists, 'some carrying iron bars and pickaxe handles.'[121] On 22 March there was an attempt to kidnap Martin Foley, who had been questioned by gardaí in connection with the shooting of Joey Flynn, from his house in Crumlin. However, his kidnappers were chased by gardaí and captured near the Phoenix Park. They turned out to be four Dublin IRA members: Liam O'Dwyer, Derek Dempsey, Seán Hick and James Dunne. Dempsey was subsequently sentenced to nine years in prison, Hick and Dunne to seven and O'Dwyer to five. The day after the failed kidnapping of Foley, Tommy Gaffney was released unharmed.

The involvement of the IRA in the kidnappings confirmed beyond doubt the links between the republican movement and the Concerned Parents, which meant that the Minister for Health, Barry Desmond, 'refused to meet members of the Concerned Parents on the grounds that they had been infiltrated by Sinn Féin.'[122]

When the Concerned Parents held their first national conference in October they adopted a motion saying the movement would

> not co-operate with the Gardaí in relation to the drug problem because, as presently constituted, they cannot achieve its objectives . . . The Inchicore group, which had been strongly influenced by members of Jim Kemmy's Democratic Socialist Party, was temporarily disaffiliated because it refused to accept this clause.[123]

A movement born of grass-roots anger and desperation had become prey to party politics and factionalism.

Chapter 14 ~

| LIVE AT THE WITCH TRIALS

1985

The story of Joanne Hayes held the country spellbound during the eighty-two days of the 'Kerry Babies' Tribunal. Strictly speaking, the tribunal should not have focused on Joanne Hayes at all. It had been set up to examine the process by which a group of innocent people had made strikingly similar confessions to the Gardaí that turned out to be false.

And strictly speaking, Joanne Hayes wasn't on trial in Tralee. But in reality she was. Yet by the time the tribunal ended and Mr Justice Kevin Lynch had produced his report it was not the 25-year-old woman who had been indicted but Irish society: its misogyny, its pretence of sanctity and its uneasy puritanism, its fear of sex, its casual authoritarianism, its secrets and lies.

Joanne Hayes's family could scarcely have been more in the traditional grain. They were a close-knit farming family with connections to the Triple Crown of Irish society: the Catholic Church (Joanne's aunt was a nun), the GAA (her brother Ned was secretary of the local club) and Fianna Fáil (the family were related to Stephen Fuller, TD for Kerry North from 1937 to 1943.) This very ordinariness was what gave the story its extraordinary power. No novel, film or political tract was as revealing about the true nature of eighties Ireland.

The story began when the body of a male infant was found at the White Strand, three miles from Cahirciveen, on Saturday 14 April. He was found face down, wedged in the rocks.[1] He had been killed within forty-eight hours of birth: his neck was broken, and he had been stabbed twenty-eight times in the neck and chest.

Enquiries by the Gardaí led them to suspect Joanne Hayes, who had recently been pregnant. She worked as a receptionist in Tralee Sports Complex and had already given birth to one child by Jeremiah Locke, a married groundsman at the sports complex, and had miscarried on another occasion. The third pregnancy meant that in their 22-month relationship 'she had become pregnant by him three times.'[2] This was hardly surprising, as '10 of the 12 pharmacies in Tralee refuse to stock condoms, as do 5 of the 6 in Listowel, 5 of the 6 in Killarney, and the sole chemist in Cahirciveen will not handle them.'[3]

The relationship between Locke and Hayes ended at Christmas 1983, and Joanne

> faced into 1984, severely burdened in mind and body. Her heart was broken, she was expecting a baby and, in February of the new year, she learned that her job was about to end. In the early hours of Friday morning 13 April she gave secret birth and hid the body of the child on the farm.[4]

Yet the gardaí who questioned her did not know this, and after interrogation she confessed to killing the baby that had been found at White Strand, admitting that she

> stabbed it with the carving knife on the chest and all over the body. I turned the baby over and I also stabbed him in the back. The baby stopped crying after I stabbed it. There was blood everywhere on the bed and there was also blood on the floor.[5]

Her family corroborated this statement, and her brother Ned confessed to dumping the body on the beach.

There was one significant problem with these confessions: 'the day after Joanne Hayes confessed to the murder of the baby found at Cahirciveen, her own baby was found on the farm.'[6] Joanne told her sister Kathleen where the body was, and her brother Mike found it in a water hole. Given that the confessions of the Hayes family contained details known only to the Gardaí (and whoever had actually killed the Cahirciveen baby), the Gardaí had some explaining to do, and even more so when it emerged that

> Joanne Hayes, Jeremiah Locke and their dead son, found on the farm at Abbeydorney, all belonged to blood group O. The Cahirciveen baby was blood group A. One of its parents would have to be blood group A.[7]

The gardaí attempted to finesse this problem by proposing that

> Joanne Hayes had had twins by two different men, one of whom was blood group A. Both had had sexual intercourse with her during a 48 hour period. She had become pregnant by both. This phenomenon, known as super-fecundation, is so rare that it is a footnote in medical journals.[8]

The Director of Public Prosecutions, Éamonn Barnes, seemed

unimpressed by this far-fetched theory and

> wrote a letter to the Kerry state solicitor in September. The letter instructed Dónal Browne to withdraw the charges in 'this amazing case' at the first opportunity. On 10 October the Hayes family learned that the case was now dropped.[9]

Six days later Joanne Hayes told the RTE television programme 'Today Tonight' that

> it was the guards that made the statement. We just agreed with them at the end. They convinced themselves that we did do it . . . They were writing down the whole time. Why I signed my statements was because they told me they were going to make Mother charged with murder as well and put my little girl into an orphanage, and going to sell the farm as well.[10]

Amid mounting public concern the Minister for Justice, Michael Noonan, decided to set up a tribunal of inquiry, which would sit in Tralee in January. The tribunal, it was presumed, would deal with the allegations of Garda misconduct. *Magill* pointed out that

> there is nothing at all surprising about the Kerry Babies scandal . . . For a decade conscientious Gardaí, lawyers, journalists and other observers have been expecting a case to come along which would be so crudely handled that even a Minister for Justice would be embarrassed.[11]

There were precedents for suspects making surprising self-incriminating statements. On 5 June 1983 Michael Ward

> signed a statement in Naas garda station admitting to 26 separate charges of burglary in the Naas area . . . He could not have committed nine of these as he was a prisoner in Mountjoy when they were committed . . . One of the offences which Ward was charged with never took place. He was charged with stealing £150 in cash from the parochial house at Saggart on 25 April 1983 (when, incidentally, Ward was in Mountjoy). However, Fr Robert Walsh of Saggart has confirmed . . . that no cash has been stolen from the parochial house in Saggart and that no such robbery was ever reported to the Gardaí.[12]

Then there was the case of Amanda McShane, who on 21 August 1982 was being questioned at Crumlin Garda Station in Dublin in connection with an armed robbery of £100,000 from Tallaght Post Office. She told her solicitor, Anne Rowland, that

> she had been asked to sign a statement which had been written out for her, which she had not made. Rowland searched the interview

room. She came across a handwritten statement. McShane confirmed that this was the statement she was asked to sign . . . admitting to having helped get the money away from the robbery.[13]

When Rowland raised the question of the statement shortly afterwards, the charges were dropped. This case was hugely important because

> in case after case . . . accused persons have claimed that they have signed statements after lengthy interrogation and that those statements were written out for them by the Gardaí, from the Gardaí's own knowledge of the case, and not from any admission by the accused. The Amanda McShane case is the only one in which it has been possible to prove that a written out statement existed before the suspect made any admissions.[14]

Also troubling was the case of Peter Matthews, who died of a heart attack in Shercock Garda Station, Co. Cavan, on 22 April 1982 after he was beaten up while being questioned about a stolen Post Office savings book. In October 1983 Sergeant Peter Diviney was found not guilty of assaulting Matthews, and during his evidence he blamed Detective-Garda Tom Jordan for the assault. In October 1984 Jordan was found not guilty of causing grievous bodily harm and actual bodily harm to Matthews. It had been

> a year of chickens coming home to roost for the Gardaí themselves. The laxity and indiscipline of previous years showed up in an unprecedented wave of prosecutions and disciplinary charges.[15]

The detection rate of indictable crime had nose-dived from 61 per cent in 1969 to 33 per cent in 1983.[16] It seemed a propitious time for an inquiry that might clear the air about alleged Garda misconduct. The terms of reference of the Kerry tribunal seemed to suggest that this was what would happen. After all,

> the primary aim and function of the tribunal was to find out how the police had conducted themselves in Tralee garda station and afterwards, to inquire 'into the circumstances of the preferment and withdrawal of charges.' The tribunal's second function was to inquire into 'the allegations made by the Hayes family against the police.' The tribunal's third function was to inquire into 'any relevant matters.'[17]

Yet from the outset it was not the Gardaí but Joanne Hayes who appeared to be on trial, as 'any relevant matters' was interpreted as allowing the lawyers representing the Gardaí *carte blanche* to lay her private life absolutely bare to public scrutiny. Tom Inglis, a sociologist at University College, Dublin, who wrote a fascinating book on the case, argued that it is likely that there was a deliberate plan to protect the state police in Irish society by blaming Joanne Hayes and her family for what had happened. In this respect, the tactic of making the Hayes family out to be immoral, uncaring liars who were obsessed with saving face was a shaming strategy used in the strategic struggle to protect the honour of the police.[18]

It became obvious how the tribunal would be conducted when Martin Kennedy, counsel for the Gardaí, asked Jeremiah Locke 'how, where and when he had had "sexual intercourse" with Joanne Hayes.'[19] When asked by Mr Justice Lynch what relevance this had to the inquiry, Kennedy replied:

> If I can show that Joanne Hayes had a previous sexual history . . . and that during her relationship she was also having sex with others; and if any one of these others had blood group A, then it will be . . . not only possible but probable that twins born of that union could have had blood group A in one, O in the other.[20]

The most cursory glance at this exchange will reveal its illogical nature. How on earth was asking Jeremiah Locke about his sex life with Joanne Hayes supposed to reveal the identity of other (fictional, as it turned out) lovers? But Mr Justice Lynch gave the go-ahead, and,

> for another 16 weeks, licence was given to the men to speculate virtually every other day on the sexuality of Joanne Hayes. The daily coupling of her name with the term 'sexual intercourse' allowed her character to pass into ferocious and lurid legend.[21]

From the start the proceedings were

> a very unequal struggle. There was very little equality between the Hayes family and the middle-aged, professional policemen and lawyers from Dublin who set about attacking their honour. The Hayes family were simply punished and branded as liars. They were denied any honour, yet the Gardaí were defined as honourable.[22]

But if the mission of defending the Gardaí had been accomplished, the attempt to destroy Joanne Hayes by making her a figure of universal opprobrium had failed. The people of Abbeydorney showed how they felt by turning up *en masse* in Tralee, some of them carrying banners reading *Abbeydorney supports Joanne*.

> The farmers came as soon as they had done their milking. They were all on the picket line by nine o'clock . . . The Abbeydorney villagers said nothing; their patience said everything to the world's media who had come to televise them. After two hours of walking up and

down they went into the Council building and stood around the walls of the packed court.[23]

The passion of Joanne Hayes struck a chord elsewhere too. Women's groups sent yellow roses; she received more than 500 letters and 142 mass cards.

> Irish Catholics, wanting genuinely to be good, struggling desperately under a yoke of bewildering rules and regulations, wrote to Joanne Hayes that no man should be allowed to sit in judgement on the human sexual condition.[24]

A forum determined to make the life of Joanne Hayes seem a squalid, sordid thing had succeeded in making something mythic of the spectacle of this woman being assailed by the forces of law and order. The telegrams of support poured in, from

> the Ennis Soroptimists' Club; the women's department of Sinn Féin; the female attendants of St Fintan's Hospital, Portlaoise; Family Aid; the principal and staff of Dunlavin National School; the ladies' club, Dundalk; the Dublin Inner City Project; workers in a Galway office; 31 villagers from Maam Cross, Co. Galway; the staff of AFRI, a third world organisation; female telephonists in the Galway exchange; the staff of Unisex hair salon in Co. Kildare; 16 teachers from Killester Vocational School, Dublin; the Connolly Youth Movement; the Kilrush tenants' association, Co. Clare; the Limerick office staff of the Irish Transport and General Workers' Trade Union; the NUJ chapel of *City Limits* magazine, London; the Galway civil rights group; a self-help women's group in Cork; and the Labour women's national council.[25]

The feminist writer Kate Shanahan, who organised a demonstration that drew women from all over the country, recalled Joanne Hayes's mother, Mary,

> up to her neck in trouble when she should have been looking forward to retirement just like my own mother. . . . If any one of us were put on public exhibition, what family would come through unblemished? You'd look at Mary Hayes and know that every mother in the country had escaped trauma by a wing and a prayer . . .[26]

In the end, the 'superfecundation' expert called by the tribunal said that the possibility that Joanne Hayes might have had twins by two different fathers was so rare that it could be ruled out. 'The bastard shot us down,' Martin Kennedy said afterwards.[27] It was an appropriately inelegant parting shot.

But the system had not finished with Joanne Hayes. On 3 October, Mr Justice Lynch issued his report, which

> rained blow upon blow on the heads of the surviving members of the family. Joanne Hayes, he found was not the mother of the Cahirciveen baby. But he exonerated the police from any major blame in charging her with its murder. She and her mother, her sister and her brother were 'barefaced liars' who had misled the police and perjured themselves before him in an attempt to cover up the death of Joanne's baby.[28]

Bizarrely, Lynch

> did not answer clearly the central question . . . How did a family come to confess to a crime that they could not have committed and supply corroborative details known only to the police, and add imaginative details of their own? By implication, though the judge does not spell out the incredible scenario, four members of the Hayes family—Joanne, Kathleen, Ned and Mike, seated in separate rooms in a police station, spelled out the exact same fantasy.[29]

The report dismissed the possibility that

> if the Hayes family confessions were false, they could not be so by accident, hysteria, confusion or because of lies told by the family. They are too detailed and similar in content for that, they contain too much detail pertaining to the Cahirciveen baby. If the Hayes family confessions are false they had to be rigged by the Gardaí and the family pressured into signing them.[30]

The unkindest cut of all was Lynch's suggestion that Joanne Hayes had murdered the baby found on the farm in Abbeydorney, a claim unsupported by the evidence before the tribunal. The judge

> bases his accusation that Joanne put her hands around her baby's neck and choked the baby on the evidence of Joanne's aunt . . . Joan Fuller. Joan Fuller gave no evidence.[31]

As for his suggestion that she 'hit the baby with the bath brush to make sure it was dead,'

> he cites no evidence for this central element in his theory . . . There is no evidence for this. There is not a shred of evidence that she hit the baby at all.[32]

There is perhaps something inadvertently revealing about Lynch's question,

> why no flowers for Mrs Locke? Why no cards or mass cards? Why no public assemblies to support her in her embarrassment and agony? Is it because she married Jeremiah Locke and thus got in the way of

the foolish hopes and ambitions of Joanne Hayes?[33]

Perhaps, one might venture to suggest, it was because Mrs Locke had not been charged with a crime she had not committed before being bullied and traduced by a team of highly paid legal professionals as her name was dragged through the mud.

The tribunal had been an unedifying spectacle that

> demonstrated an inability on the part of the legal system to mount an objective inquiry. Peripheral witnesses were insulted and made the subject of unfounded allegations and insinuations.[34]

Yet while the tribunal is now remembered as bringing to the fore the clash between a traditional, sexually conservative vision of Ireland and a newer, more liberal one that was gaining ground during the eighties, it had just as much to do with another great theme of the era: the behaviour of the Gardaí towards suspects. *Magill* pointed out that 'a system of interrogation and statement-taking which had long been suspect was seen in this case to have produced patently false results.'[35] It was not only sexual matters that were taboo in Irish society: in the words of Tom Inglis,

> most politicians knew that the Gardaí were using abusive strategies to extract confessions, but collaborated in the Gardaí's lie that they were not. We could say that in Ireland, in the years before the Kerry Babies case, people colluded and lived the lie, partly voluntarily and partly because it was imposed by the state, that terrorists and criminals voluntarily confessed to the Gardaí without being physically abused or intimidated.[36]

The definitive book on the case is *A Woman to Blame* by Nell McCafferty, a small book and yet a masterpiece. It matches a forensic clarity about the case and the convoluted tribunal proceedings with warmth, humanity and a quiet empathy with the Hayes family, their neighbours and their supporters. Underneath it all burns an anger at what Joanne Hayes was put through, firstly by the Gardaí and then by the tribunal. The finest journalist of a golden age in Irish journalism found a story that exercised her prodigious talents to their utmost.

Several gardaí involved in the investigation were briefly moved to desk jobs in the aftermath of the inquiry. In November 1989 three of them settled out of court for a record libel settlement from an Irish publisher after claiming to have been defamed by the book *My Story*, written by Joanne Hayes with John Barrett and published by Brandon Books.[37] In his report Mr Justice Lynch had 'found there was no intimidation or abuse by any of the Gardaí of members of the Hayes family.'[38]

Detectives involved were later promoted. Kevin Lynch was

subsequently appointed to the Supreme Court. Joanne Hayes has remained steadfastly silent, and in May 2006 she appealed, through her solicitor, to those planning to make a feature film about the case not to do so.

———

This was a country in which pregnant single women felt compelled to give birth in fields, on beaches and in grottoes and to leave those children between rocks, in feeding troughs and in water holes. The furore surrounding the coalition Government's attempts to liberalise the family planning laws is instructive. There was a frenzied quality to the opposition. Eleven years previously, when Liam Cosgrave had voted against his own Government's Family Planning Bill, there had been opposition, but it had not been so violent. But the time when some kind of rational debate might have taken place seemed to have passed. The opponents of the law almost seemed to feel that Irish identity depended on the denial of contraception to single people. How else could the amendment to the Family Planning Bill by the Minister for Health, Barry Desmond, have resulted in a situation in which

> the home of the Minister of State, Mr Paul Connaughton . . . was being kept under surveillance last night after members of his family were threatened with kidnap. Another Minister of State in Galway, Mr John Donnellan, had earlier been threatened by letter that he would be, 'blown out of it,' if he voted for the government's family planning bill.[39]

The zealots must have been heartened by those bishops who followed the logical implications of the 1983 referendum vote by arguing against the legislation on unabashedly theocratic grounds. The Archbishop of Dublin, Kevin McNamara, suggested that a Catholic politician must not differentiate his Catholicism from his politics.

> His lead was followed even more extremely by the Bishop of Limerick, Dr Newman, who told Catholic politicians to follow the guidance of the bishops. The combined effect of the pronouncements . . . encouraged ultra conservative lay Catholic groups to put undue pressure on politicians.[40]

Bishop McNamara asked every politician to

> ponder how he or she can justify passing a measure which, in the eyes of young people, will give the appearance of legal sanction to

what is against God's law, and will progressively result in our teenage population being presented with increased opportunities and inducements to do what is morally wrong.[41]

When Bishop Newman was asked about the position of those who did not believe that contraception was a moral evil, he replied: 'If we had a few Hottentots in our society, are we to legislate for them too?'[42] This extremist rhetoric is evident in an editorial in the *Donegal Democrat* headed 'A licence for immorality,' which said that Desmond's bill was

a proposal to license immorality, to give legal approval to promiscuousness, or, to put it bluntly, a form of prostitution. The proposed measure is not capable of any other interpretation.[43]

Though they were the most vociferous contributors to the debate, the conservatives did not have the same public support as they had mustered during the referendum. Opinion polls showed that 68 per cent of the electorate thought that contraceptives should be made available to single people and that 64 per cent felt they should be available without a doctor's prescription. Desmond's bill would

impose an age limit of 18, remove the need for a prescription and drop the qualification, *'bona fide* family planning,' for the supply of non-medical contraceptives . . .[44]

The *Kilkenny People* seemed more in tune with public opinion when it editorialised that

what an individual should not do in a free society is to insist that other people must also obey, or be forced by legislation to obey, regulations of a church to which they do not belong . . . [This] would represent a travesty of democracy and a grave infringement of personal freedom.[45]

Yet there seemed every possibility that the bill would be defeated when it came before the Dáil in February. Such ultra-conservatives as Oliver Flanagan, Alice Glenn and Tom O'Donnell of Fine Gael and Seán Treacy of the Labour Party declared their intention to vote against it, while Fianna Fáil TDs were expected to vote No *en masse*. A few more desertions and the Government would lose. TDs such as Brendan Griffin, Joe Doyle and John Conlan of Fine Gael and Frank Prendergast of the Labour Party were felt to be likely to lose their nerve when the time came to vote, and these perceived waverers were being subjected to intense pressure.

The debate opened on 14 February, and some of the contributions bring to mind Frank O'Connor's remark that he was reluctant to quote too extensively from a Seanad debate on censorship lest he tax the credulity of his readers. Oliver Flanagan was barnstorming in a speech that lasted two hours and twenty-three minutes and that only Barry Desmond and Proinsias de Rossa managed to sit through. 'Here we are taking not the first step, but one of the early steps, in throwing away the values of those who carried us to the font of baptism.'[46] Seán Treacy was prophetic: 'There is violence, there is drug addiction, and fear abounds in our land ... I will be judged at the bar of public opinion on this issue, and I will be judged in a higher place as well.'[47]

Denis Foley of Fianna Fáil declared that 'if it was considered backward to keep contraceptives away from the teenagers of Ireland then he would prefer to see Ireland staying backward,' while John O'Leary warned: 'I have it on the best of medical advice that condoms are only 70 per cent safe.' Pádraig Flynn delivered a little homespun moral homily: 'The fashion of the length of a lady's skirt may change, and the width of a gentleman's trouser leg may change, but the right of young unmarried teenagers to fornicate is still unnatural and wrong.'[48]

All this moral outrage at least seems like the honest expression of antediluvian attitudes; but a statement like that of the Fianna Fáil TD Seán McCarthy reeks of the political cynicism that lay at the heart of the party's opposition to the bill. For McCarthy

> it was a bill for which he honestly believed there was no need. Anyone opposed to it was characterised as a 'square' and it was suggested that to be opposed to contraception was to be out of touch with reality . . . He understood the needs of young people, there was no demand from them for any change.[49]

Rory O'Hanlon's similar contention drew a sharp rejoinder from the Women's Centre in Cavan, whose statement rejected

> the casual dismissal of the demand for contraceptives made by the Fianna Fáil spokesman on health, Dr Rory O'Hanlon. The need for a comprehensive family planning service was just as great in Cavan and Monaghan as it was in Dublin or other cities.[50]

Opposition to the bill had to be based on the notion that single people weren't interested in getting hold of contraception. It simply wasn't an issue for them. Why? Because Irish people didn't have sex outside marriage, and they had no intention of starting. It was self-delusion elevated to the status of a cherished principle.

The Workers' Party leader, Tomás Mac Giolla, asked Fianna Fáil to consider where they stood

> in this battle between theocracy and democracy. If they maintain their present stance they will be seen, not as great upholders of the moral values of the nation, but as a craven, weak bunch of opportunists.[51]

Yet the Fianna Fáil No vote seemed to be solid as the debate wore on. It is arguable that Oliver Flanagan's approach may have been preferable to that of a Fianna Fáil TD like Charlie McCreevy, who said that he supported the bill but would vote against it for reasons of party discipline, 'because it was not a matter of conscience for him.'[52]

There were also memorable contributions from the Government side. Mervyn Taylor of the Labour Party said that

> the argument on grounds of morality used by many of the speakers had no more credence than the writings of the Emperor Justinian who believed among other things that homosexuality was the cause of earthquakes.[53]

But in the end it would all hinge on Desmond O'Malley. In 1974, during the debate on the first Family Planning Bill, he had declared that it was the duty of the Dáil 'to deter fornication and promiscuity, to promote public morality, and to prevent, insofar as we can . . . public immorality.'[54] This time it was a very different O'Malley who spoke and gave one of the most memorable political speeches of the era, largely based on his belief that 'we will never see a 32-county republic on this island until we establish a 26-county republic.'[55] He took issue

> with the bishops who said it was possible to legislate for private morality. There were two countries in this world where this was done: Iran and Pakistan. In those countries private morality was enforced by public flogging . . . He could not accept the statement that had been made that in any country where there was contraception available along the lines suggested in the bill, that the people immediately became degenerate. There was nothing degenerate about the people of Northern Ireland.[56]

He spoke about Paddy Devlin's time as Minister of Health and Social Services in the power-sharing Executive.

> Mr Devlin extended the free availability of contraceptives and brought them within the scope of the National Health Service, making them free to everyone irrespective of age . . . How was it that if something was all right in County Armagh, something which was only half the measure was regarded as an abomination in County Louth?[57]

He concluded with words that he must have known might well sunder him from the party.

> The politics of this would be very easy. The politics would be to be one of the lads, the safest way in Ireland. But I do not believe that the interests of this state, or of our constitution and of this republic would be served by putting politics before conscience in regard to this. There

is a choice of a kind that can only be answered by saying that I stand by the republic and accordingly, I will not oppose this bill.[58]

It was that rarest of all phenomena, a Dáil speech that changed the course of a vote. The coalition rebels were limited to Flanagan, O'Donnell, Glenn and Treacy; the Labour Party TD Frank Prendergast abstained. With support from the two Workers' Party TDS and Tony Gregory, the bill passed, 83 votes to 80. O'Malley left the Dáil before the vote was taken.

It had been 'a historic public rebuff for the hierarchy.'[59] They would take their revenge the following year when the divorce referendum was defeated, and it would be another decade before anyone dared to bring forward that protocol again. Defeat for the family planning legislation in February 1985 would most probably have resulted in a similar reluctance to address the issue in the Dáil again in the near future, with a concomitant emboldening of the forces that had attempted to terrorise Paul Connaughton, John Donnellan and Joe Doyle. A Fianna Fáil party convinced that defeating the Desmond amendment was a political master-stroke would hardly have ventured such legislation itself in Government. And the idea that the bishops could never be beaten in a political argument would have taken even firmer root. That it was Fine Gael, traditionally a conservative party, that was largely responsible for mustering the numbers to put through this legislation spoke volumes for the faith FitzGerald's deputies had in him and his vision.

Desmond O'Malley paid a price for his defiance of the party leadership. On 26 February a motion for his expulsion from Fianna Fáil came before the parliamentary party.

> Haughey demanded a unanimous public decision. On three different occasions during the meeting he interceded to say: 'I want it to be unanimous for the good of the party and the organisation.' When a few speeches made it clear that a unanimous vote was out of the question, Haughey demanded an open roll-call vote. This was a flagrant violation of the party's own rules, which stipulated that all votes should be secret; nobody protested. Yet another roll-call vote was passed by 73 votes to 9.[60]

———

The death of Ann Lovett, the Kerry Babies tribunal, the bitter exchanges over the 'pro-life' amendment and the family planning legislation were painful moments for many in a country in which the public discussion of such matters had long been taboo. The stage was set for the great year of moving statues and supernatural visions, sparked off, in the words of Colm Tóibín, who had succeeded Vincent Browne as editor of *Magill,* by

> the Kerry Babies tribunal, the bad weather, the Air India crash, the death of Ann Lovett, the national debt, facts and divisions which came to light during the amendment debate, unemployment, the hunger strikes in the North, boring television programmes, the failure of Dr Garret FitzGerald to improve the lot of anyone in the country, simple piety, nostalgia for the happiness and harmony induced by the papal visit, fear that the church has moved far too away from things of the spirit and into the public domain, simple curiosity, the feeling that more sin is being committed than ever before, the sense that things cannot go on as they have been going, the need to pray in the darkness in the company of others.[61]

The phenomenon began in Asdee, Co. Kerry, near the seaside town of Ballybunion. In February seven-year-old Elizabeth Flynn went to St Mary's Church to pray to two statues,

> painted plaster images of the Blessed Virgin and the Sacred Heart which stand in the alcove at the back of the church on the left hand side ... surmounted with votive candles, and a small round stained glass porthole which lets in a dim diffuse light. Then she saw the Sacred Heart crook his finger and beckon her over to him. When she looked again, Our Lady's mouth was open.[62]

When Elizabeth told her schoolmates what had happened, all the children came to the church to look. Thirty-six of them said they saw the statues move in various ways.[63] Soon there were local people and visitors who believed that the children of Asdee might be in the great tradition of Marian visionaries. The alleged apparition at Knock in 1879 was the most famous Irish example, while the claims of fourteen-year-old Bernadette Soubirous to have seen the Blessed Virgin at Lourdes in 1858 and those of three Portuguese children to have seen her in 1917 at Fatima had also transformed those places into sites of Catholic pilgrimage. Yet these were only the best known of the many Marian apparitions that had been reported. Those of the Belgian villages of Beauraing (1932) and Banneux (1933), of Donglu in China (1900) and Akita in Japan (1973) may be little known in this part of the world, but they are all officially recognised as worthy of belief by the Vatican. The visions seen in the Spanish village of Garabandal by four schoolgirls between 1961 and 1965 were not afforded such recognition but attracted international attention and were covered at length in the Irish newspapers.

There were claims of miraculous happenings at Asdee.

> A man from Cavan who came on a Thursday evening to celebrate his wedding anniversary reached up to touch the statue of the Blessed Virgin, placing his fingertips on its hand. His fingers and thumb, he claimed, were held firm in the statue's grasp for many seconds while he tried to release its hold. A woman who came in a busload from Newry one Sunday felt the Blessed Virgin take her hand in her own. The statue's hand, she said, turned to warm flesh as it gripped her. She was crying uncontrollably.[64]

Vision-mania spread. In Co. Wexford alone there were three sites where moving statues were reported.[65] In Culleens, near Enniscrone, four teenage girls claimed to have 'seen the Blessed Virgin and Saint Bernadette' in the sky on 2 September. However,

> it took the third set of visions by the girls to boost the attendance to thousands ... They now had a public address system: a microphone and speaker had been borrowed from a local politician, Councillor Paddy Conway, so all of the 300 present could hear the hymns and prayers and respond. As usual the girls were standing together when above they could see the moon trying to break through the clouds. Her features became visible again and alongside was the headless blue statue. The lips were miming the words 'Faith and Hope,' and then continued, at pace with the hymns below, the words of 'Hail, Queen of Heaven,' and 'Be Not Afraid.' Then, to the left in the sky, they saw form in the clouds the Blessed Virgin, holding the Infant Jesus. Below, in the darkness, fervour was spiced with awe and celebration. On this occasion several spectators confessed that they had shared in the visions.[66]

But the mother of all vision sites was Ballinspittle, Co. Cork, where tens of thousands flocked 'to watch the statue from the road or from the field opposite.'[67] Ballinspittle's visionary was seventeen-year-old Clare O'Mahoney, who was

> passing Ballinspittle's grotto. She looked up from the road towards the statue, which was about 30 yards away, set in a nook high in the rocky hillside. The statue was illuminated by a halo of 11 lights. As Clare looked up, she was certain that Mary was rocking back and forward. Clare told her mother and other villagers. They looked. They also saw Mary move. Word quickly started . . . People came from other villages to see for themselves. They also saw the statue rocking to and fro. One or two people reported other movements: the twisting of Mary's body, a glint in her eyes, a gesture of her arms.[68]

But the phenomenon died away almost as suddenly as it had begun. In November, however, there was an event that really did seem to verge on the miraculous.

———

Garret FitzGerald's humiliation at Chequers the previous year seemed to confirm that Margaret Thatcher's policy on the North was based on a deep affection for the Ulster unionists, and a degree of disdain for the Irish Government. But on 15 November the signing of the Anglo-Irish Agreement confounded the critics on both sides while earning Thatcher the undying enmity of Ulster unionists.

The foundations for the agreement had been laid after Thatcher invited John Hume to talks on 17 January and four days later

> offered a joint body to discuss legal and security issues, including policing, prisons and human rights matters. There would be a joint secretariat, based in Belfast, with joint ministerial chairmanship. The joint body—subsequently called the Anglo-Irish Conference— would be charged with solving problems, rather than just reporting them back to respective governments. This was the embryo of the mould-breaking Anglo-Irish Agreement. It was a far cry from the unitary state 'preferred' by the Forum, but it was also the first time a British government had committed itself to a 'regular, continuing, constitutionalised role' for Dublin in the affairs of the North.[69]

The agreement was signed at Hillsborough Castle in Co. Down and was immediately hailed as 'the biggest Anglo-Irish initiative since 1921.'[70] Its central provisions were that

> first, both governments affirmed that any change in the status of Northern Ireland (for example, incorporation by the Republic of Ireland) would come about only with the consent of a majority of the people of Northern Ireland. Second, the governments agreed to set up an intergovernmental conference, serviced by a full-time secretariat with civil servants from both jurisdictions . . . Third, both London and Dublin supported the idea of a 'devolved' government, to deal with a range of matters within Northern Ireland that would command 'widespread acceptance throughout the community.'[71]

Supporters of the agreement in the Republic said that

> Ireland was being treated as an equal by England. Dublin officials would help administer the North from an office in Belfast. It was an incredible breakthrough.[72]

The general view was that the success

> belonged predominantly to FitzGerald. He had finally delivered an
> historic breakthrough . . . Everywhere FitzGerald travelled in the
> days after Hillsborough, he was mobbed and applauded. There was
> a national wave of good will and support for him and his
> government.[73]

Its supporters argued that

> the Agreement tackled the problem of alienation among the
> minority community head on and sought to secure, in line with the
> central requirement of the New Ireland Forum report, equal
> recognition and respect for Nationalist and Unionist traditions . . .
> Nationalists could now finally raise their heads knowing that their
> position was, and was seen to be, on an equal footing with that of
> unionists.[74]

Some nationalists, that is: because the agreement effectually ruled out
any discussions with the republican movement. In fact FitzGerald
admitted that 'it was the rise of Sinn Féin that led me to contemplate and
work towards an Agreement with Britain as the only way, it seemed to me,
of blocking the rise of Sinn Féin and showing that it didn't have the
backing of the majority of people in Ireland.'[75] The agreement came about
because FitzGerald's

> obsession with securing the SDLP's base of support and isolating
> Sinn Féin over-rode every other Irish consideration. At the heart of
> it was the explicit belief that the IRA posed a far greater threat to the
> Irish state than to the British government, and the implicit belief
> that given the necessity of seeing the IRA only in terms of 'bad'
> violence, then support for militant republicanism was the product
> of circumstance rather than conviction and ideology, that the IRA
> exploited the Catholic community rather than reflecting its
> essence.[76]

Yet this aim did not prevent unionists from reacting with fury to the
agreement, something that only added to the perception in the Republic
of a historic victory. The unionist reaction was

> even more hostile than expected. They were enraged at the idea of
> even a limited role in the affairs of the province being conceded to
> Dublin and incensed at the setting up of the joint secretariat at a
> government building in Maryfield, Co. Down. The day after the
> historic signing, the Unionist dominated Northern Ireland
> Assembly voted to demand a referendum. There were mass
> demonstrations, protests at the 'Maryfield Bunker' and fifteen

Unionist MPs resigned to fight on an Anti-Agreement platform.[77]

Twenty-one Tory backbenchers voted against the agreement when it was passed in the House of Commons, 473 votes to 47, and the Minister of State at the Treasury, Ian Gow, resigned in protest. A personal friend of Thatcher, he would be killed five years later by an IRA bomb placed under his car.

The unionists' problem was that 'the agreement fused the two most basic fears of Protestants, that they would somehow be outmanoeuvred by the South and betrayed by the British, and convinced them that dark and perfidious deeds had been plotted behind their backs.'[78] Yet complaints that the deal had been done without reference to them rang hollow, as their negative reaction to the New Ireland Forum

> made it inevitable that if Dublin could persuade London to respond to any extent to the Forum's analysis, the consequences would have to be worked out in direct discussions between them without consultation with the Unionists. Total negativity is not a negotiating position.[79]

The violence of unionist rhetoric was striking. The leader of the Democratic Unionist Party, Ian Paisley, warned Thatcher that 'the whole island could be engulfed in a situation too terrible to contemplate.'[80] The implied threat of violence was repeated by the head of the Ulster Unionist Party, James Molyneaux, who predicted that the agreement 'will not bring peace but a sword.'[81] And it was made explicit by the UDA, which declared: 'All residents of the Irish Republic will be treated as hostile and if found on Ulster soil may suffer the consequences of FitzGerald's folly.'[82]

At his Martyrs' Memorial Church in Belfast, Paisley prayed: 'O God, in wrath take vengeance upon this wicked treacherous lying woman, take vengeance upon her, O Lord, grant that we shall have a demonstration of thy power.'[83] The Lord did not oblige. For all the unionist bluster, there would be no repeat of the post-Sunningdale surrender. Thatcher's obduracy, so troublesome for the Irish Government in the past, was in this case a godsend.

Yet it was not only the unionists who came out strongly against the agreement. Charlie Haughey lamented:

> I believe the concept of Irish unity has been dealt a very major blow . . . For the first time ever, the legitimacy of the Unionist position, which is contrary to unification, has been recognised by an Irish government in an international agreement . . . From our point of view it gives everything away.[84]

Haughey's criticism was not wholly opportunist. The agreement was a watershed, after which it was accepted that securing justice for the nationalist population within the North would take priority over achieving a united Ireland.

Yet only a few months previously Fianna Fáil had been *de facto* allies of the Catholic Church and the extreme elements of the Catholic right during the family planning debate. Had the bill been defeated, as Desmond O'Malley pointed out, 'the two groups who will rejoice to high heaven will be the Unionists in Northern Ireland and the extreme Roman Catholics in this Republic.'[85] For Fianna Fáil a united Ireland had become a sacred cow to which periodic tribute must be paid but that did not require the party to think about how it might be achieved.

Haughey was not satisfied with opposing the bill in the Dáil and despatched Brian Lenihan to the United States to try to get the support of leading Irish-Americans, particularly the Speaker of the House of Representatives, Tip O'Neill. 'It did nothing to enhance Haughey's reputation when news of the intervention finally leaked out.[86] It was an ill-judged intervention, as O'Neill and other Irish-American politicians would become strong supporters of the agreement. They would not be alone in agreeing with Hume that

> though no-one among us felt it was the final solution, the agreement was a major achievement of democratic politics and was a significant step forward on the road to lasting peace and stability ... Everything that has happened in the past few years stems from the Agreement.[87]

In the Dáil, Mary Harney joined Desmond O'Malley in voting for the agreement and was promptly expelled from Fianna Fáil.

———

The Anglo-Irish Agreement may well have been FitzGerald's finest moment, but his Government had developed a reputation for economic incompetence. It was a time of record unemployment, with the figure for January exceeding 18 per cent.[88] In January the budget of the Minister for Finance, Alan Dukes, was greeted with dismay. The budget deficit of 7.9 per cent had risen from an already high 7.2 per cent in 1984 and was close to the 8.2 per cent of 1982 that had been claimed as the acme of Fianna Fáil economic fecklessness. Economists despaired. Seán Barrett of Trinity College, Dublin, declared:

> The government has not been able to tackle the public expenditure

problem ... yesterday it adopted the new public stance of not trying. The public debt is now £18 Billion. Yesterday Mr Dukes added another £2 Billion. The foreign component of state company debt is already £3 Billion. In total we owe £11 Billion abroad. In 1981 the foreign debts were £3.8 Billion for the government and £1.1 Billion for the state companies, a total of £9.4 Billion. Despite the harsh budgets in 1981 to 1984 we have managed to double our foreign debts by 1985. Despite apparent tax cuts, the real tax burden rose in the 1985 budget. Income tax will rise by 8.4% in 1985. The increase in sales taxes will be 7.8%.[89]

Alan Matthews of Trinity College spotted that

the farming sector was an important winner in this budget. Farmers now pay less than half the amount of tax (in real terms) to the exchequer than they did in 1973/74 (before the taxation of farming properties was introduced), although their incomes have risen considerably in the meantime ... Rates on agricultural land are now gone. The resource tax is gone. The removal of the VAT rebate is gone. And now the income tax system put in place by the 1974 Finance Act is going ... The absolute power of this lobby knows no bounds.[90]

That the Government coupled talk of fiscal rectitude with a determination to protect certain interest groups was most clearly illustrated in March by the bail-out of the Insurance Corporation of Ireland. By 1984 this company was

the second largest non-life insurer in the Irish market with a turnover of £380 million and a staff of more than 800. The company had offices in Britain, the U.S., France, Canada, Australia and the Channel Islands ... The company was the biggest underwriter of employers and public liability insurance; it had 25% of the market in Ireland. It was the government's sole agent for managing export credit insurance for Irish exporters and it also insured many of the state-owned companies including the national airline Aer Lingus and the transport company CIE.[91]

But ICI's foundations were built on sand. The manager of the company's London office, John Grace,

aggressively sought out new high-risk business such as insuring satellites, bloodstock and even fairground operators and circuses. These were businesses that other insurers steered well clear of. He even insured telegraph poles in the Australian Outback, items that were prone to combustion on a regular basis.[92]

The result was that, as the claims began to flood in,

> it became clear that the company was underwriting the risk far too low. The losses were immense: of the £63 million lost in 1983, £50 million was estimated to be generated by the London office.[93]

Allied Irish Banks had bought ICI outright in September 1983, but by 1985 the losses were so great that they

> threatened to bring down its parent company, AIB. The bank had ploughed tens of millions of pounds into the company trying to save it, but it could no longer afford to keep bailing the company out.[94]

On 8 March AIB told the Government that it was closing down ICI. On 15 March came the announcement that the Government was buying ICI from AIB for £1, and taking responsibility for all its debts and liabilities. It had also bought AIB's argument that it could not

> allow ICI to threaten the stability of AIB because the country was so heavily exposed to international institutional investors at that time, and if the country's largest bank failed, then the entire country could well be destabilised.[95]

In reality the chief executive of the bank, Gerry Scanlan, had

> pulled a political master-stroke . . . Dukes believed that the Irish taxpayer, not the bank, should pay for AIB's mess, even though there was huge uncertainty over the size of the losses and the length of time they last.[96]

AIB celebrated the Government's deal with drinks at its head office and soon afterwards announced profits for 1984 of £84 million. By October 1985 ICI's deficit was estimated at £164 million; AIB's contribution to paying this off was £5½ million a year.[97] But it was the taxpayer rather than the bank who covered the losses. Dukes even neglected to

> take a stake in AIB—or at least negotiate an option to acquire shares in the bank at a later date—in return for its extraordinarily generous rescue package . . . The government could have taken options over 25% of the equity. This would have meant that they wouldn't have owned any part of the bank, but over the long term they could have exercised options. Had they done this, more than 20 years on they could have had shares worth over €3 billion.[98]

Instead the Government was brought into disrepute by a bail-out that

> showed the country's taxpayers that the country's largest banks can always rely on the politicians to bail them out whenever their investments turn sour . . . The politicians stood by the big boys of Irish banking after they walked away from their mess, leaving the taxpayer to pay for the clean-up.[99]

The big boys of Irish banking would remember this.

The ICI debacle was yet another crisis that fuelled public dissatisfaction with the main political parties. The political situation might have looked propitious for the left, but the reality was that 'unemployment stood at 215,000 and an estimated one million were living on the poverty line; almost 500,000 workers were organised in trade unions; the Republic had a very young population; yet the left still struggled to win votes.'[100]

—

A hard-pressed population found heroes outside politics instead, and in 1985 few appeared more heroic than Bob Geldof, the former folk devil and punk scourge of respectable society, who with Midge Ure had corralled together the pop stars of the day to record 'Do They Know It's Christmas?' in aid of the victims of the Ethiopian famine. The success of the record prompted Geldof to try something far more ambitious.

The Live Aid concerts, held in London and Philadelphia on 13 July, were remarkable events that showed that 'rock 'n roll . . . could . . . agitate in favour of decency, compassion and real love as opposed to cheap sex.'[101]

The most memorable moments of Live Aid came from a band that had taken over from Geldof's Boomtown Rats as the standard-bearers for Irish rock music. Since releasing their first album, *Boy*, in 1980, U2 had steadily progressed to become one of the world's biggest rock bands. Their breakthrough had come in 1983 with their third album, *War*. The music magazine *Rolling Stone* had named U2 band of the year. The guitarist Dave Evans, known as the Edge, the bassist Adam Clayton and the drummer Larry Mullen all played their part in the band's success, but U2's greatest asset was their singer, Paul Hewson, who, as Bono, was becoming one of rock's great front men. In a country bedevilled by political mediocrity and economic stagnation, the success of U2 seemed like proof that a better Ireland was possible.

—

So did the Druid Theatre, founded in 1975 by two graduates of University College, Galway, Garry Hynes and Marie Mullen, and a teacher, Mick Lally, and the only professional theatre company in Ireland outside Dublin. From its first production, *The Playboy of the Western World* in the Jesuit

Hall, it was obvious that there was something special about Druid, with Hynes emerging as a director of startling power and originality. Druid's range and ambition were particularly noteworthy, and 'Jacobean revenge tragedy, eighteenth century satirical operas, Oscar Wilde and Tennessee Williams have all been produced to effect in Druid's tiny theatre . . .'[102]

A rapturously received production of John Ford's seventeenth-century tragedy *'Tis Pity She's a Whore*, with soundtrack by the electronic composer Roger Doyle and a brilliant central performance from Ciarán Hinds, garnered plaudits early in 1985. But the real triumph was to come when the combination of Druid, the playwright Tom Murphy and the actor Siobhán McKenna created a theatrical storm.

Tom Murphy had endured a lean spell of hostile critical receptions and commercial failure. *The Sanctuary Lamp*, produced by the Abbey Theatre in 1975 and now regarded as a classic, was largely met with incomprehension and indifference. It might have been enough to crush a lesser writer, but Murphy eventually came back with his most ambitious play yet and one of the finest ever to grace the stage: *The Gigli Concert* (1983). Operatic in its intensity and possessing the resonance of some previously undiscovered myth, the play stepped away from naturalism to become an extraordinary parable of the healing force of the creative element in the human spirit. It also contains the disdain for the business class that runs like a steel thread through Murphy's work. The play was a triumph. Two years later Druid would be working with a great writer at the peak of his powers.

The third pillar of their success would be Siobhán McKenna, one of the finest stage actors of her generation, who would take the leading role in *Bailegangaire*, the play Murphy wrote for Druid. While it would be stretching things to describe *Bailegangaire* as a political play, the economic hardships and the moral battles of the era are contained within it. The reaction to the play was ecstatic; it was described as 'an extraordinary, original and unique play.'

> It is a symphony for three voices, a roar of laughter in the face of misfortune, a scream of hope in a prison of despair. Siobhán McKenna's performance as the tetchy, dislocated Mommo is a tour de force, perhaps her best since Saint Joan, and as good as any theatregoer can expect to see in a lifetime.[103]

For Murphy's most perceptive critic, Fintan O'Toole, his 'achievement is highly unified and . . . what binds it together is the fact that it forms a kind of inner history of Ireland . . . Murphy has been able to dramatise an entire society.'[104]

It was not the only major play of the year. Frank McGuinness had also created a stir with *Observe the Sons of Ulster Marching Towards the Somme,* which opened in the Peacock in February. A look at a group of soldiers fated to die at the Battle of the Somme in 1916, it was an attempt to examine some of the driving forces behind Ulster Protestant identity. It was also an effort to posit some kind of understanding between the Catholic and Protestant populations, though these good intentions would have counted for naught had it not been for the passionate brilliance of McGuinness's writing and some tremendous performances, notably those of Bosco Hogan and Tom Hickey. In *Magill,* Joseph O'Connor described the play as

> an urgent communication of insight into the nature of political ideology and allegiances. It is a warning of what can happen when the psychology of reason is replaced by the psychology of surface and symbol. It is as much a prophetic play as a play about the past.[105]

The year 1985 would close with an act of political creativity that heralded the end of an era. On 21 December, Desmond O'Malley took the plunge and, accompanied by his former Fianna Fáil colleague Mary Harney, a former member of Fine Gael, Michael McDowell, Paul Mackay and Brigid Teefy, announced the formation of a new political party, the Progressive Democrats. Irish politics would never be quite the same again.

NOTES AND REFERENCES

Chapter 1: Introduction (p. 1–5)

1.   'Questions and Answers,' RTE1, 23 June 2008.
2.   *Parliamentary Debates: Dáil Éireann: Official Report*, 23 June 1993.
3.   *Irish Times*, 5 December 2007.
4.   Central Statistics Office.
5.   Bolger, *The Journey Home*.
6.   Central Statistics Office.
7.   Speech by Pat Cox, University of Limerick, 31 August 2006.
8.   *Irish Times*, 24 February 1973.
9.   Central Statistics Office.
10. *Parliamentary Debates: Dáil Éireann: Official Report*, 11 May 1983 (Dick Spring), 30 November 1977 (Brendan Griffin), *Parliamentary Debates: Seanad Éireann: Official Report*, 16 December 1981 (Seán Fallon), among others.
11. Colm Tóibín, Introduction, *The Penguin Book of Irish Fiction*.

Chapter 2: A boot up the transom (p. 6–33)

1.   *Irish Times*, 1 January 1973.
2.   Desmond, *Finally and in Conclusion*.
3.   Desmond, *Finally and in Conclusion*.
4.   Horgan, *Noël Browne*.
5.   For example in Tony Judt, *Postwar: A History of Europe since 1945*, London: Allen Lane, the Penguin Press, 2007.
6.   *Irish Times*, 24 February 1973.
7.   *Irish Times*, 24 February 1973.
8.   Speech by Pat Cox, president of the International European Movement, at the University of Limerick, 31 August 2006; *Irish Times*, 30 May 1973.
9.   Foster, *Luck and the Irish*.
10. *Irish Times*, 5 October 1973.
11. Gillmor, *Economic Activities in the Republic of Ireland*.
12. Fleming and O'Day, *Longman Handbook of Modern Irish History*.
13. Fleming and O'Day, *Longman Handbook of Modern Irish History*.
14. Fleming and O'Day, *Longman Handbook of Modern Irish History*.
15. Desmond Norton, 'Unemployment and public policy,' *Studies*, spring 1976.

16. Fleming and O'Day, *Longman Handbook of Modern Irish History.*
17. Brown, *Ireland: A Social and Cultural History.*
18. Sutton Index of Deaths at the CAIN Project (*cain.ulst.ac.uk/sutton*).
19. Keogh, *Jack Lynch.*
20. Keogh, *Jack Lynch.*
21. Keogh, *Jack Lynch.*
22. Keogh, *Jack Lynch.*
23. 'Seven Ages', programme 6: 'The Seventies,' RTE1, 2000.
24. Boland, *Up Dev!*
25. Boland, *Up Dev!*
26. 'Seven Ages', programme 6: 'The Seventies,' RTE1, 2000.
27. Dermot Keogh, on 'Seven Ages', programme 6: 'The Seventies,' RTE1, 2000.
28. Keogh, *Jack Lynch.*
29. O'Higgins, *A Double Life.*
30. O'Higgins, *A Double Life.*
31. Keogh, *Twentieth-Century Ireland.*
32. O'Higgins, *A Double Life.*
33. O'Connell, *Doctor John.*
34. Arnold, *What Kind of Country.*
35. O'Higgins, *A Double Life.*
36. Horgan, *Noël Browne.*
37. *Irish Times,* 22 February 1973.
38. Horgan, *Labour.*
39. Horgan, Labour.
40. Desmond, *Finally and in Conclusion.*
41. Irish Times, 1 January 1973.
42. *Observer,* 20 May 2001; Taylor, *Provos.*
43. Kelley, *The Longest War.*
44. Dwyer, *Nice Fellow.*
45. *Irish Times,* 17 January 1973.
46. O'Malley, *Biting at the Grave.*
47. O'Malley, *Biting at the Grave.*
48. *Irish Times,* 15 February 1973.
49. *Irish Times,* 15 February 1973.
50. *Irish Times,* 26 February 1973.
51. *Irish Times,* 27 February 1973.
52. *Irish Times,* 15 February 1973.
53. *Irish Times,* 15 February 1973.
54. Dwyer, *Nice Fellow.*
55. *Irish Times,* 23 February 1973.
56. *Irish Times,* 23 February 1973.

57.   *Irish Times,* 22 February 1973.

58.   *Irish Times,* 27 February 1973.

59.   *Irish Times,* 1 March 1973.

60.   Patrick Murray, 'Irish elections: A changing pattern,' *Studies,* autumn 1976.

61.   *Irish Times,* 27 February 1973.

62.   Browne, *Against the Tide.*

63.   Keogh, *Twentieth-Century Ireland.*

64.   Arnold, *What Kind of Country.*

65.   Foster, *Luck and the Irish.*

66.   Cruise O'Brien, *Memoir.*

67.   Brown, *Ireland: A Social and Cultural History.*

68.   Brown, *Ireland: A Social and Cultural History.*

69.   *Irish Times,* 10 November 1973.

70.   *Irish Times,* 26 February 1973.

71.   Stopper, *Mondays at Gaj's.*

72.   O'Leary and Burke, *Mary Robinson.*

73.   Dwyer, *Nice Fellow.*

74.   Foster, *Luck and the Irish.*

75.   Cooney, *John Charles McQuaid.*

76.   *Irish Times,* 9 April 1973.

77.   Browne, *Against the Tide.*

78.   Cooney, *John Charles McQuaid.*

79.   Cooney, *John Charles McQuaid.*

80.   Cooney, *John Charles McQuaid.*

81.   Cooney, *John Charles McQuaid.*

82.   Browne, *Against the Tide.*

83.   Cooney, *John Charles McQuaid.*

84.   Cooney, *John Charles McQuaid.*

85.   Dunn, *No Tigers in Africa!*

86.   Cooney, *John Charles McQuaid.*

87.   *Irish Times,* 9 April 1973.

88.   *Irish Times,* 29 March 1973.

89.   *Irish Times,* 22 May 1973.

90.   *Irish Times,* 22 May 1973.

91.   Lenihan, *For the Record.*

92.   Smith, *Garret the Enigma.*

93.   *Irish Times,* 1 June 1973.

94.   *Irish Times,* 6 August 1973.

95.   Keogh, *Jack Lynch.*

96.   *Irish Times,* 6 August 1973.

97.   *Irish Times,* 15 August 1973.

98. *Irish Times,* 15 August 1973.

99. *Irish Times,* 8 August 1973.

100. *Irish Times,* 18 September 1973.

101. *Irish Times,* 18 September 1973.

102. *Irish Times,* 23 November 1973.

103. *Irish Times,* 6 December 1973.

104. *Irish Times,* 6 December 1973.

105. Whitehead, *The Writing on the Wall.*

106. *Irish Times,* 10 December 1973.

107. *Irish Times,* 10 December 1973.

108. 'Seven Ages', programme 6: 'The Seventies,' RTE1, 2000.

109. *Irish Times,* 20 December 1973.

110. *Irish Times,* 8 December 1973.

111. *Irish Times,* 24 November 1973.

112. *Irish Times,* 2 October 1973.

113. *Irish Times,* 3 October 1973.

114. Horgan, *Noël Browne.*

115. *Irish Times,* 1 November 1973.

116. *Irish Times,* 1 November 1973.

117. *Irish Times,* 1 November 1973.

118. 'The Helicopter Song,' recorded by the Wolfe Tones, 1973.

119. Corless, GUBU *Nation.*

120. Boland, *Up Dev!*

121. C. E. Davis and Richard Sinnott, 'The controversy concerning attitudes in the Republic to the Northern Ireland problem,' *Studies,* autumn–winter 1980.

122. Desmond, *Finally and in Conclusion.*

123. *Irish Times,* 20 December 1973.

124. Catherine B. Shanahan, 'The changing face of Cathleen Ni Houlihan,' in Bradley and Galanella, *Gender and Sexuality in Modern Ireland.*

Chapter 3: Walk on hot coals (p. 34–57)

1. *Irish Times,* 14 January 1974.

2. Mullan, *The Dublin and Monaghan Bombings.*

3. Mullan, *The Dublin and Monaghan Bombings.*

4. Tiernan, *The Dublin and Monaghan Bombings and the Murder Triangle.*

5. *Irish Times,* 18 May 1974.

6. Tiernan, *The Dublin and Monaghan Bombings and the Murder Triangle.*

7. Tiernan, *The Dublin and Monaghan Bombings and the Murder Triangle.*

8. Mullan, *The Dublin and Monaghan Bombings.*

9. Mullan, *The Dublin and Monaghan Bombings.*

10. *Irish Times,* 18 May 1974.

11. Mullan, *The Dublin and Monaghan Bombings*.
12. From 'British State Papers,' *Irish Times*, 3 January 2005.
13. Mullan, *The Dublin and Monaghan Bombings*.
14. *Irish Times*, 3 January 2005.
15. Mullan, *The Dublin and Monaghan Bombings*.
16. Tiernan, *The Dublin and Monaghan Bombings and the Murder Triangle*.
17. Mullan, *The Dublin and Monaghan Bombings*.
18. *Commission of Investigation into the Dublin and Monaghan Bombings of 1974*.
19. Mullan, *The Dublin and Monaghan Bombings*.
20. *Irish Times*, 14 June 1974.
21. *Irish Times*, 14 June 1974.
22. *Irish Times*, 14 June 1974.
23. *Parliamentary Debates: Dáil Éireann: Official Report*, 26 June 1974.
24. *Parliamentary Debates: Dáil Éireann: Official Report*, 26 June 1974.
25. *Irish Times*, 7 February 1974.
26. *Irish Times*, 13 March 1974.
27. *Irish Times*, 13 March 1974.
28. *Irish Times*, 13 March 1974.
29. *Irish Times*, 8 June 1974.
30. *Irish Times*, 4 June 1974.
31. Liamy Reilly and Theresa O'Malley, 'Take Me Home to Mayo,' Mid-West Radio, 2008.
32. *Irish Times*, 4 June 1974.
33. *Irish Times*, 10 June 1974.
34. *Irish Times*, 10 June 1974.
35. *Irish Times*, 10 June 1974.
36. *Irish Times*, 10 June 1974.
37. Liamy Reilly and Theresa O'Malley, 'Take Me Home to Mayo,' Mid-West Radio, 2008.
38. *Irish Times*, 10 June 1974.
39. Liamy Reilly and Theresa O'Malley, 'Take Me Home to Mayo,' Mid-West Radio, 2008.
40. Howard, *Hostage*.
41. *Irish Times*, 9 February 1974.
42. *Irish Times*, 8 June 1974.
43. Curtis, *Ireland: The Propaganda War*.
44. *Irish Times*, 8 June 1974.
45. *Independent*, 24 September 2006.
46. *Time*, 20 May 1974.
47. *Time*, 20 May 1974.

48. *Time*, 20 May 1974.
49. Howard, *Hostage*.
50. *Irish Times*, 27 April 1974.
51. *Irish Times*, 27 April 1974.
52. *Irish Times*, 6 May 1974.
53. *Irish Times*, 26 June 1974.
54. *Irish Times*, 26 June 1974.
55. Howard, *Hostage*.
56. *Irish Independent*, 29 January 2007.
57. *Irish Times*, 19 August 1974.
58. *Irish Times*, 8 September 1974.
59. *Irish Times*, 29 May 1974.
60. *Irish Times*, 29 May 1974.
61. Bishop and Mallie, *The Provisional* IRA.
62. *Irish Times*, 29 May 1974.
63. *Irish Times*, 3 January 2005.
64. 'Seven Ages', programme 6: 'The Seventies,' RTE1, 2000.
65. *Irish Times*, 3 January 2005.
66. FitzGerald, *All in a Life*.
67. Whitehead, *The Writing on the Wall*.
68. *Irish Times*, 14 June 1974.
69. Coogan, *The Troubles*.
70. Foster, *Luck and the Irish*.
71. Lee, *Ireland, 1912–1985*.
72. O'Reilly, *Masterminds of the Right*.
73. *Parliamentary Debates: Dáil Éireann: Official Report*, 4 July 1974.
74. *Parliamentary Debates: Dáil Éireann: Official Report*, 11 July 1974.
75. *Parliamentary Debates: Dáil Éireann: Official Report*, 4 July 1974.
76. *Irish Times*, 3 January 2005.
77. *Irish Times*, 17 July 1974.
78. *Irish Times*, 17 July 1974.
79. Stopper, *Mondays at Gaj's*.
80. Stopper, *Mondays at Gaj's*.
81. *Irish Times*, 15 November 1974.
82. McCafferty, *Nell*.
83. *Irish Times*, 10 October 1974.
84. *Irish Times*, 6 November 1974.
85. Downey, *Lenihan*.
86. Downey, *Lenihan*.
87. *Irish Times*, 18 November 1974.
88. Dwyer, *Nice Fellow*.

89. Dwyer, *Nice Fellow.*
90. *Dunlop, Yes, Taoiseach.*
91. *Irish Times,* 4 December 1974.
92. *Irish Times,* 9 July 1974.
93. *Irish Times,* 11 June 1974.
94. *Irish Times,* 15 June 1974.
95. *Irish Times,* 12 July 1974.
96. Central Statistics Office.
97. *Irish Times,* 12 November 1974.
98. *Irish Times,* 12 November 1974.
99. *Irish Times,* 12 November 1974.
100. *Irish Times,* 8 January 1974.
101. *Irish Times,* 23 January 1975.
102. *Irish Times,* 26 March 1974.
103. *Irish Times,* 9 April 1974.
104. *Irish Times,* 10 April 1974.
105. *Irish Times,* 12 September 1975.
106. Harper and Hodgett, Irish Folk, Trad and Blues.
107. Harper and Hodgett, *Irish Folk, Trad and Blues.*
108. *Rory Gallagher: Irish Tour, 1974: A Film by Tony Palmer,* BMG Records, 2000.
109. Harper and Hodgett, *Irish Folk, Trad and Blues.*
110. Power, *Send 'Em Home Sweatin'.*
111. Power, *Send 'Em Home Sweatin'.*
112. *Irish Times,* 6 November 1974.
113. *Sunday Tribune,* 8 May 2005.
114. *Irish Times,* 23 September 1974.
115. *Irish Times,* 23 September 1974.
116. *Irish Times,* 24 November 1974.
117. Arnold, *What Kind of Country.*
118. *Irish Times,* 3 January 2005.
119. *Irish Times,* 3 January 2005.
120. Coogan, *The Troubles.*
121. 'Seven Ages', programme 6: 'The Seventies,' RTE1, 2000.
122. White, *Ruairí Ó Brádaigh.*
123. Bishop and Mallie, *The Provisional IRA.*
124. White, *Ruairí Ó Brádaigh.*
125. Coogan, *The Troubles.*

Chapter 4: Inflation once again (p. 58–83)

1. *Irish Times,* 13 October 1975.
2. *Irish Times,* 31 December 2005.

3. Central Statistics Office.

4. Central Statistics Office.

5. *Irish Times*, 14 August 1975.

6. *Irish Times*, 8 February 1975.

7. *Irish Times*, 14 January 1975.

8. *Irish Times*, 8 February 1975.

9. *Irish Times*, 11 March 1975.

10. *Irish Times*, 16 October 1975.

11. *Irish Times*, 16 October 1975.

12. *Irish Times*, 16 January 1975.

13. Gallagher, *The Irish Labour Party in Transition*.

14. Lee, *Ireland, 1912–1985*.

15. *Irish Times*, 6 March 1975.

16. *Irish Times*, 7 March 1975.

17. Bew et al., *The Dynamics of Irish Politics*.

18. *Irish Times*, 6 March 1975.

19. FitzGerald, *All in a Life*.

20. *Irish Times*, 6 March 1975.

21. Horgan, *Labour*.

22. Smith, *Garret the Enigma*.

23. Smith, *Garret the Enigma*.

24. Bew et al., *The Dynamics of Irish Politics*.

25. Tony Brown, 'Poverty, politics and policies,' in Kennedy, *One Million Poor*.

26. Horgan, *Labour*.

27. Roche, *Local Government in Ireland*.

28. Roche, *Local Government in Ireland*.

29. O'Connell, *Doctor John*.

30. *Irish Times*, 3 July 1975.

31. *Irish Times*, 3 July 1975.

32. *Irish Times*, 5 July 1975.

33. *Irish Times*, 8 July 1975.

34. *Irish Times*, 5 December 1975.

35. McDonald, *The Destruction of Dublin*.

36. McDonald, *The Destruction of Dublin*.

37. McDonald, *The Destruction of Dublin*.

38. McDonald, *The Destruction of Dublin*.

39. McDonald, *The Destruction of Dublin*.

40. McDonald, *The Destruction of Dublin*.

41. Gillmor, *Economic Activities in the Republic of Ireland*.

42. *Irish Independent*, 29 December 1999.

43. *Irish Independent*, 29 December 1999.

44.   Gillmor, *Economic Activities in the Republic of Ireland.*
45.   *Irish Times,* 15 February 1975.
46.   Gillmor, *Economic Activities in the Republic of Ireland.*
47.   Gillmor, *Economic Activities in the Republic of Ireland.*
48.   Gillmor, *Economic Activities in the Republic of Ireland.*
49.   *Irish Times,* 1 July 1975.
50.   *Irish Times,* 4 November 1975.
51.   Faulkner, *As I Saw It.*
52.   Dunlop, *Yes, Taoiseach.*
53.   Collins, *The Power Game.*
54.   Collins, *The Power Game.*
55.   Smith, *Garret the Enigma.*
56.   Smith, *Garret the Enigma.*
57.   Faulkner, *As I Saw It.*
58.   *Irish Times,* 31 January 1975.
59.   *Irish Times,* 31 January 1975.
60.   *Irish Times,* 23 September 1975.
61.   Collins, *The Power Game.*
62.   *Irish Times,* 30 December 2005.
63.   John Bowman in *Irish Times,* 30 December 2005.
64.   Coogan, *A Memoir.*
65.   *Irish Times,* 29 December 2005.
66.   *Irish Times,* 5 May 1975.
67.   FitzGerald, *All in a Life.*
68.   *Irish Times,* 6 May 1975.
69.   FitzGerald, *All in a Life.*
70.   Gallagher, *The Irish Labour Party in Transition.*
71.   Mac Mánais, *The Road From Ardoyne.*
72.   McCann, *War and an Irish Town.*
73.   McCann, *War and an Irish Town.*
74.   McKittrick and McVea, *Making Sense of the Troubles.*
75.   *Irish Times,* 15 October 1975.
76.   *Irish Times,* 15 October 1975.
77.   *Irish Times,* 30 October 1975.
78.   Irish Times, 21 November 1975.
79.   *Irish Times,* 21 November 1975.
80.   Kelley, *The Longest War.*
81.   Moloney, *A Secret History of the* IRA.
82.   Moloney, *A Secret History of the* IRA.
83.   Faul and Murray, *The Triangle of Death.*
84.   Power, *Send 'Em Home Sweatin'.*

85. *Irish Times*, 1 August 1975.

86. Travers and Fetherstonhaugh, *The Miami Showband Massacre*.

87. *Irish Times*, 1 August 1975.

88. Dillon, *The Dirty War*.

89. Fahy, *Death on a Country Road*.

90. Travers and Fetherstonhaugh, *The Miami Showband Massacre*.

91. Travers and Fetherstonhaugh, *The Miami Showband Massacre*.

92. *Irish Times*, 1 August 1975.

93. Fahy, *Death on a Country Road*.

94. Dillon, *The Dirty War*.

95. Seamus Heaney, 'The Strand at Lough Beg,' from *Station Island*, London: Faber and Faber, 1979.

96. Moloney, *A Secret History of the* IRA.

97. Bishop and Mallie, *The Provisional* IRA.

98. White, *Ruairí Ó Brádaigh*.

99. Bishop and Mallie, *The Provisional* IRA.

100. Bishop and Mallie, *The Provisional* IRA.

101. Jordan, *To Laugh or to Weep*.

102. *Cork Examiner*, 17 January 1975.

103. *Irish Times*, 17 February 1975.

104. *Irish Times*, 19 March 1975.

105. Barrett, *Martin Ferris*.

106. *Irish Times*, 19 March 1975.

107. *Irish Times*, 5 June 1975.

108. *Irish Times*, 24 March 1975.

109. *Irish Times*, 25 March 1975.

110. *Irish Times*, 23 June 1975.

111. Tiernan, *The Dublin and Monaghan Bombings and the Murder Triangle*.

112. Howard, *Hostage*.

113. Howard, *Hostage*.

114. Howard, *Hostage*.

115. Howard, *Hostage*.

116. Howard, *Hostage*.

117. Howard, *Hostage*.

118. Howard, *Hostage*.

119. Howard, *Hostage*.

120. *Irish Times*, 8 November 1975.

121. Connolly, *Herrema*.

122. *Irish Times*, 8 November 1975.

123. *Irish Times*, 11 November 1975.

124. Smith, *Garret the Enigma*.

125. Howard, *Hostage.*
126. Walsh, *The Final Beat.*
127. Walsh, *The Final Beat.*
128. Walsh, *The Final Beat.*
129. Walsh, *The Final Beat.*
130. Walsh, *The Final Beat.*
131. *Cork Examiner,* 9 January 1975.
132. *Irish Times,* 1 September 1975.
133. *Irish Times,* 1 September 1975.
134. *Irish Times,* 30 August 1975.
135. Kiberd, *Inventing Ireland.*
136. Browne, *Against the Tide.*
137. *Irish Times,* 1 September 1975.

Chapter 5: The war on terror (p. 84–111)

1. *Irish Times,* 30 December 1976.
2. *Irish Times,* 3 September 1976.
3. *Irish Times,* 1 September 1976.
4. Liamy Reilly and Theresa O'Malley, 'The Stolen Body,' Mid-West Radio, 2008.
5. *Irish Times,* 20 February 1976.
6. FitzGerald, *All in a Life.*
7. *Irish Times,* 20 February 1976.
8. *Irish Times,* 23 February 1976.
9. Liamy Reilly and Theresa O'Malley, 'The Stolen Body,' Mid-West Radio, 2008.
10. *Irish Times,* 21 February 1976.
11. *Irish Times,* 21 February 1976.
12. *Irish Times,* 23 February 1976.
13. *Irish Times,* 23 February 1976.
14. Liamy Reilly and Theresa O'Malley, 'The Stolen Body,' Mid-West Radio, 2008.
15. Liamy Reilly and Theresa O'Malley, 'The Stolen Body,' Mid-West Radio, 2008.
16. *Irish Times,* 16 February 1976.
17. *Irish Times,* 16 February 1976.
18. *Irish Times,* 16 February 1976.
19. Keogh, *Jack Lynch.*
20. Keogh, *Jack Lynch.*

21. Michael D. Higgins, 'Dr David Thornley TD: An intellectual in Irish politics,' in Thornley, *Unquiet Grave.*

22. Michael D. Higgins, 'Dr David Thornley TD: An intellectual in Irish politics,' in Thornley, *Unquiet Grave.*

23. *Irish Times,* 16 July 1976.

24. *Irish Times,* 16 July 1976.

25. *Irish Times,* 30 December 2006.

26. Jane Ewart-Biggs, introduction to Cruise O'Brien, *Neighbours.*

27. *Irish Times,* 22 July 1976.

28. Taylor, *Beating the Terrorists?*

29. *Irish Times,* 23 July 1976.

30. Moloney, *A Secret History of the IRA.*

31. *Irish Times,* 1 September 1976.

32. *Irish Times,* 1 September 1976.

33. *Irish Times,* 3 September 1976.

34. *Irish Times,* 2 September 1976.

35. *Irish Times,* 1 September 1976.

36. *Irish Times,* 1 September 1976.

37. *Irish Times,* 1 September 1976.

38. Smith, *Garret the Enigma.*

39. *Irish Times,* 30 December 1976.

40. Arnold, *What Kind of Country.*

41. Richard Sinnott, 'The electorate,' in Penniman, *Ireland at the Polls.*

42. *Irish Times,* 6 September 1976.

43. *Irish Times,* 6 September 1976.

44. *Irish Times,* 1 September 1976.

45. *Irish Times,* 6 September 1976.

46. Joyce and Murtagh, *Blind Justice.*

47. O'Brien, *The Irish Times: A History.*

48. *Irish Times,* 1 April 1976.

49. Joyce and Murtagh, *Blind Justice.*

50. McGarry, *While Justice Slept.*

51. Holland and McDonald, *INLA.*

52. Cruise O'Brien, *Memoir.*

53. Kerrigan and Brennan, *This Great Little Nation.*

54. FitzGerald, *All in a Life.*

55. FitzGerald, *All in a Life.*

56. McGarry, *While Justice Slept.*

57. *Irish Times,* 6 September 1976.

58. Coogan, *The Troubles.*

59. Criminal Law Act (1976).

60. *Irish Times,* 6 September 1976.
61. *Irish Times,* 6 September 1976.
62. *Irish Times,* 6 September 1976.
63. Ó hEithir, *The Begrudger's Guide to Irish Politics.*
64. Walsh, *The Final Beat.*
65. Walsh, *The Final Beat.*
66. *Irish Times,* 18 October 1976.
67. Walsh, *The Final Beat.*
68. Walsh, *The Final Beat.*
69. Coogan, *Ireland in the Twentieth Century.*
70. Walsh, *The Final Beat.*
71. Walsh, *The Final Beat.*
72. Walsh, *The Final Beat.*
73. *Irish Times,* 19 October 1976.
74. *Irish Times,* 19 October 1976.
75. Corless, GUBU *Nation.*
76. *Irish Times,* 19 October 1976.
77. *Irish Times,* 19 October 1976.
78. Smith, *Garret the Enigma.*
79. *Irish Times,* 21 October 1976.
80. *Irish Times,* 21 October 1976.
81. *Irish Times,* 23 October 1976.
82. *Irish Times,* 23 October 1976.
83. *Irish Times,* 30 December 1976.
84. *Irish Times,* 23 October 1976.
85. Keogh, *Twentieth-Century Ireland.*
86. Arnold, *What Kind of Country.*
87. *Irish Times,* 22 October 1976.
88. Ó hEithir, *The Begrudger's Guide to Irish Politics.*
89. Desmond, *Finally and in Conclusion.*
90. Desmond, *Finally and in Conclusion.*
91. *Irish Times,* 19 January 1976.
92. Walsh, *Patrick Hillery.*
93. *Irish Times,* 9 January 1976.
94. *Irish Times,* 9 January 1976.
95. *Irish Times,* 22 January 1976.
96. *Irish Times,* 22 January 1976.
97. *Irish Times,* 22 January 1976.
98. *Irish Times,* 22 January 1976.
99. Walsh, *Patrick Hillery.*
100. *Irish Times,* 12 February 1976.

101. *Irish Times,* 16 February 1976.
102. Walsh, *Patrick Hillery.*
103. *Irish Times,* 3 March 1976.
104. Walsh, *Patrick Hillery.*
105. Connolly, *The Irish Women's Movement.*
106. Connolly, *The Irish Women's Movement.*
107. Linda Connolly, 'The consequences and outcomes of second-wave feminism in Ireland,' in Connolly and Hourigan (eds.), *Social Movements and Ireland.*
108. Freedman, *The Cities of David.*
109. Freedman, *The Cities of David.*
110. Freedman, *The Cities of David.*
111. Freedman, *The Cities of David.*
112. Paul Ryan, 'Coming out of the dark: A decade of gay mobilisation in Ireland, 1970–1980,' in Connolly and Hourigan (eds.), *Social Movements and Ireland.*
113. Freedman, *The Cities of David.*
114. Paul Ryan, 'Coming out of the dark: A decade of gay mobilisation in Ireland, 1970–1980,' in Connolly and Hourigan (eds.), *Social Movements and Ireland.*
115. O'Reilly, *Masterminds of the Right.*
116. O'Reilly, *Masterminds of the Right.*
117. O'Reilly, *Masterminds of the Right.*
118. O'Reilly, *Masterminds of the Right.*
119. Foster, *Luck and the Irish.*
120. *Irish Times,* 30 December 1976.
121. *Irish Times,* 30 December 1976.
122. Appendix B, 'Labour force participation rates for 1971, 1975 and 1979, with projected rates for 1986 and 1991,' in Ryan, *Irish Industry in the Eighties.*
123. *Irish Times,* 3 March 1976.
124. *Irish Times,* 3 November 1976.
125. *Irish Times,* 3 November 1976.
126. *Irish Times,* 3 November 1976.
127. Francis Stuart, 'The soft centre of Irish writing,' in Vorm, *Paddy No More.*
128. *Observer,* 14 November 2004.
129. *Observer,* 14 November 2004.
130. *Observer,* 14 November 2004.
131. Colm Tóibín, Introduction to *The Penguin Book of Irish Fiction.*
132. 'Migrant Minds: Bono, Paul Durcan, Neil Jordan, Robert Ballagh,' in Kearney, *Navigations.*
133. Waters, *Race of Angels.*
134. 'Horslips: Return of the Dancehall Sweethearts,' television documentary by Maurice Linnane, RTE, 2007.

135. Smyth, *Noisy Island*.
136. Horslips, 'Trouble with a capital T,' *Book of Invasions: A Celtic Symphony* (CD), 1976.
137. Fleming and O'Day, *Longman Handbook of Modern Irish History*.
138. *Irish Times*, 15 May 1976.
139. Kerrigan and Brennan, *This Great Little Nation*.
140. *Irish Times*, 22 January and 23 December 1976.
141. *Irish Times*, 23 December 1976.
142. *Irish Times*, 22 January 1976.
143. *Irish Times*, 26 November 1976.
144. *Irish Times*, 15 March 1976.
145. *Irish Times*, 29 October 1976.
146. *Irish Times*, 13 November 1976.
147. *Irish Times*, 18 December 1976.
148. *Irish Times*, 20 December 1976.
149. *Irish Times*, 22 December 1976.

Chapter 6: Let's make it your kind of country (p. 112–138)

1. Mac Gréil, *Prejudice and Tolerance in Ireland*.
2. Mac Gréil, *Prejudice and Tolerance in Ireland*.
3. Mac Gréil, *Prejudice and Tolerance in Ireland*.
4. Mac Gréil, *Prejudice and Tolerance in Ireland*.
5. Mac Gréil, *Prejudice and Tolerance in Ireland*.
6. Mac Gréil, *Prejudice and Tolerance in Ireland*.
7. *Irish Times*, 11 July 1977.
8. *Irish Times*, 15 February 1977.
9. *Irish Times*, 15 February 1977.
10. *Irish Times*, 9 July 1977.
11. *Irish Times*, 20 July 1977.
12. *Irish Times*, 4 August 1977.
13. *Irish Times*, 4 August 1977.
14. *Irish Times*, 5 August 1977.
15. Irish Times, 29 October 1977.
16. *Irish Times*, 1 November 1977.
17. *Irish Times*, 3 November 1977.
18. *Irish Times*, 19 January 1977.
19. *Irish Times*, 11 January 1977.
20. *Irish Times*, 11 January 1977.
21. *Irish Times*, 11 January 1977.
22. *Irish Times*, 18 January 1977.
23. O'Reilly, *Masterminds of the Right*.

24. *Irish Times*, 26 January 1977.
25. *Irish Times*, 19 January 1977.
26. *Irish Times*, 4 October 1977.
27. Mac Gréil, *Prejudice and Tolerance in Ireland*.
28. *Irish Times*, 14 February 1977.
29. *Irish Times*, 5 February 1977.
30. *Irish Times*, 16 February 1977.
31. O'Brien, *The Irish Times: A History*.
32. *Irish Times*, 15 February 1977.
33. Coogan, *A Memoir*.
34. Barrett, *Martin Ferris*.
35. *Irish Times*, 25 April 1977.
36. Barrett, *Martin Ferris*.
37. *Irish Times*, 20, 21 and 22 April 1977.
38. *Irish Times*, 4 April 1977.
39. *Irish Times*, 4 April 1977.
40. *Irish Times*, 4 April 1977.
41. *Irish Times*, 21 April 1977.
42. *Irish Times*, 23 April 1977.
43. Barrett, *Martin Ferris*.
44. *Irish Times*, 23 April 1977.
45. Coogan, *A Memoir*.
46. *Irish Times*, 23 May 1977.
47. *Irish Times*, 23 May 1977.
48. *Irish Times*, 23 May 1977.
49. *Irish Times*, 23 May 1977.
50. *Irish Times*, 23 May 1977.
51. Lee, *Ireland, 1912–1985*.
52. FitzGerald, *All in a Life*.
53. Keogh, *Twentieth-Century Ireland*.
54. Ferriter, *The Transformation of Ireland*.
55. Richard Sinnott, 'The electorate,' in Penniman, *Ireland at the Polls*.
56. Richard Sinnott, 'The electorate,' Penniman, *Ireland at the Polls*.
57. Richard Sinnott, 'The electorate,' in Penniman, *Ireland at the Polls*.
58. *Irish Times*, 2 June 1977.
59. FitzGerald, *All in a Life*.
60. Maurice Manning, 'The political parties,' in Penniman, *Ireland at the Polls*.
61. Dwyer, *Nice Fellow*.
62. *Irish Times*, 4 June 1977.
63. Bew et al., *The Dynamics of Irish Politics*.
64. Richard Sinnott, 'The electorate,' in Penniman, *Ireland at the Polls*.

65. Richard Sinnott, 'The electorate,' in Penniman, *Ireland at the Polls*.
66. Maurice Manning, 'The political parties,' in Penniman, *Ireland at the Polls*.
67. Bew et al., *The Dynamics of Irish Politics*.
68. Bew et al., *The Dynamics of Irish Politics*.
69. Central Statistics Office.
70. FitzGerald, *All in a Life*.
71. Maurice Manning, 'The political parties,' in Penniman, *Ireland at the Polls*.
72. O'Byrnes, *Hiding Behind a Face*.
73. *Irish Times*, 10 June 1977.
74. Browne and Farrell, *The Magill Book of Irish Politics*.
75. Browne and Farrell, *The Magill Book of Irish Politics*.
76. Horgan, *Mary Robinson*.
77. *Irish Times*, 7 June 1977.
78. Jordan, *To Laugh or to Weep*.
79. *Irish Times*, 14 June 1977.
80. *Irish Times*, 9 June 1977.
81. *Irish Times*, 3 June 1977.
82. *Irish Times*, 2 June 1977.
83. Dwyer, *Nice Fellow*.
84. Brian Farrell and Maurice Manning, 'The election,' in Penniman, *Ireland at the Polls*.
85. Dwyer, *Nice Fellow*.
86. *Irish Times*,15 June 1977.
87. Brian Farrell and Maurice Manning, 'The election,' in Penniman, *Ireland at the Polls*.
88. *Irish Times*, 13 June 1977.
89. Dwyer, *Nice Fellow*.
90. Browne and Farrell, *The Magill Book of Irish Politics*.
91. Dunlop, *Yes, Taoiseach*.
92. Browne and Farrell, *The Magill Book of Irish Politics*.
93. *Irish Times*, 18 June 1977.
94. Browne and Farrell, *The Magill Book of Irish Politics*.
95. *Irish Times*, 20 June 1977.
96. Dwyer, *Nice Fellow*.
97. Browne and Farrell, *The Magill Book of Irish Politics*.
98. Browne and Farrell, *The Magill Book of Irish Politics*.
99. Arnold, *What Kind of Country*.
100. Browne and Farrell, *The Magill Book of Irish Politics*.
101. Brown, *Ireland: A Social and Cultural History*.
102. Coogan, *Ireland in the Twentieth Century*.
103. Joyce and Murtagh, *Blind Justice*.

104. Browne and Farrell, *The Magill Book of Irish Politics.*
105. O'Byrnes, *Hiding Behind a Face.*
106. O'Byrnes, *Hiding Behind a Face.*
107. Gallagher, *The Irish Labour Party in Transition.*
108. Gallagher, *The Irish Labour Party in Transition.*
109. *Irish Times,* 4 October 1977.
110. Jacobsen, *Chasing Progress in the Irish Republic.*
111. *Magill,* December 1977.
112. *Magill,* December 1977.
113. *Magill,* December 1977.
114. *Irish Times,* 14 October 1977.
115. Jacobsen, *Chasing Progress in the Irish Republic.*
116. *Irish Times,* 14 October 1977.
117. *Irish Times,* 14 November 1977.
118. *Irish Times,* 21 November 1977.
119. *Irish Times,* 28 November 1977.
120. *Irish Times,* 28 November 1977.
121. *Irish Times,* 29 November 1977.
122. *Magill,* December 1977.
123. *Irish Times,* 1 April 1977.
124. *Irish Times,* 2 July 1977.
125. *Irish Times,* 2 July 1977.
126. McNamara and Mooney, *Women in Parliament.*
127. *Magill,* November 1977.
128. *Magill,* November 1977.
129. Corless, *Party Nation.*
130. *Magill,* December 1977.
131. Waters, *Race of Angels.*
132. Fanning, *The Quest for Modern Ireland.*
133. *Crane Bag,* Spring 1977.
134. *Crane Bag,* Spring 1977.
135. Sheehan, *Irish Television Drama.*
136. McCabe, *King of the Castle.*
137. Sheehan, *Irish Television Drama.*
138. Sheehan, *Irish Television Drama.*
139. Murphy, *Conversations on a Homecoming.*
140. Sheehan, *Irish Television Drama.*
141. Sheehan, *Irish Television Drama.*
142. *Irish Times,* 22 August 1977.
143. *Irish Times,* 22 August 1977.
144. Radiators, *Cockles and Mussels* (CD), notes, 1995.

145. Radiators, *Cockles and Mussels* (CD), notes, 1995.

146. *Irish Times,* 22 August 1977.

147. *Irish Times,* 22 August 1977.

148. *Irish Times,* 22 August 1977.

149. *Irish Times,* 22 August 1977.

150. Humphries, *Dublin v. Kerry.*

151. Holland and McDonald, INLA.

152. Holland and McDonald, INLA.

153. Holland and McDonald, INLA.

154. Holland and McDonald, INLA.

155. Patterson, *The Politics of Illusion.*

Chapter 7: Boom boom boom boom (p. 139–169)

1. *Irish Times,* 28 December 1978.

2. *Irish Times,* 28 December 1978.

3. *Irish Times,* 28 December 1978.

4. *Irish Times,* 15 December 1978.

5. Jacobsen, *Chasing Progress in the Irish Republic.*

6. *Magill,* December 1978.

7. *Irish Times,* 18 October 1978.

8. Dwyer, *Nice Fellow.*

9. Central Statistics Office.

10. Lee, *Ireland, 1912–1985.*

11. *Magill,* April 1978.

12. *Magill,* July 1978.

13. *Magill,* July 1978.

14. Central Statistics Office.

15. NUI, Cork, Centre for Migration Studies.

16. *Irish Times,* 25 September 1978.

17. Heffernan, *Wood Quay.*

18. McDonald, *The Destruction of Dublin.*

19. McDonald, *The Destruction of Dublin.*

20. Heffernan, *Wood Quay.*

21. Heffernan, *Wood Quay.*

22. Heffernan, *Wood Quay.*

23. Heffernan, *Wood Quay.*

24. Heffernan, *Wood Quay.*

25. Heffernan, *Wood Quay.*

26. Heffernan, *Wood Quay.*

27. Heffernan, *Wood Quay.*

28. *Irish Times,* 9 September 1978.

29. Heffernan, *Wood Quay.*
30. McDonald, *The Destruction of Dublin.*
31. *Irish Times,* 20 February 1978.
32. *Irish Times,* 22 February 1978.
33. *Irish Times,* 28 December 1978.
34. *Irish Times,* 6 October 1978.
35. *Irish Times,* 26 April 1978.
36. Moore, *One Voice.*
37. *Irish Times,* 22 August 1978.
38. *Irish Times,* 9 May 1978.
39. *Irish Times,* 9 May 1978.
40. *Irish Times,* 18 April 1978.
41. *Irish Times,* 20 April 1978.
42. *Irish Times,* 20 April 1978.
43. Browne and Farrell, *The Magill Book of Irish Politics.*
44. *Irish Times,* 27 October 1978.
45. *Irish Times,* 20 December 1978.
46. *Irish Times,* 26 April 1978.
47. *Irish Times,* 26 April 1978.
48. *Magill,* October 1978.
49. *Magill,* October 1978.
50. *Magill,* October 1978.
51. *Magill,* October 1978.
52. *Magill,* October 1978.
53. *Irish Times,* 20 April 1978.
54. *Magill,* October 1978.
55. *Magill,* October 1978.
56. McVerry, *The Meaning Is in the Shadows.*
57. McVerry, *The Meaning Is in the Shadows.*
58. *Irish Times,* 29 July 1978.
59. *Irish Times,* 29 July 1978.
60. *Irish Times,* 29 July 1978.
61. *Irish Times,* 29 July 1978.
62. *Irish Times,* 29 July 1978.
63. *Irish Times,* 28 December 1978.
64. Bermingham and Ó Cuanaigh, *Alone Again.*
65. Bermingham and Ó Cuanaigh, *Alone Again.*
66. Bermingham and Ó Cuanaigh, *Alone Again.*
67. Bermingham and Ó Cuanaigh, *Alone Again.*
68. Brian Dillon, Lancelot O'Brien and Donal O'Mahony, 'Poverty and housing,' in Kennedy, *One Million Poor.*

69. Brian Dillon, Lancelot O'Brien and Donal O'Mahony, 'Poverty and housing,' in Kennedy, *One Million Poor.*

70. Robbie Gilligan, 'Poverty and old people,' in Kennedy, *One Million Poor.*

71. Bermingham and Ó Cuanaigh, *Alone Again.*

72. Bermingham and Ó Cuanaigh, *Alone Again.*

73. Alone, at *alone.ie.*

74. Brian Dillon, Lancelot O'Brien and Donal O'Mahony, 'Poverty and housing,' in Kennedy, *One Million Poor.*

75. Brian Dillon, Lancelot O'Brien and Donal O'Mahony, 'Poverty and housing,' in Kennedy, *One Million Poor.*

76. Dunn, *No Tigers in Africa!*

77. *Irish Times,* 23 January 1978.

78. *Magill,* February 1978.

79. *Irish Times,* 12 May 2009.

80. *Magill,* February 1978.

81. *Magill,* February 1978.

82. *Irish Times,* 24 January 1978.

83. *Irish Times,* 11 April 1978.

84. *Irish Times,* 15 July and 14 September 1978.

85. *Irish Times,* 4 March 1978.

86. *Irish Times,* 7 September 1978.

87. *Irish Times,* 2 November 1978.

88. *Irish Times,* 24 August 1978.

89. *Irish Times,* 3 January 1978.

90. *Irish Times,* 6 February 1978.

91. *Irish Times,* 14 January 1978.

92. Waters, *Race of Angels.*

93. Dunphy, *The Unforgettable Fire.*

94. *Irish Times,* 15 July 1978.

95. *Irish Times,* 15 July 1978.

96. *Irish Times,* 7 October 1978.

97. *Irish Times,* 20 January 1978.

98. *Magill,* February 1978.

99. Coogan, *Ireland in the Twentieth Century.*

100. Dunlop, *Yes, Taoiseach.*

101. Dunlop, *Yes, Taoiseach.*

102. *Magill,* February 1978.

103. *Magill,* February 1978.

104. Coogan, *Ireland in the Twentieth Century.*

105. *Magill,* February 1978.

106. Kerrigan and Brennan, *This Great Little Nation.*

107. Kerrigan and Brennan, *This Great Little Nation.*
108. Kerrigan and Brennan, *This Great Little Nation.*
109. Dunne and Kerrigan, *Round Up the Usual Suspects.*
110. Joyce and Murtagh, *Blind Justice.*
111. *Irish Times,* 2 December 1978.
112. Joyce and Murtagh, *Blind Justice.*
113. *Irish Times,* 18 January 1978.
114. *Irish Times,* 18 January 1978.
115. *Irish Times,* 18 January 1978.
116. Taylor, *Beating the Terrorists?*
117. Taylor, *Beating the Terrorists?*
118. Whitehead, *The Writing on the Wall.*
119. Moloney, *A Secret History of the* IRA.
120. Curtis, *Ireland: The Propaganda War.*
121. *Irish Times,* 11 March 1978.
122. *Irish Times,* 10 March 1978.
123. *Irish Times,* 10 March 1978.
124. *Irish Times,* 9 March 1978.
125. *Irish Times,* 13 March 1978.
126. *Irish Times,* 13 March 1978.
127. Moloney, *A Secret History of the* IRA.
128. Bishop and Mallie, *The Provisional* IRA.
129. *Irish Times,* 18 February 1978.
130. Sutton Index of Deaths at the CAIN Project (*cain.ulst.ac.uk/sutton*).
131. English, *Armed Struggle.*
132. *Magill,* January 1978.
133. O'Rawe, *Blanketmen.*
134. Coogan, *On the Blanket.*
135. Coogan, *On the Blanket.*
136. Coogan, *On the Blanket.*
137. *Irish Times,* 5 December 1978.
138. Lee, *Ireland, 1912–1985.*
139. *Irish Times,* 14 October 1978.
140. *Irish Times,* 28 December 1978.
141. *Irish Times,* 17 October 1978.
142. Dwyer, *Nice Fellow.*
143. Dwyer, *Nice Fellow.*
144. Dwyer, *Nice Fellow.*
145. *Irish Times,* 28 December 1978.
146. *Irish Times,* 28 December 1978.
147. *Irish Times,* 28 December 1978.

148. *Irish Times,* 28 December 1978.

149. Faulkner, *As I Saw It.*

150. Foster, *Luck and the Irish.*

151. *Irish Times,* 28 December 1978.

152. Sheehan, *Irish Television Drama.*

153. Sheehan, *Irish Television Drama.*

154. *Irish Times,* 7 March 1978.

155. *Irish Times,* 25 February 1978.

156. Sheehan, *Irish Television Drama.*

157. Kerrigan and Brennan, *This Great Little Nation.*

158. *Irish Times,* 3 March 1978.

159. *Irish Times,* 7 March 1978.

160. *Irish Times,* 7 March 1978.

161. *Irish Times,* 3 March 1978.

162. *Irish Times,* 25 February 1978.

163. *Irish Times,* 25 February 1978.

164. Kevin Rockett, 'History, politics and Irish cinema,' in *Cinema and Ireland.*

165. Kevin Rockett, 'History, politics and Irish cinema,' in *Cinema and Ireland.*

166. *Irish Times,* 26 October 1978.

167. *Irish Times,* 26 October 1978.

168. *Irish Times,* 21 April 1978.

169. *Irish Times,* 21 April 1978.

170. *Irish Times,* 11 March and 21 April 1978.

171. *Irish Times,* 17 July 1978.

172. *Irish Times,* 17 July 1978.

173. *Irish Times,* 17 July 1978.

174. *Magill,* July 1978.

175. *Magill,* July 1978.

176. Corless, GUBU *Nation.*

177. *Irish Times,* 18 October 1978.

178. Dwyer, *Nice Fellow.*

179. *Irish Times,* 14 October 1978.

180. *Magill,* December 1978.

Chapter 8: Things fall apart (p. 170–193)

1. *The Pope in Ireland.*

2. *Irish Times,* 2 October 1979.

3. *Irish Times,* 1 October 1979.

4. Broderick, *Fall from Grace.*

5. *The Pope in Ireland.*

6. *Irish Times,* 1 October 1979.

7. *Magill,* October 1979.
8. *Three Days in September.*
9. Scallon, *All Kinds of Everything.*
10. *Irish Times,* 1 October 1979.
11. *Irish Times,* 1 October 1979.
12. *Irish Times,* 1 October 1979.
13. Foster, *Luck and the Irish.*
14. Patterson, *Ireland since 1939.*
15. *The Pope in Ireland.*
16. Keogh, *Twentieth-Century Ireland.*
17. *Three Days in September.*
18. Raftery and O'Sullivan, *Suffer the Little Children.*
19. Raftery and O'Sullivan, *Suffer the Little Children.*
20. *Magill,* January 1979.
21. Foster, *Luck and the Irish.*
22. Sweetman, *On Our Backs.*
23. Sweetman, *On Our Backs.*
24. *Irish Times,* 3 October 1979.
25. *Three Days in September.*
26. Sutton Index of Deaths at the CAIN Project (*cain.ulst.ac.uk/sutton*).
27. Whitehead, *The Writing on the Wall.*
28. Foster, *Luck and the Irish.*
29. *Irish Times,* 2 February 1979.
30. *Irish Times,* 9 February 1979.
31. *Irish Times,* 9 February 1979.
32. Lee, *Ireland, 1912–1985.*
33. *Irish Times,* 23 February 1979.
34. *Irish Times,* 28 February 1979.
35. *Irish Times,* 1 March 1979.
36. Dwyer, *Nice Fellow.*
37. *Irish Times,* 21 March 1979.
38. *Irish Times,* 21 March 1979.
39. Allen, *Fianna Fáil and Irish Labour.*
40. *Irish Times,* 25 April 1979.
41. *Irish Times,* 25 April 1979.
42. *Irish Times,* 26 July 1979.
43. *Irish Times,* 26 July 1979
44. Fleming and O'Day, *Longman Handbook of Modern Irish History.*
45. *Irish Times,* 17 February 1979.
46. *Irish Times,* 17 February 1979.
47. *Irish Times,* 17 February 1979.

48. *Irish Times,* 19 February 1979.

49. *Irish Times,* 18 May 1979.

50. *Irish Times,* 10 May 1979.

51. Allen, *Fianna Fáil and Irish Labour.*

52. *Irish Times,* 26 June 1979.

53. *Irish Times,* 26 May 1979.

54. *Irish Times,* 23 November 1979.

55. *Irish Times,* 28 December 1979.

56. *Irish Times,* 11 December 1979.

57. *Irish Times,* 11 December 1979.

58. *Irish Times,* 11 December 1979.

59. Lee, *Ireland, 1912–1985.*

60. Lee, *Ireland, 1912–1985.*

61. Keogh, *Jack Lynch.*

62. *Irish Times,* 8 May 1979.

63. *Irish Times,* 30 May 1979.

64. Dwyer, *Nice Fellow.*

65. *Irish Times,* 21 March 1979.

66. Bew et al., *The Dynamics of Irish Politics.*

67. Dwyer, *Nice Fellow.*

68. *Irish Times,* 10 September 1979.

69. *Irish Times,* 10 September 1979.

70. *Irish Times,* 10 September 1979.

72. *Irish Times,* 10 September 1979.

73. *Irish Times,* 13 September 1979.

74. *Irish Times,* 17 September 1979.

75. *Irish Times,* 29 September 1979.

76. *Irish Times,* 29 September 1979.

77. *Irish Times,* 29 September 1979.

78. *Irish Times,* 29 September 1979.

79. Walsh, *Patrick Hillery.*

80. Walsh, *Patrick Hillery.*

81. Walsh, *Patrick Hillery.*

82. Walsh, *Patrick Hillery.*

83. Walsh, *Patrick Hillery.*

84. Walsh, *Patrick Hillery.*

85. Moloney, *A Secret History of the* IRA.

86. Arnold, *What Kind of Country.*

87. Kelley, *The Longest War.*

88. Keogh, *Jack Lynch.*

89. Bishop and Mallie, *The Provisional* IRA.

90. Bishop and Mallie, *The Provisional IRA*.
91. English, *Armed Struggle*.
92. *Irish Times*, 24 November 1979.
93. Coogan, *Ireland in the Twentieth Century*.
94. Dunlop, *Yes, Taoiseach*.
95. *Magill*, November 1979.
96. Dwyer, *Nice Fellow*.
97. Dwyer, *Nice Fellow*.
98. Dunlop, *Yes, Taoiseach*.
99. Dwyer, *Nice Fellow*.
100. Dwyer, *Nice Fellow*.
101. Dwyer, *Nice Fellow*.
102. Dwyer, *Nice Fellow*.
103. Dwyer, *Nice Fellow*.
104. Browne and Farrell, *The Magill Book of Irish Politics*.
105. Collins, *The Power Game*.
106. Browne and Farrell, *The Magill Book of Irish Politics*.
107. Browne and Farrell, *The Magill Book of Irish Politics*.
108. Browne and Farrell, *The Magill Book of Irish Politics*.
109. *Irish Times*, 21 March 1979.
110. *Magill*, May 1979.
111. Keogh, *Twentieth-Century Ireland*.
112. Keogh, *Twentieth-Century Ireland*.
113. O'Reilly, *Masterminds of the Right*.
114. *Irish Times*, 29 June 1979.
115. O'Reilly, *Masterminds of the Right*.
116. *Irish Times*, 2 March 1979.
117. *Irish Times*, 2 March 1979.
118. *Irish Times*, 1 March 1979.
119. *Irish Times*, 30 March 1979.
120. O'Reilly, *Masterminds of the Right*.
121. O'Reilly, *Masterminds of the Right*.
122. Sweetman, *On Our Backs*.
123. 'Haughey' (television documentary series).
124. 'Haughey' (television documentary series).
125. Dunlop, *Yes, Taoiseach*.
126. Collins, *The Power Game*.
127. Coogan, *Ireland in the Twentieth Century*.
128. Collins, *The Power Game*.
129. Browne and Farrell, *The Magill Book of Irish Politics*.
130. Keogh, *Twentieth-Century Ireland*.

131. *Irish Times,* 10 October 1979.
132. *Irish Times,* 10 October 1979.
133. *Irish Times,* 10 October 1979.
134. O'Morain, *Access to Justice for All.*

Chapter 9: The totality of relationships (p. 194–220)

1. *Irish Times,* 10 January 1980.
2. *Irish Times,* 15 January 1980.
3. *Irish Times,* 31 December 1980.
4. Collins, *The Power Game.*
5. Kerrigan and Brennan, *This Great Little Nation.*
6. 'Haughey' (television documentary series).
7. *Irish Times,* 10 January 1980.
8. *Irish Times,* 10 January 1980.
9. Fleming and O'Day, *Longman Handbook of Modern Irish History.*
10. *Irish Times,* 31 December 1980.
11. *Irish Times,* 31 December 1980.
12. *Irish Times,* 31 December 1980.
13. *Irish Times,* 31 December 1980.
14. Lee, *Ireland, 1912–1985.*
15. *Irish Times,* 31 December 1980.
16. *Irish Times,* 20 June 1980.
17. *Irish Times,* 23 January 1980.
18. *Irish Times,* 23 January 1980.
19. *Irish Times,* 28 February 1980.
20. *Irish Times,* 28 February 1980.
21. *Irish Times,* 31 December 1980.
22. Downey, *Lenihan.*
23. *Irish Times,* 31 December 1980.
24. *Irish Times,* 31 December 1980.
25. *Magill,* August 1980.
26. *Irish Times,* 9 July 1980.
27. *Irish Times,* 10 July 1980.
28. *Magill,* August 1980.
29. *Irish Times,* 11 July 1980.
30. *Magill,* August 1980.
31. *Magill,* May 1980.
32. *Magill,* June 1980.
33. *Magill,* December 1980.
34. *Magill,* July 1980.
35. *Magill,* July 1980.

36. *Magill,* December 1980.
37. *Magill,* July 1980.
38. O'Malley, *The Uncivil Wars.*
39. *Irish Times,* 22 May 1980.
40. *Irish Times,* 22 May 1980.
41. *Irish Times,* 22 May 1980.
42. *Irish Times,* 2 August 1980.
43. Coogan, *On the Blanket.*
44. *Cork Examiner,* 2 September 1980.
45. Paddy Logue in Morrison, *Hunger Strike.*
46. McCafferty, *The Best of Nell.*
47. McCafferty, *The Best of Nell.*
48. McCafferty, *The Best of Nell.*
49. *Irish Times,* 5 September 1980.
50. *Magill,* July 1980.
51. Holland and McDonald, INLA.
52. Holland and McDonald, INLA.
53. Holland and McDonald, INLA.
54. Dillon, *The Dirty War.*
55. Dunne and Kerrigan, *Round Up the Usual Suspects.*
56. Dunne and Kerrigan, *Round Up the Usual Suspects.*
57. McGarry, *While Justice Slept.*
58. McGarry, *While Justice Slept.*
59. Walsh, *The Final Beat.*
60. Walsh, *The Final Beat.*
61. Walsh, *The Final Beat.*
62. Walsh, *The Final Beat.*
63. *Irish Times,* 19 April 1980.
64. *Irish Times,* 19 April 1980.
65. Downey, *Lenihan.*
66. *Irish Times,* 19 April 1980.
67. Downey, *Lenihan.*
68. Downey, *Lenihan.*
69. *Irish Times,* 26 July 1980.
70. *Irish Times,* 26 July 1980.
71. *Irish Times,* 9 January 1980.
72. *Irish Times,* 9 January 1980.
73. *Hot Press,* 18 June 1987.
74. *Irish Times,* 13 May 1980.
75. *Irish Times,* 27 June 1980.
76. *Irish Times,* 27 June 1980.

77. *Irish Times,* 11 October 1980.

78. *Irish Times,* 11 October 1980.

79. Freedman, *The Cities of David.*

80. Joni Crone, 'Lesbians: The lavender women of Ireland,' in O'Carroll and Collins, *Lesbian and Gay Visions of Ireland.*

81. *Irish Times,* 12 December 1980.

82. *Irish Times,* 22 April 1980.

83. Betty Purcell, 'Interview with Mary Robinson and Mary McAleese,' in *Crane Bag,* vol. 4, no. 1, 1980.

84. O'Reilly, *Masterminds of the Right.*

85. *Irish Times,* 9 August 1980.

86. O'Reilly, *Masterminds of the Right.*

87. O'Reilly, *Masterminds of the Right.*

88. *Irish Times,* 27 September 1980.

89. *Irish Times,* 27 September 1980.

90. *Irish Times,* 29 December 1980.

91. *Irish Times,* 24 April 1980.

92. *Irish Times,* 24 April 1980.

93. *Irish Times,* 31 March 1980.

94. *Irish Times,* 8 October 1980.

95. Eric Binnie, 'Friel and Field Day,' in Harrington, *Modern Irish Drama.*

96. Eric Binnie, 'Friel and Field Day,' in Harrington, *Modern Irish Drama.*

97. Seamus Deane, Introduction, in *The Field Day Anthology of Irish Writing, Volume 3.*

98. O'Malley, *The Uncivil Wars.*

99. *Irish Times,* 9 December 1980.

100. *Irish Times,* 9 December 1980.

101. O'Malley, *The Uncivil Wars.*

102. *Irish Times,* 10 December 1980.

103. *Irish Times,* 11 December 1980.

104. *Irish Times,* 12 December 1980.

105. *Irish Times,* 12 December 1980.

106. O'Malley, *The Uncivil Wars.*

107. McKittrick and McVea, *Making Sense of the Troubles.*

108. Taylor, *Provos.*

109. McKittrick and McVea, *Making Sense of the Troubles.*

110. McKittrick and McVea, *Making Sense of the Troubles.*

111. *Irish Times,* 29 October 1980.

112. *Irish Times,* 17 November 1980.

113. *Irish Times,* 17 November 1980.

114. *Irish Times,* 17 November 1980.

115. *Irish Times,* 17 November 1980.
116. *Irish Times,* 17 November 1980.
117. *Irish Times,* 11 December 1980.
118. *Irish Times,* 3 November 1980.
119. Smith, *The Quest for Power.*
120. *Irish Times,* 4 November 1980.
121. *Irish Times,* 10 November 1980.
122. *Irish Times,* 10 November 1980.
123. *Irish Times,* 4 November 1980.
124. Taylor, *Provos.*
125. Moloney, *A Secret History of the* IRA.
126. Moloney, *A Secret History of the* IRA.
127. *Irish Times,* 19 December 1980.
128. O'Malley, *Biting at the Grave.*

Chapter 10: Death traps (p. 221–250)
1. *Irish Times,* 6 July 1982.
2. Fetherstonhaugh and McCullagh, *They Never Came Home.*
3. Fetherstonhaugh and McCullagh, *They Never Came Home.*
4. Fetherstonhaugh and McCullagh, *They Never Came Home.*
5. *Irish Times,* 16 February 1981.
6. *Irish Times,* 16 February 1981.
7. *Irish Times,* 16 February 1981.
8. *Irish Times,* 16 February 1981.
9. *Irish Times,* 16 February 1981.
10. Fetherstonhaugh and McCullagh, *They Never Came Home.*
11. *Irish Times,* 16 February 1981.
12. Fetherstonhaugh and McCullagh, *They Never Came Home.*
13. *Irish Times,* 6 July 1982.
14. *Irish Times,* 6 July 1982.
15. Fetherstonhaugh and McCullagh, *They Never Came Home.*
16. Fetherstonhaugh and McCullagh, *They Never Came Home.*
17. *Irish Times,* 16 February 1981.
18. *Irish Times,* 1 May 1981.
19. Fetherstonhaugh and McCullagh, *They Never Came Home.*
20. Fetherstonhaugh and McCullagh, *They Never Came Home.*
21. Fetherstonhaugh and McCullagh, *They Never Came Home.*
22. Fetherstonhaugh and McCullagh, *They Never Came Home.*
23. Arnold, *Haughey.*
24. *Irish Times,* 6 February 1981.
25. *Irish Times,* 10 February 1981.

26. *Irish Times,* 25 March 1981.

27. *Irish Times,* 17 April 1981.

28. *Irish Times,* 17 February 1983.

29. *Irish Times,* 17 February 1983.

30. *Irish Times,* 11 April 1981.

31. *Irish Times,* 11 April 1981.

32. *Irish Times,* 21 April 1981.

33. Clarke, *Broadening the Battlefield.*

34. Clarke, *Broadening the Battlefield.*

35. Campbell, *Nor Meekly Serve My Time.*

36. *Irish Times,* 4 May 1981.

37. *Irish Times,* 5 May 1981.

38. *Irish Times,* 8 May 1981.

39. *Irish Times,* 8 May 1981.

40. *Irish Times,* 6 May 1981.

41. *Irish Times,* 8 May 1981.

42. *Irish Times,* 9 May 1981.

43. *Irish Times,* 11 May 1981.

44. *Irish Times,* 16 May 1981.

45. *Irish Times,* 6 May 1981.

46. *Irish Times,* 14 May 1981.

47. *Irish Times,* 20 July 1981.

48. *Irish Times,* 20 July 1981.

49. *Irish Times,* 7 August 1981.

50. *Irish Times,* 7 August 1981.

51. *Irish Times,* 7 August 1981.

52. English, *Armed Struggle.*

53. English, *Armed Struggle.*

54. *Irish Times,* 1 June 1981.

55. *Irish Times,* 6 June 1981.

56. Browne and Farrell, *The Magill Book of Irish Politics.*

57. Browne and Farrell, *The Magill Book of Irish Politics.*

58. *Magill,* 14 June 1981.

59. *Irish Times,* 11 June 1981.

60. Campbell, *Nor Meekly Serve My Time.*

61. *Irish Times,* 3 August 1981.

62. *Irish Times,* 3 August 1981.

63. *Irish Times,* 5 August 1981.

64. *Magill,* August, 1981.

65. Buckley, *Memory Ireland.*

66. *Irish Times,* 8 May 1981.

67. Buckley, *Memory Ireland.*
68. *Irish Times,* 7 May 1981.
69. *Irish Times,* 25 May 1981.
70. *Coogan, Ireland in the Twentieth Century.*
71. *Irish Times,* 19 March 1981.
72. *Irish Times,* 24 March 1981.
73. *Irish Times,* 6 June 1981.
74. *Irish Times,* 30 June 1981.
75. *Irish Times,* 30 June 1981.
76. *Magill,* 31 May 1981.
77. *Irish Times,* 25 May 1981.
78. *Irish Times,* 25 May 1981.
79. *Irish Times,* 9 June 1981.
80. *Irish Times,* 9 June 1981.
81. *Irish Times,* 29 May 1981.
82. *Irish Times,* 30 May 1981.
83. *Irish Times,* 1 June 1981.
84. *Irish Times,* 29 May 1981.
85. *Irish Times,* 1 June 1981.
86. Gallagher, *The Irish Labour Party in Transition.*
87. Gallagher, *The Irish Labour Party in Transition.*
88. Gallagher, *The Irish Labour Party in Transition.*
89. O'Byrnes, *Hiding Behind a Face.*
90. O'Reilly, *Masterminds of the Right.*
91. O'Reilly, *Masterminds of the Right.*
92. O'Byrnes, *Hiding Behind a Face.*
93. *Magill,* February 1981.
94. *Irish Times,* 6 June 1981.
95. *Irish Times,* 29 May 1981.
96. *Irish Times,* 11 June 1981
97. Peter Mair, 'Party organization, vote management and candidate selection: Toward the nationalization of electoral strategy in Ireland,' in Penniman, *Ireland at the Polls.*
98. *Magill,* January, 1981.
99. *Irish Times,* 13 June 1981.
100. *Irish Times,* 13 June 1981.
101. Hanley and Millar, *The Lost Revolution.*
102. Browne and Farrell, *The Magill Book of Irish Politics.*
103. *Irish Times,* 16 June 1981.
104. Gallagher, *The Irish Labour Party in Transition.*
105. Gallagher, *The Irish Labour Party in Transition.*

106. O'Byrnes, *Hiding Behind a Face.*
107. O'Byrnes, *Hiding Behind a Face.*
108. Brian Farrell, 'The context of three elections,' in Penniman and Farrell, *Ireland at the Polls.*
109. O'Byrnes, *Hiding Behind a Face.*
110. Gallagher, *The Irish Labour Party in Transition.*
111. Gallagher, *The Irish Labour Party in Transition.*
112. Jacobsen, *Chasing Progress in the Irish Republic.*
113. O'Malley, *The Uncivil Wars.*
114. O'Byrnes, *Hiding Behind a Face.*
115. Browne and Farrell, *The Magill Book of Irish Politics.*
116. *Magill,* December 1981.
117. O'Malley, *The Uncivil Wars.*
118. O'Malley, *The Uncivil Wars.*
119. Rafter, *Martin Mansergh.*
120. *Magill,* May 1981.
121. Arnold, *What Kind of Country.*
122. *Magill,* Christmas 1981.
123. Gallagher, *The Irish Labour Party in Transition.*
124. *Magill,* Christmas 1981.
125. Flynn and Yeates, *Smack.*
126. Flynn and Yeates, *Smack.*
127. Flynn and Yeates, *Smack.*
128. Flynn and Yeates, *Smack.*
129. Flynn and Yeates, *Smack.*
130. Flynn and Yeates, *Smack.*
131. Flynn and Yeates, *Smack.*
132. Geoffrey Dean et al., 'The opiate epidemic in Dublin, 1979–1983,' *Irish Medical Journal,* 78 (4), April 1985, p. 107–10.
133. Flynn and Yeates, *Smack.*
134. *Hot Press,* 24 October 1981.
135. *Hot Press,* 1 October 1982.
136. Fetherstonhaugh and McCullagh, *They Never Came Home.*
137. Moore, *One Voice.*

Chapter 11: Gubu Roi (p. 251–279)

1. *Irish Times,* 18 August 1982.
2. *Irish Times,* 24 August 1982.
3. *Irish Times,* 28 January 1982.
4. *Irish Times,* 28 January 1982.
5. *Irish Times,* 28 January 1982.

6.   Smith, *Garret the Enigma.*
7.   Smith, *Garret the Enigma.*
8.   Keogh, *Twentieth-Century Ireland.*
9.   Arnold, *Haughey.*
10. Arnold, *Haughey.*
11. Keogh, *Twentieth-Century Ireland.*
12. *Magill,* February 1982.
13. Lee, *Ireland, 1912–1985.*
14. *Magill,* February 1982.
15. John Bowman, 'Media coverage of the Irish elections, 1981–1982,' in Penniman and Farrell, *Ireland at the Polls.*
16. Brian Farrell, 'The context of three elections,' in Penniman and Farrell, *Ireland at the Polls.*
17. *Irish Times,* 28 January 1982.
18. *Irish Times,* 15 February 1982.
19. Joseph O'Malley, 'Campaigns, manifestoes and party finances,' in Penniman and Farrell, *Ireland at the Polls.*
20. *Irish Times,* 16 February 1982.
21. Richard Sinnott, 'Voters, issues and the party system,' in Penniman and Farrell, *Ireland at the Polls.*
22. Arnold, *Haughey.*
23. Arnold, *Haughey.*
24. *Irish Times,* 4 February 1982.
25. *Irish Times,* 9 February 1982.
26. *Irish Times,* 17 February 1982.
27. *Irish Times,* 17 February 1982.
28. *Irish Times,* 17 February 1982.
29. Sunday Times, 18 June 2006.
30. *Irish Times,* 20 February 1982.
31. *Irish Times,* 19 February 1982.
32. Joyce and Murtagh, *The Boss.*
33. *Irish Times,* 21 April 1982.
34. Joyce and Murtagh, *The Boss.*
35. Joyce and Murtagh, *The Boss.*
36. Joyce and Murtagh, *The Boss.*
37. *Irish Times,* 19 February 1982.
38. *Irish Times,* 19 February 1982.
39. *Irish Times,* 25 February 1982.
40. *Irish Times,* 25 February 1982.
41. *Irish Times,* 25 February 1982.
42. Joyce and Murtagh, *The Boss.*

43. Joyce and Murtagh, *The Boss.*
44. *Irish Times,* 26 February 1982.
45. Joyce and Murtagh, *The Boss.*
46. Joyce and Murtagh, *The Boss.*
47. *Irish Times,* 26 February 1982.
48. *Magill,* 22 February 1982.
49. *Magill,* March, 1982.
50. Lyder, *Pushers Out.*
51. *Magill,* April, 1982.
52. *Magill,* March, 1982.
53. Joyce and Murtagh, *The Boss.*
54. *Magill,* March, 1982.
55. *Irish Times,* 10 March 1982.
56. *Irish Times,* 9 March 1982.
57. Hanley and Millar, *The Lost Revolution.*
58. *Irish Times,* 10 March1982.
59. *Irish Times,* 10 March 1982.
60. *Irish Times,* 10 March 1982.
61. *Irish Times,* 10 March 1982.
62. *Magill,* March 1982.
63. Smith, *Garret the Enigma.*
64. Lee, *Ireland, 1912–1985.*
65. O'Byrnes, *Hiding Behind a Face.*
66. O'Byrnes, *Hiding Behind a Face.*
67. Arnold, *Haughey.*
68. *Irish Times,* 4 May 1982.
69. *Irish Times,* 5 May 1982.
70. *Irish Times,* 7 May 1982.
71. *Irish Times,* 19 May 1982.
72. *Irish Times,* 18 May 1982.
73. *Irish Times,* 19 May 1982.
74. *Irish Times,* 25 May 1982.
75. *Irish Times,* 6 May 1982.
76. Young, *One of Us.*
77. *Magill,* June 1982.
78. *Irish Times,* 10 March 1982.
79. Joyce and Murtagh, *The Boss.*
80. Joyce and Murtagh, *The Boss.*
81. Andrews, *Kingstown Republican.*
82. Joyce and Murtagh, *The Boss.*
83. Joyce and Murtagh, *The Boss.*

84. Joyce and Murtagh, *The Boss.*
85. Joyce and Murtagh, *The Boss.*
86. Joyce and Murtagh, *The Boss.*
87. Joyce and Murtagh, *The Boss.*
88. Joyce and Murtagh, *The Boss.*
89. Joyce and Murtagh, *The Boss.*
90. Joyce and Murtagh, *The Boss.*
91. Joyce and Murtagh, *The Boss.*
92. Joyce and Murtagh, *The Boss.*
93. Joyce and Murtagh, *The Boss.*
94. Joyce and Murtagh, *The Boss.*
95. Joyce and Murtagh, *The Boss.*
96. Joyce and Murtagh, *The Boss.*
97. Joyce and Murtagh, *The Boss.*
98. Joyce and Murtagh, *The Boss.*
99. Joyce and Murtagh, *The Boss.*
100. Joyce and Murtagh, *The Boss.*
101. Joyce and Murtagh, *The Boss.*
102. *Irish Times,* 4 October 1982.
103. *Irish Times,* 4 October 1982.
104. Andrews, *Kingstown Republican.*
105. O'Byrnes, *Hiding Behind a Face.*
106. Joyce and Murtagh, *The Boss.*
107. Arnold, *What Kind of Country.*
108. O'Byrnes, *Hiding Behind a Face.*
109. FitzGerald, *All in a Life.*
110. Joseph O'Malley, 'Campaigns, manifestoes and party finances,' in Penniman and Farrell, *Ireland at the Polls.*
111. O'Byrnes, *Hiding Behind a Face.*
112. Arnold, *What Kind of Country.*
113. O'Byrnes, *Hiding Behind a Face.*
114. John Bowman, 'Media coverage of the Irish elections of 1981–1982,' in Penniman and Farrell, *Ireland at the Polls.*
115. Joseph O'Malley, 'Campaigns, manifestoes and party finances,' in Penniman and Farrell, *Ireland at the Polls.*
116. O'Byrnes, *Hiding Behind a Face.*
117. Collins, *Spring and the Labour Story.*
118. O'Byrnes, *Hiding Behind a Face.*
119. Carswell, *Something Rotten.*
120. *Irish Times,* 1 May 1982.
121. *Irish Times,* 1 May 1982.

122. *Irish Times,* 1 May 1982.
123. *Irish Times,* 1 May 1982.
124. *Irish Times,* 1 May 1982.
125. *Irish Times,* 1 May 1982.
126. *Irish Times,* 1 May 1982.
127. Central Statistics Office.
128. *Irish Times,* 6 July 1982.
129. *Irish Times,* 6 July 1982.
130. Central Statistics Office.

Chapter 12: The morals of a tomcat (p. 280–305)

1. O'Connor, *A Message from Heaven.*
2. O'Malley, *The Uncivil Wars.*
3. *Magill,* July 1982.
4. *Magill,* July 1982.
5. Commission of Investigation, *Report into the Catholic Archdiocese of Dublin.*
6. Commission of Investigation, *Report into the Catholic Archdiocese of Dublin.*
7. Commission of Investigation, *Report into the Catholic Archdiocese of Dublin.*
8. Commission of Investigation, *Report into the Catholic Archdiocese of Dublin.*
9. Commission of Investigation, *Report into the Catholic Archdiocese of Dublin.*
10. Commission of Investigation, *Report into the Catholic Archdiocese of Dublin.*
11. Murphy et al., *The Ferns Report.*
12. Keogh, *Twentieth-Century Ireland.*
13. O'Reilly, *Masterminds of the Right.*
14. O'Byrnes, *Hiding Behind a Face.*
15. O'Byrnes, *Hiding Behind a Face.*
16. O'Reilly, *Masterminds of the Right.*
17. O'Reilly, *Masterminds of the Right.*
18. O'Byrnes, *Hiding Behind a Face.*
19. O'Reilly, *Masterminds of the Right.*
20. *Irish Times,* 9 February 1983.
21. *Irish Times,* 9 February 1983.
22. *Irish Times,* 5 February 1983.
23. *Irish Times,* 28 April 1983.
24. O'Byrnes, *Hiding Behind a Face.*
25. O'Byrnes, *Hiding Behind a Face.*
26. O'Byrnes, *Hiding Behind a Face.*
27. O'Byrnes, *Hiding Behind a Face.*
28. *Irish Times,* 28 April 1983.
29. O'Byrnes, *Hiding Behind a Face.*
30. *Irish Times,* 28 April 1983.

31. *Magill*, February 1983.
32. *Magill*, February 1983.
33. *Magill*, February 1983.
34. *Magill*, September 1983.
35. *Magill*, September 1983.
36. *Magill*, September 1983.
37. Connolly, *The Irish Women's Movement.*
38. McCafferty, *Nell.*
39. Connolly, *The Irish Women's Movement.*
40. McCafferty, *Nell.*
41. *Sunday Tribune*, 30 August 2006.
42. Connolly, *The Irish Women's Movement.*
43. O'Malley, *The Uncivil Wars.*
44. *Irish Times*, 9 September 1983.
45. Keogh, *Twentieth-Century Ireland.*
46. Keogh, *Twentieth-Century Ireland.*
47. *Magill*, July 1982.
48. Downing, *Most Skilful, Most Devious, Most Cunning.*
49. Andrews, *Kingstown Republican.*
50. Joyce and Murtagh, *The Boss.*
51. *Irish Times*, 21 January 1983.
52. *Irish Times*, 21 January 1983.
53. *Irish Times*, 19 January 1983.
54. *Irish Times*, 21 January 1983.
55. Arnold, *Haughey.*
56. Andrews, *Kingstown Republican.*
57. *Irish Times*, 21 January 1983.
58. Smith, *Charles J. Haughey.*
59. *Irish Times*, 24 January 1983.
60. *Irish Times*, 27 January 1983.
61. *Irish Times*, 28 January 1983.
62. *Magill*, February 1983.
63. *Irish Times*, 29 January 1983.
64. *Irish Times*, 3 February 1983.
65. *Irish Times*, 3 February 1983.
66. *Magill*, February 1983.
67. *Irish Times*, 4 February 1983.
68. Smith, *The Quest for Power.*
69. Joyce and Murtagh, *The Boss.*
70. Smith, *The Quest for Power.*
71. Smith, *The Quest for Power.*

72. Downey, *Lenihan.*
73. Smith, *The Quest for Power.*
74. *Irish Times,* 7 February 1983.
75. *Irish Times,* 21 January 1983.
76. *Irish Times,* 22 January 1983.
77. *Irish Times,* 22 January 1983.
78. *Smith, Charles J. Haughey.*
79. *Irish Times,* 24 January 1983.
80. *Smith, Charles J. Haughey.*
81. Andrews, *Kingstown Republican.*
82. *Smith, Charles J. Haughey.*
83. Andrews, *Kingstown Republican.*
84. Smith, *The Quest for Power.*
85. Keena, *Haughey's Millions.*
86. Keena, *Haughey's Millions.*
87. Keena, *Haughey's Millions.*
88. *Irish Times,* 5 February 1983.
89. *Irish Times,* 11 February 1984.
90. *Irish Times,* 5 February 1983.
91. *Irish Times,* 9 February 1983.
92. Communist Party of Ireland, *Clondalkin: A Workers' Victory.*
93. *Irish Times,* 4 November 1983.
94. *Irish Times,* 25 January 1982.
95. *Irish Times,* 12 November 1983.
96. *Irish Times,* 17 November 1983.
97. *Irish Times,* 10 February 1983.
98. *Irish Times,* 10 February 1983.
99. Collins, *Spring and the Labour Story.*
100. Collins, *Spring and the Labour Story.*
101. O'Byrnes, *Hiding Behind a Face.*
102. O'Byrnes, *Hiding Behind a Face.*
103. Collins, *Spring and the Labour Story.*
104. *Magill,* Christmas 1983.
105. O'Byrnes, *Hiding Behind a Face.*
106. *Magill,* Christmas, 1983.
107. *Irish Times,* 10 February 1983.
108. Howard, *Hostage.*
109. Howard, *Hostage.*
110. *Irish Times,* 5 November 1983.
111. Walsh, *The Final Beat.*
112. Walsh, *The Final Beat.*

113. Walsh, *The Final Beat.*
114. Howard, *Hostage.*
115. Walsh, *The Final Beat.*
116. Howard, *Hostage.*
117. Howard, *Hostage.*
118. Howard, *Hostage.*
119. White, *Ruairí Ó Brádaigh.*
120. White, *Ruairí Ó Brádaigh.*
121. Flynn and Yeates, *Smack.*
122. Flynn and Yeates, *Smack.*
123. Lyder, *Pushers Out.*
124. Lyder, *Pushers Out.*
125. John S. Bradshaw, letter to Dr Geoffrey Dean, at 'National Documentation Centre on Drug Use' (*www.drugsandalcohol.ie*).
126. John S. Bradshaw, letter to Dr Geoffrey Dean, at 'National Documentation Centre on Drug Use' (*www.drugsandalcohol.ie*).
127. O'Donoghue and Richardson, *Pure Murder.*
128. Dean, *The Turnstone.*
129. O'Donoghue and Richardson, *Pure Murder.*
130. O'Donoghue and Richardson, *Pure Murder.*
131. O'Donoghue and Richardson, *Pure Murder.*
132. Flynn and Yeates, *Smack.*
133. Flynn and Yeates, *Smack.*
134. Flynn and Yeates, *Smack.*
135. Flynn and Yeates, *Smack.*
136. Flynn and Yeates, *Smack.*
137. Flynn and Yeates, *Smack.*
138. Flynn and Yeates, *Smack.*
139. Boyd et al., *Out for Ourselves.*
140. *Magill,* February 1983.
141. *Sunday Business Post,* 8 June 2008.
142. *Sunday Business Post,* 8 June 2008.
143. Kerrigan and Brennan, *This Great Little Nation.*
144. Boyd et al., *Out for Ourselves.*
145. Boyd et al., *Out for Ourselves.*
146. Boyd et al., *Out for Ourselves.*
147. Kerrigan and Brennan, *This Great Little Nation.*
148. Kerrigan and Brennan, *This Great Little Nation.*
149. *Irish Times,* 11 September 2008.
150. *New Ross Standard,* 18 September 2008.

Chapter 13: Out out out (p. 306–331)

1. *An Phoblacht*, 22 July 2004.
2. 'Scannal', RTE 1, 20 February 2006.
3. 'Scannal', RTE1, 20 February 2006.
4. *An Phoblacht*, 22 July 2004.
5. At *RTE.ie*, 16 April 2008.
6. Statement by Karen Gearon to United Nations Special Committee against Apartheid, 11 October 1985.
7. *Irish Examiner*, 19 July 2004.
8. Statement by Karen Gearon to United Nations Special Committee against Apartheid, 11 October 1985.
9. Statement by Karen Gearon to United Nations Special Committee against Apartheid, 11 October 1985.
10. Statement by Karen Gearon to United Nations Special Committee against Apartheid, 11 October 1985.
11. *Irish Examiner*, 19 July 2004.
12. *An Phoblacht*, 22 July 2004.
13. *An Phoblacht*, 22 July 2004.
14. O'Brien, *Seeds of Injustice*.
15. O'Brien, *Seeds of Injustice*.
16. O'Brien, *Seeds of Injustice*.
17. O'Brien, *Seeds of Injustice*.
18. Bacik, *Contemporary Theologians*.
19. *Irish Independent*, 8 August 2009.
20. Lernoux, *Cry of the People*.
21. George McGovern, 'The real cost of hunger,' *United Nations Chronicle*, no. 3, 2001.
22. O'Brien, *Seeds of Injustice*.
23. O'Brien, *Seeds of Injustice*.
24. O'Brien, *Seeds of Injustice*.
25. At *negrosnine.com*.
26. *Magill*, July 1984.
27. *Magill*, July 1984.
28. *Magill*, July 1984.
29. *Irish Times*, 15 June 1984.
30. *Irish Times*, 15 June 1984.
31. *Irish Independent*, 8 August 2009.
32. *Irish Times*, 31 May 1984.
33. *Irish Times*, 1 June 1984.
34. *Irish Times*, 1 June 1984.
35. *Irish Times*, 4 June 1984.

36. *Irish Times*, 4 June 1984.
37. *Irish Times*, 4 June 1984.
38. *Irish Times*, 4 June 1984.
39. *Irish Times*, 4 June 1984.
40. *Irish Times*, 5 June 1984.
41. *Irish Times*, 5 June 1984.
42. Routledge, *John Hume.*
43. Routledge, *John Hume.*
44. *Irish Times*, 3 May 1984.
45. New Ireland Forum, *Report.*
46. *Irish Times*, 3 May 1984.
47. *Irish Times*, 3 May 1984.
48. *Irish Times*, 3 May 1984.
49. *Irish Times*, 22 May 1984.
50. *Irish Times*, 22 May 1984.
51. *Irish Times*, 19 November 1984.
52. Smith, *Garret the Enigma.*
53. Young, *One of Us.*
54. Smith, *Garret the Enigma.*
55. Smith, *Garret the Enigma.*
56. *Irish Times*, 20 November 1984.
57. *Irish Times*, 21 November 1984.
58. Young, *One of Us.*
59. Young, *One of Us.*
60. Smith, *Garret the Enigma.*
61. Boyne, *Gunrunners.*
62. Boyne, *Gunrunners.*
63. Boyne, *Gunrunners.*
64. Boyne, *Gunrunners.*
65. Boyne, *Gunrunners.*
66. *Irish Times*, 1 October 1984.
67. *Irish Times*, 19 March 1984.
68. *Irish Times*, 19 March 1984.
69. Sutton Index of Deaths at the CAIN Project (*cain.ulst.ac.uk/sutton*).
70. *Irish Times*, 19 March 1984.
71. *Irish Times*, 19 March 1984.
72. *Irish Times*, 19 March 1984.
73. *Irish Times*, 19 March 1984.
74. *Irish Times*, 19 March 1984.
75. *Irish Times*, 19 March 1984.
76. McGarry, *While Justice Slept.*

77.   McGarry, *While Justice Slept.*
78.   *Irish Times,* 18 July 1984.
79.   *Irish Times,* 18 July 1984.
80.   *Irish Examiner,* 26 January 2004.
81.   *Irish Times,* 22 February 1984.
82.   *Irish Times,* 22 February 1984.
83.   *Irish Times,* 22 February 1984.
84.   *Irish Times,* 22 February 1984.
85.   *Irish Times,* 22 February 1984.
86.   *Times* (London), 20 March 2003.
87.   *Times* (London), 20 March 2003.
88.   *Irish Times,* 6 February 1984.
89.   *Irish Times,* 6 February 1984.
90.   *Irish Times,* 14 February 1984.
91.   *Irish Times,* 14 February 1984.
92.   *Irish Times,* 14 February 1984.
93.   O'Toole, *The Lie of the Land.*
94.   *Magill,* January 1985.
95.   *Magill,* January 1985.
96.   *Magill,* January 1985.
97.   *Irish Times,* 20 June 1984.
98.   *Irish Times,* 7 February 1984.
99.   Jacobsen, *Chasing Progress in the Irish Republic.*
100. 'The History of Ford in Ireland,' at *www.ford.ie.*
101. *Irish Times,* 18 January 1984.
102. *Irish Times,* 18 January 1984.
103. *Irish Times,* 18 January 1984.
104. *Irish Times,* 18 January 1984.
105. *Irish Times,* 15 November 1984.
106. *Irish Times,* 20 November 1984.
107. *Irish Times,* 20 November 1984.
108. *Irish Times,* 20 November 1984.
109. *Irish Times,* 20 November 1984.
110. *Irish Times,* 15 November 1984.
111. *Irish Times,* 15 November 1984.
112. *Irish Times,* 15 November 1984.
113. *Irish Times,* 15 November 1984.
114. *Irish Times,* 19 November 1984.
115. At *irishelectionliterature.wordpress.com.*
116. Flynn and Yeates, *Smack.*
117. Flynn and Yeates, *Smack.*

118. *Magill*, March 1984.
119. Flynn and Yeates, *Smack.*
120. Flynn and Yeates, *Smack.*
121. Flynn and Yeates, *Smack.*
122. Flynn and Yeates, *Smack.*
123. Flynn and Yeates, *Smack.*

Chapter 14: Live at the witch trials (p. 332–355)
1.   McCafferty, *A Woman to Blame.*
2.   McCafferty, *A Woman to Blame.*
3.   McCafferty, *A Woman to Blame.*
4.   McCafferty, *A Woman to Blame.*
5.   McCafferty, *A Woman to Blame.*
6.   McCafferty, *A Woman to Blame.*
7.   McCafferty, *A Woman to Blame.*
8.   McCafferty, *A Woman to Blame.*
9.   McCafferty, *A Woman to Blame.*
10. Inglis, *Truth, Power and Lies.*
11. *Magill*, November 1984.
12. *Magill*, April 1984.
13. *Magill*, November 1984.
14. *Magill*, November 1984.
15. *Irish Times*, 31 December 1984.
16. *Magill*, November 1984.
17. McCafferty, *A Woman to Blame.*
18. Inglis, *Truth, Power and Lies.*
19. McCafferty, *A Woman to Blame.*
20. McCafferty, *A Woman to Blame.*
21. McCafferty, *A Woman to Blame.*
22. Inglis, *Truth, Power and Lies.*
23. McCafferty, *A Woman to Blame.*
24. McCafferty, *A Woman to Blame.*
25. McCafferty, *A Woman to Blame.*
26. McCafferty, *A Woman to Blame.*
27. McCafferty, *A Woman to Blame.*
28. McCafferty, *A Woman to Blame.*
29. McCafferty, *A Woman to Blame.*
30. *Magill*, 30 May 1985.
31. *Magill*, 14 November 1985.
32. *Magill*, 14 November 1985.
33. McCafferty, *A Woman to Blame.*

34. *Magill*, 14 November 1985.
35. *Magill*, 14 November 1985.
36. Inglis, *Truth, Power and Lies.*
37. Inglis, *Truth, Power and Lies.*
38. *Sunday Independent*, 28 November 1999.
39. *Irish Times*, 15 February 1985.
40. *Irish Times*, 21 February 1985.
41. *Irish Times*, 18 February 1985.
42. *Irish Times*, 18 February 1985.
43. *Irish Times*, 19 February 1985.
44. *Irish Times*, 15 February 1985.
45. *Irish Times*, 19 February 1985.
46. *Irish Times*, 15 February 1985.
47. *Irish Times*, 15 February 1985.
48. *Irish Times*, 21 February 1985.
49. *Irish Times*, 15 February 1985.
50. *Irish Times*, 21 February 1985.
51. *Irish Times*, 16 February 1985.
52. *Irish Times*, 16 February 1985.
53. *Irish Times*, 21 February 1985.
54. *Irish Times*, 21 February 1985.
55. *Irish Times*, 21 February 1985.
56. *Irish Times*, 21 February 1985.
57. *Irish Times*, 21 February 1985.
58. *Irish Times*, 21 February 1985.
59. *Irish Times*, 21 February 1985.
60. Collins, *Breaking the Mould.*
61. Tóibín, *Seeing Is Believing.*
62. *Magill*, 16 May 1985.
63. *Magill*, 16 May 1985.
64. *Magill*, 16 May 1985.
65. Tóibín, *Seeing Is Believing.*
66. Tommie Gorman, 'A remote field in west Sligo,' in Tóibín, *Seeing Is Believing.*
67. Peter Kelleher, 'Did Mary's statue really move?' in Tóibín, *Seeing Is Believing.*
68. Peter Kelleher, 'Did Mary's statue really move?' in Tóibín, *Seeing Is Believing.*
69. *Irish Times*, 15 November 1985.
70. O'Malley, *Biting at the Grave.*
71. O'Byrnes, *Hiding Behind a Face.*
72. O'Byrnes, *Hiding Behind a Face.*
73. Routledge, *John Hume.*

74. Taylor, *Provos*.

75. O'Malley, *Biting at the Grave*.

76. Routledge, *John Hume*.

77. O'Malley, *Biting at the Grave*.

78. Lee, *Ireland, 1912–1985*.

79. *Irish Times*, 15 November 1985.

80. Routledge, *John Hume*.

81. *Irish Times*, 16 November 1985.

82. O'Malley, *Biting at the Grave*.

83. *Irish Times*, 16 November 1985.

84. *Irish Times*, 21 February 1985.

85. Inglis, *Truth, Power and Lies*.

86. Routledge, *John Hume*.

86. Routledge, *John Hume*.

88. *Irish Times*, 21 February 1985.

89. *Irish Times*, 31 January 1985.

90. *Irish Times*, 31 January 1985.

91. Carswell, *Something Rotten*.

92. Carswell, *Something Rotten*.

93. Carswell, *Something Rotten*.

94. Carswell, *Something Rotten*.

95. Carswell, *Something Rotten*.

96. Carswell, *Something Rotten*.

97. Carswell, *Something Rotten*.

98. Carswell, *Something Rotten*.

99. Carswell, *Something Rotten*.

100. Hanley and Millar, *The Lost Revolution*.

101. Dunphy, *The Unforgettable Fire*.

102. *Irish Times*, 16 June 1985.

103. *Irish Times*, 6 December 1985.

104. O'Toole, *The Politics of Magic*.

105. *Magill*, 7 March 1985.

BIBLIOGRAPHY

— Allen, Kieran, *Fianna Fáil and Irish Labour*, London: Pluto, 1997.
— Andrews, David, *Kingstown Republican*, Dublin: New Island, in association with First Law, 2007.
— Arnold, Bruce, *Haughey: His Life and Unlucky Deeds*, London: Harper Collins, 2003.
— Arnold, Bruce, *What Kind of Country: Modern Irish Politics, 1968–1983*, London: Jonathan Cape, 1984.
— Bacik, James J., *Contemporary Theologians*, Cork: Mercier Press, 1989.
— Barrett, J. J., *Martin Ferris: Man of Kerry*, Tralee: Brandon Books, 2005.
— Bermingham, Willie, and Ó Cuanaigh, Liam, *Alone Again*, Dublin: Alone, 1982.
— Bew, Paul, et al., *The Dynamics of Irish Politics*, London: Lawrence and Wishart, 1989.
— Bishop, Patrick, and Mallie, Eamonn, *The Provisional IRA*, London: Hamish Hamilton, 1987.
— Boland, Kevin, *Up Dev!*, Dublin: K. Boland, 1977.
— Bolger, Dermot, *The Journey Home*, London: Viking, 1990.
— Bolger, Dermot, *Taking My Letters Back: New and Selected Poems*, Dublin: New Island Books, 1998.
— Boyd, Clodagh, et al., *Out for Ourselves: The Lives of Irish Lesbians and Gay Men*, Dublin: Women's Community Press, 1986.
— Boyne, Sean, *Gunrunners: The Covert Arms Trail to Ireland*, Dublin: O'Brien Press, 2006.
— Bradley, Anthony, and Galanella, Marjann (eds.), *Gender and Sexuality in Modern Ireland*, Amherst (Mass.): University of Massachusetts Press, 1997.
— Broderick, Joe, *Fall from Grace*, Tralee: Brandon, 1992.
— Brown, Terence, *Ireland: A Social and Cultural History, 1922–2002*, London: Harper Collins, 2002.
— Browne, Noël C., *Against the Tide*, Dublin: Gill & Macmillan, 1986.
— Browne, Vincent, with Farrell, Michael, *The Magill Book of Irish Politics*, Dublin: Magill Publications, 1981.
— Buckley, Vincent, *Memory Ireland: Insights into the Contemporary Irish Condition*, New York: Penguin, 1985.

— Campbell, Brian, *Nor Meekly Serve My Time: The H-Block Struggle, 1976–1981*, Belfast: Beyond the Pale Publications, 1994.

— Carswell, Simon, *Something Rotten: Irish Banking Scandals*, Dublin: Gill & Macmillan, 2006.

— Clarke, Liam, *Broadening the Battlefield: The H-Blocks and the Rise of Sinn Féin*, Dublin: Gill & Macmillan, 1987.

— Clayton-Lea, Tony, and Taylor, Richie, *Irish Rock: Where It's Come from, Where It's at, Where It's Going*, London: Sidgwick and Jackson, 1992.

— Collins, Stephen, *Breaking the Mould: How the PDs Changed Irish Politics*, Dublin: Gill & Macmillan, 2005.

— Collins, Stephen, *The Power Game: Ireland under Fianna Fáil*, Dublin: O'Brien Press, 2000.

— Collins, Stephen, *Spring and the Labour Story*, Dublin: O'Brien, 1993.

— Commission of Investigation, *Report into the Catholic Archdiocese of Dublin*, July 2009.

— Commission of Investigation into the Dublin and Monaghan Bombings of 1974, *Final Report, March 2007*, Dublin: Stationery Office, 2007.

— Communist Party of Ireland, *Clondalkin: A Workers' Victory*, Dublin: CPI, 1983.

— Connolly, Colm, *Herrema: Siege at Monasterevin*, Dublin: Olympic Press, 1977.

— Connolly, Linda, *The Irish Women's Movement: From Revolution to Devolution*, New York: Palgrave Macmillan, 2002.

— Connolly, Linda, and Hourigan, Niamh (eds.), *Social Movements and Ireland*, Manchester: Manchester University Press, 2006.

— Coogan, Tim Pat, *Ireland in the Twentieth Century*, London: Hutchinson, 2003.

— Coogan, Tim Pat, *A Memoir*, London: Hutchinson, 2008.

— Coogan, Tim Pat, *On the Blanket: The H Block Story*, Dublin: Ward River Press, 1980.

— Coogan, Tim Pat, *The Troubles: Ireland's Ordeal, 1966–1995, and the Search for Peace*, London: Hutchinson, 1995.

— Cooney, John, *John Charles McQuaid: Ruler of Catholic Ireland*, Dublin: O'Brien Press, 1998.

— Corless, Damian, *GUBU Nation: Grotesque, Unbelievable, Bizarre, Unprecedented Happenings in Ireland*, Dublin: Merlin Publishing, 2004.

— Corless, Damian, *Party Nation*, Dublin: Merlin Publishing, 2007.

— Cruise O'Brien, Conor, *Memoir: My Life and Themes*, Dublin: Poolbeg Press, 1998.

— Cruise O'Brien, Conor, *Neighbours: Four Lectures* (Thomas Pakenham, ed.), London: Faber and Faber, 1980.

— Curtis, Liz, *Ireland: The Propaganda War*, London: Pluto, 1984.

— Davis, C. E., and Sinnott, Richard, 'The controversy concerning attitudes in the Republic to the Northern Ireland problem,' *Studies*, autumn-winter 1980.
— Dean, Geoffrey, *The Turnstone: A Doctor's Story*, Liverpool: Liverpool University Press, 2002.
— Deane, Seamus (gen. ed.), *The Field Day Anthology of Irish Writing, Volume 3: Political Writings and Speeches, 1900–1988*, Derry: Field Day Theatre Company, 1991.
— Desmond, Barry, *Finally and in Conclusion: A Political Memoir*, Dublin: New Island Books, 2000.
— Dillon, Martin, *The Dirty War*, London: Hutchinson, 1990.
— Downey, James, *Lenihan: His Life and Loyalties*, Dublin: New Island Books, 1998.
— Downing, John, *Most Skilful, Most Devious, Most Cunning: A Political Biography of Bertie Ahern*, Dublin: Blackwater Press, 2004.
— Dunlop, Frank, *Yes, Taoiseach: Irish Politics from Behind Closed Doors*, Dublin and London: Penguin Ireland, 2004.
— Dunn, Joseph, *No Tigers in Africa!: Recollections and Reflections on 25 years of Radharc*, Dublin: Columba Press, 1986.
— Dunne, Derek, and Kerrigan, Gene, *Round Up the Usual Suspects: Nicky Kelly and the Cosgrave Coalition*, Dublin: Magill Publications, 1984.
— Dunphy, Eamon, *Unforgettable Fire: The Story of U2*, London: Viking, 1987.
— Dwyer, T. Ryle, *Nice Fellow: A Biography of Jack Lynch*, Cork: Mercier Press, 2001.
— English, Richard, *Armed Struggle: The History of the IRA*, London: Macmillan, 2003.
— Fahy, Desmond, *Death on a Country Road*, Cork: Mercier Press, 2006.
— Fanning, Bryan, *The Quest for Modern Ireland: The Battle for Ideas, 1912–1986*, Dublin: Irish Academic Press, 2008.
— Faul, Denis, and Murray, Raymond, *The Triangle of Death: Sectarian Assassinations in the Dungannon-Moy-Portadown Area*, Dungannon: the authors, 1976.
— Faulkner, Pádraig, *As I Saw It: Reviewing Over 30 Years of Fianna Fáil and Irish Politics*, Dublin: Wolfhound Press, 2005.
— Ferriter, Diarmaid, *The Transformation of Ireland, 1900–2000*, London: Profile Books, 2004.
— Fetherstonhaugh, Neil, and McCullagh, Tony, *They Never Came Home: The Stardust Story*, Dublin: Merlin Publishing, 2001.
— Fitzgerald, Billy, *Father Tom: An Authorized Portrait of Cardinal Tomás Ó Fiaich*, London: Fount, 1990.
— FitzGerald, Garret, *All in a Life: An Autobiography*, Dublin: Gill & Macmillan, 1991.

— Fleming, N. C., and O'Day, Alan, *The Longman Handbook of Modern Irish History since 1800*, London: Longman Pearson, 2003.

— Flynn, Seán, and Yeates, Pádraig, *Smack: The Criminal Drugs Racket in Ireland*, Dublin: Gill & Macmillan, 1985.

— Foster, Roy, *Luck and the Irish: A Brief History of Change, 1970–2000*, London: Allen Lane, 2007.

— Freedman, Victoria, *The Cities of David: The Life of David Norris*, Dublin: Basement Press, 1995.

— Gallagher, Michael, *The Irish Labour Party in Transition, 1957–82*, Manchester: Manchester University Press, 1982.

— Geldof, Bob, *Is That It?*, London: Sidgwick and Jackson, 1986.

— Gillmor, Desmond A., *Economic Activities in the Republic of Ireland: A Geographical Perspective*, Dublin: Gill & Macmillan, 1985.

— Hanley, Brian, and Millar, Scott, *The Lost Revolution: The Story of the Official IRA and the Workers' Party*, Dublin: Penguin Ireland, 2009.

— Harper, Colin, and Hodgett, Trevor, *Irish Folk, Trad and Blues*, London: Collins, 2004.

— Harrington, John P. (ed.), *Modern Irish Drama . . . Backgrounds and Criticism*, New York and London: W. W. Norton, 1991.

— 'Haughey' (television documentary series), Mint Productions for RTE Television, 2005.

— Heffernan, Thomas Farel, *Wood Quay: The Clash over Dublin's Viking Past*, Austin: University of Texas Press, 1988.

— Hogan, Desmond, *The Ikon Maker: A Novel*, Dublin: Irish Writers' Co-Operative, 1976.

— Holland, Jack, and McDonald, Henry, *INLA: Deadly Divisions*, Dublin: Torc, 1994.

— Horgan, John, *Labour: The Price of Power*, Dublin: Gill & Macmillan, 1986.

— Horgan, John, *Mary Robinson: An Independent Voice*, Dublin: O'Brien Press, 1997.

— Horgan, John, *Noël Browne: Passionate Outsider*, Dublin: Gill & Macmillan, 1997.

— Howard, Paul, *Hostage: Notorious Irish Kidnappings*, Dublin: O'Brien Press, 2004.

— Humphries, Tom, *Dublin v. Kerry: The Story of the Epic Rivalry that Changed Irish Sport*, Dublin: Penguin Ireland, 2006.

— Hussey, Gemma, *At the Cutting Edge: Cabinet Diaries, 1982–1987*, Dublin: Gill & Macmillan, 1990.

— Inglis, Tom, *Truth, Power and Lies: Irish Society and the Case of the Kerry Babies*, Dublin: UCD Press, 2003.

— Jacobsen, John Kurt, *Chasing Progress in the Irish Republic: Ideology, Democracy, and Dependent Development*, Cambridge: Cambridge University Press, 1989.

— Jarry, Alfred, *The Ubu Plays*, London: Methuen, 1968.

— Jordan, Anthony J., *To Laugh or to Weep: A Biography of Conor Cruise O'Brien*, Dublin: Blackwater Press, 1994.

— Jordan, Neil, *Night in Tunisia*, Dublin: Irish Writers' Co-Operative, 1976.

— Joyce, Joe, and Murtagh, Peter, *Blind Justice*, Dublin: Poolbeg, 1984.

— Joyce, Joe, and Murtagh, Peter, *The Boss*, Dublin: Poolbeg, 1984.

— Kearney, Richard (ed.), *Navigations: Collected Irish Essays, 1976–2006*, Dublin: Lilliput Press, 2006.

— Keena, Colm, *Haughey's Millions: Charlie's Money Trail*, Dublin: Gill & Macmillan, 2001.

— Kelley, Kevin, *The Longest War: Northern Ireland and the IRA*, Tralee: Brandon Press, 1982.

— Kennedy, Stanislaus (ed.), *One Million Poor?: The Challenge of Irish Inequality*, Dublin: Turoe Press, 1981.

— Keogh, Dermot, *Jack Lynch: A Biography*, Dublin: Gill & Macmillan 2008.

— Keogh, Dermot, *Twentieth-Century Ireland: Nation and State*, Dublin: Gill & Macmillan, 1994.

— Kerrigan, Gene, and Brennan, Pat, *This Great Little Nation: The A–Z of Irish Scandals and Controversies*, Dublin: Gill & Macmillan, 1999.

— Kiberd, Declan, *Inventing Ireland*, London: Jonathan Cape, 1995.

— Lee, J. J., *Ireland, 1912–1985: Politics and Society*, Cambridge: Cambridge University Press, 1989.

— Lenihan, Brian, *For the Record*, Dublin: Blackwater Press, 1991.

— Lernoux, Penny, *Cry of the People: The Struggle for Human Rights in Latin America and the Catholic Church in Conflict with US Policy*, New York: Doubleday, 1980.

— Litton, Frank (ed.), *Unequal Achievement: The Irish Experience, 1957–1980*, Dublin: Institute of Public Administration, 1982.

— Lyder, André, *Pushers Out: The Inside Story of Dublin's Anti-Drugs Movement*, Victoria (BC): Trafford, 2005.

— McCabe, Eugene, *King of the Castle*, Oldcastle (Co. Meath): Gallery Press, 1997.

— McCafferty, Nell, *The Best of Nell*, Dublin: Attic Press, 1984.

— McCafferty, Nell, *Nell*, Dublin and London: Penguin Ireland, 2004.

— McCafferty, Nell, *A Woman to Blame*, Dublin: Attic Press, 1985.

— McCann, Eamonn, *War and an Irish Town*, London: Pluto, 1980.

— McDonald, Frank, *The Destruction of Dublin*, Dublin: Gill & Macmillan, 1985.

— McGarry, Patsy, *While Justice Slept: The True Story of Nicky Kelly and the Sallins Robbery*, Dublin: Liffey Press, 2006.

— McGovern, George, 'The real cost of hunger, *United Nations Chronicle*, no. 3, 2001.

— Mac Gréil, Mícheál, *Prejudice and Tolerance in Ireland: Based on a Survey of Intergroup Attitudes of Dublin Adults and Other Sources*, Dublin: College of Industrial Relations, 1977.

— McKittrick, David, and McVea, David, *Making Sense of the Troubles*, Belfast: Blackstaff Press, 2000.

— Mac Mánais, Ray, *The Road from Ardoyne: The Making of a President*, Tralee: Brandon Press, 2004.

— McNamara, Maedhbh, and Mooney, Paschal, *Women in Parliament: Ireland, 1918–2000*, Dublin: Wolfhound Press, 2000.

— McVerry, Peter, *The Meaning Is in the Shadows*, Dublin: Veritas, 2003.

— Moloney, Ed, *A Secret History of the IRA*, New York: W. W. Norton, 2002.

— Moore, Christy, *One Voice: My Life in Song*, London: Hodder and Stoughton, 2003.

— Morrison, Danny (ed.), *Hunger Strike: Reflections on the 1981 Hunger Strike*, Tralee: Brandon Books, 2006.

— Mullan, Don, *The Dublin and Monaghan Bombings: The Truth, the Questions and the Victims' Stories*, Dublin: Wolfhound Press, 2000.

— Murphy, Francis D., et al., *The Ferns Report: Presented by the Ferns Inquiry to the Minister for Health and Children*, Dublin: Government Publications, 2005.

— Murphy, Tom, *Conversations on a Homecoming*, London: Methuen, 1993.

— Murphy, Tom, *The Gigli Concert*, London: Methuen, 2001.

— Murray, Patrick, 'Irish elections: A changing pattern,' *Studies*, autumn 1976.

— New Ireland Forum, *Report*, Dublin: Stationery Office, 1984.

— Norton, Desmond, 'Unemployment and public policy,' *Studies*, spring 1976.

— O'Brien, Mark, *The Irish Times: A History*, Dublin: Four Courts Press, 2008.

— O'Brien, Niall, *Seeds of Injustice: Reflections on the Murder Frame-up of the Negros Nine in the Philippines: From the Prison Diary of Niall O'Brien*, Dublin: O'Brien Press, 1984.

— O'Byrnes, Stephen, *Hiding Behind a Face: Fine Gael under FitzGerald*, Dublin: Gill & Macmillan, 1986.

— O'Carroll, Ide, and Collins, Eoin (eds.), *Lesbian and Gay Visions of Ireland*, London: Cassell, 1995.

— O'Connell, John, *Doctor John: Crusading Doctor and Politician*, Dublin: Poolbeg, 1989.

— O'Connor, Alison, *A Message from Heaven: The Life and Crimes of Father Sean Fortune*, Tralee: Brandon Books, 2000.

— O'Donoghue, Noreen, and Richardson, Sue, *Pure Murder: A Book about Drug Use*, Dublin: Women's Community Press, 1984.

— Ó hEithir, Breandán, *The Begrudger's Guide to Irish Politics*, Dublin: Poolbeg, 1986.

— O'Higgins, T. F., *A Double Life*, Dublin: Town House, 1996.

— O'Leary, Olivia, and Burke, Helen, *Mary Robinson: The Authorised Biography*, London: Hodder and Stoughton, 1998.

— O'Malley, Padraig, *Biting at the Grave: The Irish Hunger Strikes and the Politics of Despair*, Belfast: Blackstaff Press, 1983.

— O'Malley, Padraig, *The Uncivil Wars: Ireland Today*, Belfast: Blackstaff Press, 1983.

— O'Morain, Padraig, *Access to Justice for All: A History of the Free Legal Advice Centres, 1969–2003*, Dublin: FLAC, 2003.

— O'Rawe, Richard, *Blanketmen: An Untold Story of the H-Block Hunger Strike*, Dublin: New Island Books, 2005.

— O'Reilly, Emily, *Masterminds of the Right*, Dublin: Attic Press, 1992.

— O'Toole, Fintan, *The Lie of the Land: Irish Identities*, Dublin: New Island Books, 1997.

— O'Toole, Fintan, *The Politics of Magic: The Work and Times of Tom Murphy*, Dublin: Raven Arts Press, 1987.

— Patterson, Henry, *Ireland since 1939*, Oxford: Oxford University Press, 2002.

— Patterson, Henry, *The Politics of Illusion: Republicanism and Socialism in Modern Ireland*, London: Hutchinson, 1989.

— Penniman, Howard R. (ed.), *Ireland at the Polls: The Dáil Election of 1977*, Washington: American Enterprise Institute for Public Policy Research, 1978.

— Penniman, Howard R., and Farrell, Brian (eds.), *Ireland at the Polls, 1981, 1982 and 1987*, Durham (NC): Duke University Press, 1987.

— *The Pope in Ireland: A Pictorial Record*, Dublin: Gill & Macmillan, 1979.

— Power, Vincent, *Send 'Em Home Sweatin': The Showband Story*, Cork: Mercier Press, 2000.

— Rafter, Kevin, *Martin Mansergh: A Biography*, Dublin: New Island Books, 2002.

— Raftery, Mary, and O'Sullivan, Eoin, *Suffer the Little Children: The Inside Story of Ireland's Industrial Schools*, Dublin: New Island Books, 1999.

— Roche, Desmond, *Local Government in Ireland*, Dublin: Institute of Public Administration, 1982.

— Rockett, Kevin, et al., *Cinema and Ireland*, London: Croom Helm, 1987.

— Routledge, Paul, *John Hume: A Biography*, London: Harper Collins, 1997.

— Ryan, Louden (ed.), *Irish Industry in the Eighties*, Dublin: Helicon, 1984.

— Savage, Jon, *England's Dreaming: Sex Pistols and Punk Rock*, London: Faber and Faber, 1991.

— Scallon, Dana Rosemary, with Murray, Ken, *All Kinds of Everything*, Gill & Macmillan, 2007.

— Sheehan, Helena, *Irish Television Drama: A Society and Its Stories,* Dublin: Raidió-Teilifís Éireann, 1987.
— Sheridan, Jim, *Leave the Fighting to McGuigan: The Official Biography of Barry McGuigan,* London: Viking, 1985.
— Smith, Raymond, *Charles J. Haughey: The Survivor,* Dublin: Aherlow Publishers, 1983.
— Smith, Raymond, *Garret the Enigma: Dr Garret Fitzgerald,* Dublin: Aherlow Publishers, 1985.
— Smith, Raymond, *The Quest for Power: Haughey and O'Malley,* Dublin: Aherlow Publications, 1986.
— Smyth, Gerry, *Noisy Island: A Short History of Irish Popular Music,* Cork: Cork University Press, 2005.
— Stopper, Anne, *Mondays at Gaj's: The Story of the Irish Women's Liberation Movement,* Dublin: Liffey Press, 2006.
— Sweetman, Rosita, *On Our Backs: Sexual Attitudes in a Changing Ireland,* London: Pan, 1979.
— Taylor, Jane, *Ubu and the Truth Commission,* Cape Town: University of Cape Town Press, 2007.
— Taylor, Peter, *Beating the Terrorists?: Interrogation at Omagh, Gough, and Castlereagh,* London: Penguin, 1980.
— Taylor, Peter, *Provos: The IRA and Sinn Fein,* London: Bloomsbury, 1997.
— Thornley, Yseult (ed.), *Unquiet Grave: Essays in Memory of David Thornley,* Dublin: Liberties Press, 2008.
— *Three Days in September: When the Pope Came to Ireland,* Dublin: Liberties Press, 2004.
— Tiernan, Joe, *The Dublin and Monaghan Bombings and the Murder Triangle,* Dundalk: the author, 2002.
— Tóibín, Colm (ed.), *The Penguin Book of Irish Fiction,* London: Viking, 1999.
— Tóibín, Colm (ed.), *Seeing Is Believing: Moving Statues in Ireland,* Mountrath (Co. Laois): Pilgrim Press, 1985.
— Travers, Stephen, and Fetherstonhaugh, Neil, *The Miami Showband Massacre: A Survivor's Search for the Truth,* Dublin: Hachette Ireland, 2007.
— Vallely, Fintan, *Sing Up!: Irish Comic Songs and Satires for Every Occasion,* Dublin: Dedalus Press, 2008.
— Vorm, William (ed.), *Paddy No More: Modern Irish Short Stories,* Dublin: Wolfhound Press, 1978.
— Walsh, John, *Patrick Hillery: The Official Biography,* Dublin: New Island Books, 2008.
— Walsh, Liz, *The Final Beat: Gardaí Killed in the Line of Duty,* Dublin: Gill & Macmillan, 2001.

— Waters, John, *Race of Angels: Ireland and the Genesis of U2*, Belfast: Blackstaff Press, 1994.
— White, Robert W., *Ruairí Ó Brádaigh: The Life and Politics of an Irish Revolutionary*, Bloomington (Ind.): Indiana University Press, 2006.
— Whitehead, Phillip, *The Writing on the Wall: Britain in the Seventies*, London: Michael Joseph, 1985.
— Young, Hugo, *One of Us: Life of Margaret Thatcher*, London: Macmillan, 1989.

INDEX